00–17

DIAGNOSIS for DISASTER

DIAGNOSIS for DISASTER

The Devastating Truth About False Memory Syndrome
and Its Impact on Accusers and Families

Claudette Wassil-Grimm, M.Ed.

The Overlook Press
Woodstock • New York

$14-

First published in 1995 by
The Overlook Press
Lewis Hollow Road
Woodstock, New York 12498

Library of Congress Cataloging-in-Publication Data

Wassil-Grimm, Claudette
    Diagnosis for Disaster : the devastating truth about false mem-
ory syndrome and its impact on accusers and families / Claudette
Wassil-Grimm.
    p. cm.
    Includes bibliographical references.
    1. False memory syndrome. I. Title.
    RC455.2.F35W37   1995
    616.85'83690651--dc20
    04-36787
    CIP

Manufactured in the United States of America on acid-free paper
Book design by Bernard Schleifer
Typeset by AeroType, Inc., Amherst, NH
ISBN: 0-87951-572-4
9 8 7 6 5 4 3 2 1

Acknowledgments

FIRST AND FOREMOST, due to the heat of this controversy, this was a very difficult book to write. I want to thank my assistant Maureen Olander and my husband Andy for their steady support across the last two years.

Others who were particularly supportive at key moments include my agent Meredith Bernstein, my editor Tracy Carns, and my friends and colleagues Anita Lampel and Jeff Victor. Carol Tavris also played a small but significant part in my decision to write the book—first by her daring to challenge the status quo, and then through her direct encouragement. Psychiatrists Harold Lief, George Ganaway and Heidi Jacke were particularly helpful in clarifying the main issues by discussing the theories and manuscript-in-progress with me.

Finally, I want to thank the survivors, retractors and families who shared their stories. I hope this book creates much healing and they are showered with all the positive energy which they have helped create.

To R.A.U.

Contents

CONTENTS

PART TWO: THE IMPACT

CONTENTS

PREFACE

Who Should Read
This Book?

THIS BOOK IS FOR any adult who has been depressed or disturbed and is wondering if he or she was sexually abused as a child. It is for those who have been told by a therapist that they have all the classic symptoms of childhood sexual abuse even though they believe they had a happy childhood and remember no incidence of sexual abuse. It is for those who have read a list of symptoms in the popular sexual abuse literature and have begun to suspect they were sexually abused.

It is also for those who remember being sexually abused and are wondering if there are more memories they might have repressed. It is for those who ask themselves, "Is my life ruined? Will I ever be well?"

Herein, you will find stories of people, mostly women, who were sexually abused and who never forgot, as well as men and women who were sexually abused and had suppressed some of the memories until brief explorations in therapy or a news item reminded them of the forgotten past. You will also find stories of women who were told they were sexually abused, spent years trying to uncover repressed memories, and later learned that the "recovered memories" were false. This book explores the impact of incest accusations on the siblings and parents of accusing adult children, as well as constructive ways to resolve related conflicts.

Finally, there are stories of those who never forgot certain incidents of sexual abuse but later fabricated additional memories of abuse while in therapy. It shows how they learned to distinguish the difference, heal from what was real, and get on with their lives.

If you are considering therapy for sexual abuse, or if you have begun therapy and are confused about which memories are real and which might be fantasy or the products of suggestion, read this book. It will help you find your truth and make an informed decision about the right program or the best therapeutic approach for you.

INTRODUCTION

Battle Lines

THERE IS A HEATED debate raging in the mental health field. Many therapists who specialize in sexual abuse issues are loath to question any accusation of sexual abuse. They have seen clients retrieve extremely painful memories of incest and feel certain that no one would want to believe anything that horrible unless it was true. At the same time, many other therapists question the zeal of the "sexual abuse recovery movement" and worry that recovered memories of abuse are the result of hypnotic suggestion and group pressure.

This controversy has polarized psychiatrists, psychologists, social workers, and psychotherapists into two strongly opposing camps and has made a thoughtful, rational interchange between the two groups nearly impossible. Therapists who support all claims of sexual abuse without question usually fear that the opposition may turn back the clocks until sexual abuse is a hidden shame again. For many therapists, the greatest concern is that children will again become silenced victims.

The treatment of children who claim they have been sexually abused is indeed a delicate issue; even when a child withdraws an accusation, the therapist may justifiably suspect that the child has been threatened by the perpetrator or other family members and told to recant. It is a brave child, indeed, who can follow through on a claim that may destroy her family. For this reason, many concerned therapists would rather err on the side of believing too readily than fail to support a child in such a vulnerable position.

However, more and more frequently adults are being encouraged to uncover "repressed" memories of sexual abuse. Because the trauma of sexual abuse can be a root of many psychological disorders, some therapists have concluded that most psychological disorders are evidence of sexual abuse. And if the client does not remember being abused, those therapists believe forgetting does not mean the abuse did not happen; it means that the memory is repressed. Sexual abuse recovery programs that specialize in helping adults retrieve repressed memories have sprung up all over the country. Though the majority of participants are women, a growing number of men are taking up this issue. Indeed, the ratio of men to women involved in the recovery movement is no different from the ratio of men to women who seek therapy for any reason. The Fitzpatrick/Porter case has raised the interest of men, and others, like Ralph whose story is presented in Chapter Two, have been drawn in through the sheer impact of the recovery movement on social intercourse.

Women (and increasingly men) are flocking to recovery programs in their search for emotional peace, and many are uncovering childhood memories of incest. Though the scenes that play across these participants' minds are obviously very painful and vivid, skeptics question whether these are recollections of actual past events or merely "false memories"—a kind of nightmare daydreaming similar to what fiction writers do when trying to create a frightening story.

Each side of the repressed memory debate has been compiling data on the nature of memory to support its own view. Bystanders are hard put to sort out the truth in this battle of the certified experts. While many adults who have recovered repressed memories of sexual abuse are adamant about the truth of their discoveries, a growing number of those who had come to believe they were sexually abused are now retracting their accusations.

In 1983, Canadian journalist Elizabeth Godley accused her mother of sexually abusing her as a child. In 1987, she realized she had been mistaken. It has been more than ten years since Elizabeth first uncovered repressed memories of sexual abuse. In a recent article in the *San Francisco Examiner* Elizabeth described how she now sees what happened to her in therapy:

> "It was on my second visit to the therapist that she shattered my composure with a single question.
>
> 'Elizabeth, do you think you might have been sexually abused by your mother?'
>
> "Suddenly, I was flooded with nausea. Alarm bells clanged in my brain. I felt light-headed and breathless. Perhaps this was the reason I'd been in and out of therapy for so many years?

"The therapist, a psychologist, was struck by my reaction to her question. (Later, when I expressed skepticism, she reminded me of this, dismissing my doubts as 'denial.') Convinced we were on to something, she asked me to remember as much as I could of this traumatic event.

"In my apartment that evening (I was 38 and living alone), I began to 'remember.' I was four years old, my mother and I were in the woods near our house, she forced me to do certain things. . . .

"My 'memories' blazed with vivid detail. I recalled the texture of the moss at the foot of a cedar tree, the smell of the damp earth, the glossy leaves and tiny red berries on a nearby bush.

"It would be four years—four years in which I had no contact with my mother, and almost none with my father—before I would come to know these memories were utterly false, that I had conjured up this scene from my imagination."[1]

Elizabeth was not a dependent child when she made her accusation, nor was she dependent on her parents when she retracted it. She is one of many adult women who have, in recent years, experienced "false memory syndrome" firsthand. As more and more women wake up from the nightmare of imagined incest, professional organizations such as the American Psychological Association and the American Psychiatric Association are investigating the problem to try to curb this trend. Sexual abuse specialists are beginning to reexamine their methods and eliminate those techniques that spark imagination to create false memories.

What has led some therapists to adopt unorthodox methods that are potentially harmful to their clients? *The Courage to Heal*, first published in 1988 and the most popular book being recommended and used by adult survivors and their counselors, was written by Ellen Bass, a creative writing teacher, and Laura Davis, a participant in one of her workshops. Bass openly admits that she began holding workshops and training professionals even though she had had no formal education or training in psychology or counseling. With sympathetic ears and unusual sensitivity, Ms. Bass and Ms. Davis were able to collect many stories from adult survivors of sexual abuse. The book offers a great deal of comfort, affirmation, and useful advice. However, the authors' narrow exposure to mental health issues has caused them to see everything through the lens of sexual abuse.

Though most professional psychologists quickly recognize the many errors of logic in this "survivor's manual," some therapists have blindly accepted the unproven assumptions of the self-help literature. For example, the symptoms of adult survivors of sexual abuse offered by Bass and Davis are so broad and all-encompassing that even a mildly emotionally disturbed person (or an emotionally healthy person having a bad day) could answer yes to many of their self-analysis questions. This is particularly true of the list of coping mechanisms believed to be caused by forgotten incest, including such behaviors as being controlling, spacing out, being super-alert, using humor to get through hard times, being busy, making lists, escaping into books or television, compulsive eating, workaholism, and high achievement.

Similarly, most of the "symptoms" the authors describe in their chapter entitled "Effects: Recognizing the Damage" are also common reactions to any stress or trauma. A Vietnam War veteran could answer yes to many of Bass's questions, and an adult child of a dysfunctional family, especially one who was physically abused, could answer yes to most. But just because most people who were sexually abused have these symptoms, it is not logical to assume that most people who have these symptoms were sexually abused. This would be as absurd as declaring they must all be Vietnam War veterans, even if they don't remember ever being in the war.

My last point brings us to the greatest fallacy of all in the book. On page 81 Bass states that

> "If you don't remember your abuse, you are not alone. Many women don't have memories, and some never get memories. This doesn't mean they weren't abused. . . .
>
> "One thirty-eight-year-old survivor described her relationship with her father as 'emotionally incestuous.' She has never had specific memories of any physical contact between them, and for a long time she was haunted by the fact that she couldn't come up with solid data. Over time, though, she's come to terms with her lack of memories."

The adult survivor takes up the story here to explain how she coped with having no memory of being sexually abused by her father despite the fact that she had many of the symptoms:

> "I obsessed for about a year on trying to remember, and then I got tired of sitting around talking about what I couldn't remember. I thought, 'All right, let's act as if . . .'

"So I'm going with the circumstantial evidence, and I'm working on healing myself. I go to these incest groups, and I tell people, 'I don't have any pictures,' and then I go on and talk all about my father, and nobody ever says, 'You don't belong here.' "[2]

Herein lies the problem. If Bass had had some formal training in psychology, she and the therapists she has trained would begin to suspect that a client who has been trying to remember sexual abuse for more than a year and has failed just might have some other problem. She might have a mood disorder, a personality disorder, depression caused by perimenopause, or any number of other problems that could produce the same symptoms. Though much of what the client receives from the incest groups—support, acceptance, sense of belonging—could be helpful for any of the above disorders, an antidepressant or estrogen might prove much more helpful. However, the sufferer will never discover these alternatives as long as the group of people she depends on keeps telling her that her whole problem and cure lie in remembering her sexual abuse.

THE RECOVERY MOVEMENT

Not long ago, the nation was swept by the adult children of alcoholics (ACOA) movement. As the leaders of that movement began to publish information and hold workshops around the country, many adults who had not had alcoholic parents began to flock to the workshops, saying that they related very strongly to the symptoms and feelings of ACOAs, and they found the meetings to be very healing. Rather than insisting that the parents of these adults must have been closet drinkers and that these adults must now force themselves to remember the smell of liquor on their parents' breath in order to be healed, the leaders of the ACOA movement acknowledged that one could have the same symptoms from a different cause. Thus, they popularized the concept of the dysfunctional family and broadened the base of people who could benefit from their workshops and advice. Out of this grew the *Recovery Movement*—an initially healthy, self-searching, grass-roots network that helps teach many adults how to overcome childhood emotional handicaps. As the "recovery" philosophy is stretched to fit many subgroups (overeaters, shopaholics, and women who love too much, to mention a few), it sometimes becomes distorted.

The adult survivors of the *Sexual Abuse Recovery Movement* is one example of how recovery philosophy, taken to the extreme, can become a destructive force. The lure of the social acceptance of these groups is very strong—so strong that the unafflicted often look in longingly from the sidelines. And, in the *Sexual Abuse Recovery Movement*, if you want to be approved of and accepted, if you want to have access to the movement's support groups, you must at least act *as if* you were sexually abused, whether or not you have any memory of being sexually abused. You are asked to suspend your judgment and trust that the other group members know more about what has happened in your life than you do.

For this book I used a number of sources to solicit interviews with women who believed they had been sexually abused. My request for interviewees ran in *Moving Forward: A Newsjournal for Survivors of Sexual Child Abuse and Those Who Care for Them*; the *Family Violence and Sexual Assault Bulletin*, and *The Retractor* (a newsletter for women who have realized their sexual abuse accusations actually stemmed from "false memories").

Commonly, such a woman goes to a therapist following a period of depression or to seek relief from a problem such as bulimia. She may be recently divorced or under some other stress. For example, one client had lost her job, witnessed her two-year-old child get hit by a car, had a miscarriage, undergone major surgery, and watched the building next door to her home burn to the ground, all within a period of eight months, before going to a therapist for depression. What was this therapist's diagnosis? The client's depression was obviously due to repressed childhood sexual abuse. Whatever the presenting problem, a poorly trained therapist enamored with the *Sexual Abuse Recovery Movement* tells the client that she has symptoms of childhood sexual abuse and that she cannot get well until she has recovered her repressed memories. The client is exhorted to read self-help books on incest, attend incest survivors' groups, and maybe attend an intensive weekend-long group therapy session.

After much exposure to others' stories of sexual abuse, the client develops some vague images of being abused. She is soon convinced that it was her father who abused her. First she believes it was one incident, but after much pressure to "remember" more she concludes that she was abused from the time she was an infant until she was in high school—and she "repressed" every memory! At this point paranoid thinking begins to take hold. The client begins to suspect that other family members were involved. She comes to believe she was also abused by her brother and her grandfather. Then she remembers the faces of neighbors during the abuse and realizes she was the victim of satanic ritual abuse that involved all her childhood friends. When she reports that she had a flashback of killing a baby and drinking the blood, she can finally stop trying to "remember." Now she can begin to recover.

But those who have been through this therapy and have recanted say that what they needed to recover from, at that point, was the therapy. As we will see, this typical scenario illustrates many of the "red flags" of bad therapy: the fostering of dependence, paranoia, isolation, peer pressure, and boundary violations.

Lynn Price Gondolf, a retractor who sought help for an eating disorder, had always remembered that her uncle had molested her when she was a child. But her therapist kept insisting that she was repressing other memories of sexual abuse, until he had pressured her to fantasize that her father had abused her too. Lynn has since recanted these accusations against her father and in a recent television appearance explained,

> "I told my doctor—I said, 'These memories feel different than the memories I have with my uncle.' And his reply was, 'Well, that's because you haven't owned these, you haven't claimed these, you haven't processed these yet.' So I believe that the therapists that do this—I know—they have all the answers to every question you're ever going to ask. . . . They believe, probably, in what they're doing."[3]

THE CONSEQUENCES

Being diverted from the best therapeutic treatment is just *one* of the tragic outcomes of being coerced to have "memories" of sexual abuse. The client is also advised to cut off all contact with anyone who doubts that she was sexually abused. This often means the loss of family and friends, increasing the client's psychological dependence on the incest survivors' group or the therapist. At the same time, false accusations are extremely painful for the accused, and in some cases the client is encouraged to file a lawsuit against the accused parent, adding financial ruin to emotional agony. If the parent has the audacity to contest the accusation and drag out court proceedings, the cost will be even higher. Confused accused parents divorce each other; siblings are torn between loyalty to sibling or parent, and friends turn away in despair, feeling as if they are talking to an automaton who can only quote slogans.

Many adults were sexually abused as children, and most of them have never forgotten. However, the number of "adult survivors" who have "recovered" so-called "repressed" memories and have had their lives painfully sidetracked is on the rise. In March 1992 a group of families falsely accused of sexual abuse formed the False Memory Syndrome Foundation (FMSF). Since then, the foundation has received eighty to one hundred phone calls a day from families who are apparent victims of false accusations. Recently, the FMSF has begun to get more and more calls from retractors—adult children swept up in the adult survivors' movement who came to believe they had been sexually abused by a parent and who now realize that their "memories" were the result of group-induced hysteria or therapist-induced fantasy.

At first the psychological community ignored the FMSF, and critics claimed that the FMSF was nothing more than an advocacy group for perpetrators of childhood sexual abuse. However, a look at the credentials of professionals who support the FMSF and serve on its board gives the organization a credibility that is hard to dismiss. Serving on the FMSF advisory board are more than forty professionals, both men and women (many of whom have doctorates in psychology and teach at prestigious universities such as the UCLA, Stanford, Harvard, and Johns Hopkins), as well as numerous teaching psychiatrists.[4]

Richard Ofshe, Professor of Sociology at the University of California, Berkeley, and board member of the FMSF, comments, "The recovered memory movement is a dangerous experiment in conformity and influence masquerading as psychotherapy. It's rapidly evolving into one of the most intriguing quackeries of this century."[5]

Understandably, many mainstream psychologists who approach each client with an open mind and who have knowledge of the various psychological problems that could be causing the client's symptoms are growing disturbed by the popularity of the sexual abuse recovery movement and its one-cure-fits-all philosophy. Yet many have been reluctant to publicly criticize the movement's methods or therapists because accepting the conclusion that someone has been sexually abused, no matter what evidence there is to the contrary, is the more "politically correct" position. Opposing the recovery movement will target them as being part of the "massive denial and justification movement started by perpetrators of child sexual abuse" as one Provo, Utah, therapist described the FMSF.[6]

However, the denial really seems to be on the part of poorly trained therapists with one-track minds who cannot accept that many psychological problems are caused by life-transition difficulties, trauma, or many other conditions besides childhood sexual abuse. Some therapists are biased by personal experience with sexual abuse, which makes them loath to question any suspicion or accusation, while others have schooling that is too narrow and is based on unprofessional self-help books rather than scientific study. In some cases, therapists have become convinced there is a national conspiracy of satanists perpetrating not only sexual abuse, but also bloody tortures, though neither the Federal Bureau of Investigation nor local police departments have been able to find any evidence to support this belief. For clients who mistakenly stumble into these therapists' offices (and for the families of these clients), therapy can become a nightmare that goes on for years, delaying treatment of the clients' real problems and costing a great deal of money and sometimes much more.

In an interview on *The Jane Whitney Show*, Lynn Gondolf, who had become convinced she was the victim not only of childhood sexual abuse, but also of satanic ritual abuse, tells what she lost when she naively began therapy for an eating disorder with a therapist who specialized in treating ritual sexual abuse:

"I went in taking no medication and had never tried to kill myself. Within a year I was taking eight different types of medication and had tried to kill myself five times. . . . The eating disorder, of course, got worse. I was taking all this medication and was paying enormous amounts for it, what insurance wouldn't cover. I lost my car. I lost a job with EDS, which to me was just the greatest opportunity in the world. It's just what a kid from the country who goes to school wishes for. I lost everything I had. I lost my family. I cut them off."[7]

Lynn has since been reunited with her family, as have a growing number of women who are beginning to "wake up" from the nightmare of falsely remembered "repressed memories."

In this book I tell the stories of many of these families—how the women fell under the cultlike influence of misguided therapists, the pain it caused the women and their families, how they broke away, and how they finally healed from not only the disorders or depression that led them to therapy in the first place, but also the misguided treatment they received.

WHERE I STAND

At times while researching this book I have felt like a traitor. I was an abused child in a time when children were the property of their parents and the parents' actions went unchallenged. When I was eighteen I informed my father that if he ever hit me again I would file charges of assault and battery. Now that I was an adult in the eyes of the law, the law was on my side, and, knowing this, he stopped beating me.

I believe the law must continue to protect children. I do not advocate turning back the clocks by rescinding laws for mandatory reporting. Rather, I sound a call for everyone to become more aware of healthy human sexual development, as well as what kind of therapy or questioning engenders false memories and false accusations. I support laws backed by government funding that not only increase the professional training requirements for anyone conducting therapy, but also provide affordable in-depth training for these therapists. This training should include an explanation of false memory syndrome, information about the long-held misgivings about the efficacy of repressed memories, and advice on how therapists can be more moderate in their efforts to help clients remember childhood trauma.

To that end, I offer this book as an educational tool for both therapist and client to help them understand what can go wrong in therapy and how to avoid the pitfalls of approaches based on repressed memory theory.

PART I
THE PROBLEM

ONE

The Tangled Web
We Weave

*When someone asks you, "Were you sexually abused
as a child?" there are only two answers: One of them
is "Yes," and one of them is "I don't know." You can't
say "No."* [1]

—ROSEANNE ARNOLD, actress and comedian

LINDA HAD BECOME suicidally depressed. For years she had fluctu-
ated between being bright, vivacious, and optimistic, and withdrawing
into deep depressions. She had trouble getting along with co-workers and
had had six different jobs in the last four years. Each new job often meant
relocation, and she had lived in three entirely different areas in the last
three years. This meant making all new friends each time. Deep in debt,
she was having a hard time managing her money. She had just turned thirty
and had never been in a relationship with a man for more than six months.
Linda was not happy being single, struggling with life alone.

Her longing for family inspired her to move back to her hometown,
though she knew there were few job opportunities there and even fewer
eligible men. She felt like she had to work something out with her family of
origin before she could give herself to a long-term relationship. She had
been the apple of her father's eye, and though he had always been proud of
her accomplishments, he had not wanted to pay for her to go to college.
Huge college loan debts had been dogging her for ten years, and she
couldn't stop being angry at her parents for not finding a way to help her.
She was trying to forgive them and get on with her life. Less than a year
after she moved back, with nothing much resolved, she learned that her

father had terminal cancer (although it was in remission). She had a very full plate.

Her parents had not been alcoholic, but she felt that she belonged among adult children. She sought out a Co-dependents Anonymous (CODA) group and began searching for a therapist (even though she owed her last therapist thousands of dollars and had no insurance). She began attending any twelve-step group she could find while reading *The Courage to Heal* (because so many people had recommended it to her). She soon discovered that she had all the classic symptoms of someone who had been sexually abused: relationship problems, low self-esteem, feeling different, headaches, depression, intermittent feelings of rage, inability to trust, a dearth of childhood memories. She asked around until she found a therapist considered to be the expert on sexual abuse in her area. If Linda had been sexually abused, that could explain it all.

After a year of therapy and groups, she had recovered a memory that an uncle had sexually abused her when she was about five years old. Her parents wouldn't believe her. There was no satisfaction in the discovery. Then she lost another job, and things started going badly with her boyfriend of the past six months. She felt certain there must be other memories causing her depression. She begged her therapist to put her into an incest survivors' group, but the therapist kept saying that Linda wasn't ready yet.

Linda bought *The Courage to Heal Workbook* and started her "incest work" on her own. Two weeks before her father died, she decided that he too had abused her. She could feel the certainty as soon as the thought entered her mind, but she didn't have details yet; she didn't have the "memories."

Her father's cancer remission abruptly ended. Her mother called and warned her that this might be the end and that her father wanted to see her. Linda dreaded the thought of seeing him, and yet, if she did not see him soon, she believed she might lose the chance to confront him and, thus, the chance to heal.

Linda came before her father and made her accusation, but he angrily denied it. She left. He swallowed his anger and asked that she come back again. She could not. She wrote letters to her relatives to explain why. A few days later he was dead, and she drifted around at the wake, isolated from all those who said what a warm and loving man her father had been.

This is an American tragedy, *circa* 1990. Although it is a "formula" story, it is the true story of one woman who is still struggling with her belief that her deceased father "incested" her.

THE SOURCE OF THE TROUBLE

In the fall of 1993 a television docudrama featured the story of Shari Karney, the California lawyer who worked almost single-handedly to change the statute of limitations for crimes of sexual abuse. Ms. Karney's basic argument is premised on the notion of repression; victims cannot be expected to press charges before they have retrieved their memories of sexual abuse. Shari Karney had become electrified by this cause when she recovered her own totally repressed memories of incest, triggered by a custody/incest case she had lost. The little girl Karney had defended later became psychotic after repeated exposure to her incestuous father.

During this trial, Karney had leapt up into the witness stand and had begun strangling the child's father when his nonchalant attitude infuriated her. In the docudrama we see that Karney was obsessed with the issue of incest, often alienating people with her uncontrolled angry outbursts, but we are left believing that all Karney's means were justified by her end—changing the statute of limitations—and that Karney is reliably knowledge-able on the incest issue.

While Karney was on *The Oprah Winfrey Show* of January 17, 1991, the following exchange took place between Karney and Winfrey:

Sherrie[*sic*]: You know, incest occurs in one in four homes in America. It occurs to one in three girls and one in five boys in the United States.

Oprah: Those are statistics that we know about. See, I believe they are much higher than that.[2]

Stop for a moment, and, without looking back at the above exchange, take this short multiple-choice exam. According to the statistics given above, how many girls have experienced father-daughter incest?

_____ a. One in two?
_____ b. One in three?
_____ c. One in twenty?
_____ d. One in a hundred?

The correct answer for the incidence of incest between a daughter and her biological father, according to the latest and most extensive studies, studies as reported in *The Characteristics of Incestuous Fathers*, a 1992 special report by Linda Meyer Williams and David Finkelhor, is d, one in a hundred.[3] (Finkelhor and Williams are researchers who not only are frequently quoted by recovery therapists, but also are highly respected by more mainstream therapists. See footnote* for a short explanation of the possible sources of the incorrect answers.)

Don't feel bad if you got this answer wrong. You were not given enough information to answer the question correctly. Many have made the mistake of jumping to conclusions when given incomplete statistics. I have attended psychology conferences that offer training to therapists where the speakers incorrectly declared that one in three women have been victims of incest. (Significant figures used in this section are illustrated on the chart on page 18.

Where does this information come from? Is Karney lying? Not exactly—she just has difficulty reading statistics. She may even have gotten her information from the same set of studies done in the last fifty years that back up the one-in-a-hundred figure for father-daughter incest.

Karney's manner of expression also causes confusion. Since none of the researchers included questions in their survey about exactly *where* the abuse happened, we just don't know how many women have been abused *in their homes*. On the other hand, the researchers were quite careful to ask exactly who the perpetrator was. We know that, by averaging the studies done between 1953 and 1985 as reported by respected researcher Diana Russell in her book *The Secret Trauma*, the figure for incestuous contact (sexual abuse by *any* family member) before the age of fourteen is actually about one in ten.[4]

Let's look at why answers a, b, and c, above, were not correct. First of all, Winfrey's estimate that the statistics are higher than one in three is conjecture, and I suspect she might now modify this opinion if asked, since she has since aired shows with retractors and their families telling about the damage that has been done to them by therapists using methods not rooted in careful study.

How did Karney come up with her estimate that one in three women have been victims of incest? Some studies have shown that one in three girls have been sexually abused if you count incidents such as a flasher

---

*a. One in two—an unfounded opinion.

b. One in three—*might* have been sexually abused by somebody, sometime, if you count noncontact encounters such as "flashing," obscene remarks, or verbal propositions not carried out.

c. One in twenty—has been abused by a father, stepfather, or mother's long-term live-in boyfriend assuming the father's role.

d. One in a hundred—has been abused by her biological father.

exposing himself to a girl under fourteen or an adult propositioning an adolescent (even if the adult did not follow through). However, you have to keep in mind that not all sexual abuse is *incest*. In Wyatt's study, which defines sexual abuse very broadly so that it even includes noncontact sexual abuse (no touching, just words), 45 percent of the 248 women surveyed said that they had been sexually abused by the time they were age eighteen. Only 21 percent of the 248 women surveyed said they had been sexually abused by a family member. However, it is important to note that Wyatt counted as family members any live-in boyfriend of Mom's, regardless of how brief the relationship was. (This also contaminated her father-daughter incest figures.) Therefore, more than half of all sexual abuse is *not* perpetrated by a family member.

Four studies done between 1940 and 1978 (which surveyed 7,474 women over age eighteen) showed that between 4 percent and 12 percent of these women had had sexual encounters with a relative. Averaged out ($4\% + 12\% = 16\% \div 2 = 8\%$), that means that about eight out of a hundred (or one out of twelve) women have had either a contact or non-contact sexual encounter with a relative before the women reached adulthood.[5] More recently, Diana Russell's 1983 survey of 930 women from all social and economic classes showed that 12 percent had been sexually abused by a relative before the age of fourteen, 4 percent more (for a total of 16 percent) had been sexually abused between ages fourteen and eighteen, and, if you count incest with any relative even after the woman is over eighteen, 19 percent of all the women surveyed had had a sexual encounter with a relative that involved physical contact.[6] Russell's very broad definition of incest yields close to a one-in-five figure, but I think including approaches to women over eighteen distorts the data, so I chose the middle figure (16 percent) for the chart on page 18.

When we look closely at the available studies we see that there is wide variation in how sexual abuse is defined, how the father-daughter relationship is defined, and consequently how incest is defined. For this reason it is best to look at a range of studies and try to find apples to compare with apples. Therefore I have created the chart on page 18 which compares apples with apples in studies done from 1940 to 1992. This chart combines data from charts and information presented in Herman's *Father-Daughter Incest*, pp. 12 and 13; Russell's *The Secret Trauma*, pp. 60 and 72; and Williams' and Finkelhor's *The Characteristics of Incestuous Fathers*, p. 4. All major studies that include relevant detail on incestuous abuse, especially father-daughter incest, were included.

SEXUAL ABUSE OF FEMALE CHILDREN (UNDER AGE 18)
TABLE OF MAJOR STUDIES DONE FROM 1940–1992

Researcher/Date	Number of Female Subjects	Abused by Any Family Member	Abused by Father, Stepfather, or Surrogate Father	Abused by Birth Father	Type of Abuse*
Landis, 1940	295	12.5%	—	—	Noncontact +
Kinsey, 1953	4,441	5.5%	1.0%		Noncontact +
Gagnon, 1965	1,200	4.0%	.6%	—	Unknown
Williams and Finkelhor, 1979 update, 1992	530	10.0% 13.0%	1.3% 5.0%	— 1.0%	Noncontact + Unknown
Russell, 1983	930	16.0%	4.5%	—	Contact only
Kilpatrick and Amick, 1984	2,004	1.0%	.4%	—	Contact only
Wyatt, 1985	248	21.0%	8.1%†	—	Contact only

*Noncontact denotes that the broadest definition of sexual abuse was used; Unknown denotes that the report of research does not make clear what definition of sexual abuse was used, and Contact only means that sexual abuse was defined as any sexual encounter that involved actual physical contact (not acts such as exposure, peeping, or verbal sexual propositions).
†Includes mother's live-in boyfriends.

So, how common is father-daughter incest? Some might say that c, — one in twenty—is the correct answer if you count both fathers *and step-fathers*. Finkelhor's and Williams' 1992 report shows that 1 percent of girls have been sexually abused by their *biological fathers*, and 5 percent of girls have been sexually abused during childhood by a father, stepfather, or adopted father.[7] So, the incidence of incest backed by research is a far cry from the "one-in-three-girls" figure that has been popularized by the media.

Misleading figures on sexual abuse abound. In the introduction to E. Sue Blume's book, *Secret Survivors*, Blume explains how she estimates that more than 50 percent of all women have been traumatized by child-hood sexual abuse:

> The statistics are disturbing; the most commonly cited is that 25% of all American women have been sexually molested in childhood, most by someone they knew and trusted. Newer research, done more carefully and accurately, indicates that as many as 38% of women were molested in childhood. . . . It is my experience that fewer than half of the women who experienced this trauma later remember or identify it as abuse. Therefore, it is not unlikely that *more than half of all women* [her italics] are survivors of childhood sexual trauma.[8]

Blume does not cite any studies or give any clues as to where she obtained these figures, which she later feels free to double. Blume's assumptions also point toward a problem that has clouded all the statistics on incest in recent years. Since we do not know how many cases of recovered memories are factual, any estimates that include reports of incest discovered for the first time in therapy have no scientific grounding. We can't determine how much the incidence of incest may have gotten inflated by uncorroborated recovered memories.

The most commonly cited study that is touted as proving that most reports of incest have been corroborated is a study by Judith Herman and Emily Schatzow done in 1987. Out of fifty-three participants in a therapy group for incest survivors, Herman and Schatzow reported that thirty-nine of the participants, or 74 percent, were able to corroborate their memories or suspicions of sexual abuse. However, on a closer examination we learn that these thirty-nine group members had had little or no amnesia to begin with, so it is not too surprising that they were able to find confirmation. What the study does not make clear, or what those who cite it try to brush under the rug, is that fourteen of the group members (or the remaining group members) had had severe amnesia regarding the incidents of sexual abuse. In other words, those with "repressed memories" did not find corroboration. Therefore, this sample does not prove anything about repressed memories of sexual abuse except that, as we already know, they are very hard to corroborate. Nonetheless, Herman and Schatzow conclude that "massive repression appeared to be the main defensive resource available to patients who were abused early in childhood," based on the fact that those who could not find corroboration of their abuse thought they were about four or five years old at the time of the abuse, and those who had always remembered the abuse reported that they were about eight to eleven years old.[9]

We see that data is corrupted in the retelling, and fantasy estimates get repeated as commentators like Oprah Winfrey say, "I believe they are much higher than that"! Tragically, such exaggerations damage the credibility of incest researchers and numb the public to the pain of real incest survivors.

WHAT BROUGHT THEM TO THERAPY

Those who are ultimately diagnosed as being "survivors" (by a therapist or through self-diagnosis) enter therapy for a number of reasons. They are often experiencing multiple problems, and few initially name sexual abuse as their reason for seeking therapy:*

- Melody Gavigan† entered therapy because she had become severely depressed following a divorce, remarriage, and relocation all within a year. She was stressed out and had no one to talk to.
- Doreen was approaching thirty and had never married. Her prestigious, high-stress job kept her flying around so much of the time that she never had time to establish relationships.

---

*Information from retractors comes from a variety of sources. Many of their stories appear in a book called *True Stories of False Memories* by Eleanor Goldstein and Kevin Farmer, published by SirS Books in Boca Raton, Florida, 1993. Other retractors spoke at the False Memory Syndrome Foundation Conference in Philadelphia, April 1993. I met or made follow-up calls to each of these retractors and to others who subscribe to *The Retractor*, a newsletter for women who developed "false memories" of sexual abuse while in therapy. Most have chosen to remain anonymous.

†A dagger by a name the first time it appears means the name is not a pseudonym.

- Lynn Gondolf† had always had problems with her weight. She'd lost and gained back the same one hundred pounds several times. She wanted to discover a way to take it off and keep it off.
- Aileen's nine-year-old son had a violent temper, and she wanted to learn how to deal with it constructively before he got any older.
- Deborah was nearly forty years old and still fuming mad at her parents. She wanted to find out why, put the anger aside, and get on with her life.
- Jane sought a therapist because she knew she had problems from growing up in an alcoholic home, and she was feeling extraordinarily overwhelmed by the arrival of her second child.
- Ralph (one of the few males who have been caught up in this movement) was ordered into therapy by his commanding officer because he had poor "social adaptation."

All of these people, with their various presenting problems—related to being single, being married, being a parent, not being a parent, and so forth—had received the same diagnosis. They were told that their problems were probably a result of repressed memories of childhood sexual abuse, and that they could not get well unless they could bring these memories to consciousness.

Through hypnosis, group therapy, sodium pentothal, writing exercises, and the exploration of "body memories," all but four of the twenty retractors I interviewed had come to believe that they had been overtly sexually abused by a parent. Seven had become convinced that they were also "survivors" of satanic ritual abuse.

Although these memories were very powerful at the time they were retrieved and caused great emotional pain and disturbance for months or years afterwards, the retractors kept feeling that the memories did not seem real. Whenever they would report this feeling to their therapists, the therapists would explain that everyone has doubts periodically—the retractors were just in *denial*. No arguments against the almighty notion of denial were acceptable.

Had these accusing adult children all entered the same incest survivors' program? No—none had the same therapist, nor did they even live in the same state. I spoke to retractors from California, Illinois, Michigan, Montana, New Hampshire, Ohio, Pennsylvania, Texas, and Canada.

Why are people jumping to the conclusion that most women are victims of incest? I think faulty logic is one prime source of the confusion.

Although many people who were sexually abused as children become depressed adults, all people who are depressed as adults have not been sexually abused as children. Depression has many causes—in fact, the most common source of depression is biochemical. Mood disorders are often inherited from mood-disordered parents, and there are medications that can, in most people, correct chemical imbalance in the brain and relieve the depression totally.

Reasoning backwards not only gets us into trouble, it can also cause some very ugly discrimination. For example, it is commonly known that most parents who physically abuse their children were physically abused themselves as children. Does this mean that all children who were physically abused will grow up to abuse their own children? No! There are many parents who are justifiably proud that they are raising their children in a very different way than they themselves were raised. The past is not *destiny*. It can be a school for learning from our parents' mistakes.

THE FORMULA

In researching this book I interviewed over a hundred people including therapists, psychology researchers, women who were sexually abused, accused parents, siblings of accusing children, neighbors, and women who realized that their accusations of sexual abuse were false. This last group, the retractors, have the most to teach us about this issue.

Although there is no doubt in my mind that many children have been sexually abused in their homes while growing up, I have also met women who had been pressured to believe they were "sexually abused" and later realized that there was not a grain of truth in the "memories" they created. This seems incredible. People ask, *Why would anyone believe anything so painful as being sexually abused by a parent if it weren't true?* The retractors can tell us how they formed their beliefs, why they clung to them, and what finally made them give up their beliefs. When I heard their stories I felt as certain that there are false accusations of sexual abuse as I am certain that most accusations of sexual abuse are true.

In a nutshell, here is how the retractors explain it. They had sought the advice of a professional because they were in pain, and they tried to accept that professional's diagnosis and cooperate with that professional's treatment. As they became more and more involved in the Recovery Movement, they began to spend more and more time in therapy sessions and groups. There were many voices confirming what their therapists had told them. They tried to put away their doubts. Soon they, too, were quoting their therapists and their self-help books as if they were the divine words of a guru. They displayed the zealousness that one often sees in recent religious converts, and they began to cut themselves off from anyone who questioned their beliefs.

Actually, the notion that all one's personal problems have been caused by traumatic sexual abuse, usually incest, and can be solved only by uncovering the repressed memory of that abuse, is not a scientific explanation, nor is it well accepted in the therapeutic community. It is simply a theory, a belief that has no more concrete proof to back it up than any of the other psychological fads or fervently held philosophies that have come and gone in the last three decades.

In the 1970s there was a flurry of new methods for achieving psychological well-being, including Erhard Seminars Training (EST), Transcendental Meditation (TM), Transactional Analysis (TA), Gestalt therapy, the Hare Krishnas, Primal Scream therapy, the Unification Church (Moonies), and Rolfing. Many of them were viable systems that helped their followers find a more peaceful, well-balanced life, but many others did not stand the test of time. They are similar to the Recovery Movement in that they are quasi-religious movements. Since they are not based on scientific research, they require a participant's trust or suspension of disbelief in their tenets before the participant can benefit from what they have to offer. Looking back, disgruntled former participants/believers regard their experiences with these alternative belief systems as wastes of time and money, at the least, and destructive forces that led to a loss of identity and mental breakdown at the worst.

I was living in California when the Moonies were at their peak. I remember an older woman friend of mine agonizing over whether she should try to kidnap her daughter and have her deprogrammed. The mother had received only one phone call from her daughter in six months. Many argued that her daughter was grown now and had a right to choose her own path. But my friend worried that her daughter had been brainwashed and was not operating on her own free will. I hear the echo of her words as I listen to FMSF parents who want to be allowed to invade their grown children's therapists' offices and demand an explanation.

The new all-pervasive concern over sexual abuse really resembles a social movement more than a psychological theory. No one has yet proved that the assumptions of the Sexual Abuse Recovery Movement are factual, so for the moment we must call them hypotheses or beliefs. This is not science. Yet any group that operates on a set of unproven beliefs and tries to convert others to those beliefs is not actually a social movement, but rather a religion or a cult.

Some of the best experts who can help us understand why so many have taken up this belief, and how to respond to it in ourselves and our loved ones, are experts on cults or other belief systems. Dr. Saul Levine, the author of *Radical Departures: Desperate Detours to Growing Up*, has linked such proselytizing behavior to the need to separate from parents and strike out as an individual — a necessary passage that all must experience. Indirectly, his book offers answers to the questions: Why would anyone give up everything for an unfounded belief? Is there a certain personality that is prone to being easily convinced of memories that are not true? Why do people stay even after the system no longer works for them?

The myth of the crippling, but forgotten, experience of sexual abuse offers an explanation for any failure to meet the impossible expectation that every woman must now, simultaneously, be an aggressive career woman, devoted wife, and perfect nurturing mother. The loud message from the mass media conveyed through everything from ads to situation comedies is that this should be a breeze; therefore anyone who can't easily accomplish all this must be defective. This leaves individual, real women wondering, "What's *wrong* with me?" The diagnoses of Multiple Personality Disorder (MPD) or Post-Traumatic Stress Disorder (PTSD) give a woman permission to stop trying to meet all these impossible demands.

ANSWER ONE

Why would anyone believe anything so painful as being sexually abused by a parent if it weren't true?

ANSWER NUMBER ONE: Because it explains why she cannot meet the modern social demand to manage careers, marriages, and children without the support of appropriate social programs (such as quality, funded daycare or paid, released time from work for essential parent/ child bonding).

One retractor, Melody Gavigan, who has appeared on a number of nationally televised programs to tell her story, had actually been told that a stay in the hospital would be like a vacation, with all expenses being paid by her insurance carrier. Stressed out from the changes wrought by remarrying before she had even had time to get over her divorce from her first husband and by moving immediately to a new area of the country, where she had to make all new friends, she thought it would be fun to go to this plush hospital in a beautiful setting and sit and talk with other women all day. Instead, Melody ended up incarcerated, unable to sign herself out, having been declared too unstable to leave until she would admit she had been sexually abused by her father. She was in living hell for six weeks until she finally did start hallucinating that her father had "incested" her.

Dr. Saul Levine interviewed and counseled many ex-cult members and found a significant pattern in those who had taken up beliefs that alienated them from their families of origin. In the majority of the cases he studied, the parents had overprotected their children, had become too involved in their children's lives, and had not opened the way for the children to make it on their own. This forced the child to select a "radical departure," as Levine calls it, in order finally to break the bonds with his or her parents.[10]

A number of the retractors recognized this pattern in their relationships with their parents. One retractor pointed out that she couldn't even come close to meeting the expectations of a woman today because she had never even had to wash her own clothes before she married and left home. She needed some excuse for being so incompetent, and incest met the need.

Similarly, Deborah's mother had planned everything for her, even down to selecting an apartment for Deborah to move into when it was time for her to leave home. Deborah recognized that she had readily succumbed to the suggestion that she had been sexually abused because she desperately needed to create space between herself and her mother. At least no one would argue she was selfish to break off contact with a mother who had sexually abused her. Besides, she had never before made a decision for herself, so she allowed her therapist to decide for her that she had been sexually abused. Deborah was just doing what she had been raised to do.

DEBORAH'S RELATIONSHIP WITH HER MOTHER

Deborah was an only child. Her mother had had great difficulty conceiving her and had miscarried another child when Deborah was about four years old, so her mother was very overprotective. Also, her mother had had a difficult and disappointing childhood. She was determined to engineer her daughter's life so that Deborah would have everything her mother had missed. Throughout her childhood Deborah drifted along, allowing her mother to make all decisions. When Deborah was nineteen, she finally had to face a crisis without her mother's help:

"I fell madly in love with this boy and I got pregnant almost the first time we slept together. This was in 1964, and abortions were illegal. After a couple of tries of my own I ended up having an illegal abortion at a doctor's office. I was five months pregnant. It was a horrible, horrible experience, and it was devastating in all sorts of ways. I had this abortion, and this guy went off to graduate school and almost immediately got married and had a child with his new wife. I was crushed. That was when I started going to therapists."

[Deborah didn't tell her parents about the pregnancy or the abortion.] "The trauma of the abortion was very fresh at that point. My mother decided that I should leave home right then, because she had wanted to leave home when she was nineteen.

[So one month after Deborah had had the abortion, her mother pushed her out of the nest, oblivious to the fact that this was a very sensitive time in her daughter's life.] "That fall I was living alone and going to school. I went completely off the rails. My grades dropped. I couldn't get up in the morning. That was my first real bout of depression. Then for years I would have three months of depression, and then three months I would be all right.

"I was in and out of therapy. I had been to one male psychologist who said to me, 'If you're having so many problems with your mother, why don't you just stop seeing her?' For a long time I thought it was her hanging on to me, and that may have been happening, but now I see that I was hanging on to her too.

[Deborah earned a university degree in Toronto and went through a series of jobs, constantly dissatisfied. After five years she was doing secretarial work far below her potential.] "I'd been under a lot of stress for years. My relationships with men were terrible. I had a lot of anger. I would just explode at people. I was really volatile and moody.

[She began looking for a therapist.] "I just happened upon Binah. I must have told her very quickly that I was having a lot of problems with my mother. At the second visit Binah said to me, 'Could you have been sexually abused by your mother?' For some reason, this struck me as a lifesaver. I thought, 'Oh, God—this explains everything!' "

ANSWER TWO

Why would anyone believe anything so painful as being sexually abused by a parent if it were not true?

ANSWER NUMBER TWO: Because it is a simple, neat explanation for a lifetime of inner turmoil and disappointment that has not been caused by any known or acknowledged trauma.

"Before I'd gone to see Binah I had had lunch with my mom one day. I was very depressed, although I'd never talked to my mother about my depression because she just didn't want to know that I was unhappy. I said to my mother at the end of this lunch, 'Mom, did something happen to me when I was a child, because I'm having so much trouble now?' My mother immediately bristled with defensiveness, and she said to me, 'Nothing happened to you when you were a child. You had a perfectly ordinary childhood.' She had this really very angry voice. She was furious with me. As we parted, she looked back at me over her shoulder with an expression of terrible pain and hurt.

So when Binah asked me if my mother had sexually abused me, I thought, 'No wonder she never wanted to talk to me about my childhood! It all fit.'

"In a lot of ways it was a very good thing for me to cut off from my mother. It was a very brutal thing—it was very hard on my mother. But during the next four years I only talked to her twice on the phone. I had to start to figure out who I was, separate from her."

SEPARATING FROM FAMILY

There are two parts to separating from family. First, there is the need to gain a sense of self and independence strong enough to be able to feel comfortable on your own. Second, there is what you will do about your obligations to your family of origin. If you do not have the confidence to think you can make it on your own, you may cling to your family, even while you find it painful to be with them. At the same time, even if you feel that you owe your family a lot because they worked so hard to put you through college to see that you got off to a good start, you may not have the resources to give much back. We are living in a time when circumstances often make it impossible to do what we think we should, and we must live with the constant discomfort of ambivalence.

For the generations who grew up before the 1960s, how and when to separate from your parents had one simple answer—when you got married. If you didn't marry, then you were the sibling chosen to take care of Mom and Dad in their old age. These were the societal expectations, and if you chose to do something differently, you knew you were going against the rules of propriety—you were a rebel, and you did not expect family sanction for it. Rebels took apartments in New York City, or Out West, or in some other place designated as rebel territory.

I was born in 1947—on the cusp of this change. Because my home was very troubled, I wanted to get out as soon as I could. Legally, my parents could have me dragged back home if I tried to leave before my twenty-first birthday. At that time you only had one chance—a bungled departure meant that you had shown your hand, and they now had the advantage. It would be even harder to escape next time.

Common wisdom had it that loving daughters got married and lived somewhere near their parents, so that the daughters could call Mom every day and have dinner with their parents at least once a week. Good daughters missed their mothers as much as mothers missed their daughters. But then all this started to change.

Graceful exits began to present themselves. Daughters could go away to college without any disgrace for the family. They could then marry some man who hadn't grown up near them, and it was understandable, though heartbreaking for any mother who had devoted her whole life to her daughter, if the daughter moved to live near her husband's parents. As jobs became more specialized it became acceptable for a couple to live near where they worked—if they would spend every holiday and vacation going "home" to their families of origin. However, many young couples couldn't help thinking they'd rather spend their vacation in Hawaii than Kansas.

ANSWER THREE

Why would anyone believe anything so painful as being sexually abused by a parent if it weren't true?

ANSWER NUMBER THREE: Because it provides a compelling and guilt-free reason for separating from his or her family and ends those awful feelings of ambivalence.

DEBORAH'S THERAPY

Deborah told me, "My therapist had said to me, 'Now go home and remember as much as you can.' So I went home and created 'memories.' I 'remembered' all sorts of details. I 'remembered' everything about the place my mother took me, and then I 'remembered' my mother forcing me to have oral sex with her.

"My therapist encouraged me to write letters to both of my parents and tell them I had remembered the abuse. When I wrote to my mother I was fairly graphic, which would have really upset her because my mother is a real prude.

"My mother replied to that letter. It was a very, very, angry letter, and it sort of just fueled the flames. She said that she had never done anything like that to me, but if she had, it would explain why I had turned into a man-hating lesbian.

"So my therapist and I sort of looked at each other and said, 'Yup.'

"Binah focused on my getting in touch with all the pain that was inflicted on me. I have pages and pages of a journal describing what I could 'remember' about what went wrong in my childhood. She introduced me to other patients who also had recovered memories.

"I spent about four years in treatment with Binah, and nothing had changed except that now I had an excuse for being so messed up. I often mentioned to Binah that I thought I might not have been sexually abused. She would get really impatient with me and say, 'Come on now. We've been over this many, many times.' She would remind me of this very strong reaction I'd had when she first brought it up. But deep down, I didn't buy it. I started to see Binah less and less."

IS THERE A BETTER WAY TO DO THIS?

Breaking away from one's roots is difficult, and though a total break often looks like the simpler and cleaner way to do it, there may be a terrible price to pay later. Things have changed so drastically since our parents were our age that we may have irreconcilable differences of opinion. Our parents have been waiting to be sought out as the wise ones, and we prefer to consult experts or our friends. We may have learned "better ways" (or at least ways thought to be better by our current social group) and now have trouble tolerating our family of origin's ways of doing things. These bones of contention may range from the picayune to the powerful.

I related to Deborah's need to break away. My parents had had a bad marriage, so my mother had made me her best friend and sometime caretaker. This was a heavy load to carry. As soon as I finished school I sought a job clear across the country. This physical distance helped enormously. My mother and I had been practically fused together as we shared the role of parent to my siblings, and I needed to get physically away to figure out who I was and which problems were *my* problems.

Under the advice of a therapist I wrote my mother a "Dear Witch" letter. There were a lot of things for which I was angry with my mother, and, although I was admirably assertive with my peers, I had always had difficulty asserting myself with my parents. Distance helped me do this. I didn't regret sending the letter. I don't think I could have done otherwise. I needed to get these things off my chest.

My mother cut off all contact with me for the next six months. During our estrangement I had time to sort out and focus on what I found truly unbearable when I was with my mother. I realized that I couldn't really hope to change her much, but I could decide what behaviors of hers were intolerable and let her know in a clear, straightforward way.

Over the years I have let my mother know what sort of conversations I didn't want to have with her, what it was OK to talk about, how I expected her to treat my son, and any number of things. I didn't present her with a list of one hundred demands right off the bat. These were things that I let her know, one need at a time, and when she forgot, I calmly and assertively reminded her.

When I left home my much younger sister (she was born when I was fourteen) became my mother's best friend. Fourteen years later my sister was trying to break away from our mother. My sister felt suffocated and controlled, and she was very angry with our mother for neglecting her as a child. (My sister really was extremely neglected.) She had just entered therapy and eventually, on the advice of her therapist, she wrote my mother a "Dear Witch" letter. This time my mother was ready to apologize right off the bat, but my sister cut her off and announced to me that she was never speaking to our mother again. I was glad I could comfort both my mother *and* my sister. I didn't try to talk my sister into forgiving our mother. I could see that my sister needed distance for her psychological health, to forge her long-overdue independence from her roots.

My sister eventually gained a clearer idea of what she did and didn't want in a relationship with our mother. After a six-month silence, she called her. They have a new relationship now. When my sister says she doesn't want anyone smoking in her car or in her house, my mother respects my sister's wish just as she would a friend's. The passage is complete.

DEBORAH'S RECONCILIATION

"I think the combination of seeing less of Binah, seeing that my life hadn't really changed very much, and doubting that the incest had happened were all building up.

"Then my grandmother died. A friend saw the obituary in the paper, and I went to the funeral. I saw my mother and father there.

"It was a very emotional encounter on many levels. I was really sad about my grandmother's death because I had really liked her. I remember during the service in the chapel I was sitting beside my mom, and she was crying and clutching my hand. She had never been that fond of my grandmother, so I had the feeling she was really crying for me. I told her that I was going to give her a call because I wanted to talk to her.

"By this time I had left Binah. I had just started seeing a psychiatrist, and I had told her that I'd been seeing this therapist who thought I'd been sexually abused by my mom.

"She said to me, 'Can you think of any other times when you were molested or abused during your childhood?' I told her about two times. One was when I ran into this guy on the beach when I was about nine years old. I described these incidents to her.

"She said in a very matter-of-fact way, 'If you can remember those incidents, I don't know why you wouldn't have clear memories about being abused by your mother. So I think we can just forget about that possibility.'

"I was very happy to do that. I felt grateful. I didn't have to torture myself about that anymore, and I could move on."

IT'S YOUR DECISION

You do not have to be a victim of incest to be allowed to put distance between yourself and your parents, for however long you need, while you sort out what you want that relationship to be. It is your inalienable right.

For years therapists have supported and enabled the process of separation. It is probably the most common problem that clients bring to them, whether the client is twenty-five or forty-five. Many, many people have extreme difficulty separating from their parents. Certainly, this had been a central conflict for many of the retractors. (We'll be looking at more explanations in upcoming chapters.)

So if you think you might have been sexually abused, but you have no "memories," or you have unearthed some memories during therapy that you are uncertain about, ask yourself what you will gain by separating from your parents. Ultimately, you are the only one who can know if your suspicions of sexual abuse are really an attempt to break away from overly close or needy parents.

There really are no classic symptoms, nor are there any sure-fire ways to test the accuracy of recovered memories other than to get corroboration (though you may have been sexually abused, and there simply is no corroboration left). Hopefully, the stories in this book will help you sort that out for yourself.

SUMMARY POINTS

1. Misinterpretations of statistics have led to gross exaggerations of the number of survivors of traumatic childhood sexual abuse.

2. Reliable studies indicate that one-fifth to one-third of all women have had some sort of childhood sexual encounter with an adult male; about 15 percent of these encounters involved physical contact. In about 75 percent of the reported cases, the women stated that the sexual encounters were not "traumatic."

3. More than half of all sexual abuse is perpetrated by a nonfamily member, a fact that seems to get lost when statements such as "one in three women have been victims of incest" get bandied about in the media.

4. Many advocates of the sexual abuse "Recovery Movement" believe that all serious, emotional problems have been caused by

"traumatic" sexual abuse, usually incest, and can be solved only by the individual recovering the repressed memory of that abuse.

5. Some mental health professionals overemphasize the possibility of "repressed memories" of sexual abuse, while ignoring the client's presenting problems.

6. Biased therapists insist that their patients must "recover" their "repressed memories" or they will not be healed. This pressure is often reinforced through participation in incest survivors' groups.

7. Why would anyone believe something so painful as being sexually abused by a parent if it weren't true?
   • Because it provides a socially sanctioned excuse for not being able to live up to society's expectations.
   • Because it is a simple, neat explanation for inner turmoil and disappointment not attributable to any other cause.
   • Because it provides a compelling and guilt-free excuse for separating from oppressive family relationships.

TWO

Psychology Fads

*As the vocabulary shared across campuses reveals,
there is an archetype, a model, for the victim's
tale. . . . As intimate details are squeezed into formulaic standards, they seem to be wrought with an
emotion more generic than heartfelt.*

KATIE ROIPHE, *The Morning After*

RALPH HAS ALWAYS had problems. When he was in high school a counselor told Ralph's parents that he should see the school psychologist because he was bookish and didn't get along well with his peers. As Ralph puts it, "You could say I was a class-one nerd." His parents permitted him to see the school psychologist, but they had no intention of going themselves. Ralph commented, "They would drop me off and burn rubber to get out of there."

Throughout his career in the Army, Ralph has repeatedly been described as having poor social adaptation. About five years ago, Ralph's chaplain and commanding officer decided Ralph must be an adult child of an alcoholic (ACOA). "I was working on bulimia at the time because of the military weight-management program. Then I was told I could either start going to Al-Anon (Alcoholics Anonymous) and ACOA meetings or I could put away my uniform for good. My duty performance was fine, but my adaptation with my co-workers and peers wasn't too good."

The chaplain had given Ralph a checklist from Claudia Black's *It Will Never Happen to Me*, Appendix A (New York: Ballantine, 1981) and decided Ralph was an ACOA. Ralph told him, "With all due respect, sir, my folks were not alcoholic."

Ralph described to me how he saw his family when he was growing up. "We always had three squares a day, we had clothes. It was never like my brother or sister had to cook because Mom and Dad were passed out. They drank socially. Sometimes my dad would come home from the NCO club with a load on, but this was the old army. That was normal for his culture."

Ralph told me about his journey through the ACOA movement and how it led him to believe he'd been sexually abused: "There I was saying, 'Hi! My name is Ralph, and my boss said I had to come here.' I did it basically for my career." Alcoholics Anonymous and Al-Anon became Ralph's social life. One of the women he met at meetings was a chemical dependency counselor who had had a massage-therapy practice for a while.

> "She started working on me to go to a meeting at the local Metropolitan Community Church. MCC is a denomination that ministers primarily to a gay and lesbian population. First I said, 'Heck no, that church is just for gays,' but she said, 'No, there are a lot of people there who are working programs, and I think you'd like it.' So I went.
>
> "Anyway, they had me diagnosed as an incest survivor as soon as I walked in the place. I said, 'Dammit, no. I know what constitutes incest and sodomy.'
>
> "At no time could I remember anything being inappropriately touched. Also, they said I seemed to be an abuse survivor, and I said, 'What in the hell do you mean by that?'
>
> "It turns out that apparently there has been a definition change since when I was growing up. In my mind, I had a normal military childhood."

Although it is clear that Ralph's family has many dysfunctional traits, focusing on the possibility of incest did much to obscure the real problems that Ralph needed to sort out.

Ralph was aware that closeness was a problem for everyone in his family. About his father, Ralph commented,

> "I wish to heck I could have had some halfway decent relationship with my dad, other than that of a private to the platoon sergeant. He was like *The Great Santini*, if you've seen that movie. And I wish I'd been able to converse with him instead of always being driven to perform. There was no intimacy—and I mean that in a good sense—between us when I was growing up.

"Standard procedure for my dad was that he would come home, change out of his uniform, get himself a drink, sit down, and watch TV, and you didn't disturb him for anything.

"When I was growing up there was very little privacy. Basically, when Dad decided to inspect your stuff, he was going to inspect your stuff. He did use corporal punishment. Sometimes he'd take off his Garrison belt and use that on us. If he said anything to us, it was done in a very belittling way. That was his idea of humor. It was very sarcastic, very acid.

"My church friends started talking about 'inappropriate boundaries' and 'predatory behavior' and all these buzz words I'd never heard before. They were a friendly, huggy-type church. Most of the women were lesbians, and I felt safe with them. The only guys in the church were very effeminate, and I'm a combat engineer, so of course I'm going to look predatory compared to them.

"Most of them claimed they were incest survivors. They kept telling me all these 'symptoms' I had that proved I was an incest survivor too. They were telling me all this stuff about covert incest, and emotional incest, and enmeshment. It's like their definition of incest is extremely elastic."

WHAT EXACTLY IS INCEST?

We can understand Ralph's confusion in the face of these vague, generalized definitions. The word *incest*, which once had a clear, specific meaning, has been overused so much that the word is now about as nondescriptive as the word *dysfunctional*. To put this in perspective for a moment, let's take a look at the dictionary definition. *Funk & Wagnalls* defines incest as "sexual intercourse between persons so closely related that marriage between them is forbidden by law or taboo."[1] In recognition of the damage that fondling and other sexual behaviors can cause to a child's psyche, researchers have been using a broader definition of incest. They define incest to be any sexual encounter (whether proposition, exposure, or actual touch) by a father, mother, brother, sister, uncle, aunt, or cousin.

Susan Smith, in her criticisms of "survivor psychology," dramatizes the dangerous potential of watering down the definition of sexual abuse or incest until it resembles the "thoughtcrimes" or "facecrimes" described in George Orwell's *1984*. Survivor psychologists often describe emotional incest or covert incest as sexual thoughts a parent might have had about a child that were never explicitly stated.

"The psychic sexual abuse or 'thoughtcrimes' theory is based on the belief that children are extremely telepathic and 'pick up' the vibrational frequency of inappropriate sexual thoughts. One therapist in the Phoenix survey explained 'covert incest' in this manner:

'Thoughts have vibrational frequency and a sexual thought that involves another person without their consent carries with it a vibration that is felt on a covert, subliminal level.' "[2]

So the term *incest* may even refer to *thoughts* a father is suspected to have had about his daughter.

Today, when a daughter calls her father up and says, "You incested me!" she might mean that her father was suffocatingly emotionally close to her, or, perhaps, that she believes he found her attractive. It's abuse of language like this that erodes sympathy for girls who are being forced to have intercourse with their fathers. In the current climate, when abused daughters reveal they've been victims of abuse, people just look up at them blandly and say, "You, too?"

Physical incest is the best term I can offer to refer to what had been the common understanding of the term *incest*. Some psychologists prefer the term *overt incest*, including any kind of physical contact of a sexual nature. Fondling, French kissing, and, of course, oral sex or intercourse would be physical incest, the most traumatic and intolerable contact a child might have with a parent. The term sexual abuse used to refer to physical contact of this type, but it is gradually coming to mean anything from telling a child a dirty joke to orgies with the child and fellow satanists. In the next chapter we'll explore physical incest in detail.

COVERT INCEST

Although I feel that the therapist quoted by Susan Smith distorted the meaning of the term *covert incest*, I think that "covert incest" is a valid concept and an attitude a parent might have toward a daughter that can be damaging. To clarify this issue, let's look at some terms that psychologists use to talk about family relationships that are considered unhealthy and are sometimes labeled "covert incest." At the lowest level is *enmeshment*, a pathologically close relationship between a parent of either sex and a child. An enmeshed mother and daughter will sometimes think like one person. It is hard for one to function without the other. Whatever the mother feels, the daughter feels as well. When the daughter tries to separate from the mother at an appropriate age, the daughter often experiences extreme guilt because she is aware of her mother's deep dependency upon her. *Emotional incest* describes the same phenomenon but is often used to describe the relationship between the child and the opposite-sex parent.

A *sexualized relationship* is more pathological. Though the father may never touch the daughter in any inappropriate way, he regards her as a sex object. He is likely to comment on her appearance in a suggestive way and acts in a flirtatious manner when he interacts with her. Dad may take an extreme interest in his daughter's dating and ask intrusive questions or offer advice on sexual matters. He is often jealous of her relationships with young men her age and may have sexual fantasies about her.

In the most severe cases the father might report his own sexual exploits and disappointments to his daughter, with the excuse that he is teaching her about sex, or might leave pornographic material around where his daughter could find it. He might be careless about walking around only partially clothed and might grab opportunities to look in on his daughter when she is dressing. Other inappropriate behaviors might include bringing the daughter little presents such as sexy lingerie. These behaviors would be legitimately termed "covert incest."

Interviews which Judith Herman conducted, with daughters whose fathers sexualized their relationship with them in this way, showed that, although the daughters of these fathers were better off than the daughters who suffered overt incest, they were still damaged by the fathers' unnatural attention. They were not as severely depressed as the physically sexually abused daughters, but many had symptoms of major depression.[3]

"Louise," one survivor I interviewed, had never forgotten some very dramatic examples of "covert incest," a sexualized relationship with her parents that was rooted in extreme invasions of privacy. Though the following incidents reported by Louise are not explicitly sexual, there is no doubt that they were sexually traumatic in nature.

Until Louise entered therapy and began to talk about her childhood, she had no idea that other people closed interior doors of their houses for privacy. Louise was always required to leave the bedroom and bathroom doors wide open even when she was undressing, bathing, or using the toilet. On through her teen years she was required to let her father and mother watch her dress or bathe. The explanation she had been given for why she should permit this, although she felt extremely self-conscious, was that her parents had seen her naked as a baby and this was no different.

Until Louise was ten years old her mother felt she was incapable of washing her genitalia adequately and would have Louise lie spreadeagled on the floor of the kitchen or living-room so that the mother could clean "every speck of dirt out of me." It was not uncommon for her father or men who came to the business which was housed in the basement to walk by during this procedure.

Louise talked about another abuse:

> "I always remembered with loathing how my dad liked to 'goose' me, often while I was standing next to my mom helping her with chores. Since I was ordered to work, I couldn't leave, and usually it gave him free access to my butt, and he acted like it was a funny joke of his to annoy me. It happened over and over again for years until I was an adult. I used to feel angry, ashamed, helpless, and violated by his groping."

Louise's father also told her dirty jokes and would frequently comment to her, "You walk like you've got a corncob stuck up your ass." He would make this comment not only at home, but also when they were walking into church or into a store. When Louise had her first menstrual period her mother promptly announced this to her father, and, as Louise recalled, "He grabbed fox scent, and sprayed me with the musk, and chortled, 'Now we have to blow the stink off you!' " We can imagine how humiliating this would be for a twelve-year-old, but it is hard to grasp how much more humiliating it was for her to have her mother check her menstrual pad to see if she was really bleeding or just faking it (presumably to see if she was trying to conceal pregnancy)—this, in front of her father, with the bathroom door open. From puberty on, Louise's mother inspected her underpants for secretions and scolded and blamed Louise if she found any.

We cannot help but cringe to hear Louise describe the emotional tortures of her childhood and how her parents insensitively invaded her privacy, violating the foundation of her budding sexuality with their crude comments and demands. The differences between Ralph's and Louise's stories and their struggles to determine if they have been victims of "covert incest" clarify the need for some specific scale or clear explanation of sexually healthy and sexually unhealthy exchanges between parents and their children. I developed the following chart to help the reader to identify appropriate behaviors for parents who hope to raise sexually healthy children.

RATING SHEET FOR
SCALE OF FAMILY SEXUAL FUNCTIONING

INSTRUCTIONS: Place an *M(Mother)* or an *F(Father)* in the space that describes how you were parented. (See the following pages for term definitions.)

	Never	Seldom	Sometimes	Often	Always
HEALTHY BEHAVIORS OF PARENTS					
Provides appropriate sex education	___	___	___	___	___
Affirms child's attractiveness	___	___	___	___	___
Is supportive of child's opposite-sex relating	___	___	___	___	___
Supports child's grooming needs	___	___	___	___	___
Is respectful of child's privacy	___	___	___	___	___
Provides basic physical care	___	___	___	___	___
DYSFUNCTIONAL BEHAVIORS OF PARENTS					
Belittles child's appearance	___	___	___	___	___
Pushes affection on child	___	___	___	___	___
Asks intrusive questions	___	___	___	___	___
Makes suggestive remarks	___	___	___	___	___
Invades child's privacy	___	___	___	___	___
Physically sexually abuses child	___	___	___	___	___

DEFINING TERMS FOR THE SCALE OF FAMILY SEXUAL FUNCTIONING

HEALTHY BEHAVIORS OF PARENTS

Provides appropriate sex education: Parent is comfortable speaking about sex when the child raises questions. Parent provides appropriate books about sexuality and reads them with the child or suggests that the child read age-appropriate books. Parents make it clear they welcome questions and let the child initiate further talk about sex.

Affirms child's attractiveness: In a pleasant, moderate way, the parent comments when the child looks nice; for example, he or she compliments the child on her hair, or her good grooming and taste in clothes. Parent also remarks on the child's pleasing personality.

Is supportive of child's opposite-sex relating: Parent unobtrusively facilitates opportunities for the child to get together with the opposite sex by planning a boy/girl party or by providing transportation and encouraging child to attend boy/girl functions such as skating parties, church groups, and school dances.

Supports child's grooming needs: Makes every effort to provide child with clothing in which he feels attractive; takes child for haircuts regularly, and allows child to select and wear styles that help him to feel good. Allows child to bathe often and use personal-care products, such as complexion aids, for problems that concern teens.

Is respectful of child's privacy: Parent avoids looking in on child while he or she is in the bathroom or bedroom; never enters child's room without knocking and obtaining permission, and permits locks for the bedroom or bathroom doors if the child requests this type of privacy. Parent leaves room when child is making personal phone calls.

Provides basic physical care: Helps child to have clean clothes available; provides toiletries so that child can be clean and attractive; takes child to doctor for any concerns about adolescent body changes.

DYSFUNCTIONAL BEHAVIORS OF PARENTS

Belittles child's appearance: Points out physical defects to the child (such as a large nose), or derides her choice of clothing or hairstyle. Comments on child's size or appearance in ways that embarrass her, particularly in front of others.

Pushes affection on child: Hugs or kisses child when he feels "too old"; does not honor child's request not to be kissed in front of friends, on the mouth, etc. Insists that the child kiss a relative that he or she does not want to kiss.

Asks intrusive questions: Questions child about his or her phone calls, social outings with friends (especially with members of the opposite sex), who he or she is dating, and whether they have kissed, etc. Pushes for answers to personal questions that seem to embarrass the child.

Makes suggestive remarks: Tells child he or she looks "sexy"; comments on the child's adolescent body changes in a lascivious way; tells the child "dirty" jokes, or makes lewd comments. Discusses, with child, own sexual experiences.

Invades child's privacy: Walks into the bathroom or bedroom unannounced when child may be dressing. Opens the child's closed door without knocking. Eavesdrops on phone calls. Walks around the house naked or too sparsely clothed.

Physically sexually abuses child: French kisses or fondles child; examines child's naked body; touches child's naked body (with the exception of very young children who need help with cleansing — in these cases child should be asked for permission before you touch his or her genitals and should be taught to take care of these functions on his or her own as early as possible); has oral sex, anal sex, mutual masturbation, or intercourse with child.

RALPH BECOMES SUSPICIOUS

Ralph continued his narrative:

"I tried to be open-minded. I was supposed to be working through all this crap with my ACOA stuff, so I was into self-improvement. Well, about this time I went home on leave. I had been primed to look for anything that might be incestuous.

"My parents and I went down to Jackpot, Nevada. I shared a room with my dad, and my mom and sister shared a room. My dad got all ballistic just because I locked the bathroom when I went in to take a shower. That might seem strange, but when I look back on his life he was raised in a big Catholic family with one bathroom. You never locked the door because someone might need to use the toilet when you were in the shower.

"But I was all super-sensitive to that stuff now. Then Mom got all huggy with me, and I blurted out, 'Dammit, Mom. I'm not your husband; I'm not your lover; hands off!' My mother was really shocked, and she said, 'What's gotten into you?'

"I found myself saying, 'Holy shit! There must be something to their allegations.'

"I went back and told my church friends about this, and they were all excited that I was finally recognizing the incest. So they gave me tapes of *The Courage to Heal* and told me that, if anything started coming up, all I had to do was call. They would be there for me.

"I started listening to the tapes while driving along in my pickup truck. I heard the prologue, and the author said, 'Any of you men that are listening, this applies to you, too.' Well, all of a sudden I had to pull off the road. I started remembering these things that happened when I was a kid. My mom was a nurse, and in her mind an enema was a cure for every kind of illness. And the book is telling me that women are sometimes perpetrators.

"I started remembering that this seemed to happen when my dad was out in the field.

"I started feeling everything the women on that tape wanted me to feel. I felt defiled; I felt plundered; I felt raped.

"When I calmed down I came home and made a couple of phone calls to my church friends and was received with open arms. As the newest incest survivor of this group I was 'in.' Suddenly I had the acceptance that I hadn't been able to get all my life."

ANSWER FOUR

Why would anyone believe anything so painful as being sexually abused by a parent if it weren't true?

ANSWER NUMBER FOUR: Because it provides a sense of belonging and acceptance that he has been searching for all of his life.

CULTS, WEEKENDS, SUPPORT GROUPS

As I explained in my introduction, the sexual abuse movement is one of the recent permutations of the recovery movement—the term used to describe the process of self-examination and healing that originated with the adult children of alcoholics movement. Most of the survivors I interviewed had read Bradshaw and scores of self-help books that were originally published for adult children of alcoholics (ACOA), and later simply adult children. Nearly half of the retractors had come to the belief that they might have been "sexually abused" as a result of their involvement in a recovery group, usually an ACOA group.

The sexual abuse recovery movement seems to borrow many of its methods from not only recovery and twelve-step groups, but also from the human potential movement, which preceded them. Group reinforcement (and also censorship) play an important part in all these movements. Like faith healers, the leaders assure their followers: Believe! And you shall be healed.

When agnostics ask for some concrete proof of God's existence, they are deemed blasphemous. Likewise, unconverted incest believers who doubt because they have no "memories" are told they are "in denial," but if they put their faith in the process of memory retrieval, they, too, can be saved. On days when their belief in their incest is strongest, they are rewarded with lots of sympathy, smiles, and approval. They are "love bombed," as the Moonies used to say. When their doubts are strong and they begin to express skepticism in front of "true believers," the leadership warns others to avoid the doubters' contaminating influence.

The most cultlike group of incest "survivors" I encountered through the stories of retractors was the disastrous therapy practice in Texas first reported in *D Magazine* in October 1991 and in a later follow-up article in January of 1992, in which Lynn Price Gondolf and four other women who had been in this notorious therapy group were interviewed.[4]

According to the later article, the program led by Dr. Richard Flournoy, formerly of Richardson's Minirth-Meier Clinic and now in private practice, and his partner, Mike Moore, was very unorthodox. Flournoy dispensed the medication, and Moore ran the groups. Both Lynn Price Gondolf (who is referred to as Price in the *D Magazine* article) and Laura Pasley (as reported in the book *True Stories of False Memories*) feel they have recovered from beliefs that Moore created. The false memories of satanic abuse that Moore inspired were reinforced by group pressure. This case will be discussed at length in the chapter on satanic abuse, but I'd like to take a quick look here at the group coercion and reinforcement used by Moore.

The women formerly in Mike Moore's group who were interviewed in the *D Magazine* article explained that Moore felt he had "a calling from God" to treat eating disorders. This calling later extended to victims of sexual abuse and then to satanic cult survivors. These patients were professionals with good jobs when they started working with Mike Moore. Some of the women had been hospitalized for a time; most were working with Moore on a one-on-one basis, and all were attending his weekly group sessions.

The group sessions had begun with people calmly talking about their feelings or their conflicts with their parents, but the group encounters grew wilder, and the tales more sordid. Former-group-member Lynn Price Gondolf explained that if one woman said she remembered someone had abused her in a certain way, another would repeat the story, changing the facts slightly. At first the copy-cat stories were all about incest or sexual abuse, but the tales became more bizarre and began to include stories of satanic abuse.

"Dick and Mike would really be watching us to see if we'd get upset during these stories," said Price. "That would mean it had happened to us."

Heidi Prior†, another member of the group, told about Moore's behavior during her hospital stay:

> "Mike kept telling me the only way I'd ever get out [of the hospital] was if I began having flashbacks and 'memories' of the abuse. I finally figured out the only way I could get out was to fake some flashbacks and say my parents were satanists. I was out in less than a week."

She actually walked out of the hospital at one point, but a nurse told her that her insurance company wouldn't pay the bills if she left against medical advice.

Callie, another group member whom we will hear more about later, decided to pay the bill and leave. She was told that she would never get well and that she would continue to struggle with mental illness until she could admit her father had "sexually abused" her. Moore was right about one thing: She is still struggling. Her staggering hospital debt has been hanging over her ever since. Many retractors I interviewed talked of finding themselves in this financial bind when trying to leave coercive hospital programs. In reality, new laws do not permit insurance companies to deny claims because the insured has left a program against medical advice, but these threats are still a widely used tactic to persuade patients to stay in the hospital when they wish to leave.

Gondolf recalled that at one point suicide attempts passed through the group in copycat fashion. Whenever a patient questioned the therapy methods, others were told that the dissenter was a sick, manipulative person whose judgment could not be trusted. Gondolf reported that Moore and Flournoy told patients that if they saw their parents, they were trying to kill their "little girl" or child within and were putting the group in jeopardy:

"None of us were able to see our parents. If we did, we got screamed at in group. You'd really get harassed if you said you wanted to see your parents. . . . We were all so dependent and enmeshed and sick. All we had was each other. Everyone else was bad. [As Price, who claims that Flournoy tried to diagnose her as having multiple personalities, looks back, she states that] "you had to get more desperate as this game went on. There's only so much you can say about sexual abuse; then it's cults; then it's multiple personalities."[5]

This story is typical of many I heard from retractors. While they suspend disbelief and try to remember sexual abuse, they experience the group as nurturing and supportive. If they begin to express doubts, they are chastised as being "in denial" and are assured that everyone doubts periodically. If they "overcome" their denial, they will be welcomed into the warm fold of the group again. If they persist in their denial and dare to challenge others about their recovered memories, they are ostracized by the group. Other group members are warned that they had better cut off all contact with any dissenters.

SOME DOUBTS ARISE

Ralph continues his story:

"I was getting all tied into this emotionally. The pastor would see things in the way I walked, the way I talked, the way I dressed— everything was proof to her that I was an incest survivor.

"Anyway, I wasn't really able to go into therapy, because the army will not pay for me to go for treatment outside of the military. I take imipramine, so I was seeing the base psychiatrist. [Ralph had been diagnosed with a rapid-cycling mood disorder, a mild form of manic depression.] I had been experiencing terrible mood swings—like the old John Denver song where he says, 'Sometimes I fly like an eagle; sometimes I'm deep in despair.' "

If someone has a mood disorder and it's caused by a biochemical imbalance, telling him that his painful mood fluctuations are really symptoms of incest can delay his getting the help he needs. Ralph was lucky that his treatment was not solely in the hands of his church friends. He reported to the base psychiatrist every few months to get his prescription renewed. Although even biochemical problems such as mood disorders respond well to medication, patients generally need therapy to help them learn how to restructure their lives. Unfortunately, Ralph's base was not staffed to provide in-depth therapy.

Nonetheless, Ralph felt good about his work with the base psychiatrist. He confided, "She sees me as one of her patients who had really worked like hell to overcome a whole bunch of crap." The base psychiatrist had not diagnosed Ralph as being an incest survivor. She saw him as having very low self-esteem. She was focusing on the present, helping him to learn ways to get along with people now instead of looking at the past so much. Ralph explained:

"She had a bodacious caseload, so she couldn't spend hours and hours talking about my childhood. But there were all these non-professionals who seemed to make almost a fetish of their non-professionalism. It was like, 'We ain't got book learning, but we've been shot at,' as my dad used to say.

"And I've always been intimidated by people in authority. These old-timers in AA and this woman with a collar on were telling me stuff, and who was I to question it?

"I started remembering stuff, not that I had 'repressed,' but I was just putting a sexual spin on all this stuff. Like I had this other memory from when I was older. I stopped in to visit my mom one day, and she was sitting around with a bunch of her RN friends. I'd just had a sky-diving accident, and she asked me to pull down my pants and show everyone my injury.

"I go, 'Come on, Mom, I don't want to do this.'

"She says, 'We're all nurses. You haven't got anything we haven't already seen.'

"So then I started thinking that not only had my mother sexually abused me, she brought all her nurse buddies in on it, too. Actually, I wasn't sure anymore what was real and what in the heck was confabu-lated details. Then a few months back, *Changes* magazine had an article on FMS [False Memory Syndrome], and it was like, 'That's it!'

"It was the first time I had seen anybody challenge any of this. It was like, 'Whoa, Nelly!' I finally felt validated.

[At last, Ralph was free to explore the real problems in his relationship with his parents.] "I've basically stopped going to all the twelve-step stuff. To me it was like quinine and malaria. Quinine is an excellent medication if a person has malaria, but if you give quinine to a person who is not malarial, they will develop malarial symptoms.

"AA is great for anybody who is an alcoholic, and NA (Narcotics Anonymous) is fine for anyone who is a drug addict, but with all this crap about co-dependency and ACOA, and with the extremely elastic definition of incest, you end up with a bunch of people who are being crippled due to misdiagnosis and 'mismedication.' "

In Ralph's case it was not a therapist who led him astray; his therapist actually saved him by being a rational voice in the midst of all this conflictual advice. He escaped relatively unharmed. He even looks back on this as positive—a test of strength that has left him feeling he can stand up for his own ideas. As Ralph explained, "I was able to keep an open mind and entertain the possibility of doubt. But they didn't overcome me and convince me of what wasn't real, despite all that pressure."

WHAT INCEST IS NOT

The "dreaded enema" was Ralph's first memory of sexual abuse. Aileen, whom we met briefly in Chapter One, spent eight years in therapy, and the only memory of sexual abuse that she could dredge up, besides being spanked on her bare bottom once, was also an enema. Though Aileen had originally sought parenting advice to help her control her unruly son, her therapist had convinced her that she needed to work on her "incest issues" first. Aileen told me:

"Finally, I remembered an incident when I was little. I was in the dining room, and I was being asked to pull down my pants to get a spanking. I thought, 'Well, maybe this is my memory.' My therapist made a really big deal out of it.

"I got really stressed out and ended up being hospitalized again. This time they put me on a special ward that was just for sexually abused women. There were all these 'survivors' meetings. People were constantly having flashbacks.

"I found myself getting all wrapped up in this. Everyone was being very reassuring, telling me not to worry. If I didn't have a 'memory' yet, one would soon come to me. After about six weeks of this, I hadn't come up with any other 'memories,' because there weren't any. I felt like a failure.

"Then a couple of weeks after I left the hospital, I was just sitting in my living room, and all of sudden I got a 'memory.' I remembered getting an enema. So I called my therapist right away.

"This enema became the focus of our therapy for the next year and a half. He would regress me so that I could describe the enema in detail—what the room was like, what I felt like—reliving the enema over and over again. It was the only memory I could come up with so we just kept processing it over and over.

"My mother really did give me an enema, just like millions of other kids got enemas in the 1950s. That's what the doctor recommended. She did not take any pleasure in doing this, as my therapist insisted."

NARRATIVE TRUTH, HISTORICAL TRUTH, EMOTIONAL TRUTH

A number of therapists are simply not concerned about whether recovered memories of sexual abuse are true or false. To them, the *historical truth*—whether or not the events reported actually happened—need not be of concern to therapists. They do not see it as their job to play "investigator." These therapists worry that a questioning stance would undermine the trust that is essential to therapy. In addition, they feel that therapy need only concern itself with *narrative* or *emotional truth*.

If the client believes he or she was "sexually abused," tortured in a previous life, or abducted by aliens, the client obviously has some feelings of fear and violation that need to be resolved before the client can let go of anxiety and be able to move on. These emotional-truth therapists believe that the abuse, if it is not real, is a metaphor for pain and betrayal that is being felt by the client. It is the feeling of betrayal that has brought the client to therapy, and it is a feeling of control and safety that will bring the client out.

Patty Sheehan, who practices psychosynthesis in New Mexico, the Land of Enchantment, explains,

"I think of it as a synthesis between the more traditional Freudian analysis and the more spiritual kind of Jungian thing that says there is a collective mind, and we do sort of know things beyond the immediate self. We may be picking up on other people's experiences. Past, present, future, there's a collective mind that we need to transcend."

Sheehan's general operating principles grow out of her belief that "whatever the psyche gives you—memories, images, body feelings—you have to take a look at and decide if it's true or false, or if it even matters."

In that New Age atmosphere, it is not surprising that many clients attribute their problems to past-life conflicts and seek a therapist who is willing to go with this imagery. Sheehan is sensitive to the disruption that past-life memories can cause, because she believes she has experienced them herself. Sheehan told me:

"In my case, I felt the sensation of being killed in my neck. I've always had an arthritic vertebrae—I have pain in the back of my neck now and then.

"During my past-life regression, I felt this real sharp pain, and I cried a lot. It was scary, and then it was over. I no longer felt this awful kind of memory.

[Sheehan felt that knowing the source was not essential to the success of the cure.] "It's like a catharsis. You just allow the feelings to be there.

"If it was a childhood trauma or a past life or whatever, chances are you didn't have an environment where you could express your feelings freely. Those feelings stayed all locked up in your body and, at some point, when the ego gets strong enough, you can let those feelings out."

In Sheehan's world, reality holds no importance. She rarely recommends that her clients confront past abusers or sue for damages. She cannot and does not judge whether the "memories" are real and, for her and for those who choose her as a therapist, the historical truth is not important:

"When they can go back and see that child being abused and they can do whatever venting or anger they need to do against the abuser, and sort of image the healing process, they feel better. I've gone out with people to a wide, open space where they can scream and yell and call the abusers every name in the book, to get that rage out. Because whatever happened to them, they've bottled up a lot of anger.

"So they'll reexperience the pain, or they'll experience it, and it feels like a reexperience. When they can do some release work, the pain goes away, and they're not so tense there."

I found it a little easier to grasp Sheehan's viewpoint when I considered how knowing the source of a physical pain does not necessarily affect its treatment. For example, one could go to the doctor complaining of back pain. The doctor might ask some questions about the patient's earlier life events, and together they might conjecture that the source of the pain might have been a high school football injury (knowing that it also might have been a basketball injury, the result of the patient's being thrown down the stairs by an alcoholic father, or a combination of all three).

Regardless of what caused an injury, the treatment is likely to be the same. Tension from working long hours could be causing the injury to flare up now. In that case, the patient needs to rest his back, strengthen the surrounding muscles to relieve the stress on the injured muscle through carefully designed physical therapy exercises, and maybe undergo psychotherapy to learn how to avoid letting tensions build up in his work life. Knowing the exact source is not essential, though determining that the patient has an old injury that he needs to keep in mind may be.

THE TRUTH ABOUT TRUTH

As therapy patients look back on their therapy, how do they feel about narrative truth versus historical truth? Since there is no absolute truth and reality is subjective, do they feel that the most important thing the therapist should concern himself or herself with is the emotional truth? Do they agree that the facts are unimportant?

Aileen, who feels she lost six years of her life to a false belief that she was an incest victim, had some very strong opinions on this subject:

"If the story isn't real, how can the emotions be real? My therapist had an expectation about the level of emotion I should have been feeling. I could sense how he expected me to react, and since I wanted his approval, I gave him what he wanted.

"The emotions they expect are unrealistic anyway. I think John Bradshaw compares growing up in an alcoholic home to being in a Nazi concentration camp. Come on! Everything is exaggerated to an absurd degree.

[Aileen was incensed by the thought that therapists consider it valid to go with the narrative truth rather than reality.] "This 'fantasy' did me terrible harm. I lost six and a half years of my life! I lost a relationship with my mother during her last years alive. My children lost a mother. I can't trust anymore. I'll never make up for what I lost financially.

"These people are out to lunch. I'm angry!"

Meanwhile very serious, well-grounded therapists like Judith Herman and Christine Courtois (backed by Gloria Steinem),* who have been pioneers of the sexual abuse movement, militantly defend the historical truth of any claims of sexual abuse. It is as if they traveled only in their own little circle and could not or would not see what less competent therapists are doing.

I have been told by a number of therapists who specialize in sexual abuse issues that there might be a small handful of therapists who are eliciting false memories, but they are the rare exceptions. The sexual abuse Recovery Movement has been scrambling to shut up the FMSF and discredit its advisers because of the atmosphere of doubt they are creating. Clients who have really suffered sexual abuse are beginning not to be believed. (Some are even beginning to doubt their own stories—we can interpret that at least two ways now.)

Doubt of real survivors of sexual abuse is indeed a terrible outcome of this debate, but the doubt actually arises from the poorly trained therapists who are eliciting false memories, not the critics who complain about the therapy methods. As a woman, a feminist, and a mental health treatment consumer, I certainly don't want my right to bad therapy protected!

When push comes to shove, therapists tend to defend their own. Like any professional group, they try not to turn against one another; they won't throw allegedly negligent therapists to the wolves at the door. They know only too well that troubled patients can misperceive, misconstrue, and

---

*Gloria Steinem spoke at the Eastern Regional Conference on Multiple Personality and Sexual Abuse in Washington, D.C., in June of 1993 and proposed investigating the FMSF to see where it gets its money. Steinem suspected it was backed by some right-wing movement and was part of the backlash against women's rights.

change their minds about many things. Patients can go from adoring a therapist to vindictive hatred in one session, and they frequently distort a therapist's words to fit their own perceptions and needs at the time.

It is every therapist's nightmare to be charged with malpractice because of a fabricated charge by an angry ex-patient. Some therapists have even been falsely accused of molesting their clients and, without tape recordings of their sessions and with, perhaps, no one else in the building during night appointments, they have no way to prove they did not make advances. It's one person's word against another's.

No, they do not want to help single out possibly negligent therapists, because they know or can imagine what it is like to be falsely accused!

Nonetheless, the tide has begun turning on this issue. Both the American Psychological Association and the American Psychiatric Association have recently appointed task forces to study this peculiar malpractice problem. Meanwhile, every therapist should be examining his or her own methods and assumptions, as well as challenging the questionable practices of any colleagues with whom they come in contact.

We need to divide the wheat from the chaff so that the public can again have confidence in the counseling professions.

SUMMARY POINTS

1. Misuse and overly broad definitions of the term *incest* by proponents of the Sexual Abuse Recovery Movement have eroded the credibility of and sympathy for victims of corroborated, remembered sexual abuse.

2. By defining what are and are not appropriate and healthy parenting behaviors related to children's sexuality, we can begin a course of prevention with this generation.

3. Participants in support groups for those recovering memories of sexual abuse are subject to extreme pressure to conform. Expression of doubts about memories is termed "denial" and is punished with loss of privileges (in a hospital setting) and group rejection.

4. Some therapists do not regard it as their job to determine the validity of repressed memories. They feel that questioning the

truth of a patient's memories is damaging to the trust that is necessary to therapy, and they concentrate instead on treating the "symptoms."

5. While the majority of mental health professionals may be appalled by the abuses of misguided or badly trained therapists, they are very reluctant to recognize the extent of the problem and to "finger" the incompetents. They forget that silence gives consent.

6. Why would anyone believe something so painful as being sexually abused by a parent if it weren't true?

   • Because assuming the role of sexual abuse "survivor" provides one with the passionate support of other "true believers." The shared sense of victimhood gives a powerful feeling of belonging in a sometimes lonely world.

THREE

Wider Perspectives

*I forgive them, and I feel sorry for them. To me, for-
giving is not forgetting; it's letting go of the right to
retaliate.*

— PAULA, a therapist

MELODY GAVIGAN, the editor of *The Retractor*, who had run an
incest survivors' group until she awoke from the nightmare of imagined
incest, has spoken about the difference she observed between those who
had been sexually abused and had never forgotten, and those who had no
memories of abuse before therapy helped them "retrieve" them.

Melody was not a therapist. She had started a group because
there were none in her area. She got literature and instructions on
how to organize a survivors' group from Survivors of Incest Anonymous
(SIA), and posted ads and flyers. Soon she had a core group of about
twelve women who met regularly. She had attracted women who had
always remembered abuse, women who had recovered memories of
abuse in therapy, and women who had not yet "gotten" any memories
of abuse.

Melody noticed that the women who had always remembered their
abuse were not interested in talking about it. They saw no benefit in
describing the abuse or reliving it and were impatient with others who
wanted to tell their abuse stories over and over, as well as with those who
wanted to search for memories. Instead, those who had always remembered their abuse wanted to focus on new skills to help them get along in
the world. One of these women finally left the group to start her own incest

survivors' group, presumably one that would deal more with present difficulties. In retrospect, Melody recalled:

"It really began to bother me that the women without any memories of abuse seemed more ill and dysfunctional than the ones who had always known about their abuse. I watched with fascination as many of these women then entered therapy to gain memories, and each became increasingly disturbed."[1]

FIVE CAMPS

We can divide therapists into five camps based on their views on the subject of "repressed memories" and "false memory syndrome":

Camp One: Therapists in camp one believe that sexual abuse is rampant and the root cause of all psychological disturbance. They believe that only "repressed memories" of sexual abuse are traumatic and that most women don't remember their abuse. Therefore, these therapists concentrate on digging up memories through various hypnotic techniques, group pressure, and challenges to the client's "denial." They will not take no for an answer when it comes to abuse.

Camp Two: Therapists who believe that incest and sex abuse are far more common than has been believed for the last few centuries. Though most of their clients never forgot any of the abuse, these therapists vociferously support those doing recovered memory work, because the therapists adamantly believe that no incest survivor should be exposed to the pain of doubt. They naively believe that all therapists behave in a professional manner.

Camp Three: Therapists who concentrate on the emotional truth of memories or images presented in therapy and are unconcerned about whether reports of sexual abuse are factual. They deal with the client's *feeling* of being raped or violated. These therapists also do not question memories of past lives or alien abductions, since they regard all material as reflective of real feelings that need to be resolved regardless of the validity or falseness of the memories presented. However, they do not advocate lawsuits based on recovered memories.

Camp Four: Therapists who believe that incest and sex abuse are far more common than has been believed but feel that sexual deviance is just one of many factors that can affect a person's mental health. They view sexual abuse as one component in the wider context that includes other causes of mental illness such as biological disorders, alcoholism, inadequate parenting, domestic violence, and various socio-economic handicaps.

Camp Five: Therapists who believe there is no such thing as a repressed memory. They suspect many accusations of sexual abuse are motivated by the desire for some secondary gain such as getting custody of a child or bilking money from an aging parent. Camp five worries that radical feminists are trying to use this movement to destroy the American family.

FATHER-DAUGHTER INCEST *CIRCA* 1980

During the last ten to fifteen years, great changes have taken place in the rhetoric of sexual abuse literature. As Martha Rogers, a forensic psychologist, points out, words such as *amnesia, dissociation*, and *memory* were not even listed in the index of Judith Herman's book, *Father-Daughter Incest*, which was published in 1981.[2] Similarly, Herman's book does not talk about repressed memories, nor does it describe protracted methods to unearth them. Neither did Herman describe the result of all unwanted sexual encounters as *traumatic*. She states:

Although the great majority of children find sexual contacts with adults disagreeable, many do not perceive themselves to be permanently harmed by the experience. . . . Thus it would be an exaggeration to state that victims of sexual abuse inevitably sustain permanent damage.[3]

As a general rule, single incidents of sexual abuse involving nonviolent encounters with a stranger were least damaging, while abuse which involved the use of force, was of long duration, or was perpetrated by a relative was most harmful. Indeed, father-daughter incest, because of the closeness of the relationship, was often traumatic for the daughter.

David Finkelhor, whose research was cited in Chapter One, points out that women who have experienced incest frequently have what he calls low "sexual self-esteem." They might fail to relax, fail to have orgasms, or be unable to enjoy sex. They feel shameful rather than attractive.[4]

Finkelhor's and Williams' most recent research has focused on the characteristics of incestuous fathers. Through the Navy Family Support Program they were able to interview 118 recently identified incestuous fathers and a matched comparison group of 116 nonabusive fathers. All of the fathers were biological parents. Along with busting some myths about incestuous fathers (they do not have a high incidence of alcohol or drug abuse), Finkelhor and Williams were able to sort out five types of abusive fathers.

TYPES OF SEXUALLY ABUSIVE FATHERS

- *Sexually Preoccupied*: These fathers had conscious sexual interest in their daughters since the daughters were very young. They often committed many abusive acts over a long period and had often penetrated their victims. They had frequently been abused as children.
- *Adolescent Regressives*: The conscious sexual interest of these fathers in their daughters began when the girls reached puberty. The fathers often sounded like adolescents when describing their feelings for their daughters.
- *Instrumental Sexual Gratifiers*: These fathers, who sporadically abused their daughters, did not feel sexually attracted to their daughters, *per se*. Rather they used the daughters for sexual gratification while they fantasized about another partner.
- *Emotionally Dependent*: These lonely, depressed fathers were trying to satisfy their needs for closeness and comfort, rather than sexual gratification. They frequently romanticized their relationships with their daughters in their minds.
- *Angry Retaliators*: These fathers were not particularly sexually aroused by their daughters but rather used them for sex to express anger at their wives for presumably neglecting them or being unfaithful.[5]

A number of other characteristics were common to the whole group. Abusing fathers were more likely to have been abused as children, to have had sexual problems as teenagers, and to have been frequent masturbators. As adults they tended to be anxious, poorly adjusted, socially isolated, violent, and avoidant of leadership. The incestuous fathers also tended to be less involved in caretaking tasks for their daughters prior to the abuse. Though the authors ultimately recommend that involving a father in early care of his daughter should decrease the risk of incest by building the family bond, some of these fathers may be at high risk of abuse in such a situation. Therefore, it is important not to assume all fathers who abuse do so out of the same motivations or impulses. What triggers the incest for each type becomes very relevant to knowing which fathers are likely to abuse and what to do about it.

One overarching cause seems to cross all types. Williams' and Finkelhor's research shows that a stepfather is five times more likely to abuse a daughter than a biological father.

JULIE—THE UNADORNED TRUTH

Julie is an incest survivor, and she has never forgotten any of her incest experiences. She was two years old when her stepfather, Skip, moved in with her, her sister, and her mom. Except for a few brief separations, he was there until she was sixteen and was the only dad she had ever known. When she was twelve, he made his first attempt at molesting her:

"I was lying on the couch late at night watching TV. Skip came and lay down on the couch next to me. He started rubbing my leg and touching my vaginal area. I had my panties on. I jumped up and went to my bedroom. Then I wrote a letter to my mom about it and gave it to her the next day.

"She showed it to my stepfather, and he said I took it the wrong way. That was it. So I told my mom, but she didn't believe me."

Miraculously, her stepfather didn't try anything for the next four years, but then when Julie was sixteen he began the incest that would last seven more years:

"When I came home from school one day Skip said something about my learning a lesson. He said I could either allow him to perform oral sex on me or I would get whipped with a switch. I had to choose. I chose the other one, and later I felt guilty like I should have chosen the switch."

The "punishment" was not for anything that Julie had done. Nonetheless, now she had done something wrong. Her stepfather told her that if she told anyone they would ask why she hadn't chosen the switch. It would look bad for her.

After this he devised other "lessons" for her two or three times a week.

"Most of the time it was when I would come from school—when my mom wasn't there. He would leave little notes on the door that said, 'It's time for your next lesson.'

[From cunnilingus they eventually moved on to intercourse.] "Skip was saying that this is what happens to everybody. He had to teach me because boys will take advantage, or something."

Julie knew that this didn't happen in other homes, but she didn't want her secret known, especially the choice she had made, so she continued to let this happen. Because of her mother's response when she was twelve, Julie didn't have much hope her mother would believe her if she told.

One day the police showed up at Julie's school. She believes her mother must have known and told her psychiatrist, who reported the incest to the authorities. "They took me out of the home, and I went to a receiving home. They have to check you over, and they gave me a pregnancy test. That's when they found out I was pregnant."

Julie's younger sister was in juvenile hall at the time for her wild behavior. Julie learned that her stepfather had tried to molest the sister, too, but the sister had fought him off. This made Julie even more ashamed of the choice she had made.

To make matters worse, during the six months of her stepfather's attentions, she had fallen in love with him. He divorced her mother and told Julie he would wait for her. When she was released from the foster home at age eighteen, she went to live with Skip. Though she had had some counseling while in the foster home, it had fallen on deaf ears.

Many therapists make the mistake of expressing anger with the offending father when the client herself does not despise him. Rather than feeling supported, the client perceives the therapist's anger to be an attack on a loved one whom she must defend, and the therapist becomes the enemy. It is important to recognize that the father can be both a perpetrator and a beloved parent or, in Julie's case, an idealized lover. If the therapist seems to indicate that rage is the only legitimate response to being sexually abused, the incest victim may feel that she is being judged and blamed if she does not hate her father, and the door to help closes:

> "I told them that I had forgotten what he did to me, and now I love him. They just took it for what I said and didn't try to tell me that this was wrong. My aunt talked to me once and said he was going to mess up my life, but I didn't want to hear it.
>
> "I had the child and kept her. She knew Skip was her father, but she doesn't yet realize that he was my father, too."

Julie had never had a boyfriend; she had never even had a date. She'd missed the whole experience of having a relationship with someone her age, someone who would be her equal, not a caretaker who made all the decisions for her. She told me,

> "I had thoughts of leaving a lot of time during the relationship. I knew I didn't love Skip. He was like a father, and then I felt sorry for him, because if I left then he wouldn't have anybody."

A little more than a year before I spoke with her, Julie had to be hospitalized. She hadn't slept for days, and she felt like she was losing her mind:

> "In a letter Skip admitted that he was putting drugs in my drinks, I guess so I wouldn't leave or something. For two and a half years he'd been putting crystal in the milk and Kool Aid and stuff. Crystal is kind of like cocaine. It makes you stay up, and it makes you talk a lot. He liked the reaction he got when he gave it to me. We would have sex more.
>
> "I would stay up for days and start crying and stuff. Then he would pretend like, 'What's wrong?' and act all concerned.
>
> [Not long after she got out of the hospital, Julie left Skip. She was twenty-three, and he was forty-one.] "I started thinking more about what had happened, how it started. I started reading books about incest. There was an article in *Cosmo* [*Cosmopolitan Magazine*] about these celebrities that got molested. The more I read, the more I began

to think that our relationship was wrong. But I didn't know how I could afford to leave and be on my own.

"One day I couldn't take it anymore, and I called a counselor on the phone and said I felt like hurting myself. The police and ambulance came and took me to the hospital. I stayed there for a week. I got help in there. I told them I didn't want to go back."

Julie has been getting counseling for the past year or so, covered by her work-provided health insurance. She was covered for one year of weekly visits, but the second year she is only covered for one visit every other week. Her therapist is very supportive, and Julie does not feel ready to cut back her visits, but she has no way to pay for more visits. However, she is young and resilient. Julie has come a long way in the last year, and it looks as if the worst is over. Still, she struggles with the past. She told me,

"I'm trying to forgive myself, but it's really hard. I should have stopped it, but I just couldn't.

[Julie has been trying to let go of her shame and be open about what happened.] "In the hospital I was in a women's group so I told them. I told a few of my friends. That's all. One friend, she's my roommate, is one I met in the hospital.

"I have another friend I told, but she doesn't really understand. She thinks, not that it was okay, but she doesn't look at it as that bad since we weren't blood-related. But he had been my father since the time I was two. I grew up calling him Daddy."

BEFORE AND AFTER

Marge, another woman I interviewed, had been sexually abused by a man her mother subsequently married, after Marge was grown. Marge is now in her early fifties and has never forgotten being molested. She is not sure how many times George molested her but recalls it was an occasional occurrence across a ten-year span. Marge told me,

"One memory has me in his room where he boarded with a neighbor who took care of me while my mother worked. Other times were in the back of his business. These times were fondling and kissing. I only recall this type of encounter and have not pushed myself to remember further (or to see if I can have more 'memory' blips). I do recall telling a neighborhood friend, probably when I was six or seven. I have a sense of the ongoing nature over several years rather than an actual chronological fix that I was a certain age when thus and such happened."

George owned a business in town, and as Marge grew older she learned never to go into the back of the store with him. Marge has always remembered this man fondling her, but more recently she has had brief flashes that suggest the molestation went farther. In what she calls "memory blips" she sees herself fondling him. She has always had an aversion to fondling a man, even her husband. She also recognizes that she has a strong need to be in charge of any sexual encounter. Marge told me,

"I ran off to get married when I was sixteen and had my first child by the time I was seventeen. I thought I was the only one George had ever molested, so it never occurred to me that he might do the same to my daughter, but he tried. She told me years later, when she was grown, that he had tried to kiss or touch her once, and she had run away. She was the only one who had been alone with him. She said he tried once, and she ran out the back door.

"I asked her, 'Why didn't you tell me at the time?'

"She said, 'Because I had taken care of it.' "

Marge had never spoken about her own molestation with her mother; in fact she had hardly spoken to anyone about it in her life. Many years later, when she and her husband were going for marriage counseling, the molestation had come up when Marge began to talk about herself as an individual rather than as a wife:

"Some of the marital problems were associated with sex and, in the process of discussing the sexual abuse, I wondered if the sexual problems might be occurring because my husband was getting to the age that George was when I first remember him abusing me. The counselor couldn't answer this.

"It was during this discussion time that I had the 'memory blips,' one of which was the fondling mentioned earlier. I am no longer having 'memory blips,' probably because I am concentrating on other things now.

"My 'memory blips' were like the flick of a camera shutter—a momentary scene and then gone. There is no face, only images of actions."

Though Marge can now talk about the incest with ease, she rates the experience as having had a fairly serious impact on her life. She rates it eight on a scale of one to ten:

"Early in my life, I always thought it was much lower on the scale when compared to others' abuse I had read about. It was only after I really looked at it that I understood the trauma that had been buried and continued to affect me.

"What made it so traumatic was the fact that I never really talked to my mother about it. My family was what you might call straitlaced—in other words, the S-word (sex) was not mentioned.

"The few times anything of this nature came up, even as a young child, I knew from the embarrassed reactions and all the shushing that went on that sex was not something to talk about. Therefore, sexual abuse could not have been a topic of conversation.

"For the most part, my conversations with my mother were genial, but only surface as far as depth—no discussion of feelings and especially sexual matters.

"I think people are too quick to decide that sexual abuse didn't really happen or isn't really important if it didn't involve penile penetration. But sexual abuse can be much more subtle than that and still be damaging.

"It can be anything from a parent being too familiar with their children or being too familiar with each other in front of their children, to not discussing sex and keeping it a taboo subject. That makes a very strong negative impression on children.

"Not talking about sex was as abusive for me as the molestation was. We give our children guidance about what they should eat to be healthy. I think we should give them as much guidance about sex so they know how to have healthy sexual relationships."

Judith Herman recommends asking about incest or sexual abuse during the initial, intake interviews and periodically during therapy if it seems appropriate. For example, since Herman's clinical experience and research showed that victims of incest frequently had ill mothers and grew up to be victims of repeated abuse, Herman sees these characteristics as signs that warn the therapist to ask about sexual abuse. Ultimately, Herman does not see incest as the cause of all ills, nor does she see remembering it in minute detail as the cure of all ills. She states:

> "Once the incest history is revealed, the patient and therapist have the opportunity to decide together whether it should be the focus of psychotherapy. . . . Simply having the opportunity to talk about the incest once, in the company of a therapist who believes the story and reacts in a calm, supportive manner, is sufficient for some women."[6]

Marge had a need to talk about the abuse since the subject had been taboo when she was a child. It is no longer important for her to report the incident for any practical reason, but she continued to be disturbed because she had not had the opportunity to talk it out of her system. In such a case the therapist can offer a lot of comfort by simply listening.

THE DANGERS OF DABBLERS

Alexandrea, another incest victim I interviewed, had taken anti-depressants for about seven years—from the time she was sixteen up until about a year before she spoke to me, when she was twenty-three. Alexandrea had always remembered her grandfather fondling her from about the age of three to the age of twelve and a half, when she told. Alexandrea's sisters had revealed that they, too, had been molested by the grandfather, and Alexandrea's parents had responded immediately by believing and protecting her. However, Alexandrea felt discounted because the mother explained away her father's behavior by talking about his hardening of the arteries—as if this would make him unaccountable for his behavior. Nonetheless, the parents did protect Alexandrea from the grandfather's further advances by making sure she was never alone with him again.

Alexandrea's parents had taken her for therapy right after she told, when she was twelve and a half. She has been in therapy ever since. By the time she was fifteen her predominant feeling was anger, coupled with suicidal urges. She would take her blankets, pillow, and stereo into her closet and live in there:

> "I just wanted to be alone. I think I told the whole world to go to hell. That's when my parents put me in the hospital. [It was shortly

after this hospital stay that Alexandrea began taking anti-depressants. To Alexandrea this hospitalization did not feel like help; it felt like a punishment.]

"I've had a lot of different labels. My mother thinks I am manic-depressive because that's what she is, but I don't believe I have a mental illness. I think all my problems come from my abuse. I have post-traumatic stress disorder and delayed memories."

Alexandrea's parents and her doctor had urged her to take the anti-depressants. Though she initially felt relief, as time wore on she found herself becoming both depressed and emotionally numb. Then she began having nightmares. She had wanted to go off the anti-depressants, but her parents had warned her against this.

When she married and her husband supported her going off the medication, she decided to give it a try. "I guess a part of me wanted to prove my parents wrong," Alexandrea admits. Alexandrea reports that she feels much more aware of her feelings now—she is a poet who will soon have her first book of poetry published—though she still has a fear of leaving her house and has withdrawn socially. Her speech is halting, and she admits that she often feels foggy, as if she were dreaming. She has been and continues to be unable to work at an outside job.

Alexandrea has also cut off contact with her parents and has moved to a new location. She would enjoy having contact with her siblings but is afraid that they might give her parents her new address. "They pretend like they are in mourning," Alexandrea told me, "but I don't believe they really love or care about me."

Alexandrea's last contact with her parents occurred when she and her husband sent them a letter of demand asking them to turn over $5,000 that had been left to her by her grandfather. Her parents had put it in a certificate-of-deposit account, and Alexandrea worried that they never intended to give it to her. After receiving the letter her parents sent her a check for $10,000, and then Alexandrea moved off to parts unknown.

After she stopped taking anti-depressants about a year ago and began therapy with a hypnotherapist, Alexandrea "recovered memories" of her father abusing her, as well as "memories" of more serious abuse by her grandfather:

"The hypnotherapist had an idea that my father must have done something to me because I told him about a dream I had.

"I was in this closet in my grandparents' house, and it was where my grandfather had abused me. There is a couch by the TV, and there are two men on the couch. I didn't know who the other man was at first, but he was tall and had dark hair. He kind of seemed like my father.

"I went from the closet and through the hall into another room. My family was there. I tried telling my mom what Papa did. She said she was busy now. My grandmother flew back in her chair and had a heart attack.

"But even before this dream I had had strong feelings that my father probably had done something sexual to me.

[Alexandrea's later memories, that had come up after hypnotherapy, closely resembled the "memory blips" that Marge described above.] "I'd watch TV movies about different things. It was like a camera flash going off in my head. And I'd see things. I remembered my grandfather trying to penetrate, but he never succeeded."

In her recovered memory she also recalled, "I put my grandfather off by telling him that he could go all the way after my periods started. That way I would be able to know if I was pregnant or not." Of course Alexandrea never intended to have intercourse with her grandfather. She called me a few months later to elaborate on this particular memory. Alexandrea explained that she was hoping to postpone intercourse with her grandfather indefinitely as she worked up the courage to report his abuse to her parents. She now remembers the exact date her period first began: about one week after she told her parents about her grandfather's molestations. Alexandrea feels she was holding back her periods until she felt safe to have them. This is all very reasonable except for two things: (1) Nothing but fondling was remembered before recovered memory therapy, so we are not certain about the grandfather pressuring for intercourse; and (2) Alexandrea was twelve and a half when she had this first period—a very normal age for menstruation to commence.

Here is her final comment on what she remembers belatedly about her grandfather and why it is so different from her early memories: "I think I must have blocked this. Sometimes I see myself in my memories, and I look like I'm blocking it."

As we listen to Alexandrea's story, we wonder if the abuse "recovered" later was real. Why would the abuse by her grandfather have been accessible to her, but not the abuse by her father? We are a bit taken aback by the hypnotherapist's jumping to the conclusion that Alexandrea was abused by her father because of something she had told the hypnotherapist about a dream.

This is in sharp contrast with Judith Herman's treatment objectives and approach as reported in *Trauma and Recovery*, her most recent book. Although Herman warns against the Freudian approach of dismissing reports of incest as "sexual fantasies" about the opposite-sex parent and advises therapists to take all reports of incest seriously, she simultaneously warns therapists to be careful not to get too emotionally caught up in the victims' abuse stories. Herman recognizes that mistakes are being made:

> "Therapists have been known to tell patients, merely on the basis of a suggestive history or 'symptom profile,' that they definitely have had a traumatic experience. Some therapists even seem to specialize in 'diagnosing' a particular type of traumatic event, such as ritual abuse. Any expression of doubt can be dismissed as 'denial.' In some cases patients with only vague, nonspecific symptoms have been informed after a single consultation that they have undoubtedly been victims of a Satanic cult."[7]

Obviously, emotionally overwrought patients do not need to have other worries suggested to them.

Right now Alexandrea's husband is the only person Alexandrea feels she can trust. She is getting counseling over the phone, since she can't bear to leave her apartment. Fortunately, the local crisis hot line was able to supply her husband with phone numbers of counselors who would hold sessions over the phone.

> "Some days I feel strong and like I'm a survivor. Then the next day I might be depressed, and I think about killing myself. I have to talk myself out of cutting on myself. Sometimes I feel so nervous, like I'm going crazy—I can't stand it."

Alexandrea perceives herself as being much better off without the antidepressants. There is no doubt that the medication was not right for her if she was having frequent nightmares, but going off medication does not seem to have improved Alexandrea's life. Her level of functioning is very low now. As she cannot bring herself to leave her apartment, she is desperately dependent on her husband and her phone therapist. Her limited ability to trust borders on paranoia. She does not even feel she can trust her old psychiatrist, whom she saw for five years, because he is also her mother's psychiatrist.

She speaks of dreams and hunches that support her current view of reality—that she is a victim of father-daughter incest and was never loved by her parents. She won't even call her sisters, whom she longs to see, because she is afraid they will tell her parents of her whereabouts.

As she spoke to me in her tentative voice I had the sense that she was very vulnerable. She seemed a long way from being healed.

BETWEEN THE CAMPS

Paula believes she is a victim of sexual abuse. She "recovered" memories of incest thirty-four years after the events. She is a counselor and has read literature on both sides of the controversy over recovered memories, striving to find the truth. In the end she has found her own personal truth. After a great deal of internal struggle, she has decided that her memories are real, even though she will never be able to find corroboration. She believes in repression, and she also believes that some memories are false.

Paula attended the FMSF Conference in April of 1993 and was impressed by the criticisms of the dynamics of repression and recovered memory therapy. The following weekend, she attended a multiple personality disorder (MPD) conference and listened to speakers who she felt had been vilified by the FMSF speakers. I was particularly interested in interviewing Paula because of her response to a survey for therapists I had distributed at each of these conferences. False memory syndrome was discussed at each conference, though from opposite points of view, and I wanted to see if therapists would change their minds when presented with new information. Out of the thirty replies I received, Paula's was the only one to note that her view had been changed by what she learned at a conference. After interviewing so many people who adamantly defended one side or the other of this controversy, it was a breath of fresh air to hear Paula's rational views. She told me,

"My goal is to be a competent practicing clinician. I don't want to harm anyone by creating false memories or by ignoring their personal history. I don't believe there are all that many therapists in the 'Let's create memories camp.' As a practitioner, I'd be reluctant to push and push on someone because I think they're 'in denial.' There's a point where you say to yourself, 'I guess it didn't happen.'

"As a therapist I feel like I need to know if the memories are real in order to treat the patient. For example, if I have a client who seems to be hallucinating abuse that doesn't make sense, I would want to check the records and see if there is any documentation. That doesn't mean I'm going to tell the client that.

[Paula told me about her own experience in therapy.] "I'd been in therapy for six or seven years, off and on, and had had some very severe depressions. I had always remembered that it was not safe to ever cross my mother. I didn't know what would happen. It was just unthinkable to do anything she didn't want me to do.

"My mother has actually bragged about how obedient I was. When I was learning to walk she taught me never to touch anything until I had made eye contact with her first to see if it was OK. That feels abusive to me—teaching a kid to never reach out for anything without getting somebody else's approval.

"Whenever I got my report card I was afraid that my parents might get rid of me if they didn't like it. My best friend had been adopted, so I knew some people did get rid of their children. I had received pretty harsh spankings, but I wouldn't say I was physically abused. My father was generally quiet and withdrawn, but occasionally he would explode. I witnessed his rage once when I was five years old. After that I tried not to set him off, but my brother stood up to them, and they were extremely physically abusive to him.

"When they would discipline him they decided they needed to spank him until he cried. It would take a long time, but they would just keep beating on him and screaming at him until he cried.

"About two years ago, I went to a new counselor and began telling her about myself, things that bothered me about myself—my weight in particular—and she was just real matter-of-fact and said, 'I've talked to you for an hour, and I don't know what is in your history, but I need to tell you that I have seven red flags already that match up with people who have been sexually abused.* I can't tell you that you were, but I just want you to be open to that possibility as we work together.'

---

*Though Paula is unaware of it, this is suggestive. The therapist is introducing an agenda (sex abuse) that the client did not bring to therapy. It is sufficient to have a question on the intake form that asks: Have you ever been sexually abused?

"At a subsequent session, I told my therapist about an image that had come to me years ago. I had seen myself as a little girl huddled in a corner, dirty and ashamed. I had always assumed that this was a metaphor for how alone I had felt as a child. But when I described this to my new therapist, she asked me, 'What happened right before then?'

"I said, 'Nothing. It's just an image.' And she said, 'OK.' But within two or three days I started believing and experiencing that image as a real memory of myself huddled in a corner as a child. And from there I saw myself being abused.

[According to Paula's new insights, she believed that all contact with her mother had had sexual overtones.] "It got so I enjoyed this contact and sought it out. I think this is why I always felt like she had the goods to destroy me. She told me I was perverted because I wanted her touch. I didn't want to push her to use her trump card, which I think might have been to expose me. I felt like she had a hold of my soul.

"My 'memories' are still very fragmented. I'm comfortable with my gut feeling of how they hang together. The initial surge of realization that I really was that little child seems so true.

"I don't know if you would consider that to be 'dragging memories out of a client' or 'providing the opportunity for memories to arise,' but the reality for me was that it helped me come to grips with why my mother has always had such strong control over me that I've had such difficulty detaching.

"It helped me believe that there wasn't anything wrong with me. I had been sinned against. Somehow that allowed me to move on. So it worked for me.

"Long after I'd recovered my 'memories,' I read *Courage to Heal*. I had some difficulty with their views because I really have no interest in discussing my abuse memory with my mother. It happened forty years ago. My mother and I have just gotten to the point where we can be civil with each other. Telling her she was sexually abusive would put an end to that. I don't think anything positive could come of discussing this with her, nor could I prove my interpretation of our relationship. I just don't buy that you have to confront the perpetrator. I have peace in my life, why would I want to stir up something like that?

"I think the purpose of therapy is healing. Sometimes it's important for some people to confront, but I think this has to be something that the victim feels. The client shouldn't confront just because the therapist says so. I don't believe you have to remember every detail to heal either.

"Right now, I have no doubts about that vision of myself being a real memory. I feel like I had experienced the horror of being abandoned, and I was forever afraid of my mother after that.

"But the exact nature of the sexual abuse is less clear to me. There is still so much shame tied to the 'memories' that it's difficult to sort it all out. It's like I have a bunch of photographic negatives of my mom and me in various sexual acts, but I can't tell you how to put those images together into any kind of narrative flow.

"I can't defend my 'memories,' but the feelings that go with them are very real to me. This understanding has made my reaction to my mom make a lot more sense. I have hated her. The memory gave me some confidence that there were good reasons to feel the way I did about my mother. Also, I've never felt comfortable with my sexuality.

"Because of this memory, I was able to get in touch with the fact that I was once a little girl with all this sexual energy as well as shame. This relates to how vulnerable I feel about looking sexually attractive and explains why I've had so much difficulty getting rid of all this extra weight.

"On the other hand, I don't go around identifying myself as a victim of sexual abuse. That is not my identity. I'm a child of God, and I'm trying to do something with my life and take care of my family. What happened, happened. My goal is to be healthy and whole. I can accomplish this without destroying my parents. God is the ultimate judge. That's enough for me.

"My parents are quite elderly now. They don't have good communication skills. When one of them dies the other will be totally alone because they don't know how to make friends. I forgive them, and I feel sorry for them. To me forgiving is not forgetting, it's letting go of the right to retaliate."

REPRESSED AND REAL—HOW DO THEY EACH FEEL?

Out of the twenty recanters I spoke to, eight had been sexually abused and had never forgotten the experience: two by strangers, five by acquaintances, five by relatives, and one by her father. (Some of the eight had been abused by more than one person.) Twelve had never been sexually abused. For all of the women who had been sexually abused prior to therapy and had never forgotten this experience, remembered abuse had served as a comparison that helped them to realize their recovered memories were false.

Their therapists' reactions to their remembered-abuse experiences were quite telling. Although Gerilena had been brutally raped by a carnival worker when she was nine years old, the therapist didn't want to spend time on that in therapy. Gerilena was told that, if she could remember the abuse, it wasn't traumatic and so did not contribute to her poor mental health. Two others who had been forcibly raped by their brothers and one who had been raped by her father were also told that this remembered abuse was not significant. Instead they were pressed to recover their repressed memories.

MEMORY TERMS

- *Recalled*: Memories never forgotten, easily brought up with minimum effort.
- *Repressed*: Memories buried away from the conscious mind; an unconscious mechanism for not remembering.
- *Recovered*: Memories that were once repressed, but have been brought to consciousness.
- *Confabulation*: A false memory created from memory fragments and imagination.

ALL KINDS OF MEMORIES

One of the most interesting stories that helps us sort out the difference between recalled, repressed, recovered, and confabulated "memories" is the story of Yvette. When Yvette was ten years old she told her older sister, Claire, that their brother had had intercourse with Yvette, and she didn't like it. Uncertain that she had any right to say no to anyone for any reason, she had actually stated that she "didn't like it" in a casual but urgent manner.

Claire, who was no longer living at home but had a lot of influence on the brother and sister, spoke to them about the incest, and it stopped. No one mentioned it again for fifteen years. Claire, who was in her twenties at the time it happened, never forgot this incest, but Yvette did. When Yvette was thinking about entering therapy, Claire recalled the brother's abuse and asked Yvette if she thought that was bothering her. Yvette remembered the incest in one full flash of memory as soon as her sister brought it up. She did not have to search for memories, nor did she doubt the memories once they came back.

This is what she recalled:

"I don't remember clearly, but I think the month before [the intercourse] he was touching me and having me come in his room and making me undress while he jerked himself off. He used to sell me to his friends and I had to do the same thing—stand there naked while they jerked themselves off. He sold me to one guy who wanted to practice kissing—all this really sick stuff."

Her brother, who was fourteen at the time, apparently collected money from his friends for these services. He was cruel and intimidating. Yvette reports that she felt dirty, disgusted, and scared. "I thought they were going to hurt me, and I felt very self-conscious of my body. I just felt really disgusting inside."

Her brother kept saying he would kill her if she told anyone. Yvette's parents were alcoholics who were rarely at home. Not only couldn't she imagine herself talking to either one of them about it, she knew she couldn't count on them to protect her. "And my sister was off at college," Yvette explained. "Whenever she called home my mother wouldn't tell me. I had no one to talk to. I was on my own with this."

Though Yvette quickly remembered the scenes of standing naked and the boys' perverse sexual reactions, she did not remember the act of intercourse with her brother:

"I knew that he had sexually abused me, but the actual intercourse I had put so deep in my mind that I didn't want to remember it. That part was just too horrible. I thought maybe my sister was mixed up, but then, when she told me what I had told her, it all came back to me."

Fortunately, Yvette's therapist did take this memory very seriously even though Yvette had not repressed it. However, the therapist was obsessed with discovering more memories. Yvette dutifully applied herself to trying to dredge up more details for the therapist. She easily recalled that the brother had started out making her take off her clothes while he masturbated. "After a while he made me jerk him off. Then he started touching me. It gradually built up."

Yvette feels certain that it all stopped after she told her older sister. She believes the intercourse only happened once. "I think that was the final straw for me, and that's what made me tell my sister. I didn't care if he killed me." She had reached the point where if she had to choose between death and incest, death would be OK.

Yvette had many memories of sexual abuse during that time, things she had recalled even without prompting from her sister Claire. Lonely and alone, she had taken up with a much older boy, Mac, who had stopped by to see her brother and found her at home by herself. She was twelve, and Mac was eighteen.

"He asked if he could come in and wait for my brother. It was dark out, and I was terrified. He had never hurt me.

"Mac kept coming around and just sitting with me until he built up my trust. Then he started touching me.

"It was painful when Mac raped me. I have a really hard time with that. I was infatuated with him. We had fooled around a lot, but things had never gone that far. He had taken me over to his house, and we had gotten pizza. He pulled out this gallon jug of wine. I didn't want any, so he sat and drank the whole jug himself. Then he raped me and took me home."

Yvette had many incidents of spontaneous recall. She had dreams and daytime images. "Things would flash before my eyes when I was just sitting." Some were memories of things she hadn't thought about in years. She realized that her father had also sexually abused her.

"I didn't know what incest was until I went into therapy. My therapist told me that my father leaving his pornographic magazines where I could see them or walking around the house in his underwear was incest. He would lie on the couch in the TV room and play with himself. I would go to watch TV, and there he would be with his hand in his pants.

"He should have done that in the privacy of his bedroom, not in front of his little girl. That is considered incest, even though he didn't touch me."

But Yvette also started to get memories that had a different quality. She felt less certain about them. She was afraid they could be imaginings.

"My therapist kept pushing on me to see if I could remember anything sexual my father had done to me because I had talked about his pornography laying around the house and how much he had cheated on my mother. Almost every session I went to my therapist would say, 'Well, do you think your father did anything? Try to remember.' When I told her that her constant questioning was making me uncomfortable she said, 'That's because you're holding back.' "

Yvette finally came up with a "memory" about her father based on a dream. She was about five years old. "We were down the shore on the beach. I was on the blanket with my father, and everyone else was down in the water. He took my hand and asked me to play with his special finger. That's all I could remember."

Yvette first remembered this while awake in a kind of reverie.

"It just sort of flashed in my mind, and I kept thinking about it.

"In the dream I had after that my family was sitting around watching home movies. I had told everybody of the abuse, and nobody had believed me. There is a scene in the home movie of all of us down the shore. Everyone else is in the water, and I'm on the blanket with my father. There is a close-up. Everyone in the room was talking, and no one was paying any attention to the sound. Then the voice in the movie came out with, 'Play with Daddy's special finger.' In the dream I jumped up and began screaming at everybody, 'Did you hear that? Did you hear that? He said he wanted me to play with his special finger.' Then I woke up because no one in the dream was paying any attention to me."

The next time Yvette went for therapy she told her therapist about the dream. "My therapist did the old 'Close your eyes and see if you can remember any more details.' Now I'm not sure what details I came up with after she asked me for more." [At the end of Yvette's session her therapist remarked,] "There'll be more coming." But nothing else came out about her father.

"The memory about my father felt different from the memories I'd had about my brother. I felt uncomfortable about it. But I could tell my therapist was really pleased with me for coming up with that memory. She said, 'Oh, that's good. That's wonderful. You're doing so well.' All this praise."

Yvette was uneasy with a number of the memories she began to come up with in therapy. For example, the memory with her father on the beach didn't mesh with what she knew about her family. Though the family occasionally went to the shore, her father never felt it was his responsibility to look after any of the kids. It's more likely she would have been on the blanket alone with her mother or sister. "I wondered," Yvette told me, "I've got this thing about pleasing people—how much did I really remember? Am I throwing in little details that didn't actually happen just because I want to please her?"

SUMMARY POINTS

1. Survivors of incest who have never forgotten seem reluctant to dwell upon the past and are more interested in developing coping skills for the future. Those who have recovered memories or are still seeking to recover them, prefer to spend group time detailing their abuse stories over and over.

2. Views among therapists on the validity of the Sexual Abuse Recovery Movement range from those who believe that sexual abuse is the cause of all psychological disturbances and that most people don't remember their abuse, to those who totally dismiss the idea of repressed memories and believe the accusations are motivated purely by personal, financial, and political goals.

3. Earlier respected sources on incest, such as Herman's *Father-Daughter Incest*, do not assume that incest memories are likely to be "repressed" and need to be recovered.

4. A balanced view toward "incest issues" during therapy is advised by Herman.

5. Some therapists dismiss never forgotten memories of sexual abuse as unimportant, believing that only repressed memories are traumatic and they direct the therapy towards a relentless search for these "memories."

6. The harder a patient must work to retrieve a memory, the more suspect it is. While painful memories may be pushed aside, true memories are easier to recall than false ones created to please an insistent therapist.

FOUR

False Memory Debate

*The controversy now unfolding around what are
called* false memories *obscures the real issue, which
is the susceptibility of human beings to adopt false beliefs at the suggestion of somebody else.*

    —MICHAEL YAPKO, "The Seductions of Memory"[1]

DR. PAUL SIMPSON, founder of Project Middle Ground in Tucson,
Arizona, was somewhat baffled when new clients began coming in with
"recovered memories" of horrific abuse. A former Child Protective Services case manager, Dr. Simpson had worked with many victims of
physical and sexual abuse, so abuse stories, *per se*, did not surprise him.
But clients began telling him that they had had no recollection of the abuse
until recently—twenty or thirty years after the abuse. Generally, they had
remembered the abuse while doing regression work with a previous
therapist or while doing explorations on their own with the help of books
like *The Courage to Heal*.

    This delayed memory of abuse did not jibe with his experiences with
abuse victims. He had always found that abused children and adolescents
had difficulty *not* thinking about the abuse—to say they had not forgotten it
would be a great understatement. "They were young adults now, and
nobody was not remembering: the problem was they were remembering
too much."

    But Dr. Simpson, whom I interviewed by phone, had been taught that
you never doubt an abuse victim. Being a responsible clinician, he tried to
learn how to help these people as quickly as possible. He began attending

training sessions that taught therapists how to help patients "recover" memories. However, he had nagging doubts, so he also decided to do his own research on repression. He was perplexed to find that there was very little published research on the subject.

Dr. Simpson had also worked with adults who had been abused twenty years earlier but had never forgotten. He noticed some differences between the repressed memory clients and those who had always remembered. "Generally those with long-standing memories are pretty reluctant to talk about it, to deal with it. Those with 'repressed memories' are pretty excited about it. They want to talk about all the details, to ruminate on different aspects, and to stay where they're at."

He was disturbed by what he was learning from recovered memory specialists and by what he was observing in recovered memory patients.

"The effects of real abuse are real; they need to be dealt with in an appropriate and effective fashion. But what I've observed in the recovery movement is that a lot of clients get into what I call myopic blaming, which is the idea that everything in my life, all my unhappiness, can be traced back to this sequence of repressed visualizations. They'll ignore some very obvious other complicating factors.

"A lot of therapists do a disservice when they oversimplify the issues involved. Someone comes in, say, for depression. This person divorced two years ago; she's having conflicts with her teenage son; she switched into a new career field a year ago, and she's not real happy with her career choice. So she goes into a therapist reasonably depressed.

"Some therapists are one-trick pony shows: 'The problem must be sexual abuse.' Rather than explore the very real stressors that exist now, they'll pull in a 'traumatic' event that occurred years ago and stay focused on that."[2]

As I pointed out in Chapter One, most of the recanters were well aware of the present problems that brought them to therapy, but the therapist made the possibility of sexual abuse the primary agenda for therapy.

WHAT IS FALSE MEMORY SYNDROME?

False Memory Syndrome is a phrase coined by the False Memory Syndrome Foundation. It is not a classified psychological illness that appears in the therapists' (and insurance companies') bible, the *Diagnostic and Statistical Manual of Mental Disorders* (DSM-IV). The phrase is meant to be descriptive, to give a name to a phenomenon so it can be discussed more easily. A number of women have come to realize that the memories they "recovered" in therapy were not memories at all; they were fantasies, fictions encouraged by their therapists that the clients were led to elaborate upon. The most common fantasy was that they had been sexually abused by a parent, and these memories often escalated over time to include involvement in satanic rituals. Dr. John Kihlstrom, Professor of Psychology at the University of Arizona, offers the clearest definition to date:

> "When the memory is distorted, or confabulated, the result can be what has been called the *False Memory Syndrome*: a condition in which a person's identity and interpersonal relationships are centered around a memory of traumatic experience which is objectively false but in which the person strongly believes. . . . [T]he memory is so deeply ingrained that it orients the individual's entire personality and life-style, in turn disrupting all sorts of other adaptive behaviors. . . . The person may become so focused on the memory that he or she may be effectively distracted from coping with the real problems in his or her life.[3]

It is a "syndrome" because of all the aftereffects of believing in these memories. There is a repeated pattern of response. The clients are generally very anxious during the remembering process, and doubts about the memories often bleed through. The clients need constant reassurance and persuasion by the therapist to maintain their faith in the reality of the memories. The clients' entire childhood is eventually "rewritten" to bring all conscious memories into line with the "recovered memories."

Dr. George Ganaway, a well-known and highly respected therapist who frequently speaks at professional conferences and is the Director of the Ridgeview Center for Dissociative Disorders, agreed to be a member of the advisory board of the False Memory Syndrome Foundation. He has since repeatedly found himself defending this choice in front of audiences of his colleagues who are incensed that the foundation is challenging therapists and questioning their methods. During a debate at the Eastern Regional Conference on Multiple Personality Disorder and Abuse in 1993, Ganaway attempted to explain his involvement. Not only did Ganaway believe it wise that therapists in his specialty have advisory influence over the FMS Foundation; but also, after meeting a group of the parents, he felt comfortable being associated with them. Ganaway commented,

> "When I listened to the families they didn't sound tremendously angry; they sounded very helpless. They sounded like folks whose children had been lured into the Moonies, abducted into some kind of a cult. They had lost complete contact with them and didn't know what to do. I'm not addressing whether or not these are true abusers, but they were very helpless and sometimes tearful individuals, and they told some very poignant stories. They wanted to know what to do about this, where to go from there, because the only thing they knew to do was to go after the people they thought might be responsible, and the only people they knew to blame were the therapists."[4]

Dr. Ganaway had to stand his ground on a panel of five on which he was the only member validating that some therapy clients had developed "false memories." He was speaking to a group of his peers, therapists who, prior to his taking this stand, considered him to be "one of them." He has defended the concept of False Memory Syndrome, not because he is a fanatic who believes all reports of abuse are false, but rather because he has come to see the issue as a blind spot among his professional colleagues, which may lead the profession astray. He commented, "I would really like to see some kind of middle ground and common ground that can be reached where the two factions really can come together and start dialoguing with each other instead of each considering their opponent to be a malevolent entity who is out to discredit them."

While I interviewed families personally involved in this phenomenon, it became clear to me that "false memories" often abound on both sides. The more the adult children exaggerate or fabricate the evils of the parents, the more the parents conjure up pristine images of home and hearth.

We all suffer from a mild form of False Memory Syndrome. It's called subjective reality. Have you ever gotten together with an old childhood friend to talk over old times? We each remember what is important to us and have elaborated our favorite memories in our minds over the years to highlight our roles as stars of the show. Our unconscious mind constantly alters our memories to bring them in line with our current view of ourselves. This is true whether our view is positive or negative. While in a depressed mood, most people have trouble remembering good things that have happened to them, and they reconstruct everything that comes to mind with a negative slant. This is not conscious, nor is it meant to deceive. Our current view of reality, and all the past events that support that reality, can shift drastically depending on our moods or our fortunes at any given time.

FALSE MEMORY DEBATES

The notion of false memories has been a hot topic for debate at psychology conferences across the nation for the past few years. All branches of therapy seem to be touched by it. The family systems therapists debated the topic at their March 1993 annual symposium. The Eastern Regional Conference (ERC) for Multiple Personality Disorder and Abuse had a panel discussion on the topic in June. The Toronto 1993 annual meeting of the American Psychiatric Association addressed the topic, and an entire two-day conference on the subject, entitled "Controversies Around Recovered Memories of Incest and Ritualistic Abuse," was held at the Center for Mental Health at Foote Hospital in Oregon. I attended two of these conferences and listened to the audio tapes of others.

Panelists at the ERC in June opened with their perceptions on the delayed memory controversy, and then the audience was invited to participate in the discussion. Panelists strove to find some common ground and focus on a shared goal: To promote good therapy and discourage bad therapy. In his address to the symposium, Dr. Ganaway spoke of the way "repressed memories" and multiple personality disorder are handled at Ridgeview Hospital, where he is director. He qualified his remarks by noting that he works almost solely with dissociative patients, so he can only speak authoritatively about that population. He discouraged digging for memories, because he believes that the patients who are preoccupied with past problems may be drained of the energy they need to work on current functioning. " 'Nonadaptive regressions'* during therapy sessions are discouraged through careful preparation and pacing of the work through mutually agreed upon goals and objectives," he explained.

"Some patients whom I've treated have grown up with histories of lots of abuse; some of them have brought up histories of little abuse,

---

*"Nonadaptive regressions" refers to regressions to an earlier age which make the patient less functional.

and some of them have come up with histories of no abuse. Their life narratives are permitted to unfold in the context of evenly suspended attention to all of their associations without any acknowledgment on my part of belief or disbelief of what they're coming up with. [He has tried to remain neutral and open, and urges his colleagues to do the same.

Ganaway sounds a warning.] "I suspect that the mental health profession, through the process of projective identification, has been drawn into acting out conflicts that really belong to the patients and their families, and that if we're not careful it's going to be we, the well-intentioned therapists, who will ultimately wind up being burned in the worst possible way."

Dr. Richard Kluft, Clinical Professor of Psychiatry at the Temple University School of Medicine, also addressed the group. He remarked that people have become so wrapped up in their own little specialties and viewpoints that they fail to read the literature of their opponents.

"Many therapists are woefully unaware of the influences of contamination, of expectation and demand characteristics, of the wish structure or agenda of the therapist or the patient, of implicit and explicit belief structures, of the patient's wish to please an authority figure who seems to be focusing, whether accurately or inaccurately, the patient's perception one way or another."

Kluft warned that certain interview styles will regularly lead to certain types of distortions of data. While Kluft acknowledged the mistakes therapists can make by unconsciously leading the client with their presuppositions, he also defended therapists against the accusation that they hypnotize the patients into believing these things. Clients who are dissociative hypnotize themselves constantly, and all clients, as part of the transference process, are prone to projecting and distorting what happens in the session. "I think when data collides, when data is incomplete, the only ethical position is informed consent," Kluft remarked, advising therapists to warn their patients about the limitations of hypnosis and other techniques. "I wish the Almighty had given us definitive answers in this area. Unfortunately, he or she did not, and consequently we'll do the best we can with our limited tools and our limited abilities."

Another panelist, Dr. Richard Lowenstein, Director of the Dissociative Disorders Program at Sheppard and Enoch Pratt Hospital, exhorted the audience of therapists to be willing to work in a scholarly way when approaching the problem of repressed memories. He reminded everyone of the responsibility to take steps to see that everyone in the therapeutic community is practicing with the highest standards and cautioned that bad practice harms everyone. He advocated careful education of therapists. "In an odd way, crises and difficulties either can produce regression, or they can produce adaptation, and they can produce growth and mastery."

Lowenstein and others see a political aspect in the criticisms of the FMSF. They worry that it is part of a backlash to silence abuse victims. "The political and social piece of this often feels assaultive to many of us because it's engaged with a direct political agenda." He cautions that when data fly in the face of therapists' most fervently held beliefs, they must be willing to modify their approach. "Perhaps this may, in the long run, have some benefit in forcing us to confront difficult ambiguities and questions that we otherwise might not—forcing us to be more rigorous in our clinical and scholarly work, and to be more effective in certain kinds of political activities."

Dr. Christine Courtois, author of *Healing the Incest Wound: Adult Survivors in Therapy* and moderator for the panel, also picked up on what she sees as the political dimension of the controversy. "I also think that there's perpetrator 'denial' and upset; there's a threat to power and privilege that's going on." Courtois was most critical of the studies that have been done on memory by Elizabeth Loftus, because all of Loftus' data have been based on laboratory experiments, not on victims of trauma. Courtois stated,

"Some studies point to the fact that 'traumatic memory' may be encoded in an abnormal way, different from normal memories. We don't have any means of proving a 'memory' true or false. But I think that we have to be very careful in generalizing from laboratory studies of ordinary 'memory' conducted on college students. [Dr. Courtois believes that some of the criticisms of therapists may be due to displacement.] We see that dynamic at play very often in the incestuous family, and now it's easy to say it's the therapist's fault for bringing these bogeymen out of the closet."

During the question-answer period Dr. Kluft expressed his opinion on one of the most frequently debated points of this controversy: Are therapists expected to act as detectives investigating the validity of all the material that clients bring up during sessions? He commented,

"Since our distinguished ancestors were dancing around with beads and chicken bones it has been known that there is a difference between healing and the search for truth. I think it is important to realize that introducing forensic criteria to the healing situation is a canard; it is also a canard for a therapist to simply accept what a patient says and make real-world interventions without circumspection. That is fraudulent and unethical. I don't think two wrongs make a right. But in essence we are healers, and it is important to understand that in many times and many places there have been effective measures of healing that we now know were effective independent of their having anything to do with the truth."

One of the most productive comments from the audience was offered by Dr. Nancy Perry, a therapist who specializes in ritual abuse, who had attended the recent FMS Foundation Conference. She came away from the Conference with a number of good ideas for ways therapists could lower their chances of being involved in a malpractice suit, a concern that was shared by many in the audience. Providentially, the measures she suggested would also serve to lower FMSF parents' anxiety about what goes on in therapy. Here are Perry's recommendations as she read them from a letter she was preparing:

"I wanted to share with you some of the things I think we need to consider. Get a second opinion if appropriate. Use hypnosis only if you have well-documented and recognized training. Obtain informed consent before using hypnosis. Avoid suggestion leading. Consider the alleged perpetrator. It's true that not all memories are accurate.

"Make it clear by progress notes and communications to the patient that the patient is responsible for the determining of abuse, not the therapist, because we're getting displacement. Continue attempts to obtain pediatric and school records. Never encourage a lawsuit.

"Use caution in the recommendation of self-help books, until you make sure a person is really ready for that. When group therapy is appropriate, refer to a group at the same level of treatment. Keep strict boundaries. Use case consultation and staffing routinely. Keep good records. Refer patients for physical assessments if appropriate. Use a team approach whenever you can. Have medical backup also."

If therapists were to follow her advice, much of the controversy would become moot. Guidelines and suggestions for therapist conduct and constructive influence will be provided in later chapters.

YAPKO AND THE POWER OF SUGGESTION

The most lucid and neutral exposition on the controversy was given by Michael Yapko at the Family Therapy Networker Symposium during the blizzard of '93, as part of a friendly debate with his colleague David Calof. In many of the other debates there was a lot of heated name calling and political grandstanding, but Calof and Yapko are friends and co-workers who happen to be on opposite sides of this issue. As a result, their debate seemed somewhat more moderate, reasonable, and respectful.

Yapko began his segment by pointing out that he is not affiliated with the FMS Foundation. As he proceeded to address his audience it was apparent that he was not launching an attack on therapists, but rather was trying to persuade therapists to take a good long look at what is happening, for the sake of their own reputations.[5]

Yapko, an expert on hypnotism who has spent his entire professional life studying suggestibility, first became alarmed in 1983 when he was working on the first edition of his textbook *Trancework*. He had begun receiving calls from therapists who wanted him to hypnotize their patients to see if they had been sexually abused. As he describes it,

"By the time I was preparing the second edition, which was in 1989, I was getting that phone call, with no exaggeration, at least once a day. It became highly apparent to me that not only was abuse becoming an epidemic issue, but that therapists were operating under a number of potentially very destructive myths—the chief myth being that you could hypnotize someone and find out in fact whether they were abused or not.

[Yapko was most disturbed by the assumptions therapists were making and the subsequent coercive methods they were using.] "The scenario I'm intensely interested in is the scenario in which someone comes in with a vague set of complaints, and it's the therapist who makes the determination, 'You were abused.' And when the person doesn't quite agree with that or isn't prepared to accept that, the therapist says 'Denial! Now I know I'm on the right track.' It becomes a very self-confirming process."

Yapko mentioned that in his second edition of *Trancework*, he included a special section called "Creating False Memories," wherein he explained that it was possible, through hypnosis, to induce someone to believe something that was patently untrue. Yapko sardonically stated,

"That is, if it was a therapeutic mission of mine to convince someone that three weeks ago they were a blueberry pancake, it would probably not be really difficult to do that with a certain percentage of people. The question became one of: How do we look at this phenomenon of suggestibility, relative to what happens in the therapy context?

"Well, by placing that section in the book—it was a lightning rod. I was bombarded beyond my wildest expectations with stories upon stories upon stories, both from accusers and the accused, that were earnestly trying to understand the process of what happened in therapy—why things happened the way that they happened.

[Yapko warned that taking a "stand" on false memories one way or the other was counterproductive.] "Bear in mind, I'm one of you. I do what you do for a living. This is not a question of not being compassionate toward victims or survivors, or of protecting the perpetrators. This is not either/or, it's both/and. There's no question that abuse is horribly epidemic, disgustingly common, and increasing exponentially. At the same time, the other side of it is that there are some people, under some conditions, who raise false accusations. It is our job to be able to make some kind of distinction between when a 'memory,' or when an allegation, has some bearing in truth and when it does not. Right now that technology does not yet exist.

[Yapko substantiates his concern about therapists' misunderstanding memory and hypnosis with an anecdote about one of his typical calls for assistance.] "How am I supposed to respond when somebody calls me and says, 'I would like to have a hypnosis session to find out if I was sexually abused or not.' My question: 'What makes you think that you might have been?' 'Well, I called another therapist, told her I had poor self-esteem and wanted to schedule an appointment with her, and she told me that I must have been sexually abused.' 'So, did you ever even see this therapist?' 'Oh no, this was a phone call where I was just calling to set up the appointment.'

[Yapko righteously complains,] "Now, when you can diagnose abuse over the telephone with someone that you've never spent five minutes with or even laid eyes on, I'm concerned about that. I doubt anybody in here would advocate that as an example of doing slick therapy. And yet I have encountered the abuse 'experts' who will say that in a crowded room, 'Oh, I can look around and I can spot the abuse victims. They stand out to me just like that.' And when I hear that kind of thing, that's what I'm concerned about. How much do a therapist's prior assumptions and belief systems impact the things that they do?"

Yapko had gotten lathered up enough about this to conduct a survey. He got 860 therapists from around the country to fill out a questionnaire that tested their knowledge about memory and hypnosis, and he shared some of these results with the audience. Nearly one-third of the therapists responded to an item showing that they believe that the mind is like a computer or camcorder which accurately records events as they occur, an assumption that has been known to be false for at least two decades. Sixty percent of his respondents believed that if you can't remember something, it must have been "traumatic." More than a third of therapists believed that early memories, even from the first year of life, are accurately stored and retrievable.

Many of the therapists surveyed were equally ignorant about hypnosis. Twenty percent believed that people cannot lie while under hypnosis. Sixty percent agreed that a "traumatic memory" reported under hypnosis affirms its accuracy. Twenty-five percent of therapists agreed that hypnosis can be used to retrieve accurate memories of past lives! Yapko explains,

"Now, the point here is, that therapists' attitudes and beliefs influence their interventions. The kind of thing that I'm reacting to specifically is when someone comes in and the therapist says, 'I believe that you were abused,' when the patient never presented that as part of the problem, and the patient has no recollection of it."[6]

In a recent article in the *Family Therapy Networker* Yapko explained that memory is a complex process that can be influenced by suggestion. Although most of the therapists Yapko surveyed believed that memory was something like an objective information-mirroring machine, they believed that they could influence clients to believe things that weren't necessarily true, but that were plausible. At the same time, hundreds of respondents admitted that they could not distinguish reality from fiction in their clients' accounts. However, they responded to this feeling of doubt by assuming that the clients' stories were true, unless evidence to the contrary was revealed.[7]

Michael Yapko has written a book that talks about this phenomenon in detail. Recently published by Simon & Schuster, Yapko's book *Suggestions of Abuse: True and False Memories of Childhood Sexual Trauma* elaborates on his study of professionals and the implications of this research.

A BRIEF HISTORY LESSON

Throughout all these debates were frequent protestations that therapists cannot make people believe stories that aren't true. Calof's comment during the debate was typical as he proclaimed, "It's somewhat unlikely that in a person who had an otherwise reasonable childhood, that I could get them to believe fifteen years of detailed memories, unwittingly, in such a way that they embraced it to such an extent that they would go sue their parents. I think that's unlikely."

Yapko does not find this unlikely, and history bears out how easily people can be led to believe that which is not true. His comeback to Calof was,

"I think that that's what happens in the context of therapy, that we can help people rewrite their entire histories and view things in ways that are really quite selective and involve a perceptual filter. . . . And you don't have to be a therapist to do that. You can have two brothers or two sisters who have been reasonably amiable all their lives. They become arch enemies when they fall in love with the same person. And then from that point on they rewrite their entire history as, 'We never got along because we were always competitive.' "

The fact is individuals and whole groups *can* be persuaded to believe something that is not true. A frequently cited example of "mass hysteria," or a whole group of people coming to believe something that had no basis in reality, is the Salem witch trials. However, many therapists bristle at that comparison, because witches are imaginary and sexual abuse is all too real. But there is another example from our history that fits the bill better: the McCarthy era.

During the 1950s, Senator Joseph McCarthy convinced many in our nation that communist spies were everywhere, infiltrating our government and our neighborhoods. Just as sexual abuse seems to symbolize all that is evil in America today, communism was the evil that terrified Americans most in the 1950s. Communism was not an imaginary entity, and there were many declared communists, so the comparison is a fair one.

In *Joe McCarthy and McCarthyism: The Hate that Haunts America* by Roberta Strauss Feurerlicht, the author explains how societies commonly choose an accursed group to blame for all their troubles. Hitler had the Jews; McCarthy had the communists; radical feminists have perpetrators. The accursed group provides an immediate simple explanation for what is wrong. The community is relieved of guilt, because there is something else to blame; the community's leaders are protected from being held accountable, and everyone is spared from facing the real problems. The majority can vent fear and rage.

Who this accursed group will be generally depends upon who is in power and who is seeking power. It is provoked by a crisis, for crises challenge the established values and beliefs and create competition for status and jobs. McCarthyism flourished in the economic crisis that followed World War II. Peace had brought inflation, unemployment, and recession. Now, in the 1990s, as women gain a foothold in the economy, a polarization has been invoked, and the tension needs to be resolved. It is politically correct to blame the "patriarchy," a group increasingly narrowly stereotyped and now redefined as men who commit incest. It is obvious who the new scapegoat is when every man is described by radical feminists as a potential rapist.

Similarly, the belief that all communists are alike, the lowest of the low, helped simplify the task of scapegoating during the McCarthy era. There were communists in America—many who simply believed in the communist philosophy of a more equal sharing of the wealth. There were also communist spies. This was the kernel of truth that inflamed the hysteria that followed. Each uncovering of a communist spy led others to speculate that there were many more communists in hiding. It was believed that they were everywhere. This growing paranoia parallels the belief that most men are out to rape you.

Truman responded to the rumors of communist infiltration by taking them literally. He ordered that all two million men and women who worked for the government submit to loyalty investigations. They singled out those who were guilty of "sympathetic association" with communists and fired the guilty, because they might be pressured to use their positions to gain intelligence for the communists. They were fired for what they might do, not for what they had done. If they liked Russian music or had Russian books in their libraries, that was enough to incriminate them as dangerous "communist sympathizers."

Similarly, siblings of accusing daughters have been reported to child protective services, because the accusing daughter believes that they are potential abusers. Because many who sexually abuse children were sexually abused as children, it has become a common, but erroneous, belief that anyone who was abused as a child is destined to abuse children as an adult. Because accusing adult children believe that their parents abused them, they assume their siblings were also abused and therefore will become child molesters. It is hysterical or paranoid to report someone because of what they might do.

During the McCarthy era people who had been accused of disloyalty to the United States government, despite a total lack of valid evidence against them, were ruined. No one else would hire them. The burden of proof was on the employee to prove that he was loyal to America and innocent of communist conspiracy. State and local governments copied the federal government, and soon fear swept the country. People grew afraid of being called communists. "For being called a communist was like being called a witch; there was just no way to prove you weren't."[8] Anyone could lose his job and reputation as the result of another's malice or misunderstanding. To be accused was often proof enough in that atmosphere of hysteria. Likewise, when people are accused of sexual abuse today, they are likely to lose their jobs (if they work with children) and will be shunned by their neighbors. Even if a jury exonerates them, their reputations are often damaged beyond repair.

How did McCarthyism—the communist craze—get started? It began with a galvanizing speech made by Senator McCarthy in Wheeling, West Virginia, in February of 1950 when he claimed to have a list of communist sympathizers. In his speech he stated, "I have here in my hand a list of two hundred five that were known to the Secretary of State as being members of the Communist Party and who nevertheless are still working and shaping the policy of the State Department."[9]

This was a purely bogus statistic. McCarthy had made up this statistic based on a loose and faulty interpretation of a statement made by Secretary of State Byrnes. Byrnes had said that 284 members of the State Department had been deemed unfit for permanent employment and seventy-nine of these had been fired. This left 205, but no one had ever said that they were communist. As a matter of fact, McCarthy's statistics were also three years old, and all but sixty-four of the incompetent employees had been fired by the time he made his speech in Wheeling. The Sexual Abuse Movement also uses bogus statistics. As I pointed out earlier, misquoted statistics, such as "one in three women have been incested," have such a ring of authority as they are repeated over and over, that all evidence to the contrary is suspect.

McCarthy eventually produced a list of names, and, though the State Department cleared these people, the press had printed the list as truth. The public panicked, and there was an outcry for an investigation. The rest is history, as they say. The investigations dragged on for years and the phenomenon of McCarthyism has gained its place in our history books as one of the most harmful hoaxes in our nation's history.[10]

Historians believe that McCarthyism succeeded for a number of reasons. I have created a table that compares these reasons with similar reasoning that has been used to stir panic over sexual abuse. (see next page)

YAPKO'S FAVORITE STORY

Yapko frequently tells a true story of an experience a therapist friend of his had with a traumatized Vietnam vet. The vet had come to this psychologist complaining that he suffered from constant nightmares from his years in Vietnam. He would awaken sweating, heart pounding, surrounded by images of his wounded buddies, visions of blood and gore everywhere. Unable to turn off the state of constant readiness that served him well in the foxhole, he startled at the slightest sound, reflexively reaching for his knife. During sessions the vet would cry about the buddies he'd seen murdered or would scream out in horror at a combat memory. The experienced psychologist treating him would reassure him that the war was over, and he was now safe at home.

Nonetheless, the vet could not be saved, and he committed suicide by inhaling carbon monoxide. Following his death, his widow attempted to get his name put on the Vietnam Memorial in Washington, D.C., since she felt he was justifiably a "casualty of the war." An extensive search of the man's military record showed that he had never set foot in Vietnam.

COMPARISON OF McCARTHYISM AND SEXUAL ABUSE HYSTERIA

1. The simplistic, self-righteous view that capitalism had all the right motives and communism all the wrong ones.

1. The simplistic, self-righteous view that all men use sex to subjugate women and sex abuse is the root not only of oppression, but of all mental illness.

2. The assumption that McCarthy's lack of evidence was not proof that his claims were wrong, but rather proof that the communists were very clever and deceitful.

2. The assumption that memories of years of nightly incest are repressed and no signs of incest were evident in childhood because perpetrators are so clever they can have undetected intercourse with one sister while the other sleeps peacefully nearby.

3. McCarthy's "documentation" showing that he had specific numbers and his spoken assurance that he had a briefcase full of documents to back up his claims.

3. The citing of official-sounding, bogus, and misleading statistics on the incidence of sexual abuse and incest.

4. Motivation of personal gain, such as reelection.

4. An assumption that the end (the curtailment of sexual abuse) justifies the means (ignoring proof or due process by making an assumption of guilt.)

5. Media overattention to the conviction of communist spies made it appear that communist spies were everywhere. Since sensationalism sold papers, the press kept the fear of communists in front of the public.

5. Media attention has sensationalized the sexual abuse issue in print media, talk shows, and television docudramas, spreading misinformation at the speed of light.

As Yapko later reported in an article in the *Family Networker Magazine*:

"This patient had suffered from excruciating symptoms of post-traumatic stress disorder, convincing his wife, his therapist and, apparently, himself that he was impaired by painful memories of events that had never actually happened. In his own mind, the memories were true, and he made them seem so real to others that anyone listening to him also believed they were true."[11]

Yapko commented, "That could just as easily have happened to me as it could to anybody else." Should therapists be expected to investigate every claim that comes up in therapy? The psychologist never even suspected that the client was fabricating the war memories. He would have had to go to the Veterans Administration and check the man's military records, something that is probably not easy to do without signed releases. "That's an awful lot of investigative work for a therapist to do," Yapko admitted. "Therapists aren't going to want to do that sort of thing, and yet, at the same time, his entire treatment proved to be based on a false premise."[12]

Yapko also emphasized that affect and testimony can be totally convincing, even when what is reported is pure fabrication. He added, "If you've ever seen someone do past-life regression therapy, and this person goes back to whatever century and relives their life as Attila the Hun, they come out telling you how much better they feel afterwards." He warned how suggestible clients can be and asked the audience to consider what impact it has on a patient when the therapist says, "You will not get better unless you face facts, unless you face your own past."

If the therapist believes the patient has been sexually abused and lets the patient know that he only has two choices—(1) to admit he was sexually abused and begin the journey to recovery or (2) to deny he was sexually abused and be in mental anguish for the rest of his life—what can we expect the patient to do?

Yapko warned that most of the methods used in recovery work are very ambiguous processes that are inherently responsive to suggestion. Hypnosis, guided meditation, journaling, and dream work are all processes of projection, and material that comes out during these processes may or may not be true. Yapko emphasized, "Hypnosis is not a lie detector; hypnosis is not a truth serum." As we will see in a later chapter, testimony that has been brought out during hypnosis is no longer admissible in court, because it has been proven that hypnosis does not increase accuracy and may cause confabulations and pseudo-memories. Once a witness has been hypno-tized, his or her testimony is forever contaminated because the hypnotized person comes to believe very strongly in what he or she has dredged up during hypnosis. It blends in with reality, and the facts can no longer be separated out.

"And the key point here," stated Yapko, "is that once the premise of abuse has been noncritically accepted, once you make that diagnosis, and you now view that person through that lens, the confirmation bias demands—cognitive dissonance demands—that you now view everything through that lens. And that is what is ultimately problematic. Because then the pressure is applied subtly, and sometimes not so subtly. Therapists will say to patients who are 'in denial,' 'If you won't face facts then I'm not going to work with you.' "

Yapko cautioned against the danger of presupposing abuse. Whether it happened should be explored before the therapist starts leading the patient to figure out when, how, where, and by whom. "You see, that's been sort of the problem all along," cautioned Yapko. "We've had people operating on the 'no pain, no gain' hypothesis—that unless you recover every single gory detail and have extraordinary catharsis experiences with them, the person is not going to get better."

Yapko conceded that therapists are not always the ones who introduce the idea of abuse. The media is so full of the incest issue that clients may come in with self-diagnoses based on something they saw on *The Oprah Winfrey Show* or read in *Readers' Digest* or *Redbook*. However, Yapko feels that therapists should not shirk their responsibility for contributing to the problem. "That's what's called being 'in denial,' " Yapko stated. "We have to consider our role in this. It's not unilaterally something that's out there, and we're the good guys. We have a role in this."

HOW BIG IS THE PROBLEM?

How many therapists are likely to overdiagnose sexual abuse? Aren't we just talking about a small minority of poorly trained therapists? Certainly the vast majority of therapists are responsible clinicians, but unsound ideas and practices have spread like wildfire over the past five years or so.

Dr. Martha Rogers, a clinical and forensic psychologist in Tustin, California, decided to survey a group of child-protective-services social workers in a county (name withheld) of California. Since she does a great deal of work on child abuse cases and has recently been asked to testify in courts on recovered memory cases, she wanted to see how frontline professionals form their judgments about whether child sexual abuse has occurred. Her survey will eventually include data on other mental health professionals, but at this writing she has only collected information on social workers.

Dr. Rogers and her colleagues are painfully aware that there are no criteria for judging the validity of accusations, and that social workers and other evaluators have been under heavy criticism. In her mind this was a first step to finding more reliable ways to interview and evaluate alleged sexual abuse victims whether they are now children or are adults making decades-delayed accusations.

The fifty-three social workers in the study had a range of three to fifteen years' experience and most held post-masters' degrees. Dr. Rogers began by collecting personal data on these social workers, such as whether they themselves had been sexually abused as children and whether they had been in therapy. About a third of them had been abused and had had therapy for problems related to that abuse. Two thirds of the sample had seen five or fewer childhood sexual abuse cases, in their professional lifetimes, that they personally believed to be false.

As part of the evaluation, the subjects were tested on general knowledge about childhood sexual abuse (receiving an average score of 75 percent) as well as developmental factors in children and memory (average score: 39 percent). So they seemed to be well-educated about sexual abuse *per se*, but had poor knowledge about child development and memory. (Rogers postulates that this is probably a result of differences in training between social workers and psychologists; psychologists are required to take more courses in child development and cognition.)

When asked how many had had adult clients who had totally repressed memories of sexual abuse in childhood, 40 percent of the workers had never seen one, and 45 percent reported they had seen between one and ten cases, while the remaining 15 percent had each seen between eleven and one hundred of these cases. This was consistent with other surveys of professionals that show that the smallest number of therapists have seen the largest number of repressed memory cases. This could indicate that these professionals overdiagnose repressed memories of sexual abuse.

Similarly, though 36 percent of those surveyed believed that only one out of ten victims of childhood sexual abuse would repress the memory, 50 percent of the social workers believed that about a third of all victims would repress the memory, and 10 percent of those surveyed believed that more than half, if not *all*, of the victims would repress all memories of abuse. So, once again, a small number of these professionals seem to have a markedly strong belief in the phenomenon of repressed memory. By looking at this information we get an idea about what sort of expectations or biases therapists may bring to their practices.

The group as a whole endorsed ideas about repressed memory that have been put forth by the popular media – for example, many believed that someone might repress all memories of abuse from childhood through late adolescence and later "recover" these memories, and that there are many people out there who do not yet know they are victims. Dr. Rogers was surprised to see that 19 percent believed that you could recover a memory from the first year of life, and that 11 percent believed that a body sensation or pain with no known cause is good evidence of prior sexual abuse.

More than 40 percent agreed that someone who can't remember any abuse, but has many of the symptoms, was abused; and 70 percent believed that hypnosis increases accuracy of memory. Curiously, though 48 percent said that if a client feels he or she has been abused, the client probably was, 57 percent indicated that some therapeutic methods can increase the chance that what is recovered in memory is inaccurate. This begs the question: How can they be so certain about vague feelings of the client when they acknowledge that some therapeutic methods can cause inaccurate memories?

Although 38 percent agreed that memory is like a videotape in the brain, 68 percent indicated that memory can be altered by post-event information. Do some believe the videotape can be altered – that future occurrences can change our perceptions of *past* events?

The study showed a lot of contradictions, uncertainty, and confusion to be present in these professionals. They weren't sure how memory really works and how accurate recovered memories might be. They had many mistaken assumptions. To be fair, Rogers admits that these professionals work primarily with *current* child victims rather than adults who have come to believe they were victimized as children. We cannot be certain what their responses would have been if they were told to comment only on adults who were retrieving memories of abuse. In later chapters I'll be presenting the most recent research on memory and hypnotism, and that should clear up some of this confusion for the reader.[13]

IT FOLLOWED HER FROM STATE TO STATE

Carol had never forgotten being sexually abused several times during her growing-up years. An uncle had molested her when she was about ten years old; the brother of a friend had taken advantage of her in early adolescence, and then later on, a high-school teacher had seduced her. "But my therapist wasn't interested in that," Carol told me. "He kept saying, 'But what happened inside your family that made you vulnerable to being abused by outsiders?' "

Carol's therapist was a minister doing pastoral counseling. She had sought counseling because she had been in a constant state of anxiety over a life-threatening illness that her infant daughter was fighting.

"The minister kept insisting that I must have been sexually abused by my father. I kept saying, 'This doesn't sound right. This can't be true.' But at the same time, he had told me repeatedly that, if I didn't believe it, my anxiety would never stop. My anxiety was so overpowering that I couldn't live a normal life at all. I felt like I had to believe it and I had to do whatever my therapist said I had to do to work it through."

ANSWER FIVE

Why would anyone believe anything so painful as being sexually abused by a parent if it weren't really true?

ANSWER NUMBER FIVE: Because someone in authority has said that belief is the only road to mental health.

"About a year into my relationship with the minister, he seduced me. As soon as he gained my trust, he took advantage of that. My marriage was in really bad shape from all the stress over my daughter. So I ended up getting into this really, really damaging relationship with this minister. Then the only way I could find to get out of that was to convince my husband that we should move. We put in for a transfer and moved to Tennessee."

Carol had tremendous difficulty leaving the diagnosis of sexual abuse behind. It seemed to dog her steps everywhere. The first therapist she chose at random from the phone book urged her to work on her "incest issues." Looking for a place that could provide a new approach, she signed up for a program in Ohio that her sister had recommended.

"So I went from Tennessee to Ohio just to go to this particular treatment center, and I spent about five weeks there. It really was a good program in many ways. They helped me with my self-esteem. But as soon as I got in there, they wanted to know if I was an incest survivor.

"We did affirmations and a lot of hugging. We would do things like one person would get in the middle of the circle and we'd all be sitting on the floor. The person in the middle would tell the group what she wished she could hear. Then she would close her eyes and everybody would take turns saying positive things to the person. It was a wonderful feeling to be in the middle. In all my therapy before that, we kept focusing on what a sick person I was. I needed a better identity, and that program helped me find more positive things about myself.

"I was ready for a total change, so when I got out I started therapy with a new therapist. The first thing she asks me was if I'm an incest survivor, and I told her that I might be, but I didn't want to work on that. I wanted to work on my self-esteem and get back on my feet again. And she said, 'We have to work on your incest issues, or you're just going to stuff it and then you'll get depressed again.' So I let her pressure me into it, and within five or six weeks I was really depressed again."

ANSWER SIX

Why would anyone believe anything so painful as being sexually abused by a parent if it were not true?

ANSWER NUMBER SIX: Because no questioning of the treatment is allowed. The clients are judged not competent to decide whether their "memories" are true. Doubting is regarded as proof of their "denial" and resistance to getting well.

"She tried to talk me into signing myself into a hospital for inpatient care again. It was an incest survivors' treatment center where all they did all day was draw and write about incest. She took me on a tour through the place, and the walls were lined with incest pictures and poems that the inmates had put on the walls. It was like walking into a torture center for me. I said I did not want to go into that place, and she said, 'Well, I really think you need this. It would do you a lot of good.'

"I decided to go back to my old therapist. I told him that I didn't want to do the incest stuff anymore because it just depressed me, and he said OK. I started cutting my appointments back to once a week. From that point on, I started feeling a lot better.

"We moved to Chicago from Tennessee and I was still on Prozac. I had to go to a psychiatrist to get the prescription. I just picked a name out of the phone book. When I went to this guy, he asked me why I was on Prozac. I told him that I had been very anxious and I got real depressed, so right away this guy asks me if I was an incest survivor. It was like these people all had the same script.

"So I started saying this is what I remember, and these are the things that I don't think are true, and I just don't want to work on it anymore. I don't think these memories are real, and when I start to work on 'incest issues' I get really crazy. So, this psychiatrist says to me, 'Well if it's so uncomfortable for you to work on these issues, then they must be significant.' So I saw him about three times, and he convinced me that I was an incest survivor again. I became totally nonfunctional again, right back where I started."

SIMPSON'S SUGGESTIONS

Because Dr. Simpson, introduced at the beginning of this chapter, had misgivings, his curiosity led him to check out a meeting of the Arizona FMSF.

"I was expecting to walk into a room full of satanists and child molesters. What I found were a lot of parents who looked like they just stepped out of Norman Rockwell paintings. I've worked with a lot of sex offenders; I'm not easily deluded by the nice presentations that a molester puts out. What I found were a lot of hurting, in-pain, families—parents who were trying to deal with something that was very bewildering. I was one of the first therapists to step into their midst, and they were very suspicious of me. There's a lot of distrust of therapists; that's beginning to dissolve as they realize there is a great body of therapists who are trying to undo damage."[14]

Indeed, Dr. Simpson was so impressed that he has begun to offer seminars to therapists in his area who were open to learning about more discriminating methods of treating patients who suspect they may have been sexually abused.

"I can tell you that there's a lot of misinformation out there. I believe that a large majority of therapists simply don't know. They take their lead from 'experts' who say that this and this is happening. There's a block of therapists who are truly somewhere in the middle, and that's where I am. Is there a phenomenon called repression? I think that there well may be, but we as a profession have done a very poor job of reliably and empirically exploring its dimensions. Are there satanic groups? Is there ritualistic abuse? Yes. It certainly is possible. But in the volume it's being described, it's just not there. The FBI, law enforcement, all the resources we've got have failed to find any evidence of the thousands of cases of ritualized murders that are being reported. If a phenomenon is being presented as occurring, it's up to the presenters of that phenomenon to demonstrate it to the scientific community."

Dr. Simpson's seminar for professionals not only strives to give both sides of the research on accusations of sexual abuse so that therapists can be better informed, he also offers suggestions for therapists that will keep them out of trouble. Below is a condensed list adapted from his suggestions[15]

If you are in therapy or thinking of going into therapy, look the list over carefully. These criteria will give you some idea how competent your chosen therapist is. If you find that your therapist uses the methods Dr. Simpson cautions against, strongly consider seeking a new therapist. At the very least, get a second opinion.

PRECAUTIONS FOR THERAPISTS

1. Watch your own agenda. If you were abused as a child or if you have a strong political bias, you may be prone to distorting the client's symptoms.

2. Help clients distinguish between free standing memories of abuse and False Memory Syndrome.

3. Reserve judgment about your clients' claims of sexual abuse if they have done any of the following: trance work, regression groups, visualizations of events prior to age three.

4. Think systematically. Interview other family members and see if you can help mediate the conflict.

5. Avoid group contagion by not putting clients into support groups until their abuse has been fully detailed and documented.

6. Do not rely on "magical" checklists such as the ones in Blume's *Secret Survivors* or Bass's and Davis' *The Courage to Heal*.

7. Keep an open mind. Do not assume guilt on the part of the accused, especially if the memories are decades-delayed or if there is no corroborating evidence.

8. If the client expresses doubts about de-repressed material, do not accuse him/her of being in denial. Encourage the client to explore other alternatives with an open mind.

9. Use standardized diagnostic tools to screen for personality characteristics, such as fantasy-prone personality, that could make the client particularly vulnerable to confabulating.

10. Never use trance induction methods to help clients retrieve possible "repressed memories."

SUMMARY POINTS

1. Effective therapy does not allow the client to wallow in an orgy of blaming all problems in his or her life on past abuses—real or imagined—to the neglect of other important issues.

2. Not all "false memories" result from poor therapy. Clients may self-diagnose after hearing stories presented in the popular media and after reading self-help books. Poor therapists, however, fail to help their clients separate fact from fiction.

3. Clients with "false memories" receive constant reassurance and persuasion by sexual abuse recovery therapists that the clients' memories are true. The clients' entire childhood is eventually rewritten to bring all conscious memories into line with the "recovered memories."

5. Current events and emotions often change our view of past events, creating an individual's subjective reality. Memories can be reinterpreted or distorted in order to fit our needs in the present.

6. Certain therapists' interview styles may lead to distortion of data. Many therapists fail to take such dangers into account, either through ignorance or personal myopia.

7. Memory recovery work such as hypnosis, guided meditation, journaling, and dream work are all processes of projection, and the resulting material may not be true.

8. The human mind is not like a videotape that accurately records all data, nor is hypnosis an infallible means to extract these memories.

9. Without intensive "detective" work that produces incontrovertible corroboration of the abuse, there is no way that a therapist can be certain whether or not a "repressed memory" is true.

10. The proper stance for the therapist should be a neutral one. Clients must be given the freedom to determine the validity of their memories without pressure, one way or the other, from the therapist.

11. Like the communist scare of the 1950s known as McCarthyism, the sexual abuse recovery movement provides its supporters with a simple solution to complex problems.

12. Studies show that a small percentage of professionals hold the most radical views, but that these people may have a tendency to overdiagnose "repressed memories" of sexual abuse.

13. Why would anyone believe anything so painful as being sexually abused by a parent if it weren't true?
    • Because someone in authority has said that belief is the only road to mental health.
    • Because no questioning is allowed. The experts do not trust the clients to know what is good for them. When the clients express doubts, the therapists tell them they are "in denial" and resistant to getting well.

FIVE

A Deadly
Dependence

*In light of the thousands of unlicensed therapists prac-
ticing all sorts of methods around the country, mental-
health consumers must protect themselves against
therapy that might be harmful.*

— ANDREW MEACHAM, *Changes Magazine*[1]

DEBORAH, THE RETRACTOR WHO had accused her mother of abuse
in Chapter One, had commented that one of the things that eroded her
belief that the memories of sexual abuse could be true was that she could
see she wasn't getting any better as a result of therapy. Indeed, all of the
retractors reported that there had been an alarming deterioration in their
functioning while their therapy was focused on retrieving memories of
abuse. Yet, some of the therapists who subscribe to the "all mental illness
is caused by sexual abuse" theory regard the client's decline in functioning as a sure sign that the diagnosis is correct. They tell their patients
to expect to get worse, and that to get worse means that healing is
beginning.

Though it is true that many patients regress somewhat after entering
therapy, largely because they are feeling safe to regress, and because the
stress of exploring one's emotional problems can leave one too tired to cope
with some everyday tasks, the majority of therapists watch to see that the
client is improving and question their therapy methods or diagnosis if the
client does not show clear signs of growing mental functioning. How do
therapists judge how a client is doing? How can you know if you are
responding well to therapy?

Below is an adaptation of the Global Assessment of Functioning Scale used by many therapists.

ASSESSMENT OF FUNCTIONING

81–90   Symptom-free. Can function well in many roles. Problems are solved before they get too big. Others seek you out because of your warmth and integrity.

71–80   Occasional symptoms in reaction to stress, but generally good functioning in all areas. Able to pursue many gratifying interests. A feeling of general satisfaction with life shared with friends and loved ones.

61–70   Occasional mild depression or insomnia or minor difficulties with social, occupational, or school functioning, but still has meaningful friendships. Most people would perceive you as mentally healthy.

51–60   Moderate degree of anxiety, depression, low self-esteem, antisocial feelings or hyped-up feelings. Difficulties with co-workers and few real friends.

41–50   Serious symptoms such as thoughts of suicide, obsessive thoughts or compulsive behaviors, frequent anxiety, antisocial behavior, or compulsive drinking.

31–40   Major difficulties with work, family relations, cloudy thinking, poor judgment, depressive withdrawal, or suicide attempt. Unable to carry out normal daily functions such as housework.

21–30   Unable to function in most areas (stays in bed all day), or suffers from delusions or hallucinations, or has serious difficulty communicating (is incoherent or unresponsive), or acts in grossly inappropriate ways.

11–20   In danger of hurting self or others (suicide attempts or violent outbursts), difficulty maintaining minimal personal hygiene, incoherent or mute.

1–10   Persistent danger of hurting self or others. No attempts at personal hygiene. Needs constant supervision.

The behavioral descriptions are ranked from highest functioning level (90) to the most dysfunctional level (1). Therapists who use this scale rate their patients periodically to make sure they are headed in the right direction in therapy. Of course we all have our ups and downs, so therapists must look for sustained evidence of health or deterioration. If after looking at this scale, you realize that you have become increasingly dysfunctional since starting therapy, you might want to seek a second opinion about your diagnosis and treatment.

If your sustained level of functioning has fallen more than ten points by the above scale since you began therapy, your current treatment may be doing you more harm than good. Consider discussing your therapy with another professional. Tips about this are given in Chapter Fourteen.

As I mentioned earlier, some sexual abuse recovery therapists believe that patients who are working to retrieve repressed memories will get worse and worse until they've dredged them all up. As one retractor told me:

> "My husband called up the therapist once and said, 'My wife seems to be getting so much worse.' But my therapist told him, 'Once you start being hospitalized again and again it's a sign that you are really working on your memories.' He tried to convince my husband that the worse I seemed, the better I was getting. And he had this attitude like my husband should be grateful that I had such a good therapist."

DEBORAH'S RE-EVALUATION

When Deborah terminated therapy with Binah, Deborah had put her name on a waiting list to see a psychiatrist. Canadian Medicare is quite overcrowded, and it can take as long as a year to get your first appointment. Deborah had turned forty and had briefly married a man she did not know very well, just to prove she could get married. Within six months the marriage ended in divorce, and Deborah was left with herself again, still unchanged, still repeating all her old patterns. "I had gotten very, very depressed about the marriage, and I was actually making plans to kill myself. When I told my psychiatrist, she immediately put me on anti-depressants."

This psychiatrist believed that no one should see a psychiatrist for more than a year. She wasted no time and pushed Deborah to examine what she was doing with her life. Whenever Deborah would try to blame her parents or others around her for her troubles, the psychiatrist would force Deborah to look at her own part in the conflict. Deborah confided,

"That was a brutal year for me. I was having problems at work; I was breaking up a marriage, and I was trying to figure out how to reconnect with my mom.

"My mother was really reluctant to forgive me. She's a real grudge holder. But she finally got over it, and I had my psychiatrist's support all through that.

[After one very intense year of therapy with this savvy psychiatrist, Deborah was ready to be on her own.] "I had needed to do some growing up. I hadn't done it in my twenties or thirties, so I had to finish growing up in my forties. I had been incredibly immature. I expected to be looked after, and I finally had to accept responsibility for myself.

[Though Deborah had been working on becoming more independent when she was working with Binah, she could not achieve this until she changed therapists.] "Binah was very sympathetic. She would point out to me things that weren't really my personal problem but problems all women had in those political times. Binah also tried to be my mother and reparent me. She wasn't hard on me except when I had doubts about the abuse.

"What I noticed about the psychiatrist right away was that she didn't allow me any excuses. Like if I had said I was having trouble with such and such, but of course who could help it in this society, she would say, 'I'm sorry, but that's not good enough. You are going to have to learn to get along in this world as it is.' And she immediately zeroed in on my anger at my mother. She really pushed me and pushed me to come to terms with that. Binah had encouraged me to see myself as a victim, but the psychiatrist really discouraged that."

As I listened to Deborah talk about her parents I was impressed with how resolved her anger at her mother, in particular, seemed to be. I wondered where all the rage had gone. Deborah explained,

"I can still complain *ad nauseam* about my mother, but I don't want to blame my parents anymore. They weren't great, but it's up to me now. I don't know where the anger went. I guess it gets eaten up by understanding. I always knew that my mother had had a really hard life.

"I can either sit around for the rest of my life saying, 'Oh, I could never do this or that because of my childhood,' or I could just get on with it. I've already wasted half of my allotted years being miserable."

ANSWER SEVEN

Why would anyone believe anything so painful as being sexually abused by a parent if it weren't true?

ANSWER NUMBER SEVEN: Because it is a socially sanctioned excuse for escaping responsibility for one's own mistakes or for failing to grow up emotionally.

OVERSIMPLIFICATION

If all the client's difficulties are being pinned on the parent, the client is forced to create a bad enough home environment to justify his or her progressively deteriorating coping ability. The "sympathy coinage" has become impossibly inflated. It's not enough anymore to report that your father beat you black and blue. As Dr. Ganaway, Director of the Dissociative Disorders Unit at Ridgeview Hospital and FMSF Advisory board member, stated in a follow-up phone interview I did with him,

"The 'garden variety' stories have no impact anymore." [It's nigh unto impossible to capture sympathetic attention unless you can report that you have been satanically abused.]

"If the person can say, 'In reality what I went through was a part of me being groomed for a position as a high priestess,' then it's not just a case of Dad doing some meaningless horrible thing to me for his gratification. This was all part of being groomed for something very special. They were all going to be priests and priestesses. But where are all the peons? They, for some reason, never wind up in therapy. It certainly suggests that the cult mythology meets some very important psychological needs, and that's why individuals might come up with a particular kind of story or feel attracted to believe it."

When clients find that they are no better off than when they started therapy and may, in fact, be more symptomatic, they are informed that there must have been more abuse that has not yet been uncovered. The party line says once you recover the memories you will be well. But after the client comes up with some memories, she often finds she does not get well. Then the therapist says, "Once you can remember your *father* abusing you, you will be well." When that doesn't work either, the client is exhorted to remember who else was there, and on and on it goes.

That is not to say that clients being drawn into repressed memory therapy really had ideal parents and have been totally duped by clever therapists. Because Ganaway is director of an inpatient unit for Multiple Personality Disorder patients, he often gets clients who have been in outpatient therapy with another therapist for a while.

"In a few cases I've had people decide there never was any abuse, but I'd have to say that out of nearly 350 patients I've seen there are very few who have said, 'I've decided that this is entirely my problem, that I really did have ideal parents and that there were never any traumas in my life.'

"Almost always there were issues that they had to go back and deal with; oftentimes it was overidealizing. They had to learn to deal with the fact that their parents were real people who had strengths, but also weaknesses. Those had to be recognized.

"They had to allow themselves to feel some of that anger and disappointment that they didn't have perfect parents. But then, who does?"

It's a normal developmental stage to realize that your parents have faults. This most often hits kids when they are in junior high school. All the faults are glaring at first, and young adolescents are perpetually mortified by their parents' dress, habits, opinions, etc. Somewhere down the line most well-adjusted older teens begin to see their parents as neither perfect nor monstrous. But if, for some reason, the adolescent had a need to idealize the parent—perhaps the father has abandoned the family, and mom is all the adolescent has—the recognition of Mom's faults can seem like the discovery of a betrayal. In reality, mom wasn't hiding her faults, but the postadolescent may believe he or she was misled by Mom because of his or her own failure to perceive Mom more realistically. Ganaway explains,

"The parents may try to convince the child, 'Hey we're not perfect,' but the child may need the parent to be perfect for whatever internal psychological reason. So no matter what the parents do, they are stuck with that label, a setup down the road for them to be vilified when their faults become harder to ignore.

"On the other hand, there are parents who feel that they should never allow themselves to look less than perfect in front of the children, so they'll never argue in front of the kids. Each parent will defend the other one if the parent makes a mistake. They'll give the impression that they really are infallible. Then those kids are never allowed to recognize that everybody is fallible.

"Unfortunately those kids may grow up with a sense of perfectionism inside themselves, filling the vacuum left by a failure on the parents' part to provide permission through example to make mistakes and still feel good about oneself."

Ganaway is also critical of therapists who take everything the client says about the parents at face value. Many people find it easier to deal with things that are divided into all black or all white. The client's inner vision of the parent is often distorted in response to the client's mood or mental state. When therapists take the client's description of the parent literally and do not gently help the client form a fuller vision of the parent, they are reinforcing the distortion and postponing the client's coming to terms with a more realistic vision of the parent.

As Ganaway explains, the way small children typically misperceive their parents illustrates the danger in relying solely on the client's view of the parents. Ganaway explains,

"For instance, the small child feels that Mom is not there when he needs her. She may have gotten sick and been in the hospital, or she may have needed to go somewhere else for some reason. But to the child it's, 'She must not love me; I must be a defective person.' So the child may fantasize that this is a malevolent mom. It may be a mom who is just inadequate in some way, just can't meet all the demands that are being placed upon her all the time.

"What we are often seeing in adult patients as we let them describe their perceptions of their parents are their own embellishments of how an individual appeared to be to them – an interpretation which may or may not have a lot to do with reality.

"When therapists take literally what patients are coming up with, i.e., their perceptions of individuals in the present and in the past, without considering the possibility that there may be some distortion based on the patient's conflicts over needs and wishes, then they're really trivializing the process of psychotherapy, oversimplifying it to what I call 'McTherapy,' a fast-food therapy that tends to boil everything down to its simplest terms."

There's always more than one side to the story. Patients who have a therapist who encourages them to become completely enraged toward the parents and to not look at anything else except their anger toward the parents are being set up for a disappointment later on. Once the therapist has jumped on the bandwagon with the patient to vilify the parent, what happens when, down the road, the patient starts talking about how wonderful this parent was in some respects, as she begins to integrate the good and bad images of the parent?

ISOLATION AND INCARCERATION

In "Captivity," a chapter from Judith Herman's book *Trauma and Recovery*, Herman explains how being in captivity increases the "traumatic" impact of any emotionally or physically threatening experience. It is not just that the trauma is prolonged, as opposed to a trauma of short duration such as a rape by a stranger, but that the experience of subjugation is soul-threatening. Psychological domination is often reinforced by the capricious enforcement of petty rules and efforts to control the victim's bodily functions by dictating when she will eat or sleep, or what she will wear.

Herman's examples are drawn from the experiences of prisoners of war, political prisoners, hostages, concentration camp survivors, kidnap victims, captives of religious cults, battered women, and victims of childhood abuse. She describes the methods used by torturers to break down their victims. Intermittent rewards let the victim know how wonderful things could be if only they would give in and share the desired information or renounce their political party. Those who have been trained to resist and outlast torture, with some remaining sense of human dignity, have been advised to take control of any part of their lives in captivity that they can. For many, a hunger strike is their only expression of free will. Those who make such a choice, though they might endanger their lives further, generally come away with less psychological damage.

In the case of the battered wife, Herman explains how the perpetrator demands her loyalty in such a way that she becomes totally, socially isolated and emotionally dependent. The perpetrator instinctively knows that any other human connections can lead the victim out of his influence. Herman states,

"But the final step in the psychological control of the victim is not completed until she has been forced to violate her own moral principles and to betray her basic human attachments. Psychologically, this is the most destructive of all coercive techniques, for the victim who has succumbed loathes herself. It is at this point, when the victim under duress participates in the sacrifice of others, that she is truly 'broken.' "[2]

As I read through this section by Herman, I kept being reminded of the retractors' horror stories of their hospital stays and even of their extreme dependence on their therapists in outpatient settings. Almost all of the retractors who had been hospitalized described "punishments" and inhumane treatments they had endured in inpatient programs. When they could not come up with memories of sexual abuse, they were sometimes put into a padded room by themselves, ostensibly to give them time to think. What they ended up thinking was that they were never going to get out of the hospital if they did not come up with some memories of sexual abuse.

Several retractors told me how they had believed that since they had gone in voluntarily, they could sign themselves out if they were unhappy with the program. However, when they attempted to exercise this right, they were told that they could sign themselves out, but that meant they were leaving against the advice of their physicians and therefore their insurance would not cover their hospital stays. At $10,000 a week, they felt their lives would be ruined if they had to pay the bill themselves. The threat of owing staggering amounts of money turned out to be a very effective coercion.

BARBARA'S ORDEAL

Barbara became suicidally depressed, and her therapist helped her find an inpatient Christian hospital.

"My very first day, when I went to see the psychiatrist, he slammed his hand down on the table and he shouted, 'You have got to pull yourself together. You are not a child. If you don't start doing what you know God wants you to do, do you know what's going to happen to you?'

"This was how it was in there. The next day I went to the telephone, and I called my therapist and I said, 'You've got to get me out of here. Please get me out of here.' I was crying and begging and screaming. It was a locked ward, which they never told me before I checked in. So my therapist told me, 'I'm sorry. There's nothing I can do.'

"So at the end of the first week, when I told the hospital I wanted to leave because I felt the program wasn't right for me, they said, 'Well, you can't leave. It's a locked ward. If you leave, you would be leaving against our medical advice, and your insurance won't cover your stay here.' And I'd already racked up a bill of about $10,000. So I felt I couldn't leave."

But when they chose to stay they often suffered daily indignities. They were allowed no phone calls or visitors, and in some cases the staff screened all their mail and decided for them what letters they would be permitted to read. If they didn't want to do the arts-and-crafts project assigned as part of their therapy they were deemed uncooperative and might be sent into isolation until their attitude improved. They had been reduced to the status of dependent children. Though they had once longed to be free of life's demands and be in a protective environment where someone else made all the decisions, they were horrified when they got their wish. Barbara continues her story:

"I was taking imipramine for depression, and Atavan and Xanax and other sleeping aids, and there were times when I would go into occupational therapy and I would just be so blah. I'm sure I didn't have any expression on my face. Everything the woman was saying was going right over my head. She would turn around to me and yell at me, 'If you're not going to listen and you're not going to be part of the group, then I'm just going to have to send you back to your room.'

"I play a flute, and I draw and I write. So one day they took my pad and my charcoals away from me; another time they took my flute away from me. Or they would confine me to the floor and I wouldn't be allowed to go downstairs and eat in the cafeteria with the rest of the people.

"After three or four weeks of this I decided that the only way I was going to get out of there was to start playing their game. I needed to supply the stories they expected. If they said that my father sexually abused me, then I would say you're absolutely right. I would say, 'He did this, and he did that,' whatever I knew they wanted to hear.

[Barbara learned what she needed to say by observing the behaviors of the other women in the group sessions.] "I would look at these other people, and I would say to myself, 'These people are getting out. I'm going to pray and everything like they do, so that I can get out too.'

"I told them what they wanted to hear, and they discharged me in about a week. But then when I left there, I was more suicidal than when I had gone in."

ANSWER EIGHT

Why would anyone believe anything so painful as being sexually abused by a parent if it weren't true?

ANSWER NUMBER EIGHT: Because he feels trapped, punished, and isolated in an inpatient program and believes he must play the "repressed memory game" in order to gain his freedom.

Indeed, the most insidious outcome of the hospital stay was when they finally got the "memories" that were the required proof that would allow them to be released from the hospital. Though many of the retractors now look back and see why they finally succumbed to making accusations of incest, at the time that they were in this high-pressure situation, it was not a *rational* choice. Instead, they would actually have a mental breakdown and begin to see images of abuse. At that point they were "living a lie" and the cognitive dissonance this caused destroyed any remaining dignity they possessed.

Melody Gavigan, like many others, described her long ordeal in an inpatient program where deciding that her father had committed incest with her was still not enough to gain her freedom. She was required to confront her parents. Just as the torturers try to get political prisoners to give evidence that will incriminate their loved ones, the hospital therapists insisted that Melody would not be on the road to recovery until she accused her father. She had to cut off her closest ties to satisfy her captors.

As Herman points out, "While it is clear that ordinary, healthy people may become entrapped in prolonged abusive situations, it is equally clear that after their escape they are no longer ordinary or healthy."[3]

MONEY: COMMITMENT OR BLACKMAIL?

Barbara was one of several retractors who told me horror stories of hospital incarceration. In each case the patient would be told she would personally have to pay the hospital charges if she left against medical advice. Women who have deteriorated to the point where they will consider signing themselves into the hospital have often already invested quite a bit of money in their therapy and may have felt too fragile to hold a job for quite a while. They are in no position to make a grand gesture of saying they will pay the bill in order to have their physical and moral freedom.

To make matters worse, this threat of insurance claim denial is not only unethical, it is now illegal. As I stated earlier, insurance companies are no longer permitted to deny claims when patients choose to leave against medical advice. Still, many hospitals continue to use this tactic to discourage patients from checking out when they hit a rough spot in the program. The intent may be to "persuade" the patient to do what they feel is in the patient's best interest, but this objective disregards the patient's need to have some sense of control over her own life.

Similarly, Aileen, whom we met in Chapter Two, found herself in difficult financial straits when she realized that the relationship with her therapist had become destructively dependent. She cut back from seeing him several times a week to seeing him once every few weeks.

"I had been paying him about $50 a week, but he kept billing me at the normal rate. I would get these horrendous bills because this was all adding up, and he would tell me not to worry about it. I should just think of it as an investment. But it was really starting to bother me. I owed him $3,800. That was just my share—he'd already collected thousands of dollars from the insurance company. So I went in to see him about it one day.

"This took a tremendous amount of courage. I had realized that I didn't want to pay it because I felt like I had wasted money on his agenda, not mine. Well, I didn't bring up the money first, he did. He said I'd better start paying him something.

"I went home and cut myself for the first time in many, many months. I wanted to let my old therapist know how angry I was. I sat down and wrote him this four-page letter telling him that I wasn't going to pay him and how I felt he had mistreated me."

This was a masterful letter. Aileen's therapist had been an authority on adult children of alcoholics, so she used his own language to explain to him what he should have realized about her as a patient. Here is an excerpt from that letter that Aileen has permitted me to reprint:

"In the beginning of my therapy with you, I took on the label of an Adult Child of an Alcoholic. I am reflecting today on how many of these classic characteristics played themselves out in my relationship with you and I must tell you that I am very frustrated that you couldn't see this happening. I'd like you to keep the following characteristics in mind as you read this letter:

1. ACOA's constantly seek approval and affirmation.
2. We are extremely loyal even when that loyalty is undeserved.
3. We become people pleasers and lose our identities in the process.
4. We get guilt feelings when we stand up for ourselves.
5. We are dependent personalities and are willing to do anything to hold onto a relationship in order not to be abandoned emotionally.

"Early on in therapy, I became overly dependent on you. I knew for a long time that this was not healthy but it seems that not only did you allow this to happen, but in some ways encouraged it. I began to depend on you totally and became terrified of being abandoned by you emotionally. I was willing to do anything to hold on to this relationship."

About that time Aileen had discovered a group called Therapist Exploitation Link Line (TELL) and started to go to their meetings. Although TELL is basically an advocacy group for clients who have been sexually exploited by their therapists, TELL was able to respond to Aileen with the supportive sympathy she needed at the time.

"When I told them my story they said, 'Oh, my God. You really have been abused.'

"I hired a lawyer to straighten out this business about the bill because I had gotten a letter from my therapist where he said he was glad I was doing so much better and had gotten sober and all while in therapy with him, but now we needed to clear up the matter with the bill.

"By this time, there was no way I was going to pay him. My lawyer asked for his records, and he finally excused the debt."

UNHEALTHY DEPENDENCIES

Aileen's claim that she had become overly dependent on her therapist is no exaggeration. When Aileen wasn't in the hospital, her therapist encouraged her to call him anytime. Aileen told me:

"he was my substitute for alcohol. I often talked to him twice a day, and I called him every night about 9:30, and he would talk to me for twenty minutes or so."

"I was so dysfunctional by then that I had to hire a babysitter to come into the house to take care of my kids. I had to hire someone to come and cook the meals. I had someone else come and clean the house, and it's not a very big house. This was draining all our money. The therapist had told me that I shouldn't have sex with my husband while I was digging up memories because I might really freak out.

"I have to give it to him. He really was going to workshops on how to work with sexual abuse victims all the time. He believed he was really educating himself and becoming a great therapist. But he lost sight of who I was.

"About ten minutes into the therapy each time, he would ask me if he could talk to the 'little girl.' So I managed to come up with a couple of little girls for him to talk to. Of course, he thought I was an MPD [Multiple Personality Disorder].

"On one level, this was all very intriguing to me too. He would ask me if I wanted him to sit with me, and of course I wanted him to sit near me. So he would come over and sit by me on the couch. I would tell him I was cold, and he would put a blanket on me. He would say to me that he'd never had a little girl, so I could be his little girl.

"I was encouraged to get an answering machine for my phone so that I could screen calls and avoid talking to my family. I was encouraged to sever the relationship with my family of origin, especially my mother, whom the therapist thought was the perpetrator.

"About that time I had seen in the paper the Dr. Margaret Bean-Bayog and Paul Lozano case. She was a psychiatrist from Harvard and had worked with this young man. She treated him much the same way my therapist treated me. He was her 'child.' She would write him these letters, which eventually became very sexual. She had convinced him that he had been sexually abused, and he ended up killing himself.

"When I read that it suddenly began to dawn on me what the therapist was doing. I was feeling stronger because of my job and I began to think that maybe I could break my dependence on him."

REPARENTING

Perhaps the most outrageous example of therapists' encouraging unhealthy dependency is the technique of "reparenting" first practiced in the '60s and recently revived by Harvard Psychiatrist Margaret Bean-Bayog, who became infamous when her patient Paul Lozano committed suicide and left behind handwritten letters from Bean-Bayog containing sexual fantasies she had shared with him.

Though the term "reparenting" is seldom used now, the techniques described as "regressive work" or "corrective parenting" are often very similar and also encourage a destructive degree of dependency on the therapist. In an article in *Changes Magazine*, writer Andrew Meacham examines the dangers of reparenting, a therapy method in which therapists become surrogate parents to their adult patients.[4]

Often encouraged to behave as if they are babies, clients are encouraged to wear diapers, pretend to nurse from their therapists' breasts, and participate nude in rebirthing experiences in hot tubs. One therapist Meacham interviewed who opposed reparenting reported that he sees patients who have broken down and become suicidally depressed as a result of this therapy.

Constructive therapeutic methods support clients becoming more and more independent and capable. A good therapist should be constantly working himself or herself out of a job. As I mentioned earlier, if you are not becoming more and more functional as defined by the Assessment of Functioning scale, you need to question the type of therapy you have chosen.

MEMORY COERCION

Many therapists I have spoken to seem to be "in denial" about the memory coercion that goes on in many therapists' offices. They insist that the FMS Foundation is making all this up. They say that therapists don't plant false memories—they go with what clients bring them. Now that criticism of memory coercion methods has been so much in the press, I find fewer and fewer therapists admitting to these techniques. But they didn't sweep the issue under the rug quickly enough. Renée Frederickson's book *Repressed Memories* is a classic treatise on "memory" coercion. I can't help quoting from her main case study, which runs throughout the book. Whether this is a composite or a true case, Frederickson finds it representative enough of the points she wants to make to open each chapter with a segment of this client's story. In the opening to Chapter Three we read:

> "Sarah was shocked and disbelieving when I suggested that her symptoms were perhaps related to unremembered sexual abuse. 'I have an excellent memory,' she asserted. 'I remember more of my childhood than most of my friends. Small things that happened to me as a little girl stand out so clearly that they seem etched in my memory. How could I remember these in so much detail and forget something as momentous as abuse?' "[5]

Notice that Frederickson admits she *suggested* to Sarah that Sarah had been abused, and this suggestion apparently took Sarah totally by surprise. Sarah reminded Dr. Frederickson that she had never forgotten her father's violence when drunk. If she could remember his traumatic beatings, why wouldn't she remember sexual abuse?

Poor Sarah—before we even read the chapter, we know she is in for the "treatment." Frederickson's book is more frightening than memories of sexual abuse. As she begins to talk about the extended family, she writes,

"Sexual abuse is always intergenerational, and everyone in a sexually abusive system takes one of these roles."[6] *Always*? Talk about self-fulfilling prophecies! If this statement is not negative enough, look at the three roles we get to pick from (remember, *everyone* in your family plays one of these roles). You must choose for yourself and your loved ones the labels of either *offender*, *denier*, or *victim*. She states, "Err on the side of overstating problems, rather than on the side of denial."[7] Here are some suggestions from Frederickson on how to get at those recalcitrant "repressed memories."

First Frederickson tells us that few survivors have spontaneous recall. So that you will not be forced to "endure months or years of fear, confusion, and doubt" waiting for your memories to surface, use Frederickson's seven major methods of memory retrieval, which I have paraphrased below:*

FREDERICKSON'S METHODS

1. Imagistic Work. Using a current image or flash as a jumping-off point, try to expand on or explore the image for abuse memories. You may need a guide to direct this process. Don't worry. Frederickson assures the reader that *all* images are fragments of "traumatic" memories ready to emerge.[8]

2. Dream Work. Frederickson believes that many dreams contain fragments of "repressed memories." Scary dreams are obviously more likely to contain these fragments. According to Frederickson, you need a therapist or guide to help you interpret these dream images.[9]

3. Journal Writing. Begin with an image or dream fragment and start free-associating in writing. The blank pages will be your prompter, so you won't need a guide. Soon you will be producing "memories".[10]

4. Body Work. According to Frederickson, massage or body manipulation will bring you "body memories" as you sense pain or

---

*I have included the page numbers of every reference so that the reader may see for himself or herself that I have not altered Frederickson's suggestions in my summaries.

discomfort in certain areas—many abuse victims experience pain in the pelvic region. Or is it an STD?[11]

5. Hypnosis. Trance states can be used to retrieve buried memories. After putting you into a very relaxed state, the hypnotist can help you focus on an image that is *inevitably* a scrap of a "repressed memory." Age regression through hypnosis is one very powerful method recommended by Frederickson.[12] Fortunately, past lives aren't mentioned.

6. Feelings Work. This is based on Frederickson's theory that feelings form a bridge to other events that prompted that same feeling. For example, since most people feel rage while being raped, Frederickson recommends you act "as if" you are being raped, feel the rage, and the feeling will probably spark the buried "memory."[13] (Warn the neighbors first!)

7. Art Therapy. Frederickson recommends beginning with the scrap of an image you suspect is an abuse "memory" and then drawing the image. Then think: "What happened next?" Get a therapist or friend to help you interpret it when you are done.[14]

Obviously, these methods would work equally well to produce fiction, and there is the problem. Renée Frederickson is director of Frederickson Associates in St. Paul, Minnesota, and codirector of Chrysalis Recovery Center in Dallas, Texas. She is a frequent lecturer and trainer of therapists throughout the United States. The above advice from Frederickson is just the tip of the iceberg.

ANSWER NINE

Why would anyone believe anything so painful as being sexually abused by a parent if it weren't true?

ANSWER NUMBER NINE: Because the therapist has used coercion and his or her aura of expertise to override the client's perceptions and convince the client that her memory cannot be trusted.

I was alarmed to learn that chiropractors now in training are being lectured on the concept of "body memories," a notion that has no scientific proof to support it. Gary Kane, the brother of one of the retractors and a medical student at the New York Chiropractic College, reported the following:

"Our class was told by a psychology teacher, at New York Chiropractic College, that if a patient comes to me with back pain of unknown origin, to think of sexual abuse.

"I foamed at the mouth; my hand shot straight up in the air and I said, 'For one, I am a doctor of chiropractic medicine. If I think that every patient who enters my office with nonspecific back pain is a sexual abuse sufferer, then I'm not qualified to call myself a doctor.'

"This is the same mindset that perpetuates the False Memory Syndrome; if they enter your office with these various general symptoms, think sexual abuse. Bam! Another family is destroyed, and we have again experienced voodoo diagnostics at its best."

BODY MEMORIES

Susan Smith, author and researcher of survivor psychology beliefs and practices, is particularly critical of the theory of "body memories." As Smith explains, the theory of body memories is used to describe feelings for which the client has no visual or auditory memory. Proponents claim that the cells, DNA, or certain body locations retain 100 percent recall of what the mind represses.

"Body memories are thought to literally be emotional, kinesthetic, or chemical recordings stored at the cellular level and retrievable by returning to or recreating the chemical, emotional, or kinesthetic conditions under which the memory recordings are filed. The theory of body memories is a fascinating example of a seemingly logical theory that is not only mistaken, it is dangerously coercive."[15]

Body memory theory is used to counter criticisms made by memory experts who point out that we cannot retrieve memories from infancy because the brain systems needed to store memory are not developed until age two or three. No problem, say body memory theorists. They believe that if they regress the patient to a stage before memory can be recorded in the brain, the body will release the memories.[16]

More commonly, recovery books and speakers claim that contact with certain body locations will release memories involving that body part. Massage therapists are warned to be prepared for the flood of memories that clients in recovery might experience during massage sessions. Proponents believe that pressure on the buttocks, for example, can release memories of anal intercourse that had been repressed until that moment of massage contact.

Similarly, as Smith reports, survivor psychologists believe that many medical diseases such as cancer of the uterus, vagina, or breasts and various gynecological problems are body-memory proofs of "repressed" sexual abuse.[17] However, there is no indication that gynecologists or oncologists have found any support for this theory.

Therapists who dream up theories without checking with knowledgeable specialists who could confirm or refute the theories are behaving irresponsibly. Therapy based on groundless conjecture can easily become misdirected and confusing, if not harmful.

SUMMARY POINTS

1. The majority of therapists periodically evaluate their clients. If there is no improvement, or if the client is getting worse, responsible therapists question the treatment.

2. The sexual abuse recovery movement regards a client's decline as a sure sign that the diagnosis is correct. According to this theory, if the client does not get well, there are more memories that need to be uncovered.

3. Hostile feelings toward a parent may be well grounded in parental failures and shortcomings. However, a therapist must not accept everything a client states about a parent as literally true. The therapist should consider that there may be distortion based on the client's needs or wishes.

4. A patient who is admitted to an inpatient treatment center which is biased toward sexual abuse recovery may be subjected to intense pressure and coercion to get in line with the diagnosis. Satisfying the staff with appropriate memories of abuse may be the only way the patient can obtain a discharge.

5. Patients in coercive hospital programs may be told that if they leave against medical advice their insurance companies will not pay the bills. However, insurance companies may no longer deny these claims.

6. Vulnerable clients who have become overly dependent on their therapists are reluctant to risk the relationship by disagreeing with the diagnosis of sexual abuse.

7. The "memory recovery" work practiced by sexual abuse recovery therapists often involves using free association, hypnosis, and quasi-hypnotic states to "recover" memories. The very act of searching for memories contains an implicit demand to come up with something. Any images created in these suggestive states are then treated as solid *facts*.

8. Why would anyone believe anything so painful as being sexually abused by a parent if it weren't true?
   • To escape from the captivity of a brutal hospital program.
   • Because, determined to prove the diagnosis correct, the therapist employs all his or her considerable authority as the "expert" to overcome the patient's doubts and objections.

Murky Memories

*We forget what happened. And then we decide on
what we think must have happened. We talk about it,
and then we remember what we said. And then eventually we think that what we said is what actually
happened.*

—HENRY GLEITMAN,[1]
from FMSF conference Speech

BOTH RECOVERY THERAPISTS and proponents of False Memory
Syndrome agree about how damaging childhood sexual abuse can be.
What is the apex of the heated debate is whether "recovered memories" of
sexual abuse are reliable. In order to understand the opposing views we
need to look at how memory and memory-enhancing methods (such as
hypnotism) work, and gain an understanding of what psychologists call
repression and dissociation.

There has been a great deal of research on memory during the last 100
years. Early theorists compared memory to photography, assuming that
everything that has been experienced is recorded in pictures in the brain,
with the most vivid memories referred to as "flashbulb memories", or
indelible images of traumatic events. As technology developed, so did the
conceptualization of memory. For awhile it was believed that memory was
akin to a telephone switchboard, where you call up and get connected to
certain memories from the past. More recently, conceptualizers of memory
borrowed much from computer science: Everything that has been experienced is somewhere on our hard disk, and all we need to do to call up a
memory is discover the pathway. Video technology has also been used as a
metaphor. This analogy assumes that we have a camera running behind our

eyes all our lives; we just need to find the video cassette that contains 1958 to know in total cinematic detail what happened to us that year.

All these metaphors have been useful for helping theorists to discover new ways to look at memory and to test out these theories. However, memory researchers have found that memory may be a bit more like "choose your own adventure" books. Recent research shows that memory is actually *reconstructive*. We remember merely the "gist" of things in what scientists call memory traces, and when we need to review an event from the past our brain first receives a bare-bones image. The actual details have often been lost, so the brain creates a "probable scenario" based on general knowledge or present related imagery borrowed from our surroundings, or movies, books, and personal accounts we have been exposed to since the event. We fill in the gaps with more recent memories.

For example, if you have not been in your childhood home in years, you may be able to remember a few sketchy details of what it was like. In my childhood home we had pinewood paneling that went up the living-room wall and hid the staircase. I think I remember this paneling because the many knots in the wood always looked like faces to me. Also, my father took family movies, and most filmed indoor scenes took place in the living room, where that staircase was located. We watched the family movies at least once a year throughout our childhoods and later at whole family gatherings, so that even long after we moved from that home (when I was eighteen) we had many reminders of how the living room looked.

However, I later discovered that the films created a distortion. Everything looks larger and farther apart on film, so that I had imagined this living room, and consequently the whole house, as being quite roomy. When I was in my early thirties my mother decided to move back to the town where I spent my childhood and nostalgically chose a house exactly like we had had—a Cape Cod, which was a very popular style during the 1950s. The first time I went back for a visit I was astonished at how small and cramped the house was, although I could see that it was indeed the same. When I pictured my parents raising five kids in this space, I had a greater appreciation for my mother's frequently frayed nerves!

MEMORY AND MOOD

In *Human Memory: Theory and Practice*, author and cognitive psychologist Alan Baddeley reports on a number of studies designed to assess the effects of mood on memory. This research shows that mood is a great distorter of memories. In one study patients with varying degrees of depression (as measured by the Beck Depression Inventory) were asked to recall stories from their lives in response to words on cue cards. Those who had scored as being quite depressed on the Beck scale recalled the greatest number of unpleasant experiences. Since this was a population of depressed patients to begin with, we might wonder if they had actually had far more unpleasant experiences. However, further studies using the same principle (where the experimenters used hypnosis to induce happy or unhappy mood states in normal subjects) confirmed that people do call up memories which are *congruent* with their present mood.

For example, different aspects or impressions of the same event will be recalled depending on mood. When depressed, patients might recall how awkward they felt at a party where they didn't know anyone. But later, when happy, they recall the party fondly, remembering the excitement of meeting new people. Of course, their feeling-state when they originally attended the party will also have an effect on which details about the party become memory traces for the event. Still, there is a great deal of evidence to show that people do rewrite their personal history based on their mood at the time of recall. One study of mood disordered patients who had predictable diurnal rhythms (depressed only at a certain time of day) had patients recall autobiographical events while in up and down moods. Not only did they have trouble recalling happy events when they were in low moods, the happy events they had recalled earlier were rated as being not so happy when the patients were reminded of the memories when they were in a low mood.[2] So, people in therapy for depression should keep in mind that they may be distorting their memories to fit their present moods.

STUDIES IN RECALL

Even important details of memories can be lost or distorted over time. Ulric Neisser, a cognitive psychologist at Emory University, an elected member of the prestigious National Academy of Sciences, and one of the most widely respected researchers of memory, used the occasion of the explosion of the space shuttle Challenger on January 26, 1986, as an opportunity to study the memory of a shocking event. The day after the explosion Neisser handed out a questionnaire to students in his freshman introductory psychology class. The students were asked to write down how they first heard about the shuttle explosion, recording who told them, where they were, with whom, what they were doing, and what time it was. Since this was just twenty-four hours after the event, Neisser assumes that these memories were accurate.

The completed questionnaires were stored until the fall of 1989 when the freshmen had become seniors. Neisser and his graduate assistant, Nicole Harsch, contacted all the original subjects who were still on campus. These forty-four students were asked to fill out another questionnaire, exactly like the one they had used before, except that Neisser had added one more feature. He asked them to rate their *confidence* on each aspect of their memories, using a five-point scale where a rating of one meant "just guessing" and a rating of five meant "absolutely certain." When Neisser and Harsch compared these with the original forms, they learned a great deal about the accuracy of memories of upsetting events.

Their rating scale went from zero (for those who were wrong about every detail of their earlier memory) to seven (for those who had remembered everything correctly). Only three of the forty-four subjects scored a seven, but eleven scored a zero—*wrong about everything*! Despite this, the confidence scores showed that thirteen of them had been "absolutely certain" that their memories were accurate, yet many of these subjects had been wrong about everything. Confidence bore no relationship to accuracy.

A SECOND CHANCE

Neisser and Harsch decided to call the students back for follow-up interviews. In these second interviews they decided to give them hints to try to trigger recall of the actual time, place, and so on when the students had first heard about the Challenger explosion. Despite many hints, no one who had been wrong ever recalled the details of the original memory. As a matter of fact, even after they were shown their original papers they made comments like, "This *is* my handwriting, so it must be right, but I still remember everything happening the way I told you! I can't help it." Some even argued that they must have been mistaken three years ago because they were certain it had happened as they now recalled it!

One student had actually heard the news in the cafeteria and had commented on her form, three years prior, that the news made her so sick that she couldn't finish her lunch. Yet, in the follow-up interview her story was as follows: "I was in my dorm room when some girl came running down the hall screaming, 'The space shuttle just blew up.' " She went on to say that she "wanted to run after the screaming girl and question her," but instead turned on the television. Neisser suspects there never was a screaming girl, since that would surely have been a detail included in the first narrative and that perhaps this student was the one who had felt like screaming. Later this image of a girl screaming had become the most vivid part of the "memory." Eventually, it became part of her remembered "reality."[3]

This study clearly shows that young adults can have vivid memories, of which they are extremely confident, that can be proven to be wrong. Further, once these "false memories" have been established, they are not easily changed by conflicting evidence even in their own handwriting.

Well, critics might say, it's easy to see how one could forget such information. It was hardly a life-threatening situation or personal trauma for these students. If patients' memories are incorrect in detail, what does it matter? It's the overall event that affects them emotionally and psychologically. They challenge: If these memories of sexual abuse are incorrect, where did they come from?

CREATING FALSE MEMORIES

Other memory researchers such as Elizabeth Loftus, have been conducting experiments that may answer this question. Loftus is a renowned memory expert who has spent much of her professional career studying the accuracy of eyewitness testimony. She wanted to see if, indeed, memories of events that had not taken place could be planted by suggestion. For this purpose, Loftus' research group decided to try to implant an early memory of "getting lost," since this is a highly charged universal fear of most parents and children.[4]

The researchers wrote to various relatives with whom they had high credibility and asked if the relatives still remembered the time they had been lost in the mall. The researchers provided only the sketchiest details and told their subjects that they had been about five years old at the time. The subjects were asked to try to recall as many details as they could about the event and to record these details in a daily journal as they recalled them. They were told to just write "I can't remember" if they could recall nothing of the event. Along with these "lost in the mall" stories were some true events described in the same brief manner.

One subject, Chris, whose older and beloved brother, Jim, had been the one to remind Chris of these bogus family stories, developed vivid memories of being lost in the mall. Chris could recall what the man who rescued him looked like: the color of his shirt, his bald head with a ring of gray hair, and his glasses. Chris recalled that he had wandered off while looking at toys in the Kay-Bee toy store and remembered how frightened he had become when he realized he had lost his family. Jim had offered none of these details, and he checked with his mother to make sure Chris hadn't been lost another time and was mixing the two events. After two weeks, Chris had been able to add many details to his "memory."

The subjects were asked to rate the various memories presented to them for consideration on a scale of one to ten, according to the vividness of the memories. Chris gave the mall memory a rating of eight, while he never could recall anything about one of the true memories that Jim had included on the list; that hard-to-remember event had actually taken place when Chris was five years old.

Though proponents of repressed memory therapy can justifiably argue that being lost in the mall is not as traumatic as being sexually abused, the experiment did indeed prove that "false memories" can be implanted. In this case, the subjects had been persuaded by a booklet with short paragraphs that had been mailed to them. If such a method is sufficient to plant detailed "false memories," then surely a therapist can implant "false memories" by repeated conversations about an event the therapist genuinely believes took place. The client, who is told that she cannot get well until she remembers these incidents, will be highly motivated to comply.

A WALK DOWN MEMORY LANE

One retractor who tells her story in great detail in the book *True Stories of False Memories* gives the clearest account of how her "false memories" developed. She chose to remain anonymous in the book, but she frequently comments on the responses of her husband, John, so, for the sake of convenience, we will call her Mrs. John.[5]

Mrs. John had never had any trouble recalling her father's alcoholism and his violent brutality toward her mother, nor had she forgotten being physically abused by her mother—memories Mrs. John found very upsetting. Although Mrs. John had sought therapy for marital problems, her therapist, Tom, told her that he suspected she had been sexually abused as a child and that she had "all the classic symptoms of an incest victim."

Mrs. John had absolutely no recollection of her father having ever done anything improper to her, though she knew she was ripe to find fault with him because he had been distant since her parents had divorced.

At her first recovered memory session with Tom, he had her relax and do a visualization. Scenes of her father violently raping her popped into Mrs. John's mind. In her picture-like flashes she saw real settings she recognized with these bizarre scenes taking place. Because Tom told her that whatever popped into her mind was a real happening, she found herself shrieking and crying. After the session, when she had gone home and begun to reflect on what happened, doubts began to arise. The feelings, which did seem real, were the same feelings she used to have when her father was in a drunken rage, but the sexually abusive details didn't feel real. However, as hypnotherapy progressed, Mrs. John strove to come up with the "memories" that would prove the diagnosis because she had such total confidence in Tom's judgment.

After some time, John noticed his wife's deterioration and insisted that she change therapists. Ann, the next therapist, had Mrs. John play with anatomically correct dolls, even though Mrs. John had told her that she felt the suspicions of incest with her father were unfounded. Ann requested that she play out a scene with the father and daughter dolls. Not surprisingly, Mrs. John found herself creating an incest scene where the daughter blames herself for the father's transgressions.

"Time and time again I questioned Ann as to whether my symptoms couldn't be related to the traumas I remembered from childhood," Mrs. John relates. "Time and time again she firmly rebuked me with the pet phrase, 'Trust me! It happened!' "[6]

Then Ann recommended that Mrs. John start coming to group therapy so that she could "piggy-back" off the other women's stories. The therapist saw listening to the stories of others as a good way to get "memories." When Mrs. John entered the group it was a mixture of women who had been abused in childhood either physically or sexually. Mrs. John saw that women who entered the group believing only that they had been physically abused soon got "memories" of being sexually abused. Those who had been sexually abused and had never forgotten it began to believe that they had "repressed" abuse by other perpetrators.

One therapeutic technique used during group sessions was something Mrs. John calls "make-up-a-story." When someone in the group would tell about a nightmare she had during the week, Ann would ask the woman where in her body she felt the fear. Then she would tell the woman to go back to a time in childhood when she felt the same physical sensation. If the client did not get any "memories," Ann would tell her to make up a story. Inevitably, the stories were "repressed memories" of sexual abuse.

Mrs. John was reading *The Courage to Heal Workbook*, and its warnings began to affect her like scripts. If the workbook said she would probably feel suicidal, she did. If the workbook said that doubts were an expected part of the struggle to overcome denial, she interpreted her doubts that way. After four years had passed without any improvement, Mrs. John's husband and minister convinced her to consider quitting therapy. The spell broke when Mrs. John told Ann that she would be leaving the group soon, and Ann pondered aloud that maybe Mrs. John's "memories" weren't real after all. She asked Mrs. John, "What do you think happened?"[7]

Mrs. John was astonished that, after years of being told she was "in denial," the therapist now wanted to know what Mrs. John thought. She went home to think for herself.

HYPNOSIS

Hypnosis, trance work, image work: these are all forms of hypnosis. Whether through formal induction by a certified hypnotist, or through self-hypnosis, the images or thoughts that come up in an uncensored "altered state of consciousness" are believed to carry some magical message from the unconscious. But does that have anything to do with truth?

Hypnosis has been described as "structured dissociation." In order for hypnosis to be successful, three components must be in place. The first is total absorption in one perception, idea, or memory to the exclusion of all else. The second component is dissociation or the compartmentalization of experience. The first two, combined, cause the subject to focus very single-mindedly, relegating most of his or her sensations to the periphery of awareness. This enables a hypnotized subject to respond to commands without any conscious awareness. Third, the subject must have a heightened responsiveness to social cues. This responsiveness is what is meant by suggestibility. In this state, a subject is less likely to judge or evaluate the meaning of the experience or the motivation of the person giving the instructions or suggestions. In fact, subjects often experience others' suggestions as *their own ideas*.[8]

Some psychological theoreticians note that many highly hypnotizable patients are also highly dissociative and have histories of child abuse, and these theoreticians conclude from this that anyone who is highly hypnotizable must have been sexually abused as a child. Once again we have a logical fallacy. There is no reason to assume cause-and-effect works in reverse.

Studies have shown that hypnotizability may be hereditary. Imaginative absorption is also characteristic of highly hypnotizable subjects.[9] When we consider the fact that subjects are very vulnerable to suggestion when hypnotized, we understand why it is easy for therapists' hypnotic probing to produce "stories" on their preferred theme.

THE POWER OF SUGGESTION

Dr. George Ganaway, Director of the Ridgeview Center for Dissociative Disorders, likes to tell the story of when he hypnotized a close relative by marriage. This relative is one of the super high-hypnotizables called hypnotic virtuosos. Ganaway explains, "When such a person slips into the trance state, she can actively hallucinate anything that the hypnotist suggests very easily. She can visualize James Dean standing in front of her and go up and get his autograph, and this all seems very real to her." Here is Ganaway's tale:

"She agreed to allow me to implant an hypnotic suggestion for a period of lost time. I asked her to go back to that period of lost time and see if she could piece together what happened. She came up with an elaborate alien abduction experience. Interestingly, later on, even though she knew that she had confabulated the experience, she actually had some flashback experiences where some brightly colored lights triggered her to go back and actually feel like she was on board the spacecraft. I used some leading questions, but not heavily leading questions, to continue to push her to come up with this very elaborate story.

"When I would first ask her, 'Were you experimented upon inside the spacecraft?' she would say, 'No.' I would say, 'Try harder and see what you can remember.' I'd see her knit her brow and she'd be trying really hard, and all of a sudden she'd say, 'Oh yeah,' and then she'd start describing the experiments.

"She described the process afterward in a debriefing interview as, 'It was a lot like "Let's Make a Deal." Choose door number one, door number two, or door number three. I wanted to choose door number one, but you kept saying, 'How about door number two, or number three?'

"Then, as a kind of a bonus, since I hadn't even asked about it, she went back to an earlier part of her life when she'd been abducted by aliens previously as a three-year-old. When she got back to that point, after describing that, she started to spiral back even further. I thought, we'll go with this and see what happens, so I suggested she head on back to age two, age one, age zero, minus one, minus two, 'as far back as you need to go, and let's see what you find.' She started to go through what I can only describe as an identity transformation, and turned into an aristocratic lady who lived in a castle in England. She talked with a British accent, and started to tell me about her experiences in this castle.

"After that she came out of the trance state, and I debriefed her, then showed her the whole videotape. Before she saw it she only remembered a little bit about the alien abduction experience. It's very normal to have some posthypnotic amnesia if you're highly hypnotizable. When she watched the videotape and saw that she had gone back into a past life, it freaked her out. She was mostly embarrassed; she said, 'That's not me.'

"Afterward, as she was talking about it on camera, she said, 'That was such a weird thing to see that person sitting there talking about those things. It looks like me, but it's not me.' Well, that's very, very similar to how people diagnosed with MPD describe their alternate 'identities.' Yet, this is a person who clearly doesn't have multiple personalities and no history of childhood trauma. Yet I would suspect that, if we wanted to, we could go back and come up with several other entities. Before she knew it, she could have a whole repertoire of identities that could be called out on demand.

"There was much 'day residue' in what she came up with in both the abduction experience and the reincarnation experience. For example, mundane things she had been doing the previous day got incorporated into these events that she was describing. She had said that when they experimented on her they took a tissue sample and left a little mark in the shape of a clover leaf on her shoulder. Later in the debriefing, when I asked why she chose the shape of a clover leaf she said, 'Today I was wrapping up a brass shamrock that I was going to pack away to take on a trip.'

"There were many other things like that that she could trace to bits and pieces of actual 'memories' of actual things. They were just little vignettes that she had incorporated in her story. Some of them were things of the past day or two; some went back to when she was a child in school. She incorporated these into the life of her reincarnation person as well. It shows how the mind can take a bunch of things, and under the expectations of the demand characteristics of a trance interview, piece them together in a confabulated story that sounds very vivid in detail."[10]

AN OFFICIAL WARNING

The Council on Scientific Affairs of the American Medical Association makes no bones about its view of hypnosis as a memory enhancer. A special commission studied the subject of refreshing recollection by the use of hypnosis and prepared a report on the present scientific status of this matter. Their summary of findings was as follows:

"The council finds that recollections obtained during hypnosis can involve confabulations and pseudo memories and not only fail to be more accurate, but actually appear to be less reliable than nonhypnotic recall. The use of hypnosis with witnesses and victims may have serious consequences for the legal process when testimony is based on material that is elicited from a witness who has been hypnotized for the purposes of refreshing recollection."[11]

This report explains that since hypnosis produces an increased responsiveness to suggestions, as well as the suspension of disbelief accompanied by a lowering of critical judgment, one cannot assume that "memories" recalled while under hypnosis are factual. Although during hypnotic age regression the subject appears to behave in a manner that is appropriate for the age at which the "traumatic" event occurred and despite the fact that the subject may describe myriad details, the hypnotic experience is simply the subjective reliving of earlier experiences *as though they were real* but does not necessarily replicate earlier events. Even Freud came to realize that though these hypnotic remembrances reflected an emotional reality, they were actually just a combination of fantasies, desires, and fears mixed in with details that may have come from real life.[12]

Unfortunately, too many practitioners perceive and explain hypnosis as being able to call up "memories" and play them for the subject like a video camcorder. This is not accurate. The AMA council's review of the literature showed that when hypnosis is used to refresh recollection, one of the following outcomes occurs:

1. Hypnosis produces recollections that are not substantially different from nonhypnotic recollections;
2. it yields recollections that are more inaccurate than nonhypnotic memory; or, most frequently,
3. it results in more information being reported, but these recollections contain both accurate and inaccurate details.[13]

In the case of the latter, a hypnotized subject has more difficulty discriminating between accurate and inaccurate recollections. Nonetheless, hypnosis does increase the subject's *confidence* in the truth of his recollections. Hypnosis may still be a valid therapeutic technique. Even though the recall may not be *historically* accurate, there may be an emotional validity. Though it can be valuable for the patient to work through such feelings, responsible clinicians should keep in mind that *processing** invalid recollections could have detrimental effects on the client's relationships with others. More important, the council found that individuals who had been hypnotized to recall disturbing events sometimes remained disturbed for some time afterward.

The council also concluded that hypnosis can lead to increased distortion in recall. Both the expectations of the hypnotist and the preconceived notions of the subject may produce confabulations or pseudo-memories during hypnosis.

The council recommends that therapists avoid any specific questions and instead encourage elaboration by stating neutral phrases such as "go

---

*Processing is the therapeutic technique of helping the client to relive the "memories" in order to purge or resolve the anxiety connected with them.

on," "continue," or "yes." When it is necessary to ask a question the subject should be told that the answer, "I don't know," is acceptable.

THE BATH TUB

Yvette, whom we met in Chapter Three, changed therapists shortly after I interviewed her for the first time. I had two sessions with her which were one month apart, and during that month the nagging doubts she had had about her therapist had turned into open criticism and disenchantment. Yvette's insurance had stopped covering her visits, and there was another psychologist closer to her home who accepted payments from a disability program for which Yvette had just qualified. In a later chapter we will see how Yvette's survivors' group handled her farewell.

Changing therapists caused Yvette to begin questioning material that had come up with her first therapist. She began to believe that some of her memories weren't true, and she struggled to sort out fact from fantasy for her own peace of mind. Looking back, she told me, "At one session I remembered something awful that my brother had done to me, and I started going downhill health-wise."

During group one night, one of the other women began talking about abuse that had happened to her in a bathtub. "By the end of the session I was really anxious, and tears started welling up in my eyes," Yvette told me. "I had this flashback that my brother had taken this shower brush with a long handle and stuck it up inside of me."

Though all her other memories had taken place in the bedroom, this memory seemed plausible because her brother had never respected her privacy in the bathroom. Still she was aware at the time that this memory had a different quality from the rest of her abuse memories. Strangely, it affected her more than any of the other memories. She recalled thinking,

"It hurt like hell. Just thinking about it makes me sick.

"The night I remembered what happened in the tub, I came home hysterical. I parked the car in the garage and locked the doors and wouldn't get out of the car. I sat there and cried and cried. I didn't want to come out of the car because I felt safe in there. My husband finally coaxed me out of the car and held me while I cried. He was appalled when I told him what I had remembered.

[But she has always been uncomfortable with that particular memory.] "There's a part of me that wonders if I just made it up so I would have a good story to tell the group. I had been feeling left out. My brother did so many horrible things that I do remember, that it wasn't hard to believe that he would do something like that to me.

"Then lately, I've been so sick and all, and my therapist keeps telling me it's about the bathtub scene. I think I have some physical problem and I need to get a thorough check-up. But she just keeps telling me that it's all in my head. I went to this one specialist, and he said that I have permanent nerve damage from my car accident. My mind couldn't have caused that."

FALSE OR REAL?

How can a therapist tell a real memory from a false one? How can the client herself tell what is real and what is made up? These questions have become pivotal in the last year or so, and yet no one has come up with any certain answers. Memories have been attacked for having too little detail and for having too much detail.

In 1986 Loftus offered the opinion that real memories reflect more perceptual processing, greater sensory detail, and greater mention of geographic components. However, critics point out that, since that time, therapists who have become aware of these criteria have asked clients to supply more sensory details. Also, the recovery movement literature, including *The Courage to Heal*, first published in 1988, has alerted survivors that their memories should be very detailed, so that factor has been contaminated and is no longer a valid criterion.

Speculations have also been made about the amount of emotion that is shown with the memory. Sexual abuse recovery therapists point to the painful *abreactions** they have witnessed as proof of the memories' authenticity. However, trauma experts tell us that one of the effects of trauma is that our emotions become split off, and traumatized victims most often report memories of the trauma in a flat unemotional voice. Who is right? All these observations are true depending on the circumstances.

---

*Abreaction is a Freudian term for the dramatic emotional release of feelings connected to a past trauma.

There have been several attempts to assess the reliability of "memories." The most extensive and careful system of evaluation was created by Martha L. Rogers, a forensic psychologist who has had to testify in many sexual abuse cases that have come to court. Surprisingly enough, Rogers testifies at child abuse cases on either side, but most often for the prosecution. Sometimes the victim's attorney has asked Rogers to testify, and at other times she testified for the defense. She has striven to be as neutral as possible and devised a decision tree to objectify her search for the truth.[14] (However, I must add the disclaimer that this is her personal professional judgment and has not been validated by research.)

Rogers first addresses whether or not the complainant has been in therapy because she could not endure painful or stressful pressures which she is now motivated to change. If the patient has not selected or changed therapists in order to find one who is likely to testify on her behalf in court, Rogers believes it is more likely that the accusation is legitimate. Next she checks to see if the patient claims to have forgotten or "repressed" her memories of abuse. If the memory of abuse had always been present, Rogers considers this a "go." If the complainant has been heavily influenced by self-help books, groups, or seminars, Rogers considers the possibility that the memories may be false or exaggerated. If there have been no major outside influences, Rogers assumes that the case is more likely to be valid.

Rogers is suspicious of any claimants who are financially stressed and may see a lawsuit as a way to solve their problems, those who have only "recovered memories" of abuse, those who may have been influenced by a third party such as the attorney, therapist, or therapy-group friends, and anyone who has had intrusive techniques such as hypnosis used on them in treatment. Rogers does not necessarily believe the above factors mean that the complainant is fabricating stories of abuse, but rather that her memories have been contaminated by other influences and pressures so that the truth may be hopelessly obscured. Rogers emphasizes, however, that the current state of knowledge does not yet permit reliable categorization of cases based only on "memory" characteristics.

Paul McHugh, Professor of Psychiatry at Johns Hopkins University, has also attempted to find some distinguishing criteria for what he calls "pseudo-memories." Unfortunately, this list, like the many survivor lists, is only speculative and based on too small a sample to be considered scientifically supported. So, use McHugh's list of distinguishing characteristics, given below, with caution.

CHARACTERISTICS OF PSEUDO-MEMORIES

1. They occur in distressed people with many different diagnoses.

2. They begin as vague and uncertain suspicions.

3. They are affect-laden. *

4. The initial "memory" is envisioned with difficulty.

5. Later "memories" flood in, swelling to astonishing tales.

6. Such memories are sensitive to suggestion and contagious.

7. They expand in group settings and with hypnotism.

8. "Post-traumatic stress" responses *follow* the memories.

9. The "memories" tend to block all therapy toward the here and now.[15]

Most retractors have had moments of doubt. If they had had any support for their doubts, they would have figured out much earlier that their memories of sexual abuse were fabricated. If you are uncertain of your memories and your therapist tells you that you are lapsing into "denial," be suspicious of your therapist rather than yourself. It is agreed by most rational surveyors of the delayed-memory controversy that there is absolutely no evidence to support the serial repression of years of abusive episodes, nor is there any scientific evidence showing that memories can be retrieved from before the age of three. If you have recovered memories that began in infancy and spanned ten years or more, they are probably false. If, on the other hand, you have retrieved a couple of memories from age three to five, they are less likely to be false. But this also depends on how much coercion was used to "bring up" those "memories." Remember, most therapists who have worked with trauma victims find that they have trouble forgetting the trauma—not trouble remembering it—even for a moment.

Psychology is not a mysterious, complicated system with secrets you can't understand. Trust your common sense. If something your therapist

---

*Full of intense emotion.

says sounds "off the wall," get a second opinion. When Yvette began to feel uncertain about her memories, she changed therapists. We can hear her doubts as she reported to me:

"I know for a fact that he used to come into the bathroom when I was in there. I had no privacy. But I don't remember the brush incident like I remembered the others."

Question, always question.

SUMMARY POINTS

1. Current research shows that the concept of memory as an infallible recorder of events is wrong and that memory is actually *reconstructive*. We remember the "gist" of things and then fill in missing details drawn from various sources.

2. Mood can have an effect on memory recall. People in a depressive state tend to view past events in a negative light.

3. Young adults can have vivid memories, of which they are extremely confident, but they can be proven wrong.

4. "False memories" can be implanted by someone considered to be a credible source.

5. The American Medical Association has explicitly warned against using hypnosis as a memory enhancer. Since hypnosis produces an increased responsiveness to suggestions and the suspension of disbelief, accompanied by a lowering of critical judgment, one cannot assume that memories recalled while under hypnosis are factual.

6. Although hypnotic remembrances may reflect an emotional reality, they may also be a combination of fantasies, desires, and fears mixed in with real-life facts.

7. There is no evidence to support the serial repression of years of abusive episodes, nor is there any scientific evidence showing that memories can be retrieved from before the age of three.

8. Determining the veracity of memories is not, and doubtless never will be, an exact science. There are, however, some common-sense factors that can be applied in trying to make a determination.

SEVEN

Dense Defenses

The substantive part of the controversy can be resolved by determining the answers to two questions: Does the repression mechanism exist and function as the therapy presumes? And are the techniques employed capable of producing false memories of abuse even if no abuse occurred?

—RICHARD OFSHE and ETHAN WATTERS,
"Making Monsters"[1]

REPRESSION, DENIAL AND DISSOCIATION have become buzz words used so frequently they have nearly lost their meaning. Like the game Telephone, these words have been passed from therapist to client to self-help book, becoming fuzzier and fuzzier as they work their way down the line. Though many people use the terms, few can define them. We have also lost a sense of these concepts in context. Repression and dissociation are actually just two of many "defense mechanisms" that have been identified by psychologists, beginning with Freud.

REPRESSION

Many critics assert that repression is just a theory that has never been proven by any controlled study, while recovered memory therapists point out that laboratory studies, such as those conducted by Loftus, which examine the memories of normal college students, cannot legitimately be compared with the experiences of women who have been sexually abused. Clinical psychologists—those who do actual therapy rather than research—prefer to rely on their own perceptions and intuitions as their patients present their memories. They feel that the theory of repression has been proven over and over again in their offices. To study trauma, they argue, you have to work with people who have been traumatized.

SOME DEFENSE MECHANISMS DEFINED

- **Denial:** Avoiding awareness of some painful external reality. When properly used, denial slows down the absorption of bad news until it can be taken in. It is only maladaptive if it blocks awareness indefinitely and stands in the way of a solution.
- **Regression:** Lapsing into an earlier level of development when confronted with uncomfortable levels of stress; becoming childlike in terms of demands, demeanor, and dependence on others. If not indulged too long, this can be a valid means to draw back and recuperate. However, regression is destructive when we regress to former dysfunctional behaviors such as alcoholism.
- **Suppression:** Dealing with emotional conflicts or stressors by purposely avoiding thinking about disturbing problems, wishes, feelings, or experiences for which there is no immediate means of resolution.
- **Repression:** Involuntarily withholding an idea or feeling from conscious awareness, for example, excluding a traumatic event from conscious awareness or remaining unaware of a sexual attraction toward an inappropriate person.
- **Dissociation:** Emotional conflicts and stresses are dealt with by a temporary disintegration of self-concept, or an alteration in the normally integrative functions of identity, memory, or consciousness.

In an effort to find such a group to study, the Dutch psychologist Willem Wagenaar examined the testimony of seventy-eight witnesses involved in a case against Marinus DeRijke, who was accused of atrocities at a Nazi concentration camp in the Netherlands. Many of the witnesses had been questioned shortly after being released from the camp (1943–47) and then again nearly forty years later (1984–87). Of those examined forty years later, 80 percent who had recently seen a television program on the camps containing DeRijke's picture were able to identify him, while only 58 percent of those who had not seen the program could identify DeRijke. All easily recalled his name, and those who had been tortured by DeRijke were only slightly more likely to remember him (80 percent) than those who had not (74 percent).

In general, all the survivors were able to remember a great deal about the camps, particularly the punishments, though other details had been lost. Those who had been questioned in both the 1940s and 1980s gave instances of very dramatic events which were subsequently totally forgotten. For example, one who had reported a severe beating by DeRijke when questioned in 1940 had reduced the memory to an occasional kick from DeRijke when he recalled the events forty years later. For the most part, the prisoners could recall events, but the emotional intensity was usually distorted to be much milder after the passage of forty years.[2]

I would like to add that there was no evidence that any prisoners had "repressed" their memories of the concentration camps; rather, their psyches had toned down the impact so that time could "heal the wounds." It would have been cruel for the examiners to induce them to recapture the original level of pain, as many sexual abuse recovery therapists believe is necessary. It would be like tearing open a nicely healing wound. Herman, in her book *Trauma and Recovery*, looks at many different traumatized groups. In addition to concentration camp victims, her investigations include other victims of captivity such as prisoners of war, tortured political prisoners, and battered women. For the record, none of them seem to have forgotten much of their traumatic experiences, nor have any in Lenore Terr's group of Chowchilla schoolchildren forgotten their bus being kidnapped.

On the other hand, the study most often cited to affirm the existence of repression as a response to a traumatic event was conducted by Linda Meyer Williams of the Family Violence Research Laboratory at the University of New Hampshire. In a twenty-year follow-up study of 200 children who had documented reports of childhood sexual abuse on file, one-third did not voluntarily recall the incident for which they had been brought to the hospital. It is important to note, however, that the interviewers never directly asked the subjects if they had been sexually abused, nor did they make any reference to the incident that had caused the subject to come to the hospital, because the researchers did not want to contaminate the results with any kind of suggestive reminder.

Williams and her research assistant called in each of the 129 subjects willing to be interviewed and had one-on-one interviews with them during which the researchers indirectly tried to cue the memory of sexual abuse. Subjects were not reminded of the sexual abuse that had been reported but were asked if they knew anyone who had been sexually abused. Despite much indirect prompting, 38 percent (or forty-nine of the subjects) made no mention of the particular incident of sexual abuse that had brought them to the hospital twenty years earlier, though two-thirds of these forty-nine women did recall other equally traumatic incidents of sexual abuse. In other words, all but sixteen of the 129 women did recall being sexually abused.[3] Hence, we do not know if the incident was *repressed* because it was too traumatic, or if it was merely *forgotten* because it was not significant in the context of the subject's whole life. We'll be taking a deeper look at the probable incidence of repressed memories of abuse when we examine the Father Porter case below.

The interviewers were not familiar with the details of past abuse during the interview so that they would not contaminate the results. However, detailed notes were taken during the session, and in one remarkable story the subject reported that she recalled hearing about her cousin's being sexually abused and that family rumor had it that her aunt had stabbed the abuser. When the researcher checked the hospital record, the report showed that this was the story of the subject's own abuse, and she had witnessed the stabbing.[4] This does appear to be protective amnesia. What remains unknown is if the woman would feel better if she were forced to remember the truth, or if her repression is a positive protective device that should not be tampered with.

FATHER PORTER AND THE QUESTION OF REPRESSED MEMORY

Does repression really exist? How common is it? Has media attention focused on repressed memories of sexual abuse hopelessly mixed up the concepts of repression, suppression, and normal forgetting, so that the public has no clear understanding of the differences? Two cases that have been much in the media in the past few years illustrate the confusion that exists over repressed memories: the Fitzpatrick/Porter and the Cook/ Bernardin cases where priests were accused of abuse that took place decades earlier. Early in 1994 Stephen Cook had accused Cardinal Joseph Bernardin of molesting him seventeen years ago, but within a few months Cook realized he had made a false accusation. On a *Today Show* newscast (March 16, 1994) Cook released this statement to the press: "Based on information I have learned since filing the lawsuit, I now realize that the memories which arose during and after hypnosis are unreliable. In fact, if I knew at the time I filed the lawsuit what I know today, I would never have included Cardinal Bernardin in it." At the same time, the case against Father Porter presented a classic example of how far memories of abuse can recede into the mind when there is shame and fear about reporting them.

Father Porter was a Catholic priest who molested scores of preadoles-cent boys more than two decades ago. This first came to light in 1989, when Frank Fitzpatrick, then thirty-nine, uncovered repressed memories of being molested by the priest. The following information on this case comes from a variety of sources, including articles in *The Minneapolis Star Tribune* and from a "Justice Trials" segment hosted by Jay Shadler.

in one article in *The Minneapolis Star Tribune*, Fitzpatrick explains that he was happily married, a proud father, and a successful businessman, but he found himself inexplicably depressed much of the time. He sat alone for hours one day trying to dredge up the source of his unhappiness and began to have vague memories of being molested. Fitzpatrick told the *Star Tribune* reporter, "The first memories were of pain and betrayal, and then sounds came back . . . the sound of him breathing, the sounds of bedclothes rustling . . . I realized that I had been molested as a child. I had repressed the memory all those years."[5] At this point, Fitzpatrick sought therapy.

During the next few weeks Fitzpatrick was able to flesh out his recollec-tions, and he remembered being molested when he was twelve years old and an altar boy at St. Mary's Catholic Church in North Attleboro, Massa-chusetts. The bishop of Fitzpatrick's former diocese told him that the priest had left the priesthood, and Fitzpatrick should just forget about it. But Fitzpatrick was used to doing detective work because he was an insurance adjuster. He did not want to let it go; he wanted to pursue it.

Fitzpatrick began calling boyhood friends whom he hadn't seen in twenty years and learned that they all remembered their abuse by Father Porter. In a later phone conversation that Fitzpatrick had with Porter, the ex-priest admitted to molesting as many as one hundred children when he was a priest. There was plenty of corroboration because the diocese was aware of Porter's nefarious activities and had sent him for treatment. After being in a treatment program, Porter went on to molest more boys before he finally left the priesthood in the early '70s. Since then Porter had married and become a family man, hoping to leave his past behind.

In the course of his career, Porter had served churches in five different states, and in all of those states men came forward to tell of their sexual abuse at the hands of Porter more than twenty years earlier. One man, Dan Dow, thirty-four, of Bemidji, Minnesota, opened his *Newsweek* and read of the case. The news report on Dow's epiphany stated that for Dow, "What had been blocked for more than 20 years came rushing back into his consciousness."[6]

What blurs in this story is how many of Porter's victims repressed the memory, suppressed the memory, just plain forgot, hadn't thought about the incident in years, or never forgot. Below are the reactions reported in *The Star Tribune* and other sources. (Unless otherwise noted, quotes are from *The Star Tribune*, July 19, 1992.)

- Fitzpatrick had repressed the memory and initially got only vague impressions before he remembered who, when, and where, within a few weeks of his first recall.
- Boyhood friends who had served as altar boys with Fitzpatrick were able to immediately confirm that Porter had molested them when they each received a phone call from Fitzpatrick. Of these phone calls, Fitzpatrick stated, "Every one I called, when I told them why I was calling, they said, 'Yes, I was a victim, too.'" This implies they each remembered immediately once reminded of the event and may never have forgotten.
- Many victims immediately remembered their abuse by Porter when they read an ad Fitzpatrick had run in his local newspaper that said: "If you remember Father Porter . . ." Fitzpatrick received many letters and phone calls from former victims. The mention of Father Porter's name was apparently enough to make these victims remember.
- Dan Dow remembered being abused by the priest as soon as he read the *Newsweek* article.
- Jim Grim remembered being abused by Porter when he read a news service report; when Dan Dow called him, he confirmed that Porter was the one who had abused the two friends twenty

years earlier. In a later article in the *Star Tribune* Grim stated, "When the memories came flooding back, I thought my head would explode."[7]

- Michael Huber, a former neighbor of Porter's, had apparently never forgotten Porter's attempt at abuse. When his father showed him a news article about Porter, Michael Huber said, "Well, that doesn't surprise me. He tried something on me once, too."

- John Vigorito stated in court, "I want you to know, James Porter, that you may have forgotten me and my face and my name, but I will never forget what you did to me."[8]

All together, more than a hundred of Father Porter's victims who were molested twenty years ago or more have come forward to declare their abuse. Many were abused repeatedly across a period of a few years, and the abuses included kissing, fondling, and rape. With the exception of Fitzpatrick, none of them had repressed the memory or needed therapy to "uncover" it. Even in the case of Fitzpatrick, retrieving the memories had only taken him weeks, not years. Reporters are often rather sloppy in distinguishing who remembered and who "repressed." A glaring example of this can be found in the *Newsweek* article:

"Ten days ago, dozens of Porter's former charges gathered to recall those early days—with mounting horror at memories they had for so long repressed."[9]

This is an irresponsible misuse of the term "repressed" and adds to the public's confusion. I am not questioning whether Porter molested anyone twenty years ago. It is quite clear that he did, and he has been found guilty in Minnesota. But did all these people really repress these memories for twenty years? Nowhere else, even in the cited *Newsweek* article, is it claimed that anyone other than Fitzpatrick had repressed memories. In addition, unlike the many "survivors" who spend years "recovering memories" of sexual abuse in therapy, Fitzpatrick, once reminded, had retrieved all his memories within weeks. It might seem like nit-picking for me to demand specificity about how well these incidents were remembered or if they were definitely "repressed." However, whether repression exists and how common it is for people to repress things are central to the false memory controversy.

Porter's case is one of the most extensive, well-documented stories of abuse recalled after a twenty-year time period. From the reports on Porter and his victims it appears that only one out of a hundred people who experience traumatic sexual abuse will repress it. That makes repression a quite uncommon phenomenon. Also, the abuse suffered by the one boy who did repress was no more "traumatic" than the abuses of the many who hadn't repressed it. This flies in the face of many assumptions made by the sexual abuse recovery movement. At the same time, this case is a fair comparison. Unlike the laboratory studies criticized by repressed memory supporters for their sterility, the molestation of many of the boys was both repeated and brutal. As their priest, Porter had inspired awe, love, and fear equal to the emotional dependence an abused child would have felt toward a parent. This is indisputable, real-life trauma.

Furthermore, the priest was not just a pedophile, he was a beloved youth minister who enjoyed and courted the trust of his young parishioners. The betrayal by this "man of God" would have been no less traumatic than a betrayal by their own fathers.

If it is actually quite rare for someone to repress sexual abuse, then the scores of adult children recovering decades-delayed "memories" of incest, which no one else in their families can corroborate, seem much more suspect.

In my interviews I put a lot of effort into trying to stay clear about which sexual abuse incidents have always been remembered and which ones were totally nonexistent before recovered memory therapy. I try to find out if there is a qualitative difference. Many therapists have offered me the opinion that the more traumatic the memory, the more likely it is to be repressed. It is hard to refute their proof of this when their patients are telling them that not only were they sexually abused, they were also forced to eat the baby who was the result of the rape. But how much is therapist or client *expectation* at work here?

In Chapter Three, I presented some stories of individuals who had always remembered their abuse. Julie's story was quite practical and down-to-earth. She had been molested by her stepfather and later married him. Neither she nor anyone in her family has ever had much money, and her therapy coverage and personal resources were limited. No one tried to help her recover repressed memories, so her story remains very straightforward.

Alexandrea, on the other hand, had very clear memories of her grandfather fondling her, and she had therapy for the problem at the time.

But years later, while using memory recovery techniques, her hypnotist told her he suspected that her father had also molested her. Sure enough, she then began to have "memories" of Dad molesting her. Also, she began to have "memories" of having intercourse with Grandpa—something that had not come up at all ten years earlier when she had therapy immediately following the incidents. Those "memories" seem suspect to me.

I had a lot of trouble getting people to pin down what things they had always remembered and what had been recently "recovered." They would keep using the phrase, "I remembered." I would push them, saying, "Was this a recovered memory or something you had always remembered?"

I would usually try to screen out contamination by asking people first to pretend that I was interviewing them before they had begun their search for "repressed memories" and to tell me exactly what they could remember at that time. Next, I would ask them to tell me about their "recovered memories." Finally, I would let them relax and tell me their story as they were comfortable telling it. They would usually go back and tell their stories as if the "recovered memories" were now a remembered part of the story, merging the old and new sets of information into one narrative with the phrase, "I remember." The result was frequently some very ordinary incidents enhanced by incongruously fantastic or super-sinister details. (For example, one interviewee talked about memories from when she was about eleven years old. She would go out rock hunting or fishing with her family during the day and at night gave birth to a baby who was later kept chained up in the garage.)

Memory research shows that, often, stories that people tell about very early childhood events are actually things that have become family stories and have been repeated in front of the children. They join in with the storytelling, sometimes even remembering things that happened before they were born! Such family stories become solid, elaborate memories, noting details and nuances that a three-year-old could never grasp. Who hasn't seen this happen with a younger sibling?

When the sexual abuse victims I interviewed mixed together their long-remembered details with new information from recovered memory work, I did not have the sense that they were trying to confuse or deceive me. They could no longer tell the difference. When I would ask, "Why do you think you remembered this detail, but repressed that one?" they seemed to be irritated by the question. I had the feeling that I was stirring up cognitive dissonance.

After all my research I have no definitive answer to my questions about what kinds of *"memories"* are *"repressed,"* but I still think it is a very valid and important question to ask. Well-controlled scientific research needs to be done in this area.

TRAUMA THEORY AND PTSD

One of the cornerstones of Freudian psychoanalytic thinking and therapy was that psychological problems stem from childhood trauma. Popular conceptions of analysis show the therapist searching endlessly for the key "memory" that caused his patient's psychological pain and dysfunction. This theme has been reinforced by Hollywood movies such as *The Three Faces of Eve* and Alfred Hitchcock's *Marni*. Trauma theory was all we had to go on before psychology branched out and incorporated other concepts such as behaviorism, systems theory, or psychobiological etiologies. Now we know that psychological disturbances can have many different origins, but there remains little doubt that traumatic events are, in fact, true causes of many psychological ailments.

Trauma is psychological shock or severe distress in reaction to extremely upsetting events that, to us, feel beyond our control, such as earthquakes, war, or a frightening physical threat like rape. Dissociation during such an experience is not only normal and expected, it can be helpful for surviving the experience. At the time of the assault many people recall "out-of-body experiences" that blotted out the pain and helped them think more calmly. Some will even block out the experience entirely, though they can remember the surrounding events and recall that they have been raped, for example. Unfortunately, if a person persists in not remembering the event, he or she will probably still experience the post-event upset. Blocked realizations of this type differ from simple forgetting because the victim will often feel depressed or numb until he or she is ready to deal with the emotions connected to the event.

There are two levels of reaction to trauma that concern psychologists. Psychologists classify symptoms such as amnesia or numbing, which persist and interfere with normal functioning for more than a few days but for less than four weeks, as brief reaction dissociative disorder. Most people experience the greatest amount of disturbance in the days immediately following the event. For example, if they have flashbacks or intrusive memories of the event, these disturbances will gradually decrease in frequency as the event is distanced by the healing power of time passing.

If the symptoms persist for more than a month, it is characterized as post traumatic stress disorder, or PTSD. Since PTSD is a deeper disturbance, there are more symptoms to watch out for. Flashbacks, nightmares, intense anxiety when near the location where the trauma took place, or on anniversaries of the event are common. Clients suffering from PTSD frequently show little interest in what were once significant activities, feel estranged from others, and cannot respond to situations with their usual emotions. They may be ever-ready for danger as exhibited by difficulty sleeping, an exaggerated startle response, trouble concentrating, or frequent unexpected outbursts of anger.[10] In other words, they are nervous wrecks.

It is important to keep in mind that PTSD is a kind of extension of the traumatic reaction. It is not common or expected that the person would have no reaction at the time the trauma occurs and suddenly experience symptoms sometime later. In the case of Vietnam veterans, the flashbacks and disturbances persist for years. Sometimes symptoms that have abated for a considerable amount of time later return as a result of another, perhaps milder, traumatic experience. Just as certain moods cause us to recall other events that produced that mood in the past (emotional congruence), a violent argument can trigger a flashback to a moment in a war zone.

What has not been proven to be characteristic of PTSD is that one would experience a "traumatic" event, go happily on with normal activities for twenty years (as do women who purportedly were socially adept, high achievers as children while they were being abused nightly), and then have a sudden full-blown PTSD "breakdown." However, this sequence does seem to be the assumption underlying diagnosis of decades-delayed reaction to traumatic sexual abuse in childhood as PTSD.

Take, for example, someone who was sexually assaulted when she was seven years old and reacted by wetting her bed, being very cranky and insecure, and failing a number of tests at school because of poor concentration. If she gradually got over the event and was fine for twenty years until an abusive husband came home drunk one night and raped her, we could attribute the return of symptoms to PTSD. If she never really got over the incident and had periodic anxiety attacks during the next twenty years, we could say that the damage was long-term but could not meet the criteria for PTSD. Furthermore, there is no evidence to support the notion that someone could have had a traumatic experience (or especially a series of traumatic experiences) twenty years ago, had absolutely no reaction at the time, and then suddenly could have had a "postponed breakdown," exhibiting many PTSD symptoms.

People who have been through genuinely traumatic experiences certainly are not eager to have those intrude and will generally make every effort to block them out. These people typically either consciously suppress the memories by finding other things to occupy their minds, or they may temporarily repress the memories. For example, someone who has recently been through a severe trauma, such as witnessing his family burned up in the house, may initially totally deny that it happened. It is a temporary psychosis confined to one memory in his life. The event is so unbearably horrible that he needs to deny the reality at that point. It's not really considered abnormal for someone to temporarily deny the loss of a loved one or even to cling to an idealized image of a lost loved one.

NONPATHOLOGICAL STRESSORS

The chart below of relative reactions to common stressors such as divorce or job loss, shows the many present-life circumstances that can cause stress-related symptoms such as fatigue, inner turmoil, sleep difficulties, headaches, stomachaches, chest pains, tearfulness, asthma, migraine, peptic ulcers, irritable bowel syndrome, rashes, excessive sweating, and heavy, prolonged menstrual periods or cessation of periods. These sensations are not "body memories" of past trauma, but rather are body reactions to *present* psychological stress. They do not necessarily indicate PTSD.

The following chart assigns numerical values to various life events. Studies indicate that a person who accumulates 150 to 300 points within a twelve-month period has a 50 percent chance of coming down with an illness requiring hospitalization. A twelve-month score of 300 points raises the risk of serious illness to 90 percent. How many stress factors have you experienced in the last twelve months—or in the twelve months before you sought therapy? You may not be suffering from PTSD, but rather, from PSD (Present Stress Disorder).

ROBUST REPRESSION

The "repressed memories" that have engendered the most disbelief are the cases of what has been called "robust repression" or claims that repeated incidents of sexual abuse were repressed as soon as they happened. It is most suspect when clients who previously believed they had a normal childhood "recover," during therapy, incidents of sexual abuse

ADULT STRESS CHART[11]

1. Death of a spouse	100
2. Divorce	73
3. Marital separation	65
4. Death of a close family member	63
5. Personal injury or illness	53
6. Marriage	50
7. Dismissal from job	47
8. Marital reconciliation	45
9. Change in health of a family member	44
10. Pregnancy	39
11. Sex difficulties	39
12. Gain of a new family member	39
13. Change in financial state	38
14. Death of a close friend	37
15. Change to a different line of work	36
16. Change in responsibilities at work	29
17. Son or daughter leaving home	29
18. Trouble with in-laws	29
19. Outstanding personal achievement	28
20. Beginning or ending of school	26
21. Change in living conditions	25
22. Trouble with boss	23
23. Change of residence	20
24. Change in sleeping habits	16
25. Change in eating habits	15
26. Vacation	13
27. Christmas	12

that began when they were infants and continued into their teens, while no memory of these happenings has ever been part of their conscious awareness.

Before we look at the concept of "robust repression," let's see what experts believe about these early memories. Loftus, Baddeley, Neisser, and most other cognitive psychologists agree that it would be extremely rare for anyone to remember an event that happened before his or her third year. Occasionally, someone may remember an event that was very significant to him, such as the birth of a sibling, that took place before he was three, but even in such cases we cannot be sure if the person is truly remembering the incident or is instead remembering what he was later told about the incident. It is very difficult to sort out family stories from early memories. In any event, before Repressed Memory Therapy became popular, people did not generally believe they remembered anything from infancy. Most neurological experts assert that infants have not developed the brain capacity to store memories. Life events are considered "episodic" memory and depend on a key midbrain structure called the *hippocampus*. Scientists know this because damage to the hippocampus of an adult can cause severe amnesia. Research shows that the hippocampus and its connections do not fully mature until the child's second year of life.[12]

So we begin with doubts about memories of sexual abuse which have allegedly taken place before the age of two. What about the reports that a woman has recovered memories of being repeatedly and brutally raped from early childhood on into adolescence? Psychological historians point out that even Freud had never conceived of repression operating this way. The only evidence in support of such a notion is anecdotal—that is to say only those undergoing therapy with therapists who believe that this is the way repression works are producing stories of repeated rapes, serially forgotten.

The only kind of traumatic amnesia that has been documented is the partial forgetting of moments or details in a terrifying event. For example, a teenager raped at knife point may have memory lapses in the sequence of events. She might remember feeling the knife at her throat, and the next thing she recalls is lying alone under a bush. The actual rape may have been so traumatic that the normal biological process underlying information storage was disrupted. This would be similar to what happens to an alcoholic in a "blackout." A disruption in the biochemical process of memory prevents information from being stored in the long-term memory. However, the person experiencing the "blackout" recalls events up to the point of unbearable anxiety and is later aware that memory loss occurred.

Yvette, from Chapters Three and Six, was actually most similar to the subjects studied by Meyer Williams who did not seem to recall their abuse. Only after Yvette's sister reminded her of the abuse was she able to recall most details. However, she repressed one detail: the penetration of intercourse. Yvette told me,

"I still haven't gotten to the point where I can really believe it happened. In my mind—and I still picture it this way after all this therapy and stuff—I'm on his bed. He's on top of me. My mind will not let me believe that he actually had intercourse with me. There's a hole in the mattress. And in my mind he's sticking his penis in the hole in the mattress, not me. I can recall that the next day after it happened, in the morning after he left for school, I pulled back his covers and looked at the mattress and there wasn't any hole there. But my mind will not allow me to believe that he actually raped me."

We see that Yvette has truly repressed the one portion of the experience that she found too painful to absorb. Like an alcoholic's "blackout," the memory is intact up to a point. The rest is *ego-dystonic* or so noxious to her self-concept that her psyche refused to record it in her memory. As anyone who has experienced this knows, no amount of prompting, reliving, or listening will ever call up such an image from memory. Alcoholics who have blackouts come to know whose stories about themselves they can trust. Alcoholics will not deny what a reliable source tells them they did. But they do not *remember* it.

Therefore, the missing segment can never truly be remembered. Yvette believes the intercourse happened, because her sister Claire is a reliable witness. Yvette apparently knew intellectually that the intercourse had taken place. She did not find the hole she'd imagined in the mattress, and she'd told her sister Claire that their brother had "had sex" with her. Claire confirmed that she was not given any actual description of what had happened at the time. However, Yvette's psyche recorded the entire scene in her memory except for the actual moment of intercourse. Since it was never recorded in her memory, it cannot be retrieved.

Those who make claims for the existence of "robust repression" believe that victims can be totally unaware of the circumstances that led up to the attack. Before Recovered Memory Therapy, the client does not even recall getting up at night or going down the basement stairs to join the satanists. She does not remember being tired at school the next day from lack of sleep, nor do these traumatic experiences keep her from getting all A's. By contrast, rape victims, even those who temporarily forget the whole event, are all too aware that something horrible happened, and they experience the terror both before the memory returns and for a long time afterward.[13]

DISSOCIATION

There are many levels of dissociation, and some levels function as good defenses. Dissociation is really a continuum. At one end we might have problems switching gears from work role to parent role, and at the other end of the spectrum is multiple personality disorder, where we have a whole other personality with an existence beyond the host personality's conscious awareness. Hypnotic states are also a great deal like dissociation, and there is a correlation between hypnotizability and degree of dissociation in the same person. The more easily you are hypnotized, the more dissociative you are.

All people frequently experience mild dissociation, such as episodes of "spacing out" while driving and such intense absorption while reading or watching television that they are totally unaware of their surroundings. In a study using individuals who were not in therapy, it was found that 5 percent had the ability to dissociate to a pathological degree.[14] However, this does not mean they were mentally ill; rather dissociation would be a defense readily available to them if they were in a traumatic situation. Highly hypnotizable people are also more susceptible to suggestion.

Hypnotizability and dissociative behaviors are more common in childhood, peak at about age nine or ten, and then gradually fade as we grow older.[15] Some theorists believe that if a child is exposed to severe punishments or other traumatic experiences, he or she is more likely to retain the ability to dissociate. This belief supports the link between childhood sexual abuse, dissociation, and, ultimately, multiple personality disorder (MPD).

Whether or not one's degree of dissociability is considered maladaptive depends a lot on the culture in which one lives. In cultures that emphasize religion, ritual, healing, and magic, dissociability is a valued trait. On the other hand, here in America, where one must put on a suit, drive in heavy traffic, and answer telephones all day, dissociability is a disadvantage. Officially, as we noted above, dissociation is a psychological problem if it invokes a disturbance in identity, memory, or consciousness.

The most serious symptoms of dissociation are amnesia, time loss, and identity confusion. Severely ill MPD patients experience "blackouts," or amnesia, while performing complex tasks such as going to a strange city and making new friends. They have no conscious memory of these events unless they come back to themselves midstream in the experience. Also, they usually have large memory blanks that date back to childhood. We'll be looking at MPD in greater depth later.

ROLES, LIFE STRATEGIES, AND MULTIPLICITY

The notion of a split psyche is not confined to certifiable MPD patients. The average person plays different roles. We often see people behaving in a way that is contradictory to what they say they believe. The people who come closer to being labeled "multiples" are the ones that can pull up each side of their inner conflicts as a separate voice. This ability can be a strength that allows them to understand an internal conflict better than somebody who is less self-aware. Before we have pulled it up into conscious awareness we often feel the conflict but cannot clearly "hear" the different viewpoints, or the subliminal thoughts or beliefs, that can undermine us. For example, your job performance may be slipping because you'd really rather be home with your kids, but that awareness has been blocked from consciousness because you need the money, and being a stay-at-home parent is not an option. This uncomfortable feeling is called ambivalence. Most people just live with it.

However, someone who is higher up the scale of dissociative disorders and could be considered psychologically unsound might be driving to work saying to himself, "Why do I have to go to work when I'd rather be home with my kids?" Those even farther up the scale, who have actually given that internal, nurturing voice a name, might recall the internal conversation like this: "So I said to Susie, why do I have to go to work?"

Some people feel relieved when they can separate their opposing feelings and assign them to different "personalities." Indeed, there is a central conflict among the MPD experts about how advisable it is to draw out the various "personalities." Some feel that it helps the client to see internal conflicts more clearly, so that they can work on them. Dr. George Ganaway disagrees.

In our phone interview, Dr. Ganaway shared his concern that the more discrete these two entities become, the more rigid the defense becomes.

"At first it's just a case of 'I can't make up my mind.' Then it becomes a case of, 'I have two minds really, and the two minds just can't agree.' It can even become a case of one part of the mind disowning the other. Rather than saying, 'These are thoughts and impulses that I can't accept,' the patient says, 'It's not even me.' But the 'multiple' will tend to stop at the point of saying, 'It's another me.' "

Ganaway believes that the danger in completely externalizing the conflicting thought as belonging to another personality increases the loss of control. States Ganaway,

"MPD is sort of one step removed from possession, in that the person is able to say, 'I can't own this collection of thoughts and feelings. It just doesn't feel like me.' He or she gives it another name, another description, and then it's easier to say, 'It's not me.' "

Ganaway admits that "naming the alters" can have some advantages. It gives the patient and the therapist something more concrete to build upon.

"That's the rationale that some therapists use when they say, 'Well, even if I am being iatrogenic when asking to meet certain personalities, that process of concretizing has to happen before you can integrate the personality parts.' I used to buy that, but I've long since discovered that it's really risky to push things that far in terms of crystallizing those into entities."

IATROGENESIS

Iatrogenesis is the creation of an illness as a result of the treatment. Critics have pointed toward False Memory Syndrome as an iatrogenic effect of recovered memory methods. The controversy in the MPD field is over the creation of increasing numbers of "personalities." Whereas most MPD patients used to have about twelve alter personalities, many therapists are now reporting clients who have over 200 "personalities"! More conservative therapists believe that it is the therapists who are creating these "personalities" with their excessive probing. As Dr. Ganaway explained,

"When a therapist starts looking at descriptions and names and such, what he is really doing is focusing on the differences rather than trying to look at the similarities and the manner in which all the 'parts' fit together." [He feels this is counterproductive to the ultimate goal of integration.] "You're sort of breaching a barrier that may never have been breached before, in such a way as to begin to confuse reality with fantasy for that person.

"Say a person comes to me and says, 'I have different conversations inside my head that seem to be different aspects of me that talk among themselves. I realize I'm arguing with myself, but it really feels weird. Sometimes I can even picture these different entities.' My tack would be to continue to try to understand more about all this and to talk about it, but not necessarily to talk directly to the entities, because once one of those entities takes executive control by talking to me directly, then it's living in the *outside* world."

Ganaway feels that addressing various "alters" directly can get very confusing for the patient. He doesn't want to tamper with the fantasy world inside that's serving some very important defensive or restorative function. Ganaway explains,

"I still wind up learning all about the differences and similarities within this internal world. It's just that I don't show an interest in the specific parts themselves, in the sense of wanting to meet them and learn their ages and when they first appeared. As long as I keep referring to it as all *aspects of the larger self*, or entities that the patient created for a very important reason that we can begin to understand, it never needs to take on the quality of true multiplicity, that is, 'individuals' taking turns in having control."

There are conflicts in the MPD literature over what exactly constitutes Multiple Personality Disorder. The top guns, such as Kluft and Braun, do not agree with Ganaway. According to Ganaway, Kluft believes that most "multiples" do not have different "personalities" that take executive control, nor do they come out without the person remembering. He classifies a client as a "multiple" if the client simply feels a sense of influence or co-presence from another part of the mind. Kluft believes that in MPDs the other parts of the mind may still be aware of what's going on and feel that they're just going along for the ride. Ganaway and many others believe that before a therapist can classify someone as MPD they should observe a true identity alteration, where it is visibly apparent that this person has switched to another personality.

One psychologist who specializes in MPD (name withheld at his request) stated that,

"Multiple Personality Disorder, as well as a large number of psychiatric diagnostic labels, are metaphors for (sometimes) poorly defined domains of behavior. There is a lot of smoke about whether it is real or not. Of course, it is not 'real.' It is a metaphor for a cluster of observable behaviors, for which better metaphors have not been described. By better, I mean more useful. The same can be said for Bipolar Disorder. There, what is observable is mood swings that, at either extreme, are disruptive to living. The biochemical mechanism is not understood. That it is biochemical is *inferred* from the observation that major or total relief is had by ingesting lithium carbonate, for a majority of sufferers.

In the same vein, dissociation is a model, a metaphor, for a cluster of behaviors. The question is not whether these metaphors are proven or disproven (see above), but whether or not they are useful, at least for relieving human suffering. Dissociation is a more useful metaphor than repression, encompassing a larger domain of behaviors.

As I listen to the sides of this debate, it seems to me that they often reflect different techniques rather than different diagnoses. Kluft has watered down the definition of MPD to the point that anyone with dissociative behaviors could qualify as having MPD. By assigning the label arbitrarily when a more accurate diagnosis might be Dissociative Identity Disorder (DID) or Dissociative Disorders Not Otherwise Specified (DDNOS), clinicians contribute to the overuse of the MPD label. Not only does this lead to confusion, movies like *The Three Faces of Eve* have made MPD a "glamorous" diagnosis. Clients casually labeled MPD when they really have a more mild dissociative disorder, may be "flattered" into getting worse to keep their new status.

If MPD really is just a "metaphor" instead of a diagnosis of a psychiatric disorder and working with "alters" can help people understand their own minds and resolve their ambivalences, why not do this with everyone?

GESTALT, PSYCHODRAMA, AND TRANSACTIONAL ANALYSIS

MPD is really nothing new under the sun. Twenty years ago everyone sat around having conversations with their "alters." This unique approach was available to almost everyone at a low cost. Sensitivity groups were springing up all over America and the Human Potential Movement taught converts many powerful ways to commune with their psyches.

One of the first forms was psychodrama. A psychodrama workshop ran regularly in a round theater building on the Columbia University campus. Subjects were invited up from the audience to act out a childhood conflict. Therapists in training would take various roles in the subject's life and act out an old conflict, speaking out the thoughts of the opponent, when appropriate, to increase the understanding of the subject. Sometimes the subject played his or her adversary, and the therapist played the subject, modeling another way the subject could behave in the situation. This was a very dramatic, powerful, and affecting method that sparked enlightenment in many ordinary people. It was not reserved for the very damaged. Sensitivity groups, the forerunner of today's self-help groups, used psychodrama to help participants explore conflicts in their relationships and lives. When a group was well run, and the leadership did not try to take on people with severe emotional problems, the method was helpful and entertaining at the same time.

From psychodrama, where you talk to someone else playing the person with whom you are in conflict, popular psychology went on to Gestalt therapy, where you address your adversary in an empty chair placed across from you. Once you have stated your side, you move to the other chair and argue back as you know your opponent would. When one has become really proficient at this skill, one could move on to addressing part of the self. For example, according to Jung, *everything* in your dream is you. Participants spent time not only talking to every person who appeared in their dreams, but also to objects such as tables and rugs.

But the fine art of talking to yourself really reached its zenith when Transactional Analysis (TA) hit the circuit. According to the precepts of TA, invented by Eric Berne but made popular by Tom Harris' book, *I'm OK—You're OK*, we each contain, at a minimum, an Adult, a Parent, and a Child. This was *twenty years* before John Bradshaw announced the birth of the inner child!

The beauty of TA was that everyone had a Parent, an Adult, and a Child. (This was based on Freud's Superego, Ego, and Id.) This wasn't the case of an ordinary one-dimensional person bringing out the multiple personalities of another. It was two "multiples" talking to each other. Not only could your Child get a chance to talk, she could actually talk to another Child. But I'm getting ahead of myself. Let me stop and explain this for those who weren't around twenty-five years ago.

In a nutshell, the Adult inside you was always logical. It operated on factual information. The Parent portion was controlled by the shoulds in life (which are derived from the "parent tapes" that play in your head), and the Child portion was pure feeling with a total disregard for the facts. "I wanna do it, because I wanna do it, and I wanna do it *now!*" Harris elaborates by saying the Parent represents the "taught concept" of life, while the Adult represents the "thought concept," and the child, the "felt concept."

The practical application was to analyze which entity you were when you communicated with others. For example, a man who was in his Parent mode, hurrying to get ready for a party, was bound to have a fight with his wife if she was in her Child mode, playing with her makeup. Truly, TA was an invaluable tool for sorting out conflicts with those around you. If you could stay in Adult mode, you could avoid most arguments, but you wanted to get out of Adult mode by the time you hit the sheets with your spouse.

Advanced courses taught the finer permutations of these transactions. For example, one could have more than one Child. You might be in your playful Child mode, or you might be in your frightened Child mode. You might be in your stern Parent mode or in your nurturing Parent mode. The number of characters available to be played was limited only by your imagination.

This was a great concept! And it was not confined to the rich and the well-insured. Anyone could use this stuff. You could do it in your home with a simple book as your guide. We were all "multiples," and we were all OK! It was, once again, a tool available to the average person interested in gaining insight into himself or herself. Unlike the person with MPD, one could use and benefit from Transactional Analysis without having to have had a serious psychological disease (caused by some forgotten, horrendous, permanently damaging experience).

If you think I exaggerate its similarity to MPD, read this excerpt from the beginning of Chapter Two in *I'm OK– You're OK*:

> "Early in his work in the development of Transactional Analysis, Berne observed that as you watch and listen to people you can see them change before your eyes. It is a total kind of change. There are simultaneous changes in facial expression, vocabulary, gestures, posture, and body functions, which may cause the face to flush, the heart to pound, or the breathing to become rapid.
>
> "We can observe these abrupt changes in everyone. . . ."16

Viewing the ability to change mood states as a *resource* (as TA does) instead of an illness (MPD) puts a very different slant on the discussion. In one case using your Parent, Adult, and Child parts to your maximum benefit is something you need to get educated about; in the other case having alter "personalities" is something of which you need to be cured.

It is actually very common for people to have a work *persona* — a way they act among professional peers. They dress differently, act differently (no feet up on the boardroom table), and often speak in jargon that no one but their co-workers can understand. When these people come home to family, different behaviors are required. Those who can switch quickly into a parental or playful persona as needed are at an advantage. Many normal healthy people can do this, and many normal healthy people get "stuck" in the "wrong personality" when stressed.

Just as changing "personalities" is not necessarily pathological, forgetting large portions of one's childhood does not mean there is some dark secret one is blocking from consciousness. There is a wide range of normal variability in how much is remembered. Events may be forgotten because they were unremarkable or unimportant. Unpleasant events may be forgotten as a healthy defense mechanism, as when a woman forgets the pain of childbirth, or we forget how truly painful it was to lose our first love.

But most of the time, most of what happens in anyone's life is forgotten, unless there is good reason to remember it: to be able to avoid things that cause pain or to be able to recall moments of pleasure and relive them.

Much of what has been assumed about memory by the promulgators of Recovered Memory Therapy is simply inaccurate and unfounded. Beware of any therapist who is too quick to jump to negative conclusions. How we frame things in our minds affects how we live our lives. Be sure you know where you're going when your companion suggests a stroll down a dark lane without a light.

SUMMARY POINTS

1. There is reason to believe that people may repress the details of a traumatic event for a relatively short time after the event, until the psyche is ready to cope with it. However, the only kind of traumatic amnesia that has been documented is the partial forgetting of moments or details in a terrifying event.

2. The ability to totally repress for decades all "memories" of a series of "traumatic" events, with no symptoms whatsoever in the interim, has never been scientifically proven and is based solely on anecdotal evidence.

3. While there is little doubt that traumatic events are true causes of many psychological ailments, sexual abuse recovery therapists focus exclusively on the search for "the" traumatic memory while ignoring all progress made in the field of psychology since Freud's time.

4. Post Traumatic Stress Disorder is an extreme reaction to a traumatic event, with a variety of symptoms. It is not common or expected that a person would have no reaction at the time a trauma occurs and then suddenly experience symptoms many years later.

5. Multiple Personality Disorder (MPD) is a dissociative disease frequently diagnosed in the sexual abuse recovery field. Different mental health professionals have their own opinions on what is a true "multiple" personality.

6. The current popularity of Multiple Personality Disorder diagnosis is reminiscent of the Gestalt, psychodrama, and Transactional Analysis theories propagated in the '60s and '70s.

7. While the true cause of MPD is unclear, many mental health professionals believe it is always caused by sexual abuse or extreme physical abuse. If the client does not remember any such abuse these therapists begin a relentless search for the "repressed" memory.

8. There seems to be a strong correlation between the ability to dissociate and hypnotic susceptibility. This correlation poses a particular danger of memory contamination while using hypnotic techniques on a dissociative client.

EIGHT

Dubious
Diagnoses

*The cure of multiple personality disorder leaves the
patient afflicted with single personality disorder, the
state in which most patients seek psychotherapy.*

— RICHARD P. KLUFT, M.D., MPD specialist[1]

AS MENTIONED EARLIER, reports from accused families and retractors show that many of the accusers' stories follow a patterned progression. They enter therapy for a variety of reasons, from depression over a recent divorce to stress-related anxiety. A poorly trained sexual abuse recovery therapist tells them that they show symptoms of sexual abuse, even though the clients may have no memories whatsoever of having been sexually abused. So they begin searching for "memories." When the patient finally accepts this diagnosis and is able to come up with some memories of being sexually abused, she is often functioning at a lower level of psychological health than when she entered therapy.

The therapist interprets this to mean that the pathology is more serious, and the patient is told that she may be a multiple personality. This is followed by many probing sessions with the therapist to call out and meet all the various personalities, or "alters." As more and more "alters" are discovered, the therapist begins to suspect the client has been a victim of the most serious of traumatic experiences — satanic ritual abuse.

If we look at the current understanding among therapists about Multiple Personality Disorder (MPD), as they talk about it at their conferences and in their literature, we can see how a "mythology" of causes has been developed and reinforced. Like self-fulfilling prophecies, if therapists do not hang onto a healthy amount of skepticism, they will find, if not *produce*, what they are looking for, even if they have to create it themselves. The whole field has been contaminated by a circular "proof," based on clinical experience, that has not been backed up by any scientific studies.

Dr. Ganaway has often seen patients who experienced some kind of trauma or abuse who were diagnosed as having MPD, but sexual abuse was not part of the trauma. One patient had been extremely humiliated and embarrassed by her father who used to drink too much and could say things in front of other people that were very embarrassing to her. She would crawl under her bed to escape the embarrassment. She had a lot of mixed feelings about both her father and her mother. They had committed sins of commission and omission when it came to parenting but not those behaviors that comprise the standard stories of physical and sexual abuse. Ganaway (in our telephone interview) stated:

"However, at one point in time she wound up in a psychiatric hospital where the staff was heavily into satanic cult stories. Before she got out of the hospital she had begun to imagine herself being involved in these rituals. When she was transferred to Ridgeview all that stuff started evaporating. It had taken a short exposure to that group of patients claiming ritual abuse for her to start imagining she'd been ritually abused too. They were all telling her, 'You just don't know yet. You haven't gotten the memories yet,' and she started to get them. Once she got to us she gradually began to decide, 'No, that wasn't true.' "

THE MPD MYTHOLOGY

As both critics and proponents of the rapidly increasing number of diagnoses of MPD are quick to point out, before the 1980s only a few hundred cases of MPD had been reported in two hundred years, but during the 1980s thousands of cases have been reported in the U.S. and Canada. Critics say this points to irresponsible overdiagnosis or a therapeutic "fad" gone wild.

Proponents believe that we have finally refined our methods of diagnosis and expanded our knowledge of MPD enough to diagnose it properly more frequently. They assert that many of the clients who are diagnosed as having MPD have been in the mental health system for a number of years and have often had two or more previous diagnoses which led to ineffective treatment. They say many MPD cases have been misdiagnosed or overlooked because of the *mistaken* belief that MPD is rare. Further, they see the expanded recognition of MPD as a logical result of our society's increased willingness to recognize child abuse, especially childhood sexual abuse.

Here is where the dangerous circular reasoning begins. As we have discussed in previous chapters, there has been so much "leading the witness" evident in treatment of suspected sexual abuse, that we no longer know how many cases of reported sexual abuse are real. Intrusive methods of hypnosis, guided imagery, and outright forceful argument ("You're in denial!") have been used to convince many clients that they were sexually abused. These cases are then tabulated and reported as statistics of childhood sexual abuse, without any corroborating evidence. "Evidence" based solely on repressed memories of sexual abuse is pretty shaky ground with which to support the statistics needed to uphold the idea that MPD is an epidemic in North America.

Bennett G. Braun, Clinical Associate Professor of the Department of Psychology at the University of Illinois in Chicago, is recognized as one of the leading authorities on MPD. In a paper he co-authored with Roberta G. Sachs (a psychologist in private practice) in 1985, Braun describes MPD, its roots, and the factors that aggravate and prolong the condition.[2] Braun and Sachs begin by summarizing the definition of MPD (below), paraphrasing the Third Edition of the *Diagnostic and Statistical Manual of Mental Disorders*, or the DSM-III:

1) the existence within an individual of two (or more) distinct personalities, each of which is in control of the body at different times;
2) the personality that is dominant determines ongoing behavior; and
3) each personality is complex and has its own unique history, behavior patterns, and social relationships."[3]

But what is believed to cause MPD? The authors describe the two main factors that MPD therapists currently believe are the etiology of most cases of MPD. Braun and Sachs concluded that:

1. Clients who develop MPD have an inborn capacity to dissociate.
2. These clients have experienced serious trauma, particularly in a relationship during childhood with caretakers that were unpredictably, alternately, abusive and loving.[4]

Braun and Sachs emphasize that neither of these factors are strong enough to cause dissociation as serious as MPD by themselves, but *both* must be present in the patient to create a condition as serious as MPD. The authors state that these observations are based on clinical observations over the last few years.[5] Though the authors never mention how many of the clients reported the abuse only after regressive therapy to help them uncover repressed memories, their research and conclusions were drawn from clinical practice before 1985, so their results should be free of contamination by overzealous ill-defined MPD diagnoses.

Sachs and Braun do point out that the "inborn capacity to dissociate" is determined by the patient's hypnotizability, noting that studies using hypnotizability scales show that MPD patients are more hypnotizable than clients suffering from other disorders. It is easy to see how cause and effect may have been muddled in the conclusions being drawn about MPD patients. First, since people have differing susceptibilities to hypnotism, and many therapists use hypnotism to draw out the separate personalities, it logically follows that easily hypnotizable people would be very vulnerable to being convinced they are multiples. As has been mentioned earlier, high-hypnotizables are also very susceptible to suggestion. Therefore, MPD may be the result of hypnotic techniques used by the therapist. If we add to this a therapist's predisposition to find MPD, the outcome is doubly contaminated.

Similarly, the evident cause and effect of child abuse and MPD may have been reversed by therapist expectation. For MPD clients who were not aware of any abuse before they entered therapy, their discovery of repressed memories of childhood abuse is not proof that MPD is *caused* by childhood abuse. Before we can come to any conclusions about the cause-and-effect relationship between MPD and childhood abuse, we need to know if the reports of abuse are factual. Richard P. Kluft, Clinical Professor of Psychiatry at Temple University and much-respected authority on MPD, calls for caution in assessing the validity of patients' stories:

> "Retrospective recollection is prone to several forms of distortion, revision, and reworking. Furthermore (and without implying disregard for or disbelief in patients' representations), unless there is documentation from sources other than the person who is recounting his or her life, it is difficult to transpose what is offered, however convincingly, from the realm of retrospective account into the domain of scientific record."[6]

Indeed, in the last decade the conclusions and current beliefs about MPD have become so wound up in the dubious proofs of "recovered memories" that we need to take about four steps back and look at beliefs about MPD before the 1980s. Before the story of "Sybil" was recounted in novel form, the only case of multiple personality in recent times, which was widely recognized as genuine, was the case made famous by the movie *The Three Faces of Eve*. By looking at the story of Eve (whose real name was later revealed to be Chris Sizemore) we can learn a great deal that will help us put the current MPD craze in perspective. We not only have the detailed account written by Drs. Thigpen and Cleckley, the psychiatrists involved in this case, we also have two books written by Eve herself: the first published in 1977, some time after the movie came out, and a later book in 1989, in which she is able to look back from the distance of many years.[7] The doctors also published a revised edition of their book in 1992.

EVE SPEAKS FOR HERSELF

It is important to keep in mind that Eve's multiple personality was discovered in a time when multiple personality was not a fad, so the doctors' observations were not contaminated by any preconceived notions or expectations. The case of Eve should serve as a model for subsequent speculations about multiple personality. It is fair to ask if the case of Eve confirms Braun's and Sachs's absolute declarations about what is always present in genuine cases of MPD. Did Eve have an inborn capacity to dissociate, and was she traumatically abused as a child?

The answer to the first question is a definite yes. There are some stories from Eve's childhood (confirmed separately by her parents in interviews with Thigpen) that show Eve had two separate personalities as early as age five. (Thigpen apparently believed in checking his patients' views of reality by interviewing other family members.) Within her family circle, Eve had a reputation for being a liar. Several times she had totally denied a misbehavior when she was guilty beyond any doubt.

For example, one day when Eve's twin baby sisters were only a few months old, Eve's mother had left the infants sleeping on a bed, while she went outside to do some yard work. When she heard the babies crying, she rushed to the window to see what had happened and saw Eve angrily biting the toes of the babies. The mother banged on the window and then rushed around to the door. By the time she reached the bedroom, her daughter Eve was standing idly by looking as if nothing had happened. When her mother began scolding her, Eve could not remember harming the babies and told her mother that someone else had done it.

As Eve White, the original personality the doctors had met, explained her recollection of this incident, she again proclaimed her innocence. She could remember another girl biting the toes of the babies – a girl who had run out when the mother banged on the window and left Eve White with the blame. At this point of her therapy, Eve White genuinely believed that she was innocent and had been falsely accused and punished for this transgression. She had a number of other similar memories in which she believed she had been blamed for something someone else had done. We needn't suspect the mother of "messing with little Eve's mind." A number of Eve's teachers had also accused her of bad deeds she swore she had not done.

Later, when Dr. Thigpen met Eve's first alter, referred to as Eve Black, the doctor got another view of these incidents. Eve Black stated that she had bitten the babies' toes, and she had no regrets about it. She habitually ducked out and left Eve White to receive the punishment for her misdeeds. The changes in personality displayed in the doctor's office were initially brought about by the doctor inducing a hypnotic state, but as therapy progressed Eve was able to put herself quickly into a trance. Her early confirmed dissociations and her later easy ability to enter a hypnotic trance show that she has one of the necessary antecedents to multiple personality as described by Braun and Sachs.

What about the second vital component – a history of traumatic abuse, especially by a primary caretaker? Throughout both of Eve's written accounts and her childhood as reported by her doctor, Eve's parents appear to be extraordinarily supportive. Despite Eve's difficult personality, the parents continued to treat her lovingly. Eve felt supported and cared for, and the doctors confirm her positive impression of her parents. When Eve got involved in a brief abusive marriage, her father came and got her so she could escape it. When Eve encountered difficulties in her second marriage and was feeling very unstable, her parents cared for her child while she continued her therapy and prepared to live apart from her husband. They were happy to care for her child and willingly gave her up when Eve felt secure enough to care for her. They were always cooperative about talking to her doctors and tried earnestly to help the doctors discover what traumatic event could have caused the split in her personality.

MPD WITHOUT TRAUMA

So Eve was definitely not a victim of child abuse, and Eve, her parents, and her doctors ultimately failed to come up with a memory traumatic enough to have caused a major mental disorder. Though they did discover that Eve had seen two dead bodies during her very early years and when five years old was asked to touch her dead grandmother (a regular custom of the times that was believed to help the child get over her grief more quickly), the doctors acknowledged that these incidents were really not terribly traumatic and certainly wouldn't have caused a normal child to become emotionally disturbed. So we must conclude that Eve was not "normal" to begin with. Indeed, she later turned out to be a rather accomplished artist, implying that she may have been an especially sensitive child.

At the same time, there is ample confirmation from Eve's parents, doctors, husband, children, and her own incomplete memories to show that she was a true multiple. So much for Braun and Sachs' second absolute criterion.

Drs. Thigpen and Cleckley as recently at 1992 have viewed and commented upon the current MPD fad with rancorous skepticism. In the "Thirty-five-year Addendum" to the revised edition of *The Three Faces of Eve*, the doctors emphasize the caution with which they approached the case of Eve. Only after a year of working with Eve did the doctors rule out psychosis, partial dissociation, secondary gain (such as attention-getting), or feigning ("acting" the other personalities).

In the thirty years following their diagnosis of Eve, the doctors saw thousands of psychiatric patients, and in all that time they saw only one other case that appeared to be a genuine multiple personality. Since 'the doctors had been able to recognize Eve as a multiple when they had had no prior experience in this area, we can safely assume that they would be able to recognize another example of MPD if they saw one. Though many psychiatrists referred suspected multiples to Thigpen and Cleckley and the doctors were contacted by many self-diagnosed multiples, the doctors have found no proof that MPD is rampant. Rather they believe that therapists are jumping to conclusions, because of either naiveté or ignorance. Thigpen and Cleckley maintain that most cases that appear to be multiples are hysterical-personality types seeking the limelight through dramatic symptoms. Further, they believe that some of these patients may have dissociative tendencies, and it is the overzealousness of therapists which causes these split-off feelings to become full-blown separate "personalities."[8]

WHAT ABOUT SYBIL?

Those who support the belief that most cases of MPD are caused by severe child abuse most frequently cite the case of Sybil as reported in the book of that name by Flora Rheta Schreiber. The book, which was written with the cooperation of Sybil's psychiatrist, Cornelia Wilbur, portrays a mother who was a heinous sadist. Sybil recalled that when she was two or younger her mother used to hang her from the ceiling and fill her bladder with water or put sharp objects in her vagina. However, more recent research into Sybil's history casts doubt not only on the certainty of these memories, but also on the fact that she was a multiple personality.

Author John Taylor tracked down Sybil's relief psychiatrist, Herbert Spiegel, since Cornelia Wilbur is now deceased. Spiegel, a former professor at Columbia medical school who specializes in hypnosis, diagnosed and treated Sybil when Dr. Wilbur had reached an impasse and subsequently became Sybil's therapist when Dr. Wilbur went on summer break. Taylor quotes Spiegel as saying that,

> "She was suicidal and would come to see me when Wilbur was out of town. When I talked to her about aspects of her life, she would say, 'Do I have to become Helen or can we just discuss this?'
>
> "I said, 'Why are you asking?'
>
> "She said, 'Dr. Wilbur would want me to.'
>
> "I said, 'You can if you want to,' and she would not. She would discuss her problems, her suicidal tendencies, without switching personalities."[9]

Spiegel went on to explain that Sybil's mother was definitely schizophrenic, but that the sexual abuse had never been corroborated. Neither had Sybil been diagnosed as having MPD.

The diagnosis of MPD was mentioned to Spiegel only after Sybil had stopped treatment, and Wilbur and Schreiber had begun collaborating on a book about her. Schreiber came to see Spiegel about helping with the book by opening his files and mentioned that she was going to call Sybil's condition MPD. When Spiegel objected that Sybil was not a multiple personality, Schreiber got angry. Spiegel explains that,

"Schreiber [who died in 1988] said that publishing companies wouldn't be able to sell it unless it was MPD. I said that was a hell of a reason for a medical diagnosis. She got mad as hell and left the room in a huff. She wouldn't talk to me after that and neither would Wilbur. Their goal was to do something to capture the imagination of the public. They succeeded."[10]

Sybil's and Eve's stories are just two of the MPD stories promulgated by the media. In the book, *Multiple Personalities, Multiple Disorders: Psychiatric Classification and Media Influence*, authors North, Ryall, Ricci, and Wetzel delve into the history of all the well-publicized MPD stories of the past century, showing that most of the clients had enough clear symptoms of Briquet's syndrome (very similar to the earlier classification of hysteria) to qualify clearly for that diagnosis.[11] The implication of the book is that MPD is a new name for an old disorder that has a slightly less dramatic description. When one finishes reading *Multiple Personalities, Multiple Disorders* he or she might suspect that the diagnosis of MPD is just a scheme to create new jobs for conference speakers and special unit hospital workers.

MANUFACTURED MPD

Dr. Paul McHugh, Director of Psychiatry and Behavioral Science at Johns Hopkins, sees the overdiagnosis of MPD as a problem related to False Memory Syndrome. He attempts to answer the question, "Why would anyone believe anything so painful as being sexually abused by a parent if it weren't true?" by pointing out past errors in the field of psychiatry. His favorite comparison is the story of the neurologist Jean-Martin Charcot, who thought he had discovered a new disease he called "hystero-epilepsy," a disorder of the mind and the brain that combined features of hysteria and epilepsy. Symptoms of the disease included convulsions, contortions, fainting, and transient impairment of consciousness.

Joseph Babinski, a student of Charcot's, was skeptical of both the diagnosis and the disease. He noticed that the patients had come to the hospital with vague complaints of depression, which Charcot took to be the beginning signs of hystero-epilepsy. Once they had signed into the hospital, they declined rapidly and began displaying the same symptoms as the other patients.

Babinski believed that these patients were showing signs of epilepsy because hysterical patients (the then-current term for a special kind of emotional disorder) were housed with the epileptics. He believed these very suggestible women (the precursors of today's MPD patients) were imitating the behavior they saw around them—epileptic fits. Fortunately, he was able to persuade Charcot to consider this possible iatrogenic cause of hystero-epilepsy and change his procedures.

The hystero-epileptic patients were transferred to general wards of the hospital and kept apart from one another. Once they had been separated from everyone else who behaved that way and from all the staff members who had come to expect them to have epileptic fits, the symptoms subsided.

As a second measure, they decided to ignore any hystero-epileptic symptoms and focus on the patients' present circumstances. The patients were suffering from many stressors and fears. The staff refused to respond to any hysterical behavior, assuring the patients that they were in recovery and needed to focus on the aspects of their home lives that may have brought on the disease.

Dr. McHugh states his opinion on MPD clearly:

"The rules discovered by Babinski and Charcot, now embedded in psychiatric textbooks and confirmed by decades of research in social psychology, are being overlooked in the midst of a nationwide epidemic of alleged MPD that is wreaking havoc on both patients and therapists. MPD is an iatrogenic behavioral syndrome, promoted by suggestion and maintained by clinical attention, social consequences, and group loyalties. It rests on ideas about the self that obscure reality, and it responds to standard treatments."[12]

McHugh points out that it is particularly tragic because the myth of MPD includes the presumption that the client has suffered a childhood sexual trauma. Not only is therapy directed at reinforcing the symptoms, by drawing out "alters," but the patient's real problems are ignored as any remaining session time is occupied by the search for *the* traumatic memory.

ANSWER TEN

Why would anyone believe anything so painful as being sexually abused by a parent if it weren't true?

ANSWER NUMBER TEN: Because many therapists have failed to study the history of psychiatric practices, theory, and past grave errors, and these therapists do not realize that they can be mistaken.

A CONTEMPORARY CLIENT'S REPORT

At the 1993 conference entitled "Memory and Reality: Emerging Crisis," sponsored by the False Memory Syndrome Foundation in Philadelphia, one of the retractors who spoke made it abundantly clear how this issue of sloppy misdiagnosis of MPD affects individuals in therapy. Elizabeth Carlson told how she had sought therapy for depression following a nine-month separation from her husband. Almost immediately Ms. Carlson was diagnosed as having MPD, and the therapist began enumerating Elizabeth's many "personalities." Elizabeth described the experience from the patient's point of view beautifully:

> "I was told that the sadness I had was not me; it was another personality. I was told the part of me that liked to get on the floor and play with my kids was not me; it was another personality. I had to keep index cards with me all the time so I could figure out who I was. I could not go into my psychiatrist's office and say: 'I'm feeling sad today.' I had to say, 'I'm Sarah.' "

After attending a conference on Multiple Personality Disorder, Elizabeth's therapist returned and told her that she had other "personalities" they had yet to uncover: lesbians, men, animals, and demons. The therapist warned Elizabeth that until she let these personalities come out, she could not be healed. As is the common pattern in these cases of poor therapy, Elizabeth was also exhorted to try to recall being sexually abused during satanic rituals. Whenever Elizabeth questioned the validity of her therapy, she was told she was in denial.[13]

ARE THERE ANY REAL MPDS?

This has become a moot question because the new DSM-IV will eliminate MPD as a category and will rely instead on a continuum of dissociation. Dr. Ganaway has kept a conservative position on MPD that allows him to slip comfortably into using this new concept of classification. He has seen many patients suffering varying degrees of dissociation, but unlike many of his contemporaries in the MPD business, he finds few patients he would diagnose as multiple personalities. Since he runs an inpatient clinic, he often gets referrals from therapists who work only in outpatient settings. During the past six years, patients referred to his clinic have arrived with increasingly large numbers of alternate "personalities." The experiences related by the patients have also become increasingly bizarre; many recent referrals have told tales of recovered memories of satanic ritual abuse. Ganaway is aware of no evidence that supports these recollections.

Though Ganaway does not believe patients' claims of ritual abuse are founded in fact, he has seen the damage the belief alone can do. After many sessions of "memory work" with the referring therapist, these patients often display frequent and dramatic spontaneous alterations of consciousness and regressions to primitive self-destructive states. Rather than continuing the focus on uncovering more "personalities," Ganaway's clinic concentrates on supportive techniques that help the patients get reoriented to normal life in the here and now. In contrast to techniques that encourage clients to excuse their negative behaviors by pointing to an "alter" who "did it," Ganaway's staff members hold the patients fully responsible for all of their impulses and behaviors. As Ganaway explains, "The patients' belief in their multiple semi-autonomous 'selves' is respected, but not indulged."[14]

If, as Thigpen, Cleckley, and Ganaway imply, MPD is often a misdiagnosis, how do we explain the "cures" that many MPD therapists report? Ganaway believes that MPD and survivor therapies educate the client to externalize the cause of their symptoms. Instead of facing and resolving an inner conflict, for example, the common conflict over separating from one's parents while still feeling dependent upon them, the client is encouraged to blame the parents for the conflictual feelings and difficulty with separation. Both client and therapist seem to be unaware that *symptom substitution* gives some relief and hence a feeling of progress when the client transfers his dependency on his parents to a dependency on the therapist. By mounting up evidence of the hateful aspects of the parents, separation is perceived as not only desirable, but just. It may even be that, the stronger the attachment the client has to his or her parents, the more heinous and numerous the crimes must be to justify separation.

JUDY IN JEOPARDY

In 1985 Judy was diagnosed as having MPD; however, after two years of therapy, it was decided Judy had a mood disorder instead. How could this error have occurred? What harm, if any, did that year and a half of misdirected therapy do to her? Is it possible that the second diagnosis was the incorrect one? Should Judy sue her therapist or her parents?

There are a couple of reasons why her therapist began to suspect Judy had MPD. The basic problem that brought her to therapy was that Judy was a first-time mother, struggling with her very demanding and intense child. Prior to that Judy had led a quiet life as a student, writing teacher, and writer. Judy like spending long, silent hours with herself.

Then along came this little person who demanded her notice every minute and was endlessly inventive about ways to get Judy's attention. In order to spend more time with her, Judy's little son had managed to get himself thrown out of a series of pre-schools. So, from a life of solitude, Judy was thrown into a life of total togetherness. When Judy would get a few hours to herself, she could not write. Judy could not switch out of her mom "gear" into her writer "gear."

Her life as a mother was totally different from her life as a writer. Judy had two separate sets of friends. She thought different thoughts and behaved differently. Judy used to do editing out of her home, and if a client called while Judy was attending her son, she had a terrible time sounding professional or thinking clearly.

Judy is not the first or the last person to have experienced this split. Most women with strong personal or professional lives of their own experience this conflict when they become mothers. Though many find it difficult to be both career woman and mother, Judy found the pressure of this double life devastating. It had thrown her into a deep depression, and she felt as if her personality had disintegrated. Judy felt fragmented, unable to concentrate on any task.

Being a mother restimulated her childhood role as the "little mother," caring for her two younger brothers and sister while her mother worked and then stayed out drinking. The role of mother was overwhelming when Judy was twelve, and she found it overwhelming again when she was thirty-seven.

Besides her current rigid inability to flow in and out of her various roles, Judy had told her therapist about the double life she had led in high school. Judy had had two separate sets of friends and two different names. As Judith, she was a cheerleader, vice president of her class, president of the Pep Club, and a popular, vivacious extrovert. As "Jude," she lead an alternate existence, mainly on the telephone, with a bunch of "beat" introverts as her friends. They were all very cynical—the antithesis of cheerleaders. Jude used to fantasize about moving into her closet with a telephone, so she wouldn't have to interact with people except when she chose.

When her therapist asked if there were only two of her, Judy began her life as a model of MPD. Judy was a writer who had been writing stories for years, so she had no difficulty coming up with identities. Judy had always been aware of a moderating self that oversaw the discussion when her introverted/depressed self decided on suicide and her extroverted/manic self would deny anything was wrong. This third "personality" (whom she later dubbed Judy) would acknowledge that life was horribly painful right now, but if "Jude" killed herself it was forever. The moderator would urge "Jude" to hang on one more day and see if things would improve. She promised that "Jude" could always kill herself later.

Judy came up with permutations of the two major identities. "Little Mother" had an "alter" named "Big Mama," who was a resentful, surly disciplinarian who believed that kids' misbehavior was calculated and purposeful. Some personalities were plotting to kill her (by making her step off a curb in front of a moving car, which Judy had plainly seen), and others were trying to save her (by pulling her back up onto the curb before the car hit). Judy and her therapist had uncovered about thirteen "alters" when, because Judy wasn't getting any better despite many positive changes in her life, they decided she should see the staff psychiatrist about medication.

The psychiatrist asked Judy about her multiple "personalities." Judy told him about "Judith" and "Jude" in high school, the split life Judy had always led that had caused her great embarrassment at times. As "Judith," she would volunteer to do a speech in front of fifty people, but then, when the day arrived, "Jude" would be in charge, and she was speechless. There had been times when Judy was in the right "personality" at the right time, too, but Judy could never predict or control who Judy would be on a given day.

After asking her a lot of questions, the psychiatrist and Judy came to the understanding that she was really dealing with two main characters: introverted, depressed "Jude" and extroverted, manic "Judith." The psychiatrist asked about Judy's family history and finally concluded that she was not a multiple personality, but rather a person with a rapid-cycling mood disorder. Judy was cyclothymic, a mild form of manic-depression— or bipolar disorder, as they now call it. Judy was not experiencing different "personalities," rather she was experiencing gripping and intense mood variations. She began taking antidepressants, and within six months she was one, integrated person.

Her therapist apologized profusely. He seemed very embarrassed, and he worried that he had wasted her time in therapy and made her suffer needlessly. But Judy hadn't felt that the two years had been a waste of time at all. Though she and her therapist had meandered down a number of blind alleys, he had been supportive and sympathetic throughout the therapy, and Judy had healed from many deep wounds in the warmth of his concern. Besides, Judy found the multiple personality work to be very useful for clarifying her opposing desires, learning to live with the ambivalence caused by motherhood, and understanding how stress made her feel fragmented and unable to act. It was a very useful metaphor for what Judy was experiencing.

Though her therapist was taken with MPD theory, a field that was emerging into popularity at the time, he had always been eclectic in his approach. He had never really pushed the MPD theory, but Judy had gone along with it because it worked as an explanation for what Judy was feeling at the time. When the psychiatrist and her response to antidepressant medication indicated that Judy was not a victim of MPD, her therapist was quick to admit his mistake and go with her in a new direction.

Though he had made an error, he was a good therapist. He was flexible; he was kind; he let Judy unfold. He had a pet theory, but he could see beyond it. When the shoe no longer fit, he didn't insist that Judy go on wearing it.

When Judy realized she was mood-disordered, and not suffering from MPD, he didn't tell her she was "in denial."

Good therapy is supportive, not coercive. It is flexible, and good therapists listen to what clients have to say about themselves. When a client doesn't remember being sexually abused, a good therapist assumes she was not. When a client does not improve, a good therapist questions his own diagnosis and treatment, and considers other options.

SUMMARY POINTS

1. The history of psychiatry shows that heinous errors have been made in the past. Therapist overconfidence coupled with a lack of adequate regulation of the profession can yield a very harmful outcome.

2. There has been a veritable explosion of MPD diagnoses in the past decade or so. Some consider this to be a therapeutic "fad" gone wild, while others believe therapists have just become more proficient at recognizing the disease.

3. The theory that MPD is always caused by childhood sexual abuse is a recent one, based solely on anecdotal evidence drawn from the experiences of mental health professionals who treat sexual abuse survivors.

4. Though there are people who are highly dissociative to the point of developing true, separate, and distinct personalities, they are extremely rare.

5. Since dissociative people tend to be highly susceptible to hypnotic suggestion, the very act of using hypnosis to "uncover" different "personalities" may become a self-fulfilling prophecy.

6. Why would anyone believe anything so painful as being sexually abused by a parent if it weren't true?
   Because many therapists have an incomplete education in the history of psychiatric practices, including great errors of the past. Those who fail to learn from their profession's mistakes are doomed to repeat them.

NINE

Satanic Ritual Abuse

Little by little I have come face to face with the extent of what I do not know. And just as gradually, like a squirrel gathering acorns, I have collected bits and pieces here and there of what I can find bankable, reliable and sure.[1]

— LAWRENCE R. KLEIN, PhD.,
President, Ohio Society for the Study of MPD

THE ULTIMATE ACCUSATION is the claim that one's parents abused one as part of satanic rituals. Indeed, some naive, poorly trained therapists mistakenly believe that anyone who has MPD must have been ritually abused, because only the traumatic impact of satanic abuse could cause such a "split." A whole belief system about satanic cult conspiracies has developed in the past ten years or so, and testimonials by patients have convinced many therapists that the stories are true. Because claims of satanic abuse are met with much skepticism, these therapists have come to feel that it is their mission to support these claims. Believers point to the fact that not long ago no one would believe incest survivors, and any child making an accusation of sexual abuse was usually discredited. They urge others not to make the same injurious mistake by doubting these vulnerable survivors.

SATANIC RITUAL ABUSE (SRA)

Whether claims of satanic abuse are founded in fact has been a subject of debate in the International Society for the Study of Multiple Personality

Disorder (ISSMPD) at its conferences for the past several years. At the Seventh International Conference on Multiple Personality and Dissociative States held in Chicago, Illinois, in 1989, a panel of professionals highly respected in their field presented their views to a large audience of conference attendees. The workshop title was "Satanic Ritual Abuse: Critical Issues and Alternative Hypotheses." Panel Chair Roland Summit opened the session by summarizing remarks that had been made at earlier sessions that weekend. There was a growing concern that the skepticism about satanic ritual abuse was damaging the therapists' credibility and would destroy the gains they had made in getting their profession to recognize their work with MPD patients as legitimate.

Frank W. Putnam of the National Institute of Mental Health (NIMH) was the first to speak. He implored his colleagues to be cognizant of the known memory disturbances in most people with dissociative disorders and to keep some healthy skepticism while listening to clients' stories. He reported that studies and clinical experience show that the vast majority of MPD clients have trouble differentiating between what was real and what was imagined. For example, material that occurred in a dream becomes incorporated into memory as a real event. There is very strong documented proof that MPDs and other dissociative patients also have memory deficits for autobiographical material, as well as general knowledge (implicit memory). The fact that these patients confabulate to fill in blanks in their memories has been very well-established in laboratory studies. The tendency for these patients to create pseudo-memories has been known since Pierre Janet's time. In fact Janet, one of the first psychologists and an expert on hysteria, would heal his patients by implanting positive pseudo-memories in place of disturbing memories. Janet apparently believed in the power of positive thinking long before Norman Vincent Peale.

Putnam reminded his colleagues that MPDs also have a great deal of difficulty remembering the source of much of their knowledge. Because of all these memory difficulties, he cautioned that patients who give specifics of cult rituals and state that they never read it or heard it before may have very earnestly forgotten that someone reported that detail in a phone conversation last week. Subconsciously, they may be calling up satanic ritual abuse memories to avoid remembering actual childhood traumas. Finally, he urged therapists to keep in mind that MPD patients have a strong information network. They have their own newsletter and frequently attend professional conferences, so the similarities in their stories do not stand as corroboration for one another, but rather show how quickly information travels in this group.[2]

The next speaker, Dr. George Ganaway, followed up on Putnam's remarks by explaining why MPDs would choose to call up heinous memories of ritual abuse rather than discuss real childhood trauma. Many dissociative patients use pseudo-memories of life-threatening experiences to practice dealing with their fears of abandonment and death. After working through a satanic memory with a therapist, the inconsistencies and cruelties of their actual childhoods seem surmountable by comparison. For those who have suffered traumatic garden-variety abuse and gross neglect, fantasies of ritualized abuse allow them to contain their rage in a "structure" while offering an explanation for their parents' otherwise senseless abuse. If they can weave their memories of abuse into a "memory" of satanic abuse, they can justify their parents' cruel behavior with the belief that their parents were preparing them for their future role as high priests or priestesses.[3]

In my later telephone interview with Ganaway, he elaborated on this theme. "One of the most interesting things is that patients who come to me with really bizarre 'memories' find it much easier to go on and on about these experiences than to talk about what relationships were like during their normal times at home." They avoid talking about family interactions or more reality-based types of abuse. Ganaway suspects that many SRA stories may be distraction techniques to avoid talking about the thing that really hurt the clients—lack of love from their parents.[4]

ANSWER ELEVEN

Why would anyone believe anything so painful as being sexually abused by a parent if it weren't true?

ANSWER NUMBER ELEVEN: Because he or she finds focusing on a fantasy of satanic abuse to be less painful than the mundane reality of parental neglect and emotional abandonment.

"By putting the parents into the roles of high priest and high priestess of a satanic cult, the patient doesn't have to deal with the fact that she really did have some problems with Mom and Dad, in their other roles as real people during the daytime."

Ganaway is continually astonished by the lack of real-world difficulties in these narratives. He was told that a father was the principal of a school in the daytime, working six and seven days a week, and Ganaway was expected to believe that the father had time to run a highly organized satanic cult that met throughout the night. There was no accounting for when people would sleep or do the laundry.

"One patient, who was struggling with the validity of cult memories and I knew had a wonderful sense of humor and a good working alliance, was describing the encapsulated quality of these memories, and I commented, 'You describe these rituals where nothing ever goes wrong. These are human beings who are trying to set up and perform a ceremony. You know how things can go wrong in weddings. Didn't the candles ever blow out accidentally? What if somebody sneezed in the middle of something and laughed, and what happens after these ceremonies? Did everybody go to the Waffle House for coffee?' She laughed and said, 'It just doesn't seem like part of the real world,' and she was betraying herself when she said that. It *wasn't* part of the real world."

In addition to these subconscious motivations that help patients avoid feeling their real childhood pain, they often reap the benefit of suddenly being treated very specially by the therapist. Being a survivor of satanic ritual abuse can serve as the ultimate excuse for all irresponsible behaviors. They can plead that they are too damaged to concentrate on their family responsibilities or that they have been "programmed" to act out in certain destructive ways.

AN ANTHROPOLOGIST'S VIEW

Sherrill Mulhern, an anthropologist and the next speaker at the 1989 conference, seemed to know her remarks would probably fall on deaf ears. She had just spent the past two years attending seminars on ritual abuse all over North America. In an attempt to get a complete picture of this growing belief system, she had made it a point to attend conferences sponsored by churches, mental health professionals, law enforcement officers, and anyone else who claimed expertise in the area of satanic ritual abuse. In her explorations she realized that the belief in satanic abuse was

strong, especially among dedicated clinicians. Those who had been working with satanic abuse survivors had repeatedly backed up their beliefs
with their clinical experience with these patients. Four factors were
sighted over and over as "proof" of the validity of these claims:

1. the violence of the abreaction
2. the abundance of detail in the accounts
3. the manifestation of "body memories"
4. the similarities in victims' stories[5]

At the conferences I've attended, I have also heard therapists say, "If
you work with these people you become a believer." As the clients "experience" these memories in therapy, their whole aspect is extremely
convincing.

Law enforcement officers and Federal Bureau of Investigation (FBI)
officials such as Kenneth Lanning have asserted time and time again that
despite hundreds of hours of investigations and the expenditure of huge
sums of money, no physical evidence has been found to support the notion
of a satanic cult conspiracy. Yet many patients report and believe such
tales. One interviewee, not a recanter, told me:

"My father came up here to threaten me. He broke into my house,
and he brought cult members with him. They have a national network
like the Mafia; in fact, they have a lot of associations with each other. If
you know somebody in Timbuktu who is having memories and you
want to make sure they repress those memories again, you can contact
the local cult, and they will start a little terror program to get that
person to repress them again. That's why there have been so many
recanters. They're so highly organized."

Until recently, such a statement by a patient would be labeled a
paranoid delusion. Now, therapists who specialize in SRA share the
paranoia.

Lanning has stated that, in the early 1980s when these investigations
began, he, too, was a believer, because he had been dealing with bizarre
deviant behavior in connection with the sexual victimization of children
for years as an FBI agent. He knew that many unbelievable things are
possible. The recent case of Jeffrey Dahmer, who found a way to dispose of
bodies without detection and who escaped detection for so long, reminds
us of how clever psychopaths can be.

But Lanning began to have doubts when the number of alleged cases grew beyond credibility. In a report he prepared for the FBI, Lanning stated, "We now have hundreds of victims alleging that thousands of offenders are abusing and even murdering tens of thousands of people as part of organized satanic cults, and there is little or no corroborative evidence."[6]

Other critics have also cited the number of allegations as the key factor that strains credulity beyond the breaking point. In most cases, victims of ritual abuse are "recovering memories" in therapy of events that would have taken place in the 1950s or 1960s. A healthy majority of the alleged incidents took place in small towns in an era of extreme stability. Families were not divorcing and moving to new towns every few years as they are today. A missing child (sacrificed in a satanic ritual) or a pregnant pre-teener (breeding a baby for infant sacrifice) would not have gone unnoticed. The sheer number of cases being reported means, at the very least, that many, if not most, cases of reported satanic abuse are fictitious. So why do so many therapists believe these accounts are true?

SPREADING THE WORD

Mulhern explained how seminars support and perpetuate the belief in satanic ritual abuse. First, although there has been no evidence found that substantiates claims of a satanic conspiracy, seminar speakers all refer to the problem of satanic ritual abuse as a proven phenomenon. They present themselves as authorities on something that has not been proven to exist, but fail to mention that their "information" is all theoretical. According to Mulhern, the seminars attempt to "convert" people into belief in the existence of satanic cults by employing four methods that are standard approaches used by proselytizing groups.

1. the encyclopedic method of gathering data or using facts taken out of context
2. proof texting or grouping together unrelated proofs such as photos used with an unrelated text.
3. personal testimony offered as proof
4. group participation that creates pressure for conformity

Mulhern explained that the last two methods taken together are especially effective for creating conformity and offering little or no opportunity to express dissenting views or even to question the material being presented. Personal testimonies spark certain behaviors in the audience. Listeners become very emotional, and there are often standing ovations for the speakers, which make anyone left sitting down look like a traitor. There are frequent calls from the podium for a show of hands from those who are working with survivors or who have experienced ritual abuse. The presence of "survivors" at professional seminars also inhibits open discussion, as therapists must worry about the psychological effect of their comments.

During the question-and-answer period following Mulhern's presentation, one audience participant gave an impassioned speech about how, during World War II, no one believed that Jews were being incarcerated and annihilated in concentration camps. In response, Mulhern pointed out that during the Holocaust there were many Christians who hid Jews in their homes and did not fail to notice that Jews were being sent off in droves. Why has no one noticed the absence of the tens of thousands of children who have allegedly been sacrificed by cults?[7]

George Ganaway talks about the elaborate rationalizations that cult believers offer to any challenge for proof:

> "I've watched the cult stories over the past decades change according to the need to change. For instance, 'The bodies were being burned on an open fire' story—it didn't take long for a forensic pathologist to say, 'You can't destroy bodies in an open fire; it isn't hot enough.' So the next thing you know the patients were coming up with new stories: they had undertakers who were burning them up in crematoriums. Law enforcement officials staked out crematoriums and found no evidence that this was going on. So then the ritual abuse believers said the satanists had crematoriums on wheels, which they hid in caves and other secret places like that."[8]

Ganaway watched a similar string of rationalizations develop in response to the question "Where are they getting the sacrificial victims?" Cult survivors said the victims were all the missing children, but then statistics showed that the vast majority of "missing children" had been abducted by noncustodial parents and were very much alive. So the next rationalization was that victims were being smuggled in across the border from other countries. When no proof of that could be found, the stories of adolescent breeders took hold. Ganaway explained:

"It's the 'but, can you explain this one?' phenomenon, where each time the authorities can explain why it can't have happened, they come up with another 'but can you explain this one?' Similarly, when 'cattle mutilations' were offered as examples of satanic sacrifice rituals, a pathologist was called in to determine the cause of death, and for cow after cow he identified what disease or ailment had killed each one. Finally he said, 'You can bring me one more that I might not be able to explain, but just because I can't explain it doesn't mean that the cow either was experimented on by UFOs or was part of a sacrifice by a satanic cult.' The people come with the belief systems already in place, and then they look for evidence to support it."

WHY SO MANY SIMILARITIES?

The bottom line for many, even the most skeptical, is how one can account for the many similarities in stories reported independently to therapists in different parts of the country if there is no satanic network. The clearest explanation for this phenomenon that I have read is sociologist Jeffrey Victor's theory of the contemporary legend.

We have all heard contemporary legends, for example, stories of the ghost hitchhiker, a girl who was killed alongside the highway whose ghost shows up each year at the time of her death at the spot where she died; or the story of the man with the hook who escaped from an insane asylum and attacked two teenagers parked in the woods necking. There are many areas of the country that claim to be the place where these events happened. Similarly, the recent nationwide panic over reports of syringes found in Pepsi cans had begun to look like a bizarre epidemic (similar to the Tylenol scare a few years back) before it was traced to its origins and revealed as a hoax. Just as many around the nation imitate and falsify reports of syringes in Pepsi cans, it is not uncommon for teenagers to engage in mayhem (such as a cat mutilation) and leave a sign of satanists they have read or heard about to add to the impact of their action. These isolated incidents are then interpreted as evidence of an organized network that is already drawing in teen followers. If we stop for a moment and remember that adolescent fascination with Ouija boards and the occult is a stage many pass through, we realize how quite normal behavior can become misconstrued—another mountain out of a molehill.

In his book *Satanic Panic*, Victor also explained how the "rumor stories" spread from area to area by a variety of methods. For example, some spread rapidly by word-of-mouth as stories of something that happened to a friend of a friend. Because we trust the friend telling us the story (and she has trusted the friend who told her), the stories are repeated as if they were true stories. Victor also traced individual "news" items to show how a rumor panic spreads to different areas. There is a pattern to the way the media deal with these sensational items.

The news of a dig to excavate some land, in response to information from "reliable sources" about remains of sacrificial children buried in the area, would be a front-page item before the dig takes place. When the police find nothing or admit they have made a mistake, this news would customarily be printed as a small paragraph on a back page. In this way, stories brought to the attention of the public continue to circulate because the retractions have gone unnoticed. As they spread by word of mouth, the locations are soon forgotten and transformed so that a dig which took place in Town A is later reported as digs that took place in Towns A, B, C, D, E, and F.

The spread of stories through the therapeutic network can be even more rapid. Perhaps Patient A recalls images from a television show on satanism she saw three years ago but has long forgotten, and believes the images are not recollections of a television show but rather are "memories" from childhood. Patient B (who saw the same television show) does not know Patient A, though they share the same therapist. When B recounts a similar memory to the therapist, a cult network is born. The shocked therapist has heard "two stories from independent sources that corroborate the cult activity in the area" with their strikingly similar details. The therapist rushes to tell her colleague, who is also working with cult survivors, and learns that he, too, *independently* heard a very similar story last month from a patient who couldn't possibly know A or B. And on it goes, until the similar stories are reported nationwide by the many patients who saw the same television show three years ago but have forgotten this source of their images.

Victor's view of the problem is more complex as he considers the feelings that fuel these beliefs and the social conditions that keep such fears alive. In the course of his book he answers all the tough questions that stump those trying to make sense of this irrational phenomenon.[9]

CULT SURVIVORS

Ironically, some therapy groups exploring satanic ritual abuse become cults themselves, focused around finding more and more memories of abuse. One of the best-documented cases of this was Mike Moore's inpatient group at a clinic for eating disorders in Dallas, which I touched upon in Chapter Two. The first to come forward with a retraction and details about what went on in the group was Lynn Price Gondolf, whom I introduced briefly in the Introduction. Lynn has told her story on numerous talk shows and in many magazine and newspaper stories; she has also been a speaker at the FMS Foundation–sponsored Conference, "Memory and Reality: An Emerging Crisis."[10] In an appearance on *The Jane Whitney Show*, Gondolf stated,

"I believed that my parents—that my mother and father—participated in abusing me sexually, like on a table with a doctor way out in the country. And that they had cut on me—that they had forced me to eat flesh, drink blood, urine, different things of this sort. I believed it so much that I could visualize it. I believed that they knowingly allowed me to be used and abused by just anybody who wanted to. I believed that they killed babies."[11]

One of the reasons that Lynn Gondolf started speaking out was that she was appalled to read, in a magazine article published in 1991, that one of the members from her old group was still hospitalized and believing she was part of a satanic cult. "I had thought that this girl had probably gotten out by now," Lynn told the audience at the FMSF Conference.

"This girl, for a year, said, 'I don't know why I am the way that I am, nothing bad ever happened to me.' And near the end this girl believed that her parents had cut on her and had her bear babies and all this stuff for the cult. She was such a wonderful person when she came in. I'll tell you, her parents were part of FMS, and we were so scared of them. And the mother couldn't even swat a fly and not feel guilty. But during this period I had believed that she had done all these awful things. I still, today, really hurt for her daughter, and I wish her well and hope that she's better."[12]

That girl was Gloria Grady,** the daughter of Lee and Jean Grady.** Though the Gradys have contact with several of their daughter's old group members who have since retracted, their daughter still maintains the belief that they abused her in a satanic cult.

THE ONE THAT GOT AWAY

Like Lynn, Callie, whom I mentioned briefly in Chapter Two, had an eating disorder and learned that her insurance would cover her stay in the hospital in Mike Moore's program. Callie checked herself out against doctor's orders and was told she would have to pay the bills herself. Although it is now against the law for insurance companies to refuse these claims, therapists have told me that some hospital programs still tell patients this to discourage their leaving. For those patients who do not have the correct information about the current state of the law, this threat is very effective indeed for keeping them "trapped" in the hospital.

Prior to signing into the hospital, Callie had been in therapy with Doug, a warm therapist whom she trusted, but after Callie entered the hospital this therapist was not allowed to see her. This is standard hospital procedure when a therapist is not affiliated with that hospital. Nonetheless, it seems unwise to prohibit emotionally disturbed patients from seeing someone they trust deeply.

Callie's parents were not allowed to visit her either. When Mike Moore learned that Callie's father had been a Mason, he informed Callie that the Masons were a satanic cult and that her father must have satanically abused her. "He told me that I had all these repressed memories," Callie recalled. "Whenever I started to tell him about a disturbing incident from childhood, he would add things to it. I would say, 'No, it didn't happen like that.' And he would say, 'Something else happened. You're just not ready to remember it yet.' "

Callie found the stories that were told in group to be preposterous. She believed that there were cults, but the women's stories about having babies that were sacrificed did not make sense to her. She was sure the police or FBI would have noticed if all these murders had really taken place.

"I would ask questions like, 'Didn't anyone ever notice that you were pregnant? What would they think if all of a sudden you're not pregnant anymore, but there isn't any baby?'

"Mike would say they could just say they had a miscarriage. Then he would belittle me and say, 'You're in total denial, so you're just going to keep asking me these ridiculous questions until you can accept what happened to you.' "

Callie had the definite impression that the stories grew increasingly elaborate in order to gain the attention of Moore. There was constant note comparing about whom he had confided in outside of group in their individual sessions. Though he has been described as a short, squat man with plain features, he had a charismatic hold on the women in the group. The better the story, the more attention they got, and they wanted his attention. Callie told me:

"One day this girl in the group started crying. She said, 'I'm just bulimic and I don't have any stories like this. I came from a dysfunctional family, but nothing like this ever happened to me. I feel really abnormal here.'

"And Mike said to her, 'You will feel abnormal until you remember.' "

There are a number of reasons why Callie might have been able to resist succumbing to the group beliefs. She actually was a survivor of incest. She had been abused by her brothers, and she never forgot it, so she had a good, solid idea of what memories of sexual abuse are like.

Callie had also had good therapy in the past. A few years back she had had therapy in an incest survivors' group that was properly run, and her recent therapist had been warm and supportive. So Callie knew what therapy was supposed to be like.

"I had been in a support group before I went into the hospital, and they were very, very strict on their boundaries. They said that the members of the group shouldn't have relationships with one another, or the therapists, outside of the group.

"There were three of us who started to get together, and the therapists got wind of it, and they straight out told us, 'You can either go by the rules, or you can leave the group.' "

The therapists firmly explained that the rules were for their protection. Cliques and subgroups erode trust. Callie could see why her previous therapists had been so careful about mixing social life and therapy when she watched the interaction of the members of Moore's group.

"When the members of Mike Moore's group would get together outside of group it was a very, very sick thing. I tried going with them a few times, but I found myself so confused and depressed afterward that I decided that it wasn't good for me."

However, Callie would occasionally talk to the other women in the group on the phone. She was even more disturbed by the things that she learned during phone calls. Moore had revealed things that were told to him during private sessions, discussing clients with his chosen confidante of the week. "I was very careful about what I said to Mike during our private sessions," Callie told me, "because I knew he would bring it up in group if I wasn't cooperating."

Callie came to dread her private sessions with Moore and tried to avoid telling him anything she did not want made public. A very "low-hypnotizable," Callie feigned hypnosis.

"When he thought he had hypnotized me he would say things that didn't make any sense. Once he said, 'Beware of the man in the hardware store. Look out for the tools he picks up.'

"He was always bringing up tools and a hardware store. I don't know what that's supposed to symbolize."

Moore was probably trying out satanic ritual codes. Many SRA therapists believe that certain nonsensical phrases or series of numbers will "break the spell" over ritual abuse "survivors," so that they no longer obey commands to keep the secrets. He told Callie that she must have been part of a cult because her mother was born in Austria. Moore believed that Hitler had run a large satanic cult there during the war.

HOW IT SHOULD BE

With Callie's permission I contacted her former therapist—the one who had run the incest survivors' group that Callie considered to be legitimate. I wanted to find out what rules and approaches create a productive incest group. Therapist Eileen Goldman explained to me some of her philosophy, guidelines, and approaches.

Goldman begins by trying to construct the groups so that the participants are all working on the same level. She is aware that when group members have experienced very different types of trauma, those who may have only been fondled once, when teamed up with someone who suffered years of abuse, tend to feel as if they have no right to be angry or hurt. When she must put people with widely varying abuse experiences together, Goldman tries to teach the group that everyone's feelings are valid.

Relationships outside the group between members are discouraged for two reasons. First, Goldman has a rule: "Don't leak during the week." She believes that talking outside of group might serve as a pressure release that would cause members not to bring up needed issues in group. A second reason for discouraging out-of-group relationships was that cliques might form and threaten the trust important between members during group sessions.

Trust is an important concern of Goldman's. She feels that it is important for everyone to use first names only and that therapists never take notes during group. Goldman also feels strongly about working with a male co-leader so that women can deal with their mistrust of males in a safe setting. "For the first time they meet a male who is not going to make a sexual pass, who is not going to let that happen." Both therapists should be available to group members outside of group, and there should be an understanding that whatever was said in private sessions would never be brought up in group by the therapists.

"Charlie (Goldman's co-leader) and I let all the memories come from them. We were very careful not to lead or suggest anything. We didn't want to influence memory recall. I felt very strongly that when you are at a certain point the unconscious will release to you anything you need to remember. So you don't have to struggle for the memories. They will come forth as needed, because the unconscious knows better than I do when to release them.

"Another reason I don't lead, I don't suggest anything, is because I want them to have clear memories without interference so that they know what happened. I don't need to know if it happened or not; they need to know."[13]

Goldman is also opposed to "anger therapy." When clients become angry at a perpetrator, Goldman agrees that the perpetrator violated them, and they have a right to be angry, but she prefers to emphasize the healthier relationship the perpetrator had or could have had with the client but, in effect, gave up. She points out how much the perpetrator lost in doing so. This approach focuses on the client as someone valuable, whom it is a gift to know. It is the perpetrator's loss. "I won't join them in their anger," Goldman explained, "because I think that can be terribly destructive."

A SEASONED VIEW

Dr. Lawrence Klein, currently Director of Emergency Services at Wood County Mental Health Center in Bowling Green, Ohio, has presented papers at annual conferences of the International Society for the Study of Multiple Personality and Dissociation (ISSMPD) on the topic of working with people who have memories of being in satanic cults. He has been such a respected authority on the topic of working with SRA survivors that he still receives many requests for unpublished papers he co-authored in 1987 and 1989. For this reason he was asked to speak on the topic of satanic ritual abuse at the Foote Hospital Center for Mental Health Conference held in August 1993. However, when he was approached to speak, his first response was extreme hesitancy. He explained to the conferees:

> "Being asked to present at a conference having to do with recovered memories of Satanic Ritual Abuse was like being asked to retrace my steps along an arduous passage, long since survived and behind me now, thank God. No way—thanks, but no thanks—were my initial thoughts."[14]

Klein realizes that his view on satanic ritual abuse has shifted considerably. Though five years ago he would have identified himself as one who believed that SRA reports must be true, he now finds his commitment on the issue has cooled. His opinions have been tempered by information he has come across since that time. For example, he found his doubts rising when a colleague told him about her patient who, after reporting that she had been a cult breeder, had gynecological surgery and was informed that she had never been pregnant.

The most pronounced change Klein feels is his loss of certainty. He no longer feels as if he knows whether there is a widespread network of satanists. He states,

"I have had to put my questions about SRA on hold while I tread psychic water, awaiting new information or insight, holding fast to the dictum of 'First, do no harm.' "

Though he still sees some self-identified SRA patients, his approach is more neutral. First, he does not initiate discussion of SRA, but listens respectfully if they bring it up. If asked, he tells them that he believes that satanic ritual abuse exists, but he has no way of knowing if they themselves have been satanically abused. Klein confessed,

"I no longer know that specific instances of horrific abuse, reportedly suffered by a number of my clients, are representational and not essentially symbolic, or even suggested and merely imagined."

Klein is aware of the desire to have closure, just to decide one way or the other and end the ambiguity, but he can no longer approach the SRA issue with conviction. Klein told the conferees:

"I believe that the current state of knowledge and insight with regard to the widespread incidence of SRA phenomena and the specific accuracy of so-called 'repressed memories' is insufficient to support extreme positions on either side of these questions. I believe we simply do not yet know enough or yet grasp the shape of truth."

Klein admits that these patients are more susceptible to suggestion, but he feels it is as wrong to refuse to hear the patient's complaints of ritual abuse, because the therapist does not find it plausible, as it is to encourage the patient to provide more details when the therapist does find it plausible.

Klein had found himself accepting the reports of his clients at face value and operating on those reports as though they were literal fact. For a time he suspended his accustomed practice of maintaining predictable boundaries, getting swept up in the intrigue of reported ritual practice, missing the forest of good psychotherapy for the trees of cult detail. At times the fact of the patient's pain got lost in the shuffle.[15] Then two influences caused Klein to take the time to reassess his approach.

Dr. Ganaway's paper "The Historical Truth Versus Narrative Fiction" challenged what Klein felt he knew about SRA and forced him to revise his position. Klein stated, "Dr. Ganaway, in head-on fashion, has made us all aware that what we hear from clients, though heartfelt, may not always be literal truth."

At the same time Klein had just learned that he had multiple sclerosis and needed to lower his stress for the sake of his health. He had been allowing clients to disturb him at all hours and had been spending inordinate amounts of time learning about the complex subculture of SRA.

"Imagine me trying to keep track of the endless stream of satanic holidays in order to anticipate anniversary reactions—learning all the symbols; studying Enochian as a second language; learning about satanic philosophy and world view; keeping up with all the various practices, rituals, and ceremonial objects; reviewing client mail in an effort to screen it for triggers—imagine that.

"Clients lugging in unopened mail from their Aunt Bessie; waiting for me to open it, read it, determine if it was safe for them to see— imagine me doing this.

"Imagine who it was who was the certifiable nutcase here—trying to remember which color flower carried with it which potentially life-threatening message; helping clients to devise elaborate strategies for screening triggers that would hearken them back to the cult."

A pattern of overwork has been a common problem for therapists who specialize in SRA as evidenced by the many references to the exhaustion of working in this field that are heard at SRA conferences. Klein now feels he was spending so much time on these details that he did not have time to do good therapy, push his clients toward independence, or save energy for his health.

"Something had to give in how I was living my life and practicing as a therapist, and it was doubtful that much therapy was getting done. So much energy was taken up with plugging leaks and dikes; moving from crisis to crisis; being caught up in all the details, the apparatus, accouterments, and procedures of abuse, it left little place for unhurried attention to the thematic elements associated with victimization: loss, rage, grief, helplessness, hopelessness, shame. My willingness to assume so much of the burden of the change promotion in treatment served to divert clients from their own difficult choices.[16]

Since then Klein has come to respect running modulated sessions that avoid retraumatizing the patient and has embraced Kluft's dictum "The slower you go, the faster you get there."

SUMMARY POINTS

1. Some sexual abuse recovery therapists believe that anyone who has MPD must have been ritually abused because the traumatic impact of such abuse would undoubtedly cause a "split."

2. Belief in the existence of satanic ritual abuse perpetrated by well-organized satanic cults is based on purely theoretical evidence—primarily testimonials by clients diagnosed with a dissociative disorder such as MPD.

3. Studies and clinical experience show that the vast majority of MPD clients have trouble differentiating between what was real and what was imagined.

4. Dissociative clients have memory deficits for autobiographical and general knowledge. Well-established laboratory studies show that these clients tend to fill in the blanks with confabulated pseudo-memories.

5. Pseudo-memories of life-threatening ritual abuse may serve a variety of purposes for a troubled client: to practice dealing with fear of abandonment and death, to contain rage in a "structure" while offering an explanation for parents' otherwise senseless abuse, to gain special attention from the therapist, as a distraction technique to avoid talking about painful family relationships or more reality-based types of abuse, as an excuse to avoid taking responsibility for his or her own actions.

6. Law enforcement officers and FBI officials, after many extensive investigations, have found no physical evidence to support the notion of a satanic cult conspiracy.

7. Why would anyone believe anything so painful as being sexually abused by a parent if it weren't true?
   • Because he finds focusing on a fantasy of satanic abuse to be less painful than the mundane reality that his parents neglected and emotionally abandoned him.

PART TWO
THE IMPACT

TEN

When
Everything
Isn't Enough

*I'd like to say that we would continue to love her, but I
think that's difficult without the trust part. Things have
really changed, and the fact that she has inflicted so
much pain on my parents is something that she'll have
to work her way back from.*

ALAN, a brother

THE HANSEN FAMILY HAS seven children. Paul Ayres has been the
eighth child in the family since he was about nine years old. Paul's father
died when he was five, and when Paul and his mother moved into the
Hansens' neighborhood, it was obvious that the Hansen house was the
place to be. Paul told me:

"It was utter chaos. There were the seven Hansen kids to start
with, and then there were about ten other neighborhood kids hanging
around all the time. The doors were never locked. Everyone just ran in
and out of their house. It got so I never knocked.

"When I was in high school I think I spent every weekend there.
Alan [the middle Hansen son] and I and maybe Doreen [Alan's sister
who later became an accusing daughter] and a few of the other kids
would go out to a movie and then come back and lie around the living
room watching TV for hours. I was often the last one up. Everyone else
would have gone to bed or fallen asleep, and I would let myself out and
go home. Terry [the father] worked long hours, and he was always
sound asleep by eight o'clock. Sometimes he would fall asleep in the

living room and start snoring. It was awful hard to wake him or get him to move. There's no way he would have had the energy to get up and molest anyone the way Doreen describes it.

"If you wanted privacy in that house it seemed almost impossible to get it; all seven children had to fit in this four-bedroom house. For Doreen to say that abuse of any kind happened during this period is hard for me to believe."

Paul's mother died recently, and he went back to the old neighborhood for the funeral. The Hansens helped out by letting some of Paul's relatives stay there.

"They babysat my stepdaughter, Elena, and when I spoke to Doreen later she was appalled that I'd left Elena there, but there isn't anyone I would trust more.

"A few months before she died, my mom had written a letter to the Hansens telling them how much she appreciated the way they had let me be a part of their family. It really meant a lot to her, and the Hansens cried when they read the letter. My mother was very perceptive. If there was anything wrong happening there, she would have known it, and she wouldn't have allowed me to go there.

"Doreen and I kept in touch for years after she left Wisconsin. To me it seemed she would struggle at times with her relationships, maybe putting too much pressure on them too early. Also, it may have been her inner drive to succeed in her career, which in my eyes she certainly has done.

"Another problem for her was trying to balance a good Christian life with being a single twenty-five-year-old female. I don't know which one won out, but I believe this was a problem for her.

"At one time she told me I would someday have to choose whom I believed—Doreen or her parents. As much as I value her and miss her friendship, from my own experience I can't believe anything—even remotely close to what she says—happened in the Hansen house when we were growing up.

"I remember a girl who, for being a child with six brothers and sisters, got as much attention and was given as many opportunities to expand her knowledge as anyone could expect. I don't recall any incidents of physical abuse of any kind in their house, and I certainly didn't see any sexual abuse.

"Now this therapist has her convinced that she was neglected as a child. That's absolutely not true. Her family went through a real rough time because of the bankruptcy. Maybe that's where she gets her bad memories. Her father was very discouraged, but they all managed. Kids were still welcome in the house; everything went on as usual. They got through it. She might not have gotten everything she wanted then, but her parents took good care of them all, no matter what was happening."

THE HANSEN FAMILY

Mother: Colette, Age 57   Father: Terry, Age 58

Ursula	Mark	Alan	Doreen*	Karin	Beth	John
Age 35	Age 34	Age 31	Age 30	Age 29	Age 28	Age 27

*Accusing daughter

CONSISTENT FAMILY EVALUATIONS

For my first book, *How To Avoid Your Parents' Mistakes When You Raise Your Children* (Pocket Books, 1990), I developed a scale to chart family functioning based on my research on healthy and dysfunctional families. In addition, I sought out families with problems and, through their stories, illustrated how healthy and dysfunctional families each deal with problems. I used similar techniques when I interviewed families who claimed to have been falsely accused of sexual abuse by an adult daughter. I began with a survey (below) of each child in the family and then followed up with extensive interviews with the siblings of the accusers and, in some cases, the neighbors. In each case I attempted to interview the accusing daughter but was repeatedly rejected.

RATING SHEET FOR
SCALE OF FAMILY SEXUAL FUNCTIONING

INSTRUCTIONS: Place an M(Mother) or an F(Father) in the space that describes how you were parented.

	Never	Seldom	Sometimes	Often	Always
HEALTHY BEHAVIORS OF PARENTS					
Esteem building	——	——	——	——	——
Support	——	——	——	——	——
Consistency	——	——	——	——	——
Encouragement	——	——	——	——	——
Praise	——	——	——	——	——
Physical care	——	——	——	——	——
DYSFUNCTIONAL BEHAVIORS OF PARENTS					
Corporal Punishment (mild spanking)	——	——	——	——	——
Verbal/Emotional Abuse	——	——	——	——	——
Addictions and Compulsions	——	——	——	——	——
Physical Abuse (hitting, bruises)	——	——	——	——	——
Sexual Abuse	——	——	——	——	——
Extreme Violence	——	——	——	——	——

THE MEANING OF THE SCALE

All families have both healthy and dysfunctional behaviors. The degree of overall healthy functioning in a family is determined in part by how much the healthy behaviors outweigh or outnumber the dysfunctional behaviors. Because family dynamics change over time, each child's perception of the family may be different. Also, as each child's personality comes up against the parents' personalities, each child's experience of the parents and family life may be different. If you anticipate that your perception of the family will be different due to your particular experience or personality traits, please explain your special circumstances on the back.

Following is an explanation of the terms used in the Scale of Family Functioning, including what they do and do not mean. Please read these before filling out the scale so that our results will have consistency. Place an M(Mother) and an F(Father) in the appropriate boxes on each line to show whether this parenting behavior occurred Never, Seldom, Sometimes, Often, or Always.

DEFINING TERMS FOR THE SCALE
OF FAMILY FUNCTIONING

HEALTHY BEHAVIORS

Esteem Building: Parents consciously look for behaviors to praise, show children they are important by spending time with them, and frequently express their joy at being with their children—unconditional love.

Support: Parents are on the alert for what they can do to help each child with his or her goals in life. They make time to listen to the child's problems and advocate for the child in unobtrusive ways, helping the child find his or her own solution whenever possible.

Consistency: Parents not only have clear rules and consequences, they also keep their own promises and commitments to their children. Children are one of the top priorities in the parents' lives. Family schedules and activities keep the needs of the children in mind, and children have a secure sense of knowing what is expected of them. Discipline is not harsh or physical.

Encouragement: Parents boost the children's confidence with declarations that the children can accomplish what they set out to do. The parent stands behind the children, cheering them on, as opposed to taking over tasks and leaving the children feeling inadequate.

Praise: Parents are quick to compliment children on their behavior, appearance, skills, talents, and accomplishments. They constantly mirror the child's better self to him or her.

Physical Care: The children have no worries about food, clothing, or shelter. In the best homes (top of scale) parents prepare meals, wash clothes, and provide a stable home environment. In less than ideal homes the parents might provide clothing and food but expect children ten or under to care for themselves. The homeless represent the bottom of this scale.

DYSFUNCTIONAL BEHAVIORS

Corporal Punishment: Parents dispassionately use mild physical punishment as a deterrent, such as spanking, squeezing the child's arm, physically pulling children apart, or taking them bodily to their rooms. The parent is objective as opposed to full of rage.

Verbal/Emotional Abuse: Parents use put downs, sarcasm, scoldings, insults, and the "silent treatment" as primary means of discipline and interaction. They are a negative mirror to the child, emphasizing the child's faults and failures.

Addictions and Compulsions: Due to a parent's addiction to a substance or compulsive pursuit of an activity, children are ignored, neglected, discounted, witnesses to violence, and generally made to feel unimportant. Promises are broken, and children often have an inordinate amount of responsibility.

Physical Abuse: Beatings with fists or objects for the purpose of inflicting pain on the child. Discipline is harsh and meted out in accordance with the parents' moods and inability to control their rage, rather than in appropriate response to the transgression of the child.

Sexual Abuse: Parents repeatedly fondle the child in inappropriate ways, comment on the child's sexuality in a leering fashion, or force or coerce sexual contact such as intercourse or fellatio.

Extreme Violence: Parents are out of control. They beat the children with all their might, fiercely drag or shake the children, hit them with heavy objects. Includes bruises, broken bones, injuries to the head or organs, and brutal rape.

Concepts taken from *How to Avoid Your Parents' Mistakes When You Raise Your Children* by Claudette Wassil-Grimm, Pocket Books, 1990.

The Hansen family surveys were remarkably consistent. All of the children (with the exception of Doreen, a middle child and accusing daughter, who would not participate) gave their parents very high ratings on healthy behaviors. Most checked that both the mother and the father were generous with esteem-building behaviors, support, consistency, encouragement, praise, and good physical care. Their marks fell mainly in the "Always" category with the few exceptions in the "Often" category. The toughest family critic gave the parents a "Sometimes" for praise.

The dysfunctional behaviors rated by the children were similarly congruent. All agreed there were no addictions, compulsions, physical abuse, sexual abuse, or extreme violence. There was also total agreement on mild corporal punishment, with each child giving the parents a "Seldom" rating. However, most added notes on the back explained that though spankings were occasionally used for discipline, they were always mild and always expected. The Hansen kids knew when they crossed the line, and on the few occasions when they had been spanked, they felt they had deserved it. The spankings were not done with rage, and none worried it could get out of control. The two toughest critics among the children checked that the parents were "Seldom" verbally or emotionally abusive. The rest had never felt verbally or emotionally abused.

In addition to the remarkable degree of agreement on this objective measure, their comments during interviews unanimously supported the impression of a healthy, happy, highly functional family. The old est daughter, Ursula, commented, "It was a fun house; my parents were really good about having other kids in. If any of our friends were there they could stay to dinner because with seven kids around, what was one more?"

This impression of harmony pervaded all their descriptions of childhood in the Hansen home. Alan, a middle child and Doreen's closest brother, described these years as "idyllic." "We could ride our bikes down to the river and go fishing, up to the playground, or anywhere. I enjoyed growing up in a large family. You had so many different personalities. I don't think there was anything all that different about our family except that I felt our family stood out in terms of where we were going."

John, the youngest son, reinforced this impression: "My parents always made every effort to give us everything, despite having seven kids, while my father was making what you might call a modest salary. For example, my brother Alan and I went to a preparatory school. With every one of us they made a sacrifice at one time or another. Doreen was sent over to Japan during high school, and that cost some big bucks. They tried their hardest to do their best for us."

Though they were a farming family, both parents and grandparents were college-educated, a remarkable feat in those times. Beth, the youngest daughter, who has a master's degree in counseling, had done a genogram of the family and only found one family member with any emotional disturbance: an eccentric great uncle who was a mathematical genius and had drinking problems. Outside of this, the Hansen family is typical of healthy families in that strong values and good parenting behaviors have been passed down for generations.

The kids all helped with the family poultry business, which Terry had taken over from his father. Doreen later complained that the father was sexist and favored the boys. Her older sister Ursula remarked, "My dad wanted me sitting in the hatchery doing office work and vaccinating chicks, not driving tractors in the field. I didn't mind that; it wasn't a boy/girl thing." But the best evidence to support the family's basic nonsexist attitude was the fact that all the girls were encouraged to go to college and have careers. Doreen became a highly successful business executive.

Dr. Stephen Landman, a speaker at the Foote Hospital Conference on the "repressed memory" controversy, stated that he believed that all the FMSF families were enmeshed with their daughters.[1] Yet, the freedom allowed the Hansen children, and the encouragement and support they received to spread their wings and fly as high as they could go, is in stark contrast to Landman's prediction. Two of the boys chose to go to a prep school away from home during high school, and both Doreen and her brother Alan spent a year of high school in a foreign country as part of student exchange programs. Alan commented,

"When I was in the eighth grade I told my parents I wanted to go to St. John's. My father was excited by the idea; my mother was not. She didn't want her fourteen-year-old son going away, which is very understandable. [*But she did not stand in her son's way*.]

"For me, being young and idealistic, it was a place where I could develop my intellect. It turned out to be a terrific experience."

Colette Hansen, their mother, didn't want to let go of her children when they were teenagers, but she didn't let her sentimentality hold them back. That's not enmeshment; it is a wonderful example of putting what is best for your child before your own feelings.

Another hallmark of a truly healthy family is how it deals with problems. Mark, the oldest son, has vivid memories of the most difficult problem the family ever faced before Doreen's accusation.

"Dad owned a business with his father that went bankrupt in '76. It was pretty tough on him. He was a working maniac the last year and went here and there to get financing, borrowing from Peter to pay

Paul, and things were going downhill fast. It was that way in the whole poultry business at the time, in Wisconsin. Mom was always there for him. I remember a lot of tears, a lot of pressure. I remember Dad being on the phone a lot that year. I think their faith in God and their faith in each other pulled them through. It was important for us as a family to see them make it, because that gives the rest of us hope. We can say, 'No matter what happens, you can make it as a family, as a married couple.' "

Similarly, when Doreen made her accusation, the Hansens didn't hide in their house and hope no one would find out. They were open from the start. When the neighbors asked about the kids, they told them about Doreen's accusation, just as they would have told about any accomplishment or setback that was affecting their children's lives. Colette reported,

"My neighbors howled because our house was never locked. It was full of kids from early morning until 2 a.m. My next-door neighbor started laughing and said, 'I'm really sorry; I know it isn't funny, but when would Terry have had time?' Terry and his dad always worked six days a week when they could, sometimes seven. They worked from dawn until dark, and many times Terry would get up at 4 a.m., come home after dark, get up at 4 a.m. again the next day, go up to the hatchery at the other end of town, and start taking the chicks out of the incubator, so when the help came at six o'clock they could start sexing the chickens. He lived that business twenty-four hours a day for all the time Doreen was growing up. He was on the road into Iowa and Michigan selling chicken. He was also the mayor of our town. He was a busy man."

UNDERSTANDING HEALTHY, AVERAGE AND DYSFUNCTIONAL FAMILIES

Popular writers such as John Bradshaw postulate that over 90 percent of families are dysfunctional. I have had recovery therapists tell me that they don't believe there is such a thing as a healthy family. People in the mental health field can lose their perspective. All day long they see people who struggle with depression and anxiety, and they may forget that there is a vast population they may never meet—those who don't need mental health services. Not only are they seeing the least functional members of society, research shows that when depressed, even normally highly functioning people will begin to rewrite their histories through smoke-colored glasses.

Many recovery therapists and much recovery literature also tend to describe things in black and white terms. If a family isn't totally healthy twenty-four hours a day, seven days a week, family members may mistakenly believe that proves them dysfunctional. But there is a lot of gray area between healthy and dysfunctional. In fact, average families cover a vast portion called middle ground. Like a bell-shaped curve, we have severely dysfunctional families at around 10 percent, somewhat dysfunctional families in the next 15 percent, average families in the middle 50 percent, somewhat healthy families in the next 15 percent, and the top 10 percent are healthy families. The normal families are going to do about as many things right as they do wrong, and most kids in these families will turn out to be competent adults. Above those average families are the families who manage to nurture more than they do harm. The kids in these families will often have an easier time growing up. However, a child with a difficult temperament who is born into a healthy family will sometimes do worse than a child with an easy-going temperament who has grown up in the worst of families. There are no hard and fast rules. The important thing is to keep one's perspective and not fall prey to overly simple explanations.

All families have problems; all kids have bad days. A crisis such as a serious illness, a financial downturn, or a death in the family may create a bad time that can cast a shadow over several years in even the healthiest of families. If we learn from our mistakes and retain the ability to change when circumstances demand it, we will have rewarding lives in the long run.

DOREEN'S PERSONALITY

I asked the Hansen parents to tell me about Doreen, what she was like as a little girl. Despite their recent difficulties with her, Colette responded as if I'd pushed her "pride" button:

"I knew right away that she was bright because she was very curious. If there were mud pies we made, she was right in the middle, and she was very good at making mud pies. She was always a very good student and achiever. Doreen was well liked by teachers, by friends, real active in Girl Scouts, a very busy girl, very talented musically, all kinds of crafts, read a lot, always could easily entertain herself.

"The only complaint that anyone ever made about her was that the teachers said she talked too much.

"She was an AFS student to Japan for a year. When she picked going to Japan she said, 'I want to go to someplace different! Anybody can go to Europe.'

"She said later that for the first six months it was a lot of work because she didn't have the language. We heard from the head of the school where she went in Japan that she was the best AFS student they'd ever had. She was very outgoing, and she was very nice to everybody. She never got involved in the clique of the more wealthy girls or anything like that."

This sounds like a very emotionally healthy child who has been taught to embrace opportunities.

How did her siblings see her? They all remembered her as competitive and tomboyish. She was a middle child and preferred to be identified with the older half of the kids. This meant tagging along after the boys, trying to get in on their games. When she couldn't get her way, she would tattle on them. Still, her brothers remember her fondly. Alan told me,

"She was very fun-loving, rather on the mischievous side. Being the middle child and following two boys was probably a challenge for her, because my brother is a very competitive person; I'm somewhat competitive. She was constantly competing against us. I always thought that she rather enjoyed that.

"Generally, I think we got along fairly well. She excelled at everything she did. She was very good at music, excellent in languages, and she's beautiful. I don't think the sparring ever got her down. She's a pretty worthy opponent."

The siblings were also unanimous about Doreen being their mother's favorite. Doreen and her mother, Colette, had very similar personalities, and Doreen reminded her mother a lot of herself. They related well together and were interested in the same things. Doreen liked to help in the kitchen, to sew, and to make crafty things while visiting with her mother.

Though this favoritism didn't seem to bother the older kids, Doreen's younger sister, Karin, recognized that it was a bit of a barrier between Doreen and her two younger sisters:

"I was jealous of her for a long time. I think it kind of caused me and my sister, Beth, to gang up on her sometimes—you know, say mean things to her—and Doreen did her share to cause a rift. Beth did do some of the same things that Doreen did, and she would always put Beth down for it. Doreen just couldn't stand the competition. Beth ended up being a better piano player than she did, and that always got on Doreen's nerves."

Most of the siblings also described Doreen as someone who always needed to have attention, and it was not difficult for her to get it because she was very accomplished at everything. The only tragedy that clouded Doreen's growing-up years was the fact that she had to wear a scoliosis brace on her back through junior high and high school. However, this did not stop her from shooting baskets with her brothers or canoeing with the Girl Scouts. Neither was she singled out in the family as the sickly child. Her older sister Ursula had had to lie in bed in a cast for six months because her scoliosis had been too far along to be cured by a back brace.

On the other hand, Ursula thinks that Doreen may have been more affected by the scoliosis because she had to wear her brace in public, and Doreen's mother did remark that Doreen had never had a date until she went to college. Both the parents and all the siblings commented that they traced the beginning of Doreen's depression back to when her five-year relationship with her college boyfriend abruptly ended. She had counted on marriage, but he backed out of the relationship when she suggested that they live together. Ursula observed that Doreen had gone from depending on her parents to depending on the boyfriend and had never developed an independent life of supportive relationships with girlfriends.

Doreen had taken the breakup with Brian very hard, and, after a few more broken relationships, she began to be chronically depressed. She had told her sister Karin that she didn't know if she wanted to go on with life. Ursula explained the family's first reaction to Doreen's desire to go for therapy. "None of us had a real belief in therapy. I think it was concern for Doreen and confusion about what was going on—why she felt things were so bad that she had to go to therapy. I think we had a feeling of—why couldn't she just come to one of us and talk about what was going on? We've always been real supportive of one another."

Alan had been the most supportive about Doreen's therapy. He and his wife Katie had become Doreen's closest friends. Though she lived a considerable distance away, Doreen frequently flew out to spend a weekend with them and their children.

"During the early stages of her therapy, I was probably the one person she was talking to about it somewhat. She seemed to be in the stage of exploring, which I thought was good. Maybe she'll find out who she really is, what she wants.

"She didn't say that she had a specific problem; I think it was more a matter of identifying the problem. She was happy in her career, but when it came to her personal life, I think she had this feeling of emptiness which I personally, without telling her this, identified as depression of some kind. I didn't know what the source of it was.

I encouraged her, also, because she had been through this series of relationships and nothing seemed to work out. That was making her unhappy. In a lot of ways, I don't think she knew what she wanted. Ever-looming was the breakup of her five-year relationship with Brian."

Alan remembers Doreen going through what seemed like a change of character. She had been very involved in her parish: singles groups, liturgy planning, scripture reading, whatever interested her. Alan explained,

"I think the church, for a while, was her guiding force, and then she kind of did a turnabout.

"Our sisters told me she was recounting to them all her various sexual experiences. She thought it was entertaining that she could just go to a bar and pick up a man and sleep with him. Of course, my sisters were aghast. Not in a moral sense, but in a sense that that's really screwed-up. I think, again, that sort of behavior shows that she was probably seeking solace in all the wrong places."

When Doreen first started therapy she began to be mildly critical of her parents. Beth recalled,

"It started with the boys were more important than the girls and that our family didn't know how to communicate, and we weren't affectionate. Then one Christmas, Doreen and I got in a big fight. I said I hoped I could do as good a job with my kids as Mom and Dad had done with us. She said something about 'Well, I hope you'll be a lot better than that.' I said, 'What do you mean by that?' And she said, 'Beth, you don't even know, do you?' I said, 'Know what?' and she said 'Things that Mom and Dad did to us as children.' I said, 'Don't give me your therapy bull, I don't want to hear it.' So I was kind of aced out, and she didn't communicate with me any more."

John had noticed a change in Doreen, too. "I always used to kid her with sexist comments because I knew it made her mad, but it was in fun. One of the things that happened to her is she lost her sense of humor. In engineering school we always poked fun at the business students, and Doreen was a business major. I poked fun at her, and usually she'd shoot it right back. As she got more and more into therapy she got more and more defensive. Suddenly I was a chauvinist or a sexist."

Everyone in the family told me she was closest to Karin. Doreen changed jobs, and it meant a move to Milwaukee. Karin remembered Doreen's unhappiness starting there. She was on the rebound from another relationship and was very confused. Karin recalled,

"She had all this money; she had everything she could want; she still wasn't happy. She thought if she talked to somebody it would make her feel better.

"When she started her therapy, she started to talk about how she really felt like she was getting to know herself like she had never really known herself. She even said she had a lot of fake personalities, but that she was trying to become her real self.

"A lot of people at her office have all gone to this same therapist. I met some of them when I went to visit her. One was a girl who had just finished her therapy, and she was just shaky and everything. She had to learn not to depend on her therapist anymore, and Doreen was being very supportive of her. Everybody that I met was in therapy. I thought it was very odd."

THE ACCUSATION

Alan was the first to hear of Doreen's accusations, and ultimately the only family member to get the story straight from Doreen. Alan told me,

> "Doreen thought that somebody had abused her, and she was very nondescript; she could not remember anything about it, other than it was just a feeling that she was exploring. And then she came back with a specific memory of abuse, but she still didn't know *who* it was — it could have been someone in the family.
>
> "At that point I was well, hell, who knows? I wasn't there every minute; I'm not going to discount it. I said, 'I can remember playing doctor with you, the typical I'll-show-you-mine-if-you'll-show-me-yours. If I did anything to offend you I'm really sorry about it.' That was as far as it went. After that I didn't hear from her for the longest time, and the next thing we knew she was coming back with allegations that were constantly changing, always involving members of the family."

Doreen ultimately accused her father of sexually abusing her since infancy and her two older brothers of abetting him. The stories grew to describe orgies that involved the whole family and even some of the neighborhood children. These orgies took place on Saturday afternoons. Karin reported,

> "She never did tell my parents. She told a friend of our family, Paul Ayers. First it was two of our brothers and our father; then the stories changed, and it was just our father."

Beth remarked,

> "If she would have said 'I was sexually abused, and it was only me,' I might have believed her, because, of course, I'm conditioned to believe her.
>
> "But that's not what she said. She said we were all sexually abused by my parents. We've all thought about it and really tried to think, 'Did this happen, and I don't remember?' We've all discussed this without my parents around, and none of us can think of anything that even comes close to sexual abuse. But, what I'm hearing now is there's covert and overt sexual abuse. That my dad walking around in his underwear is covert sexual abuse, which is absolutely crazy."

As we hear testimony by the Hansen family siblings and their neighbors, we get a picture of a hard-working bunch whose house was brimming with activity. It had an atmosphere of openness, acceptance, and support. We begin to appreciate the feelings expressed in the following quote from the *FMS Foundation Newsletter*:

IT CAN HAPPEN TO ANYONE

If a person goes to a therapist who already assumes that most patients have been sexually abused in childhood . . .

And if that therapist believes that most memories of abuse are repressed . . .

And if the patient reads books that make the same assumptions . . .

And if the patient joins a group made up of women who all believe they have been sexually abused . . .

And if they all tell their horrible stories . . .

And if the patient has a suggestible personality . . .

And if the patient spends months, sometimes years, in therapy and groups seeking the identity of the abusers—is it not likely that the identity of the abuser or abusers and recollections of the abuse will finally, after all that work, finally emerge?

How would you like to be accused of horrendous acts of child sexual abuse on the basis of such recalled memories?

And what if these reconstructed memories were ten, twenty, thirty, forty years old?

Beware!! It can happen to you. Accusations of child sexual abuse based on repressed memories that are decade-delayed discoveries are running rampant—an epidemic is emerging. This is the mental health crisis of the decade—if not of the century![2]

CHILDHOOD SEXUAL ABUSE AS THE ROOT OF ALL PROBLEMS

Freud initially theorized that all mental health problems stemmed from early childhood sexual abuse, because he had drawn out stories of father-daughter incest from most of his female patients. He later rescinded this theory and decided that the women were only telling early fantasies they had had about their fathers. And so the Electra/Oedipus complex was born.

Many feminist psychologists now cry that Freud was hushed up by strong disapproval from his male colleagues, and he only took back his theory to save his reputation. Radical feminists see father-daughter incest as the cause of mental illness that has been hushed up for over a hundred years. At this point we will never know if Freud's patients were real victims of incest, but we do know that incest is not the cause of all mental illness.

Researchers have established genetic patterns that show that schizophrenia and mood disorders are hereditary. Scientists have discovered the brain chemistry that produces depression and have developed medications to correct the brain chemistry in sufferers from mood disorders. Scientists have even discovered the gene which marks extreme shyness as a personality trait, and genetic markers have been discovered in alcoholic families.

But the simplicity of the "all mental illness is caused by sexual abuse" theory has great appeal for some therapists. While attending a conference on sexual abuse last summer, I was astonished when a school counselor turned to me and said that he had recently realized that all attention deficit disorder (ADD) kids have been sexually abused. As a school counselor he probably hasn't been required to read information on medication and chemical origins of mental illness. Many of the grave errors made in therapy today result from expertise that is much too narrow.

In my best conflict-resolution style, I tried to help this counselor save face by educating him with a parable from my own life. I recalled how when I was a young, single, special education teacher of ADD kids I used to say to myself, "What do the parents do to make these kids this way?!" I felt morally superior and very certain that if I had been their parent, they would not be like this. To teach me a lesson, God rewarded me with one of the most hyperactive, contrary kids ever to be born. Now that I was a mother of an ADD kid, I asked instead, "How did the parents ever manage to cope with those kids?"

I saw my companion's eyes glaze over, and I realized that he thought I was a perpetrator "in denial." During the next break he changed his seat so he wouldn't have to sit next to me—or have his ideas challenged one iota.

RECONCILIATION?

The Hansens hoped this problem could be worked out through Doreen's therapist. Colleen explained, "I wrote a lengthy letter to this therapist. We offered to come to Milwaukee to talk with him; we offered to meet with him someplace; we offered to talk with him on the phone."

"We offered family therapy for the whole family," Terry added. "He refused."

"He's never talked to anyone except our daughter," Colette clarified.

They were at a loss for what else to do about their daughter's strange secondhand accusations, so they sought counseling for themselves to help them cope with the situation and try to find some solution. Their counselor wrote to Doreen's counselor hoping to open some kind of exchange.

Below is Doreen's counselor's reply. I have copied it verbatim, and in its entirety except for inserting the Hansen pseudonyms. All the Hansens I spoke to were willing to be named, but it was decided that names would be changed to protect Doreen's privacy. In the article that follows this section, I have also changed only the names.

"I write in response to your letter dated September 16, 1991, regarding the Hansen family, which you have seen for consultation.

"I began seeing the Hansens' daughter Doreen in March 1988. At that time she was experiencing mild depression and anxiety related to her recent move from Minneapolis to Milwaukee. I initially diagnosed her as having an Adjustment Reaction with Mixed Emotional Features (309.28).

"During the first year of therapy Ms. Hansen always presented her family in terms of high praise, rarely even subject to the normal frictions that are present in families. Beginning in February 1989, Ms. Hansen began to have confused and disturbing fragmentary memories of sexual abuse. At that time I changed her diagnosis to Post Traumatic Stress Disorder (309.89).

"As Ms. Hansen continued to recover and organize her memory it became clear that she had been the victim of extensive sexual abuse, probably beginning in infancy, perpetrated and orchestrated by her father. Her memory is that this abuse was perpetrated on all seven children in the family and that her mother was knowledgeable about and participant in this abuse.

"Ms. Hansen has shared with me letters from her father, mother, and paternal grandmother, all of which lend credence to my belief that this is a sexually abusive family.

"As I understand your letter, you do not have a therapeutic contract with any member of Ms. Hansen's family. I am unclear from your letter how you understand your role as a consultant to the family.

"You do have my permission to share with the family the information in this letter. You may also share with them my complete certainty that Ms. Hansen's memories of sexual abuse from infancy until she left home at age 18 are true and accurate."

One can't help wondering how this therapist can be so certain of the historical accuracy of Doreen's accusations. Why is it easier for him to believe that the parents sexually abused all seven children than it was for him to believe that Doreen's description of her family during the first year of therapy—as a happy trouble-free family—was true? Perhaps he has never met a healthy family and doesn't realize that people can be depressed as adults no matter how secure a childhood they have had. As he pointed out, when he first met her, Doreen was only mildly depressed. What happened in therapy that made her change, so drastically, her vision of her family?

It appeared that the Hansens had come up against a brick wall. It was more than six months before any attempt to contact them was made. Colette explained,

"In June of '92 we got a letter saying, Dear Mom and Dad, I am writing this letter to ask you to come to a meeting at the blah, blah hotel in downtown Milwaukee. At this meeting I will express to you the incest that I experienced while growing up in our home. This will give you an opportunity to admit your guilt.

"These are the rules: my therapist will act as a referee. I will have three support people there. The parents may have one support person—it's right out of *The Courage to Heal*.

"Everyone will stay seated at all times. There will be no physical contact whatsoever. She would speak to Terry for half an hour; he could reply for ten minutes. She would speak to me for half an hour; I could reply for ten minutes. There would be no further contact that day. On the basis of this confrontation, it would be decided if there would be any further contact."

Terry added,

"We counter offered and said if her therapist and our therapist would pick a neutral referee that we would meet with her and the three of them at a neutral site. Everyone would have equal speaking time.

"We got a letter from Australia saying she could not accept our offer, and that's the last we heard of that. The confrontation was supposed to be on July 21st. She got married that August to someone we've never met.

"I'm wondering if she was trying to clean up her old life and get on with the new, or if, on the basis of that confrontation, she was going to decide if we were going to be invited to the wedding."

That was the last anyone in the family heard from or about Doreen until a newspaper reporter interviewed the Hansens and attempted to interview Doreen. The following ran as a sidebar to the article on the family:

Dᴏʀᴇᴇɴ Hᴀɴsᴇɴ's ʀᴇsᴩᴏɴsᴇ
ᴛᴏ ʀᴇǫᴜᴇsᴛs ғᴏʀ ɪɴᴛᴇʀᴠɪᴇᴡs

This is a written response from Doreen Hansen in reply to several requests for an interview. "I did not feel comfortable answering your questions directly," she wrote. "Therefore, I have issued a statement instead."

"I am a survivor of incest. In 1992, I arranged to meet with my parents privately to discuss the specific issues and circumstances regarding the abuse within our family. Unfortunately, they were not willing to participate in the manner in which I requested. Consequently, that meeting was never held. To this day, my parents have never asked me any questions, nor have they been informed by me about the specific details of the abuse. At no time has it been my desire to discuss or reveal any of the outstanding issues with my parents in a public forum. I do not understand why my parents have decided to open our private family situation to the public media rather than in a private fashion."[3]

CAUSES FOR DOREEN'S BREAKDOWN

Doreen's sister Beth speculated on the causes of Doreen's depression:

"I think a lot of it came from, she was this big career woman, and I think she found it demeaning and degrading to want to be married and have a family, but on the inside, that's a lot of what she wanted. Because she had this career, she didn't want to admit to people that marriage and a family were important to her."

The ads on television show us that the successful woman has a career, a few kids, and time to pamper her husband. She skips along full of energy. It's a breeze. But even without a husband or child to care for (or to care about her) Doreen's high-test career was taking its toll on her. Along with the move to Milwaukee, she had gotten a job as an international sales representative. She was constantly traveling and had no time to make friends. She called and told her parents that she felt like jumping off a bridge.

Doreen's parents think she may have been experiencing painful conflict between her "modern woman" behavior and their family sexual mores. Colette recalls Doreen coming home one weekend from college and telling her, "Mom, I want to sleep with Brian." Colette told her, "Well, Doreen, you know all the moral implications. I think it would be a big, big mistake." Colette explained,

"After she got back to campus she called her dad, and he told her pretty much the same thing. I assumed that she had taken my advice.

"It wasn't until after she moved to Milwaukee that my two other daughters said that it had been a sexual relationship with Brian, and that there had been others since then. My husband thinks this is her guilty conscience, that she felt she was being promiscuous and, in therapy, blamed it on the fact that she was sexually abused.

[Colette tried to give her daughter the acceptance she seemed to need.] "She came home for Thanksgiving that first year she was in therapy, and the day after Thanksgiving she and I sat and talked for most of the day.

"I realized afterward that she was picking my brain. At that point I knew that she'd had intercourse with her college boyfriend, and she was depressed and everything, and I'm putting two and two together. She had been telling me that she had problems with the Catholic Church because those priests were so dang hung up on sex it was ridiculous.

"I said, 'I think I've figured this out. Your relationship with Brian was a sexual relationship,' and she said, 'Yes, it was.'

"I said, 'If you're feeling guilty about that, there's worse; I don't want to say this is OK, but the ways people treat each other in this society, there are worse things than having sex with your boyfriend.'

"She assured me, 'Oh, I blew that off a long time ago. It's not a problem at all.' "

However, Alan felt that Doreen had never outgrown her need for her parents' approval. He explained,

"I think that everyone goes through a stage where they take charge of their own lives. With me it was probably sometime in college where you sit down and say, 'All right, I'm doing this because I want to do it. I don't really care what my parents think. They've brought me up, and now I've got to make my own decisions. I have to do it for me, rather than do it for them.'

"You go through your childhood constantly trying to please your parents, and at some point you have to make that break and spread your wings.

"Doreen had a very difficult time making that break, and I don't know if she's done it yet. I found her, even going through college and after she graduated, constantly seeking their approval. Maybe this whole thing was her way of making the break.

"I don't think she was emotionally self-aware. In retrospect, maybe she was reaching out for some way not to be so dependent. I don't know.

"I've got to tell you, [Alan said, suddenly letting his feelings break through the tone of analysis] the times we spent with her were very happy times. They were wonderful. This whole thing came as quite a shock to us. My wife really feels like she's lost a friend. My children still ask about Aunt Doreen."

ANSWER TWELVE

Why would anyone believe anything so painful as being sexually abused by a parent if it weren't true?

ANSWER NUMBER TWELVE: Because it provides one, simple, graspable reason for being unhappy when he or she "has it all."

THE AFTERMATH

The greatest challenge for the Hansen family in recent years was pretending everything was OK for the sake of Beth on her wedding day. Beth told me, "Everyone else had found out about the accusations a week before my wedding, and they tried to shelter me from it. They tried to make sure I had a nice day."

Before the wedding Terry (the father) had gotten a letter from Doreen. The letter said, "This letter is very hard to write. I want to come to Beth's wedding, and I want you to do me a really big favor. I want you to stay at least three feet away from me and not touch me. If you can't do this, I will not be able to come." Terry wrote back right away: "I understand where you're coming from. There are women in my office who have been to therapy and I understand how they need their space. By all means come." Colette added,

"And then, dumb us, we said at the bottom—Doreen could get attention away from other people because she's very outgoing and can take the limelight, and we didn't want her to take the limelight from Beth—so we said, 'This is just between you and us, and we won't tell anyone about this.' Well, the therapist loved that. That was proof. We just fell into the trap.

"All we meant was that we didn't want to spoil Beth's day. We didn't want her worrying that there was the potential for some big family blowup."

Terry commented,

"Well, in the end that's what happened anyway, because the word got out that she'd been abused by her brothers and her mother and I. She had told Paul that, and he delivered the message, of course. That was the only thing that anybody talked about, almost, on that wedding day."

Colette clarified,

"We discussed it after everybody was gone, pretty much. The guests weren't aware; it was strictly the family. Beth wasn't aware that this was going on. We didn't let it spoil her day."

John had been hyper-alert for a family blowup. He told me,

"At the reception Doreen made every effort, in a way that drew attention to herself, that every time Dad came into the room she would get up and stomp out. If he would come over and try to be on decent terms with her, she would just not talk to him and make it very obvious: 'I'm not speaking to you.'

"She tried to sneak out. I'm probably the only one who saw this. She walked right past me, didn't say a word. She said goodbye to my brother and then walked straight out the front door. My mom ran out and said, 'You're not going to leave just like that.'

"Doreen was a real bitch to my mother, and my mom walked back into the house crying. It was a big leaving scene, even though there were only three witnesses. It was Beth's day, her wedding, and Doreen was trying to make this crappy commotion in her own way."

John obviously feels protective of his parents in this painful family situation, but now Beth is the one who lives nearby and sees the effect on her parents.

"I used to go to lunch with my dad, and he would sit in the restaurant and cry. I'd say, 'Oh, Dad, things are going to work out. There's a reason for this.'

"I guess I never realized how hard it is for them every day. I have a lot of mixed feelings about contacting Doreen. My parents have told us all, 'You're adults, and you can have your own relationship with Doreen.' I think they wish that somebody did have a relationship with her.

"I don't know how I would deal with a relationship with her. I don't want to hear her accusations and everything else. Then, part of me thinks, 'Well, she doesn't have anyone there telling her she's wrong. How is she ever going to know?' "

Ursula, the oldest girl, gave me her perspective:

"I think my parents are really strong people, but all this with Doreen has really hurt them. The only good thing that has come out of this is that they are involved in the FMS society and trying to help other people who have been going through this without support for years. They are really trying to keep their lives together with the other kids and stuff. They try not to think about Doreen, but I know my mom can't help herself.

"I know my dad still thinks of her, too, because that's how he is, though my dad is better at putting things aside and going on. I think because of that he's been real helpful to Mom. They'll come out OK because they're strong people. They appreciate their other kids and their grandkids. They feel real bad that Doreen's not part of our life, and I know my mom feels better since we found out that she got married. Just because she has somebody."

The Hansens recently heard about their daughter Doreen's marriage through Paul Ayers, who received a wedding announcement from Doreen. Beth reflected on how much Doreen has missed:

"I feel bad for Doreen because she's missed out on a lot of family things and a lot of fun. We had a tacky gift contest for Christmas last year, and she missed that. Watching my parents grow older, that's a thing that's an experience for people.

"I don't think that my parents were ever human to her. I've found that since I've gotten married my relationship with my parents changed a lot. It was kind of like, they view me in different ways than they did before. That's something that she's going to miss.

"For a while, I was really tired of talking about Doreen. I told my parents, 'I'm sick of this.' It was all they talked about. Now, they've gone beyond that stage. It's really a grieving process. But it's hard to grieve when somebody's not dead."

Perhaps the one who is most hurt is Alan. According to his mother, Colette, he felt deeply betrayed when Doreen accused him of abusing her, particularly because he had been so supportive during her searching. Colette told me,

"Oh, he was so furious and angry when Doreen told him he'd abused her. He went through the whole grieving process. Very, very hurt and he just could not believe it. He said, 'Mom, I've supported her through this whole therapy thing, and she's been at my house, and we've been wonderful to her; I can't believe this.' "

Ursula had a final comment:

"I just want to add that this whole situation has brought the rest of our family closer together and has made us think more of how important we are to each other and how much we love each other."

WHAT SIBLINGS CAN DO TO HELP
THEMSELVES AND THEIR FAMILIES

REMAIN NEUTRAL

Even if you know where you stand, try to avoid saying so in a very direct way. Remember the wisdom of Keri O'Neill (a sibling whom we will meet in the next chapter):

"Once in a while I get pissed or sad that it's my family. But then I step back and watch it because I don't think it's my role to change or fix it. I told her that even if it's true, I'm not going to hate Mom and Dad. I'm going to help them get better. If it's not true, I feel sorry that you're being taken through all this pain. But I'm not going to hate you. You are all my family and I love you all and will support you all."

Siblings have the best chance of keeping that tenuous thread of contact. If you can avoid a confrontation, at least someone in the family will know where the sibling lives.

The sibling closest to the accusing sib can be elected to do this. The parents should be told that this sibling is the "contact" sibling and will not be making any public declarations to relatives in support of the parents, lest it get back to the accusing sib.

PROTECT YOUR HEALTH AND SANITY

—Don't take on the role of the "contact" sib if it is so strongly opposed to your way of operating that you will get ulcers pretending to be neutral.

—Find a therapist, minister or wise friend to talk to about the family situation so that you can get some objective feedback when things get hot.

—If anyone demands your loyalty, tell them you don't respond to emotional blackmail.

—Trust your own memory. You were there. You *do* know what happened. People don't repress years of abuse.

—Take frequent breaks from the situation. Make sure you have plenty of other things happening in your life. Do not give up your activities, plans, or interests to run to the aid of your parent or sib.

—Remember that you are not responsible for anyone else's feelings, but you are responsible for your own. You don't have to be a ball of anxiety about this unless you allow yourself to be one.

—Read the best material you can find on the subject. Read it *critically* to see if it is based on science or superstition.

WHAT IF SHE COMES BACK?

I asked the members of the Hansen family how they each would feel if Doreen decided to come back. Some accusing daughters have suddenly called their families after years of silence and never brought up the accusation again. They have neither apologized nor reversed their position. Rather, they have come back agreeing to disagree. Parents are often afraid that bringing up the subject would break the fragile new bond. How would the Hansens feel?

Beth doesn't know if the family can ever forgive Doreen:

"Karin tried to keep in touch with her. Last year she lost her job and called Doreen. She left a message but got no acknowledgment at all. That really hurt Karin very much. She feels like she was there to support Doreen for lots of things, and then, because she didn't agree with her about the sexual abuse, because she wouldn't say, 'Yeah, you were sexually abused,' Doreen just cut her off.

"I don't know what I would do. I'm kind of wimpy, so I would say, 'Oh, that's okay.' She is important to me and I do miss her. Still, I don't think I could ever trust her. It's difficult."

Beth is right about Karin. One can hear the deep disillusionment in her voice when she talks about Doreen. Karin is not sure what she would do if Doreen showed up on her doorstep:

"I don't think I would speak to her. I know I could never trust her again. I don't feel I have to give her any respect or the time of day. She's not a part of my life; I'm not a part of her life. We just happen to be born from the same parents. You don't have to like all your relatives.

"She just hurt me too badly. I wouldn't open myself up to that again."

Karin may have already begun to rewrite her history with her sister. After so many members of the family had told me that Karin was Doreen's closest friend, I was surprised to hear Karin deny it:

"In reality, I don't know if it's because so much time has passed, but I feel like we weren't really ever close, because she talked to me and stuff, but underneath she wanted people to see what she wanted them to see.

"If you would have asked me four years ago if we were close, I would have said, 'Yeah, we're close,' but now I don't know. It was like every time she had a boyfriend, the boyfriend was the most important thing, and we'd hear from her once in a blue moon. If he was gone somewhere and she needed somebody to talk to or hang out with, she'd call.

"When we talked, it was more Doreen talking about herself. Talking about her and her boyfriends and her job. I've always felt I was just there to listen."

John is bitter, too. He is not sure if he can ever forgive Doreen. He would need her to make a clear statement that she was wrong, and she is sorry. He told me,

"Number one, my dad is such a good person. Number two, it's total bull. It never happened. What bothers me so much is that my father gave us such a great foundation. They instilled in us such good values and religion, and here's somebody coming and trying to crush the cornerstone. I just can't go for that, it doesn't matter whether she's family or not."

Karin explained, "We never thought we'd have to deal with something like this. It's made all of us angry. Nobody's divorced; nobody's into drugs or alcohol. We all go to church. I guess we always felt we had the perfect family. We have to realize that we don't. That's hard." I asked Karin what she felt was imperfect about the family at this point. Her reply: "Doreen."

Even Alan, who had the most loving and forgiving things to say throughout our interview, was uncertain if he could ever trust Doreen again. Like many accused families, the Hansens do not know if they could accept Doreen back unless she explicitly withdraws her accusations. Alan told me,

"I don't think I could accept it if she just came back and pretended like nothing had happened. Something did happen [her accusation and the pain for the family, which followed], and I think that it will be many, many years, if ever, before any of us could ever trust her again, which is unfortunate. I think she has completely severed the ties.

[Alan relented for a minute.] "I love her dearly and she's a great person. I think she's lost."

[I reminded Alan that he told me he hadn't even sent her a Christmas card last year. I challenged, "You love her dearly and think she's a great person, but you won't even send her a Christmas card?"]

"No, [Alan told me,] "I loved the *old* Doreen."

[I countered, "She dwells in the same body."]

"I wonder. [Alan replied.] I think this other thing has taken over. We tried for a while to continue to contact her. The birthday that she had after Beth's wedding, I didn't think she wanted to hear from me, but my son Terrence is her godson, and I told Terrence, 'Why don't I call Aunt Doreen, and you can tell her happy birthday?' She was very rude to my children, rather on the mean side. That sort of put an end to my trying to contact her."

Beth observed, "My mom and dad would take her back in a second. It would just be hard. I know Mom and Dad have a lot of hope, but Doreen's a really stubborn person, and she has always had a problem believing she was wrong about anything. So I really don't see her ever recanting whatever she said. I think she believes that she's right and to hell with the rest of us."

SUMMARY POINTS

1. The notion that 90 percent of all families are dysfunctional is an idea that has taken firm hold in the pop-psychology mentality and is a virtual article of faith in the Sexual Abuse Recovery Movement. The term "dysfunctional" has been expanded to include all families that aren't totally healthy twenty-four hours a day, seven days a week—a standard few families can achieve.

2. Recovery therapists believe that a "dysfunctional" family will always produce "dysfunctional" children. These "dysfunctional" children then turn up in their offices as "dysfunctional" adults. This attitude ignores
   - Inborn temperament that may exacerbate or mitigate a child's reaction to a less-than-perfect family.
   - The entire body of psychiatric work pointing to a multiplicity of other possible causes for mental disturbances.

3. Early in his carer, Freud theorized that all mental health problems stemmed from early childhood sexual abuse, usually father-daughter incest. He later changed his mind, but the beautiful simplicity of this idea holds great appeal for some therapists. This theory has also found credence among the radical feminist population, who insist that Freud caved in to pressure from his male colleagues.

4. Why would anyone believe anything so painful as being sexually abused by a parent if it weren't true?
   - If your childhood was pretty good and there were no obvious reasons for your unhappiness, placing blame on "repressed memories" of sexual abuse by diabolically clever parents gives one a simple, one-size-fits-all answer to the question "Why can't I be happy?"

ELEVEN

Families in Pain

*I love my dad; I love my mom, and I love my sister,
too. You can quote me on that.*

— DONALD O'NEILL, a brother

JASON, THE OLDEST O'Neill child, realizes his birth position gives
him a very different perspective on his family. Unlike his siblings, who are
a few years younger, he did not grow up while his parents were drinking
heavily. That began after he had left for college. The business problems
between his uncle and his father had not become serious before then.

It was a large family, six kids in all, crammed into a modest house in
Great Neck, New York. Jason had a lot of responsibility. He not only
helped care for his younger brothers and sisters, he was his father's right-
hand man in the family grocery store. He remembers his parents as being
warm and responsive. He got lots of positive attention for the work he
performed, and he feels the praise and encouragement he received from his
parents was the source of his solid self-esteem.

However, Jason is aware that his siblings grew up in a different family.
On his visits home from college, his brothers and sisters began complaining
to him about his parents' drinking. He could see that family routines had
been severely disrupted. He instinctively knew that the problem needed to be
talked about. The kids talked it over first, and then they invited their parents
in to hear them out. They let Mom and Dad know that their parents' drinking
was making them miserable, and they made demands about what needed to
be changed. Dinner should be served predictably at 6:00 each evening, and
Mom and Dad were to sit down and eat with the family.

This began a turn-around that eventually led to Dad's quitting drinking. The parents began attending Alcoholics Anonymous meetings, and despite a few slips, home life improved from then on. For the most part, the kids have accepted their parents' imperfections and have forgiven them for past hurts—all but one.

Jane, the oldest daughter, believes her parents sexually abused her from the age of six months to ten years. To her, the alcoholism that they all remember is proof of the sexual abuse she suffered that none of them remember. Jason told me of his reaction to Jane's accusation, "I tried to be totally neutral at first. I strained to remember something that might help Jane. She's very convincing. I was really confused for a while, but then when she started talking about my parents taking her out in the middle of the night to attend satanic rituals, she lost credibility with me. There is no way I could have failed to notice something like that. It was a small house. You heard everything."

Now Jason is certain that his father did not molest his sister, Jane, but takes care not to challenge her on this point unless she pushes him to take sides. The whole family has coped with this situation very constructively. All the "adult children" are in touch with the accusing sister and still love her dearly. Since the sister would not come to the parents' house at Christmastime, Mom and Dad volunteered to watch all the grandchildren while the siblings went out to dinner with Jane. Needless to say, Jane would not leave her kids at Grandma and Grandpa's, and she was shocked that Jason trusted his daughter with them.

Jason wasn't worried, but when he got back to the house and learned that Grandma had gone shopping and left his daughter alone with Grandpa, he felt a lurch of panic and questioned his father about why he (Jason) had not been told his daughter would be alone with his father. As soon as the words were out of Jason's mouth he could see the effect on his father.

"It's the most I've ever hurt him," Jason recalled. "I'd give anything to take it back, but it's been said. It was a hard blow for my father when he was so vulnerable."

Jason got a hold of himself and realized that since he really didn't believe Jane's stories, he need not fear his father's babysitting and has since left his daughter at his parents' home without questioning who exactly would be at home. He is satisfied that his father has never done anything to harm his daughter and that he never would.

One of the more tragic aspects Jason sees in the current standoff is that Jane's children have not seen their precious "Pop" in years. As Jason explained, Jane's oldest son is now eleven, and he has been told why Mom doesn't want to see her father anymore. Jane's husband had been very close to Jane's father, but now he has embraced his wife's beliefs about her father.

On the other hand, Mr. O'Neill was recently in the hospital for a heart attack, and Jason was moved that Jane broke her vow and came to see her father.

> "She leaned over and told him that she forgave him, and I saw my father jerk in his tubes. I could tell he wanted to shout, 'For what?' but he lay back and calmed himself. Carl stood by looking grim and cold, but he came. I have to give them a lot of credit for that. I know it wasn't easy for them. I guess my sister was worried that Dad might die.
>
> "It's been really hard sometimes. We've all tried to rally around both of them. We can see they are both in a lot of pain, and we want to be supportive, but it's hard to walk on both sides of the street at once."

They all get together, minus Jane, at important family times, and then try to schedule a side activity with Jane. They'll take the kids and meet at a park, or have a get-together at someone's house. Mom and Dad give them their blessing to have a good time without them. They are worried about Jane and want her to have the support of her brothers and sisters. Jason confessed,

> "I have to say I don't think I've been as supportive as I think I should. I tend to avoid calling Jane. The conversation always works its way around to Dad, and I just don't want to hear it. I haven't called her in a long time now, and I feel guilty. If she decided to come back to the family I know we'd all greet her with open arms—no questions asked."

THE O'NEILL FAMILY

Mother: Mary, Age 65　　　Father: Jack, Age 67

Jason	Jane*	Ruth Ann	Mike	Donald	Keri
Age 42	Age 40	Age 38	Age 36	Age 33	Age 31

*The accusing daughter.

GROWING UP IN THE O'NEILL HOUSE

As we have seen already, the O'Neill family is not a perfect family. There were a lot of dysfunctional family behaviors, but somehow, in the midst of all this chaos, something was going right. The O'Neill siblings have had the most accepting and forgiving attitude toward their accusing sister that I have seen in any of the families I have interviewed. They are all still in touch with their sister, a remarkable feat among FMSF families. Perhaps it is their faults, their acknowledged imperfect childhood, that make it easier for them to forgive their sister. After all, they have been forgiving their parents for years.

Here's what it was like. Ruth Ann, as the third oldest—just two years younger than Jane—was the last of the older children. She was in the middle in many ways. She could still remember the innocent childhood times—the times before her parents started escaping their problems with liquor.

"We played outside all the time. My father wasn't around much; he was at the grocery store night and day. We went to the shore once in a while for a week or so. It was a normal childhood. My sister Jane and I shared a small room with twin beds. It was a four-bedroom house, six kids, two adults, one bathroom. We had a nice backyard. We all had friends in the neighborhood that we played with all the time."

[Discipline was simple, and not harsh by Ruth Ann's standards. She told me:] "My mother believed in 'A pat on the back, low enough and hard enough, once in a while, keeps them in line,' which means spanking. When she thought it was necessary, we got a swat. I remember once she told a friend I couldn't come out till my chores were done. We didn't scrub the floor or anything, but, unlike other kids, we couldn't go out and play all the time. I think my mother, who's a teacher, was very structured. With six kids, I think she kept a good hand on things. My father was around on Sundays and at night occasionally, when he didn't work late."

[Ruth Ann remembered the one rare occasion when her father totally lost his temper and slammed her up against a door:] "One time in high school I threw a big party when my parents were out. My father came home early, and he saw a couple kids out front, peeing on the bushes. He pulled into the driveway, kicked everybody out, and he beat me. He beat me up against the back door. That's the only time I was ever hit by my father. He just lost it on me.

"Then we had a meeting with my mother. A friend was living with us at the time whose mother had died. We had to make a list of everyone who was at the party, and my parents called every parent and said, 'Your child was at a party at my house that was not supervised, and there was drinking.' That's the way they handled things.

"My father apologized later, and then over the years, whenever it would come up, he'd feel bad about it. He lost it, and I completely understand. I got caught red-handed."

It was about that time, the early '70s, that her father and mother started drinking heavily. He and his brother were partners in a grocery store, and they didn't get along. Her father would come home tense every night. It would begin with a drink before dinner:

"My parents started this habit of cocktail hour with a couple of neighbors. It was like a new thing—cocktail hour. Dinner would get pushed back later and later. One of the neighbors would stop on the way home from work for cocktail hour. They would play music and drink. After a while that stopped, but then my father and mother would just drink. Every night before dinner—cocktail hour. A lot of time it developed into arguments, because he was so frustrated with his business. I guess they were having marital problems too.

"My room was at the top of the stairs, and I remember standing at that banister, listening to them argue on and on and on. I could hear every word clearly—the grocery store and who did what, constant arguing about that."

Her parents finally stopped drinking in the late '70s, when her father got out of the grocery business and went into real estate. Ruth Ann knows she was affected by the alcoholism, but by the time the drinking got bad she was already rather independent. However, this period in the family history was especially hard on her younger brother, Mike, who felt he had neither a father nor a mother then. Mike told me,

"I had a lot of brothers and sisters, so we fended for ourselves. Both parents worked too, so I pretty much grew up with my peers, a lot of first cousins, and siblings. My mother worked all day and marked papers all night. It seemed like the mornings and afternoons were OK, normal family stuff. It got hectic in the evening when they both drank a lot. All hell would break loose sometimes."

One can hear the loneliness and helplessness in Mike's voice and choice of expression. He obviously felt abandoned. There were no stable adults in his environment, and he did the best he could. But he felt the loss deeply. "The relationships weren't there; important activities, anything to do with the school, they missed. They were either working or busy. They basically missed it."

Mike is much more careful with his own kids now. "I work long hours, but they get the first free time. My other activities are second." But his parents never understood how much they had hurt him with their neglect. He had tried to tell them how he felt, but his comments fell on deaf ears.

"In our family you weren't allowed to have a problem. Everything had to be smiles, even if you were hurt. If you were it was like, 'Oh, what's the matter? There's nothing wrong.' It was always brushed under the rug. Especially my father, he had the attitude, 'Oh, there's no problem.' "

Although their parents drank throughout her childhood, Keri, the youngest, seemed less affected, perhaps because of the stabilizing presence of Ruth Ann. But the alcoholism was obvious to her.

"When I was seven or eight, I remember things being kind of fun and happy. Then in second or third grade I began to realize how much my parents were drinking. From then on, I remember bad drinking and fighting. They didn't have fun when they drank; they fought.

"Even so, I remember having nice Christmases and birthday dinners and such. I was a bookworm, so I got into school and books a lot. By sixth or seventh grade I knew that my house was totally out of control. My brothers could drink and smoke pot in the house, and my parents didn't have a clue."

The surveys help sort out how the various children were affected by the chaos of alcoholism. Though there was, generally, consistency among the O'Neill evaluations of family functioning, there was more individual variance than among the Hansen family members. There seemed to be evidence of the interplay between personalities. For example, Mike, who had the most negative recollections of his childhood home, was the only who had been described as "a scrappy little kid" by his mother on her child evaluation form. Apparently, trying to keep this "scrappy" kid under control sometimes provoked the parents to use harsher discipline. Though all the children admitted that the parents used spanking as discipline (and most of the children did not object to this method), Mike was the only one who indicated that his mother was "Seldom" violent and his father was "Sometimes" violent.

Jason, the oldest child, who had received his parents' most beneficial attention before their drinking had started to interfere with their functioning, saw his parents as having few dysfunctional behaviors, although he admitted to their drinking and use of spanking as a discipline, on occasion.

All the children agreed that their parents sometimes used positive esteem-building behaviors, but the younger children marked "Seldom" more often than the older siblings. Though rarely praised, they all agreed that they also were seldom punished, and rarely were punishments harsh. No one, except presumably Jane (who refused to fill out a form or to let me interview her), stated that the siblings had been sexually abused by a parent—ever. All the siblings indicated that their parents often drank to excess.

In this family, birth order seems very important at first glance, but closer analysis shows that temperament mattered more than birth order. Jason extols the virtues of his family because he feels that, as the oldest, he was privileged to have responsibilities that built character in him. One would assume that as the first girl, Jane would have had a lot of responsibility caring for the younger siblings. However, that was not the case. Jane was not the nurturing type, but her younger sister Ruth Ann was, so Ruth Ann inherited the child-care duties. For children growing up in this family, their lives and their degree of satisfaction or disappointment with their childhoods are as different as their personalities.

THE PARENTAL MIRROR

The inability to form close relationships usually has its root in early childhood experiences, especially with the main caretaker. Children depend on their parents to reflect the children's best traits. They look into their parents' faces hoping to find appreciation and approval.

But the relationship between parent and child is a two-way street, heavily influenced by the temperaments of both the parent and child. An easy-going child can emerge with a positive view of himself and life in general even when raised by the worst parent, while a very sensitive or poorly adaptable child may grow up feeling neglected and unappreciated despite the supportive efforts of a good parent. Regardless of the reality, how the child *perceives* the parent/child relationship significantly influences the child's entire life-view.

For this reason, some therapists believe the patient's subjective reality is more important to address than the objective reality of what really went on in the patient's childhood home. Current conflicts raised by the controversy over False Memory Syndrome and its potential effect on third parties have brought this therapeutic approach under fire. The effect of the parent/child bond on the mental health of the child is a complex problem that sparks continuing debate.

Not long ago it was believed that schizophrenia and autism were caused by poor mothering, but observers were really reversing cause and effect. For example, the autistic child does not respond to the mother's overtures from birth onward. After repeated lack of response from her child, the mother gradually stops attempting to stimulate the child or to gain his or her attention. The mother realizes that something is wrong and seeks help. The expert to whom she turns observes that the mother doesn't exhibit the normal "mothering behaviors" with her child—she doesn't grin and coo at the baby. The expert concludes that the infant is suffering from a lack of mothering. Today research has shown that schizophrenia and autism are usually genetic—the child was born that way, and the mother has responded normally to a totally unresponsive child.

Psychiatry has been moving away from blaming the mother for the last few decades. A good therapist considers what the client's part is in any poor relationship. Whether instigator or responder, the client can do things to lessen the damage of even the worst parent. A therapist who assures the client that none of the conflict was his or her fault takes away half the client's resources for healing. This attitude robs the client of his or her sense of mastery over the client's own life and can leave the client feeling helpless and overly dependent upon the therapist for guidance.

TEMPERAMENT

There are two sides to every story, and on each side of the story there is a temperament at work. Our temperaments, or personality traits, influence how we perceive things, and in so doing, create a reality that is unique to each person. Some people are extremely sensitive. As a result, a minor incident for the average person is perceived as a grievous slight by the sensitive person. All parents make mistakes. How those mistakes affect their children is determined by each child's temperament.

PARENT ASSESSMENT OF CHILDREN DURING CHILDHOOD[1]

Turecki's Temperamental Variables Checklist

Trait	Column 1 (difficult)		Column 2 (easy)
	extreme------------ mid-range		--------------extreme
Activity Level	Very active	to	Sedentary
Distractibility	Easily distracted	to	Attends easily
Adaptability	Resists change*	to	Very adaptable
Approach / Withdrawal	Introverted or shy*	to	Extroverted
Intensity	Very intense*	to	Quiet and easygoing
Regularity	Unpredictable	to	Creature of habit
Sensory Threshold	Very sensitive	to	Mellow
Mood	Pessimistic*	to	Optimistic

*These are the most critical variables in determining if a child will be easy or difficult to raise. Negative, highly reactive, emotional, or withdrawn children with poor adaptability are very difficult to raise. They are also very vulnerable to stress, especially high parental expectations.

As we will see, the O'Neill family's problems were, for some of the children, important learning experiences that taught them good coping skills. Donald, the youngest son, doesn't remember any family problems. As far as he's concerned he had a happy childhood. Mike, on the other hand, was very hurt by his parents lack of participation in his activities. Jason, Ruth Ann, and Keri were all made stronger by the exercise of dealing with their parents' business troubles and alcoholism. Jane, who wanted everything to be perfect, was apparently deeply damaged while growing up with the same set of parents.

Above is a chart that presents some of the variables of temperament. I have used this to help the parents describe the personalities of each child. A concept that continually comes up when temperament issues are discussed is "goodness of fit." An extremely sensitive child with many negative or difficult traits may have a relatively carefree and harmonious childhood if he or she is born to a mother who is very easygoing. Similarly, an easy child may suffer no damage if she or he is parented by a cantankerous, moody mother or father. When two positives collide, parent and child live an idyllic life. When two negatives collide, all hell breaks loose. The parent and child will each suffer from the impact.

JANE'S STYLE OF COPING

As a young girl Jane had everything totally under control. As Ruth Ann recalls it, Jane always had her homework done and her uniform laid out by 8:00 p.m. She hung out with the "preppies." Keri backs this up with her own examples:

> "Jane was always this perfect child who was really spoiled. She was always called 'the pretty one.' She was never her own person. She did what the crowd did, did what the cool people did.
>
> "She never did any chores. She was totally a brat. We used to joke about it. She used to come home from school and do her thing; her room was perfect. She and Ruth Ann fought so badly in their room because they were like Felix and Oscar; my parents split them up, and I lived with Ruth Ann for a while.
>
> "Jane would say to my mother, 'The kids did this, or the kids did that' meaning us, me, the little ones. My mother would be like, 'Jane, just go. Go be with your friends.'

"I could never go in and sit on her bed when I was a little kid. She would say, 'Get off my bed.' I could go sit on Ruth Ann's bed, and she'd ruffle my hair and say, 'What did you do today?' It was just different.

"Jane got married and left when she was twenty-one. She never checked in. At that time Ruthie and I were really upset about the drinking. Jane wouldn't even acknowledge it. She just wanted a perfect little house. She never got upset about the drinking until she was thirty-four.

"I think when she had kids it was the first time she really had to be responsible. Having children really threw her for a loop. Even when she only had one baby, we were surprised because she just couldn't handle it. We would be down at the shore, and there were a couple of little babies around. Everyone would take turns with everybody's baby, and it was fun. If a baby cried the mother would go get it if she was close, and if she wasn't someone else certainly would.

"Jane's baby would always be crying, and Jane would have this blank look on her face. We'd say, 'Jane, just pick him up. He just wants you to hold him.'

"And she'd say, 'God, he's so needy.'

" 'Yeah, Jane, he's three months old,' I would say. 'That's how they are.' "

"Now looking back, Jane says, 'It started when I had those kids. That's when my memories started.' "

Ruth Ann confirms Jane's lack of mothering skills and talks of the strain it seemed to be for Jane to be a mother. It seemed to push her over the edge:

"She was on her second marriage, she had two kids—talk about a mother with stress. She could never really handle those kids. Looking back on it, we thought it was funny at the time; she used to take her infant son and go to the shore for a weekend with her pocketbook. No baby pack. She would get down there and buy diapers and feed him.

"Looking back on it, I think she was neglectful. She did what was right for Jane. It was hard for her to think of other people, even her own kids.

"Even now, she goes to therapy twice a week; she goes riding three times a week; her husband works full time. Everything is for Jane. I think some people are too selfish to be mothers.

"Her little boy was kind of high strung. When the second one came along my mother and I helped her a lot. At one point she was thinking of having a third one. This was after the accusations came out.

"I said, 'Jane, you've got to be kidding. First of all, Mom's not around to help you.'

"She just looked at me. I doubt she'll have any more now."

Ruth Ann is angry that extended family members do not ask the other four kids their opinion of Jane's perceptions:

"We have a cousin named Cindy who just got her masters in psychology from Princeton. Cindy believes everything that Jane is saying, and she's convinced a lot of people in the family that Jane is an incest survivor.

[Astonishingly, Ruth Ann added,] "Cindy thinks that when she has children, she'll probably have memories of her own childhood sexual abuse — even though she doesn't have them now.

"I mean, she's *planning* on that happening. She says a lot of people who go through childbirth then have memories."

The truth of the matter is that having children is very stressful, whether it's the first, or second, or whatever. Kids are a lot of work. Sometimes the first child, though always an abrupt awakening to how much care children need, may not be the most stressful because everyone offers help. But by the second or third kid, babies are "old hat," and family and friends don't perceive a need to rally around the mother. However, the mother may need help all the more when the second one comes along and abruptly doubles her work. Parenting difficulties, and anxiety and depression at the time of increased childcare responsibilities, are not signs of past sexual abuse. We don't need to look for hidden reasons why mothers have trouble coping with their children. It's hard work!

KIDS' EFFECT ON PARENTS

Many books have been written on the effect parents have on their children, but very little has been researched on children's effects on their parents. One sociologist, Dr. Anne-Marie Ambert, has written a book entitled *The Effect of Children on Parents* (Hawthorne Press, 1992) that looks at this other side of the coin.

Parenting is difficult, and our society is not very supportive of families. Because of our shortage of good child care, many mothers who would rather work than be stay-at-home moms are forced to quit their jobs. Without paid work, many women begin losing self-esteem. They may find the things that children enjoy doing excruciatingly boring. The days become long, and, as their irritability increases, mothers may end up screaming at their children. If there is no alternative to being with the kids all day again tomorrow, mothers may helplessly watch their worst selves emerge.

Difficulties with parenting can be especially painful and conflictual for perfectionist personalities like Jane. Children always seem to act up in public, and the more it bothers us, the more they act up. Someone as meticulous as Jane might find public scenes painfully embarrassing. At the same time, the inability to change the child's behavior can leave a mother feeling like a total failure, especially if she is a perfectionist who tends to see things in black and white. It can relieve the pressure somewhat to point to one's own parents as poor role models, but parent blaming is a double-edged sword. If we believe our parents are responsible for all our problems, then when we become parents we must believe, perhaps only on a subconscious level, that we are responsible for all our children's difficult behaviors. This can create tremendous psychological pressure and uncomfortable feelings of guilt.

PARENT BASHING

In the recent era of parent bashing, there has been a damaging over-emphasis on the effect parents have on their children. Not only does the exaggerated importance placed on the mother/child interaction during the first six years of life place an enormous burden on the mother, it carries with it the implication that any damage we suffered twenty years ago has left us irreparably damaged.

When someone comes to a therapist's office troubled because he or she cannot form a good love relationship or cannot parent effectively, the problem is not necessarily rooted in the client's childhood. The client may be having trouble finding someone to love because he or she works such long hours that the only place to meet people is in a bar after work on Fridays. They don't have time to form healthier social connections through volunteer work or leisure activities.

Some may be having trouble parenting because their parents were poor role models, while others may never have been very interested in parenting while they were growing up and have no idea how to do it. In the O'Neill family we see that Ruth Ann, though not the oldest sister, was the one who looked after the little ones. Her parenting has gone smoothly because she has had lots of practice. But Jane was always more interested in her own activities. That's her temperament. She needs help learning how to parent and meet her own needs for excitement at the same time. But, apparently, that's not where her therapy is focused. According to her sisters, Jane's therapist did not consider Jane's parenting difficulties to be a significant contributor to Jane's emotional distress. Rather the therapist immediately assumed they were an effect rather than a cause of Jane's mental illness.

Instead of guidance on how to meet her own needs while meeting the needs of her children, Jane was encouraged to think mainly in terms of blaming her parents. As she worries about her own failings, she learns that the only socially acceptable excuse for being a less-than-ideal mother is that you had a terrible childhood. Jane is boxed in. She either has to create a good story that excuses her limitations, or she has to change. Since the therapist is not offering constructive suggestions for Jane to change herself, parent blaming has become her only face-saving resource.

ANSWER THIRTEEN

Why would anyone believe anything so painful as being sexually abused by a parent if it weren't true?

ANSWER NUMBER THIRTEEN: Because it's less painful to blame someone else than to examine one's own personal failings and do all the arduous work of changing from within.

THE PRESSURE BUILDS

It all began over Mother's drinking. Dad had stopped long ago, but Mom had started up again. Ruth Ann told me,

"Jane and I went to counseling together. Jane was having marital problems; I was having problems with our mother's drinking. The first thing Marjorie [the counselor] told us was to go get *Co-dependent No More*. That really helped us both. I stayed in therapy for six months, and Marjorie really did me a lot of good. I was ready to quit therapy, but she didn't want me to stop. Marjorie said I had so much to work on that I should keep coming in. Now Jane's still going twice a week, and it's been four years."

Keri, the youngest sister, also went along for a few sessions because she was trying to work out her own solution to the problem of their mother's drinking. Keri told me:

"Jane and I were leading up to a meeting with my mom. I said to my mom, 'I'm not going to watch you drink anymore. I'm never coming to your house for dinner again. I can't stand it. But I'll always stop by in the morning, because I love you.' That's what I did and what Jane did too, but Jane kept going to see Marjorie. I stopped because I was done."

At about the same time they had started going to Adult Children of Alcoholics (ACOA) meetings. Ruth Ann described the meeting:

"Half the people in the room were incest survivors. I remember Jane saying one time, 'Thank God we're not incest survivors.' When I confront her with that now she says, 'Oh, I was in such denial.'

"Half the people around that room were clutching teddy bears and talking about their inner children. That's all part of it. Jane got swallowed up in the whole thing.

[Ruth Ann saw Jane become more and more obsessed with her therapy.] "She drones on and on and on. Even her friends in therapy complain about it. She ignores everything, her kids and all. A truck could be coming at her, and she would stand there and drone on and on about her therapy, her abuse. It's like she's in a trance. I told her, 'I can't get together with you if you're going to go on about this all the time.'

"She had me in a parking lot for an hour and a half, after lunching with the kids. I could not get away from her. The kids were in both cars crying. She's oblivious to that. She always has been."

ACCUSATIONS

Mary O'Neill, Jane's mother, told me about how it all began:

"Jane [then 36 years old] called early one morning in an agitated state, asking if we would go to her therapist that morning with her. She said she wasn't coping, she couldn't go on. We knew she had been getting some kind of help, because she would often leave her children with us when she had appointments. We assumed she was having marriage counseling, although she never discussed her problems with us.

"When we got to her therapist's office, her husband Carl and two-year-old daughter were there. During the hour or so she made the statement that when she was a baby 'someone put something into her.'

"Jack's [the father's] reaction was to ask astonished, 'What do you mean?' Mine was to take her in my arms, she was trembling so.

"It was proposed by the therapist that Jane should be hospitalized so she could have some space and work on her 'memories.' This wasn't feasible financially. Also, we all (including the therapist) agreed that the stigma of being in a mental hospital was not necessary. So I moved in and took over her household.

"Jane's husband, Carl, was a kind, patient man, utterly at a loss as to what to do now to help her and very grateful for my complete support. The next several months were an insidious nightmare! With my support she was free to go to daily therapy, to visit aunts, uncles, cousins, friends—anyone who could help her recreate her early years, of which she had no memory."

Mary was distressed to realize that Jane had spent her time questioning everyone on both sides of the family about alcoholism in the family history. Mary felt that Jane's investigations had supported an unfair generalization, which Mary states thus,

"All Irish are alcoholics, and all alcoholism leads to incest.

"Her demands were unending. She insisted that her husband and I read all the books she was reading to help her get well.

"Acting on the therapist's recommendation, I was the one who bought her a copy of *The Courage to Heal*!"

Jane's four-year-old boy was extremely active, and the two-year-old daughter was sullen and cried a lot for her absent mother. It was an exhausting job for Mary, and her other children felt that Jane was taking advantage of her. Since Jane's home is an hour-and-a-half drive from her parents' home, Mary was virtually living at Jane's, coming home only twice a week to see her husband and other children. After two months of this, Mary was too tired to continue, and she went home to stay a week or so before Thanksgiving. Jane said she could not attend the family meal because she wasn't "up to seeing everyone." The day before Thanksgiving, Jane's father drove for an hour and a half to deliver a complete turkey dinner to her. Mary told me,

"One night the following week, around midnight, she called, awakening us. I answered, and she began screaming over and over, 'It was him. It was Dad. It was him.' She sounded drunk, which was most unusual. I became hysterical and screamed back, 'No! No! No!'

"Jack took the receiver and spoke to her very calmly, telling her she was wrong. She was tired and should get some sleep. We would see her in the morning. After I got control of myself, we discussed going to her that night and decided against it.

"Early the next morning, I arrived at her doorstep to be greeted by horrible abuse. She hated me because I allowed this to happen to her. She told me that I was probably abused as a child myself, and on and on."

Looking back, Mary believes that Jane was following a "plan" outlined by the therapist. First came the belief that "something" had happened. Then would come the "who and what."

Jane's parents asked for a family meeting at the therapist's office. A week or so later the whole family gathered there: Mom, Dad, Ruth Ann, Mike, Donald, and Keri (Jason lived too far away). With the therapist were Jane and her husband Carl. Mary described Jane's behavior as hostile:

"She accused her father of molesting her from the age of six months until ten years. When asked, she would not give any specific details but was furious that no one believed her. The therapist told us all that we were a dysfunctional family and needed help to get over our denial – she would be happy to treat the entire family. We declined."

HOW JANE'S SIBLINGS SEE IT

Keri shared her first reaction to Jane's accusation:

"You know, my dad bought her a horse at a time when nobody was getting anything. I always knew she was his pet. At first I was thinking, 'God, maybe this could fit.' But I never told her, 'Yes, I believe you,' and I never said to my father, 'I know you never did anything.'

"I was open to both of them but never committed myself. I just figured, even if it did happen, that that was her relationship with her father; my father was a different person to me. But as it went on—and even from the beginning she was doing such intense hypnotherapy—I thought, 'That's not right.' I don't even think this is good therapy.' I asked myself, 'Why is this therapist digging so vigorously with this person who is so suggestible?'

"I even called Marjorie and said, 'I just want you to know that you're working with a very suggestible person who blows everything up anyway.' But Marjorie didn't really want my input on how to do therapy. So I was worried from the beginning about this therapy process.

"I know incest survivors who have done different types of therapy who are not in major nightmare trauma for four years. Jane believes that she has to remember every memory, every awful moment. She says, 'Another year or two and I might have remembered everything.' "

Ruth Ann also gave me her perspective:

"At first Jane was saying she was raped when she was little; she didn't know who it was. We were all trying to think, 'What family friend could have done it?' Then she said it was my father.

"She would ask aunts and uncles questions, trying to figure out where it happened. I don't know if she's come up with a place yet. Except that, in some of her memories, my parents were wearing black cloaks with rosary beads over their hands, and it was at night with candles burning. Apparently, she thinks they got her up at night, maybe even took her somewhere in the car, then had her back in bed by the time we all woke up.

"She has blanked out every good memory. She doesn't remember anything normal or anything good. When I ask her something like 'Do you remember the time you were going to tell on me because I was painting in the basement, and I threatened to tell on you because you rode your bike to the park and you weren't allowed to?' She'd say, 'Oh, I don't remember anything like that.' But before she went into therapy she could remember all kinds of things from her childhood. She would talk and laugh about it a lot."

A MIXED BAG

As we have seen, this family does not have the clean lines of the Hansen family. There is no doubt that this family is dysfunctional in some ways, but they also show vigorous signs of health. The one central criterion for the difference between a healthy family and a dysfunctional family is not whether they have problems; rather, it is how they deal with the problems that they have—for all families have problems.

This family, as a whole, has shown a remarkable ability to confront its problems. Jason helped orchestrate the first family confrontation when all but he were still children in the home. As a result of the children talking to the parents about the parents' drinking and how it was affecting them, the parents immediately began to be more reliable about mealtimes, and, shortly after, both parents started attending AA meetings.

As they grew older, Ruth Ann and Keri began to attend Al-Anon to better understand their family situation. In the years since, all the siblings have sought whatever help they needed to overcome the effects of their parents' alcoholism. Mike has even quit drinking recently, because he worried that he couldn't control it and wants to be sure that he is "there" for his children. Admittedly, the parents still have denial about the alcohol problems. The mother still drinks, and the father pretends she doesn't. But the children have been wide awake, in touch with reality, the whole time.

As we have seen above, in our culture we often exaggerate the influence of parents and tend to ignore how strong the influence of a peer group is. The siblings are Jane's peer group and, as such, represent a lot of support and verification that could be healing for Jane, if she allowed it. They have not been "in denial," unavailable to commiserate with Jane about the serious family problems that they all faced together. Their long history of dealing with the parents' drinking in such a forthright manner makes them reliable witnesses, and we cannot help but wonder why they are so aware of the alcohol problems but cannot corroborate Jane's accusations of sexual and satanic ritual abuse, if they are true.

Healthy families also come through during times of stress. Jane's siblings, though distressed about her accusations and the pain they have caused their parents, have continued to have contact with her. The parents have been there, too. Jane's mother had taken over childcare for her many times before her crisis. The mother gave everything she had in response to the daughter's emotional breakdown. They all do their best to include Jane in family functions in a way that won't be uncomfortable for her. Despite their irritation with her accusations, they are trying to stand by her and make it easier for Jane to return to the family if she should change her mind. Unlike the Hansens, this family is even willing to take Jane back without extracting a retraction from her.

They have done what they can on their end. They willingly went to talk with Jane and her therapist when requested. Both Keri and Ruth Ann have gone back for follow-up visits. They have all sought the advice of a therapist on how to deal with the problem and offered to have a second meeting. The door is still open.

BOUNDARIES

Ruth Ann told me,

"I went to see Jane and her therapist for two hours, last spring. Jane said that she played 'possum' when I was being abused and that I must have done the same—blocked it out and ignored it so we could get up in the morning and eat our cereal.

She's sure that we were all abused, that my father has gotten to hundreds of children, and that he's still getting to hundreds of children. We have about sixty cousins, and I asked her to give me one name of anybody who can say anything happened. I want to believe you, give me a name. She said there is one cousin, but she couldn't tell me the name. I told her to have that cousin call me. I'm still waiting for that call.

"After the meeting we all had, Jane went out to lunch with her therapist, Marjorie. They're buddies now, where before we started therapy together Jane and I were buddies. I am resentful of that. Jane and I weren't close when we were growing up, but after she had kids we got together once a week, taking the kids on day trips. I miss that."

The whole controversy over repressed memory therapy and incest is replete with boundary violations. There is, of course, the sexual boundary that the daughters accuse their fathers and mothers of violating. But there are many other subtle (and some not subtle) boundary violations taking place. Boundaries are the containing walls healthy people build around not only their bodies, but also different areas of their lives. The need for boundaries is just beginning to be understood in all its ramifications. But we must keep in mind that it is not a heading in even the revised edition of Dr. Spock's childcare book. Though we can expect parents of the last generation to know they should not have overt sexual contact with their children, it is unreasonable to expect them to have known when they were committing "covert" incest, as it is currently being defined.

As you may recall from Chapter Two, "covert" incest is parental behavior that might have sexual overtones. However, this is very hard to define and becomes a matter of opinion and personal sensitivity. Though some therapists feel an act (such as parading around in one's underwear) can only be considered "covert" incest if the parent feels some sexual stimulation, this definition only makes the issue murkier as client and therapist speculate about how a parent *felt* (the thought police again) one day, twenty years ago.

In addition, behaviors that would not have been considered even covertly incestuous a generation ago are now considered near crimes by the Sexual Abuse Recovery Movement. Asking a child not to lock the bathroom door so others may use the toilet while they are showering was an example provided by Ralph. A generation ago most families were larger, and most had only one bathroom. Families didn't have the physical facilities to be able to provide absolute privacy. It is not fair to look back and expect our parents to have known what the social/sexual mores were going to be in the 1990s. If "covert" incest is a "crime," it was not a crime in the 1950s.

Parents are not soothsayers. They are no more guilty of "covert" incest than their grandparents were guilty of neglect if they failed to give their children penicillin or polio shots (which had not yet been developed).

But parents are not the only ones who have violated boundaries. It is also a boundary violation when accusing daughters tell all the relatives and even former neighbors that the daughters were sexually abused. In the case of the Griffith family, whom we will meet in the next chapter, the accusing daughter not only mailed a thirty-two-page document describing the alleged rapes by her father to all the relatives, she also called child-protective services in the towns of each of her brothers because they were "in denial," and she therefore believed they were probably molesting their children. That certainly felt like a boundary violation to her brothers!

The accusing daughters frequently violate their own boundaries and the boundaries of their children as they indiscriminately tell their "story" to anyone who will listen (willingly or not). Mothers have told their children's teachers the gruesome details of their uncorroborated "recovered memories," presumably to explain why the children are acting up in class. Not only do the children feel embarrassed and humiliated that their families' private business is known by all, the children's own child/parent boundaries are being violated when their parents share these grown-up problems with them.

I'm not suggesting we reinstitute Victorian "denial." There is a wide berth between sweeping problems under the rug and announcing them on public radio. Some therapists do not seem to be very effective in guiding their patients toward appropriate behavior—when and where it is appropriate to tell your story, and when it is not. Just as Ruth Ann has grown tired of hearing Jane's "story," Jane's friends have probably grown tired of it, too. I'm sure that each of us has run into people who obsessively discuss their "abuse." Retractors have told me that they eventually alienated any friends who managed to stay friends when their therapists advised the clients to avoid contact with those who didn't believe them.

This brings us to another category of boundary violation—between therapist and client. As we see above, Jane's therapist now pals around with her, and Ruth Ann is gradually losing her place in her sister's life. Retractors have told me stories of therapists having sex with them, confiding their own personal problems to the clients, and creating dependence in clients by encouraging daily phone calls to their homes. When the client's alienating behavior teams up with the therapist's unhealthy availability (their failure to set appropriate boundaries with their clients), the therapist becomes the client's entire support system.

PROFESSIONAL ETHICS

Therapists talk about transference, displacement, and projection. We have probably all experienced displacement or projection in our everyday relationships with people. We find that there are certain people who really set us off. We may inexplicably blow up about some trivial incident, or we may find we are the target for someone else's disproportionate anger over some small slight.

If I still have a lot of conflict about my mother trying to control me and haven't found a way to stand up to her, adult to adult, then when my spouse tries to tell me what to do (even if it's a gentle request), I may vent on him all my pent-up anger at my mother. I think I'm angry with my spouse, and my spouse thinks I'm angry with him, but actually I have transferred my unresolved anger with my mother to my spouse.

If my spouse's father always blew up at him instead of listening to his requests and discussing differences calmly, then when I blow up at my spouse he is likely to react to me the way he would have reacted to his father. For example, he may get depressed, withdraw, and sulk. It looks like a fight between my spouse and me, but it is really a fight between my mother, me, my spouse, and his father.

It is part of a therapist's training to become aware of occasions when the client's anger, sadness, or seductiveness are really "old routines" they used to act out with a parent. When clients displace their feelings toward their parents onto the therapist, it is called transference. The therapist needs to distance himself and think through his reactions, so that he can use the transference to help the client. It is an opportunity for the client to learn a new way of interpreting the behaviors of others or a new way of responding that gets better results. The therapist is better able to "keep her cool" if she is aware of her own early-formed, knee-jerk, emotional reactions and can avoid countertransference or acting out her unresolved conflicts with the client.

Unfortunately, one of the consequences of the kind of sharing that takes place in therapy, coupled with the therapist's accepting attitude, is that the client often falls in love with the therapist. In addition, it is common for therapists to feel not only protective of the client, but also attracted to the client. One therapist may begin to feel a parent-like desire to soothe and fix things for the client—an urge to give unconditional love, be a best friend, and more. Another therapist may find himself drawn into a sexual affair with a client. These feelings are extremely common in therapy, and all good training programs spend time forewarning therapists and helping them think through appropriate responses when these feelings come up. In other words, therapists need to know what to do to avoid forming unhealthy ties with clients. In the clinical jargon, they need to learn to set boundaries.

There are many sources that discuss this problem and offer suggestions for the kind of boundary setting that will make it easier for therapists to avoid mistakes. Here are some guidelines gleaned from the literature:

DO'S AND DON'TS FOR THERAPISTS

1. DO have a question on the intake form that asks: Have you ever been sexually abused? DO be ready to take "no" for an answer.

1. DON'T tell your clients that others with her symptoms were sexually abused.

2. DO end therapy on time. Give a five-minute warning and assure them that they can finish discussing pressing issues at the next session.

2. DON'T let sessions run over except for very infrequent crises.

3. DO tell your client that professional ethics prevent you from socializing with clients. It could harm your trusting therapeutic relationship.

3. DON'T spend social time outside of the session with the client. Don't go to lunch or lectures together.

4. DO set limits on phone calls. Use an answering service so clients do not call your home directly. Unless it is an emergency, return their calls during your workday.

4. DON'T allow frequent or lengthy phone calls, or exceptions to your rules about calling because the patient has "special needs."

5. DO explain the limits of your time and attention in a gentle way, explaining what constitutes an "emergency."

5. DON'T promise you can always be there for your clients. Remember, you have human limitations.

6. DO help the client make concrete plans for meeting people and forming healthy friendships. Keep the pressure on for the client to "fix" his or her own isolation.

6. DON'T become your client's best and only friend.

7. DO encourage the client to keep a realistic view of your limitations as a human being.

7. DON'T let yourself believe that you are the only person who can save the client.

8. DO let your clients know that you prefer to keep your personal problems private. This is *their* hour.

8. DON'T share personal problems or discuss other clients with any patient.

9. DO emphasize that the way to better health is through the clients' own efforts.	9. DON'T "rescue" patients or feel responsible for making up for all their past traumas.
10. DO be patient and allow the client to set the pace. Avoid using the power of your position.	10. DON'T let yourself be goaded into becoming angry at your client's resistance.

Among the personal stories I listened to while researching this book, I found every conceivable kind of boundary violation between therapist and client. The most obvious was Carol, who was drawn into a sexual affair with her therapist. Another retractor reported listening to her therapist's personal problems during her session. Members of a Texas satanic ritual abuse group were made to feel special when the therapist shared confidences from other clients' sessions. Aileen was encouraged to call her therapist every night and couldn't get to sleep without this good-night call. Ruth Ann talked about her sister going off to lunch with her therapist. All these actions are boundary violations: They are inappropriate conduct for a therapist, and they will result in an unhealthy dependence upon the therapist. If your therapist is having a "dual relationship" with you, beware. These boundary violations are considered unethical by most professional therapists because they confuse the patient and interfere with the patient's forming a healthy therapeutic relationship. You will probably need to switch therapists before you can become an independent, fully functioning person.

THE AFTERMATH

Above, we saw that Jane had tried to convince Ruth Ann that she, too, had been abused by their father. This was Jane's way of answering Ruth Ann's challenge that since they shared a bedroom, she didn't believe that Jane was abused in the night by their father, or Ruth Ann would have noticed.

Jane also tried to convince her brother, Mike, that he had been abused. "The age that she was talking about," Mike told me, "I would have remembered. As far as I'm concerned, there was nothing done to me. I'm sure of that." However, Mike says he can't judge what went on between his sister and their father. "I don't know what happened, but I guess it's possible he could have abused her."

I asked Mike if he thought his sister Jane might be mixing things up—if she was really angry about their parents' alcoholism and had taken real problems and mixed them up with fantasy. He replied, "She's definitely stretching it, especially with the pedophile accusations. They're way off base, I think." Mike admitted that Jane had tried to convince him that their father was abusing his children. Mike thinks Jane may be picking up ever more elaborate accusations from her therapy or her groups.

Keri put in a good word for the therapist. Marjorie had given Keri excellent and compassionate advice on how to deal with their mother's drinking. Keri feels that Marjorie has been a good therapist but had been led astray by the Sexual Abuse Recovery Movement. Keri told me,

> "I think she has a good heart, and she does give some good advice, but I think she has just fallen on that bandwagon, and I don't think she's clear in her own work, not clear in herself. My sister-in-law, Gail, went to her for years. Gail was an abused child and never forgot it. She's not a 'repressed memory' person. Gail to this day says Marjorie helped her. But Gail also says, looking back, she knows there is a lot of projection.
>
> "When Gail decided to quit therapy, she told the therapist, 'Marjorie, I'm feeling pretty good; Mike and I are doing better. I'm going to take a couple months off and see how I do.' But Marjorie said, 'No, Gail, you cannot live without me. You cannot stop therapy.' I think a good therapist would say, 'Hey, you're feeling pretty strong. Give it a try, and if you need me, I'm here.' She definitely has too much attachment for a therapist."

Keri has ultimately come upon a low-intensity way of dealing with this family conflict. She told her sister Jane, "I don't know what happened." Keri recognizes that neutrality is harder for Ruth Ann. Keri explained that

> "Ruth Ann is hell-bent on proving my parents innocent. Jane wants to prove them guilty. I don't have a vested interest in proving anything. I think people have to go through different lessons in their life, and Jane is picking this drama for a certain reason. In a way it's helped my parents get closer. I listen to Jane, and I tell her I love her and her kids. I told her I felt like someone watching a play unfold.

"Once in a while I get pissed or sad that it's my family. But then I step back and watch it because I don't think it's my role to change or fix it. I told her that, even if it's true, I'm not going to hate Mom and Dad. I'm going to help them get better. 'If it's not true, I feel sorry that you're being taken through all this pain, but I'm not going to hate you. You are all my family, and I love you all and will support you all.' She appreciates my honesty, but finds it hard to be around people who have any sense of love for my father."

Ruth Ann has been more able to let go of her anger lately, but the feelings inevitably flare up at times:

"My father had a heart attack in July and was in the hospital for a month. My mother had to call around to a lot of aunts and uncles, and this one niece was really rude to my mother on the phone, just about hung up on her. So I went to see that cousin's sister, whom I'm a little bit friendly with. I said, 'Linda, everything that Jane is saying is bullshit. I know, I was there.'

"My word is just as important as hers, and I want people to know that I have a voice too. It really got me mad that this girl, who's in college, was so rude to my mother at a time like that. I realized that, God, there are a lot of people out there who believe this is true."

Mary and Jack, the parents, tried to arrange another family meeting, this time with a therapist of their choice. They had begun to see a psychologist to help them cope with the turmoil brought on by the accusation and had encouraged the other kids to see him also, at the parents' expense. Their son, Jason, was making a special trip to town to have a private session with the psychologist, and the family hoped to have a joint session the next day. The family invited Jane, her husband, and her therapist to attend the session. Jane's therapist replied that such a meeting would be too traumatic for Jane.

The next month they received a threatening letter from a lawyer representing Jane. For $25,000, the letter informed them, Jane was willing to sign a release absolving them from all future claims. If they didn't pay it, they could expect his client to "press ahead with the full court process, including a jury trial if necessary." The O'Neills were more fortunate than a number of other accused families. A letter from a lawyer representing the family, stating that no one else in the family supports the claims and threatening a countersuit against the lawyer and Jane for filing a frivolous suit, has ended the matter of litigation for now.

This is a rather grim ending, and the tone may be misleading. The O'Neills are not going to be intimidated, but despite Jane's behavior, they all love her dearly. Though Jane will have no contact with the parents, the siblings are all still in touch with her, and Jane has been able to respond at important times, such as when her father was in the hospital's intensive care unit, critically ill. Among accused families, they have done best tolerating one another other's viewpoints and not allowing this crisis to harden into bitter enmity.

I'm going to give Donald, the brother who didn't want to be interviewed, the last word here. Taciturn, he very succinctly told me about his family from his perspective. "Everything in my family was fine as far as I'm concerned. I was a happy kid, and I'm raising happy kids. I don't want to say anything that will hurt anybody. We've all tried talking about this, and it doesn't seem to help. It just gets everybody more upset. I love my dad, I love my mom, and I love my sister, too. You can quote me on that."

A CHANGING VIEW

Many retractors are "adult children" of alcoholics, and many of their parents quit drinking before being accused. Nonetheless, there seems to be a lag in forgiveness. It is almost as if the adult children don't feel free to get angry until the parents acknowledge their own alcoholism. Before they can forgive, the accusing daughters need to express their anger. The way this is played out in reality is that while the parent was behaving abominably, no one said anything, but as soon as parents begin to clean up their act, they are hit with twenty years worth of pent-up anger and criticism.

How an "adult child" feels toward and perceives her parents is not always reflective of current reality, or reality of any time past. As an experiment I asked a number of retractors to fill out a set of three parent-evaluation forms to reflect how they believe they would have described their parents before their "memories," during their period of belief in the accusation, and after they realized the memories were false.

In Chapter Four, Carol, the retractor whose infant daughter's life-threatening illness sparked the anxiety that sent Carol into therapy, was the adult child of an alcoholic. Let's take a look at her changing view of her parents.

Before Carol had gotten "memories," she described her parents' strengths as follows: She often felt unconditional love and acceptance from her mother and sometimes from her father. However, they seldom paid enough attention to her needs for her to feel supported, encouraged, or secure. They were not quick to praise, but she always felt sure she would have her physical needs for food, clothing, and so on satisfied. On the down side, both her father and mother were frequently verbally abusive, and they both had drinking problems. Though they rarely used even mild corporal punishment, they sometimes had violent outbursts during which they were frighteningly enraged.

In the midst of Carol's therapy she saw her parents mainly in terms of black and white. She forgot all the positives and reported that she recalled that they *never* complimented her, boosted her confidence, acted in a consistent manner, encouraged her, or expressed their love. She begrudgingly admitted that they sometimes provided adequate physical care. She perceived her parents as both having been constantly verbally abusive, extremely violent, and sexually abusive. She had begun to believe that her parents had often hit her.

When I interviewed her, about a year after she had quit therapy and given up her memories, her beliefs about her parents were leaning more toward the middle on many things. She was able to admit again that they had always taken care of her physical needs, and she now saw them as sometimes exhibiting all the positive behaviors—that she had received as much encouragement, support, love, and praise as most children. Gone were the memories of physical and sexual abuse, though she did still believe that her parents had often been verbally abusive and did indeed have a drinking problem throughout her childhood. Though she had indicated in her first evaluation that her parents were sometimes extremely violent, she now believes they were never so. She seems to have gained more perspective and has less polarized thinking about the incidents of her childhood.

CAROL—LOOKING BACK

Carol told me,

"Whether I was, or was not, sexually abused as a child is not important to me anymore. I have things in my life right now that I need to work on, and I'm just going to stick to solving those problems. I need to learn to function. I still have a long way to go. I may have to work on this for the rest of my life. But what I want to work on is what concerns me now, and my future.

"I have three really good friends I can talk to, and I feel comfortable talking to my husband now. So that's where I get my support. I don't need a support group. I just want to take care of my family. I'm back in school, and I'm working on improving my life. When I hear the words 'support group' or 'recovery,' I just want to throw up. As far as I'm concerned, that's for people who want to be sick. I want to be well.

"I've never told my parents I thought they had sexually abused me, and I don't ever intend to. I want to be anonymous so they never have to know I believed such awful things about them. They're elderly, and they're not well. They don't need to know about those kind of things. That's the last thing I want them to hear during their last years. They don't drink anymore, and they don't deserve to suffer. I've been closer to my parents since I contacted [FMS]. I look at them as two adults who have their faults just like anybody else, and I can forgive them for it.

"The people at the False Memory Syndrome Foundation were just great when I called them. They told me, 'We understand what happened to you. We've heard this story before, and you're not alone. It's OK to question, so you can decide whether or not you really are an incest survivor. You are the only one who knows the answer to that. It's up to you to make that decision.'

"And when they validated my power to make that decision, I suddenly knew that my instincts had been right all along. It helped so much to know that I was not the only one who had thought that of their parents. FMS didn't tell me what to do. I had needed someone just to help me understand that my parents weren't perfect, but that's OK. Life is hard, and that's OK too. We all go through stages, and some are difficult, and some are wonderful, but if we just hang in there, the bad times will pass. Your parents had their stages too. My parents shouldn't have drunk so much. They made some mistakes, and I'm making my mistakes as a parent now.

"I needed someone to sit me down and tell me that I couldn't expect life to be wonderful all the time. Talking about bad stuff all the time isn't what makes bad stuff go away. Instead, you need to say, 'This is really bad, but I've got to get on with my life.' "

SUMMARY POINTS

1. The relationship between parent and child is a two-way street. A child's inborn temperament and sensitivities may minimize or exaggerate reactions to parental failings. Regardless of the reality, how the child *perceives* the parent/child relationship significantly influences the child's entire life view.

2. A therapist who assures the client that none of the conflict was his or her fault takes away half of the client's resources for healing. This robs the client of his or her sense of mastery over life, leaving the client feeling helpless and dependent upon the therapist to guide the way out.

3. While the inability to form relationships is usually rooted in early childhood experiences, especially with the primary caretaker, an exaggerated overemphasis on the parent/child interaction during early childhood carries with it the implication that any harm we suffered twenty years ago has left us irreparably damaged.

4. A good therapist desires to help her clients solve their own problems and to find strength within themselves. A poor therapist desires to solve the client's problems personally and encourages the client to draw strength from the therapist, leading to an unhealthy dependency. In this case, the client will never feel ready to "solo," to face life without the constant support and reassurance of the therapist.

5. Everyone has "boundaries," personal containing walls that healthy people build around their bodies and different areas of their lives. Defining and respecting appropriate "boundaries," emotional and physical, are important for the client and the therapist.

6. Alcoholics, on the whole, tend to make poor parents. False accusations of sexual abuse may be an expression of pent-up anger over very real damage suffered during childhood.

7. Why would anyone believe anything so painful as being sexually abused by a parent if it weren't true?
- It's easier to blame someone else than to acknowledge personal failings and responsibilities. Personal change is difficult but worth the effort.

TWELVE

Guilty Until
Proven Innocent

*This is the most important statement that needs to be
brought out in your book: Had she gotten into the
hands of proper medical care, she could have been
treated early on.*

—BOB GRIFFITH, an accused father

IN 1990, CHRISTY GRIFFITH, then age thirty-five, began calling old
family friends, neighbors, relatives, law enforcement agencies, and child-
protective services in Arizona, West Virginia, and Illinois in an attempt
to corroborate her "recovered repressed memories" of childhood sexual
abuse. She told people with whom she talked that she intended to sue her
parents. During the next year the charges expanded to include drug abuse,
satanic rituals, and murder. On October 3, 1991, Bob and Lorna Griffith, a
retired couple in their sixties who had raised five children, received a
certified letter from an attorney in Arizona offering to negotiate a financial
settlement for injuries they had allegedly perpetrated on their daughter
when she was a child. The parents, who had by then retired to West
Virginia, had lived in Arizona with their children during most of Christy's
childhood.

About six weeks later, the Griffiths received notice that Christy had
filed her lawsuit against them in a civil action in federal district court in
Arizona. The nine pages of charges were extremely detailed and covered a
period of thirty years; The charges included alleged abuse that was still
occurring when Christy was a married adult and mother living a thousand
miles away from her parents! (She stated that her father had followed her

on her drive home and raped her en route. However, toll charges to the Griffiths' phone in West Virginia showed that Bob Griffith was at home on the phone with her at the time of the rape.)

In February 1992, Bob and Lorna each received a summons from the daughter's attorney in Arizona. The Griffiths' attorney advised them to get an attorney in Arizona who would be familiar with that state's laws and procedures. Though they were required to send this attorney a $1,000 retainer, they were relieved to learn that the situation should be covered by the homeowner's insurance policy they had at the time the alleged assaults took place. Initially, the insurance company tried to deny responsibility, stating that the policy did not cover rape, murder, or cannibalism, but the Griffiths countered with the argument that they had committed none of these crimes and so were being threatened with a frivolous suit.

While the daughter applied for extension after extension, the Griffiths began compiling any evidence they could find to prove they could not have committed the alleged crimes. They got affidavits from the other four children, and from twenty-five friends and neighbors, and dug out photographs and home movies that showed, for example, that the daughter could not have given birth to a baby at age eleven, as she had claimed. They worked night and day searching out report cards, family history, genealogy, awards, activity cards, church records, employment records, medical records, and hundreds of letters Christy had written to them that showed she had been a loving, caring daughter before she began therapy in 1989, shortly after the birth of her first baby. Bob explains, "We were able to show we are a perfectly normal, hard-working, God-fearing, church-oriented American family . . . not likely to have been involved in satanic cult worship, drug abuse, murder, cannibalism, and other depravities."[1]

As Christy's accusations expanded to cover a wider time frame, another insurance company was brought into the defense. The Griffiths drove 2,000 miles to Arizona to meet with their attorney and the two attorneys representing the insurance companies. The attorneys had borrowed *The Courage to Heal* from the library at the Griffiths' suggestion and had concluded that the issue had more to do with pernicious influences than it did with the guilt of the Griffiths. Christy had sent the Griffiths her copy of *The Courage to Heal* with certain pages underlined to show her parents what she believed they had done to her.

About this time, the Griffiths learned about the FMS Foundation (from a childhood friend whom Christy had reported to child-protective services after the friend would not acknowledge or support Christy's case against her parents) and began to collect articles on false memory phenomena. Christy kept updating and expanding her account of their atrocities, and it now numbered about twenty-five pages. The Griffiths combed her treatise for contradictions that they could prove with their collection of school records, pediatric records, and so forth.

In July 1992, Christy's attorney wrote them a letter stating that Christy was willing to settle out of court, but the insurance companies declined. By September 1992, the Griffiths and their insurance companies had involved in their case six different attorneys and a federal district judge, in addition to the daughter's lawyer. The Griffiths' attorney had demanded that the daughter produce all of her therapy records. She had begun therapy after a lengthy and difficult labor with the birth of her first child. During the following three and a half years, she had seen six different therapists, attended group therapy, joined support groups for "survivors" of incest and childhood sexual abuse, read volumes of self-help books, and traveled to two different states to see specialists who gave tests to "survivors" of satanic rituals. The Griffiths' attorney had gotten an order for the daughter to be examined and evaluated by a psychiatrist.

On September 29, 1992, Christy called the Griffiths' attorney and offered to drop the charges. Her attorney had advised her to offer to dismiss *with prejudice* if the Griffiths' insurance companies agreed not to sue her for the expenses they had incurred. (*With prejudice* means that the case can never be reopened.) On October 5, 1992, the charges against the Griffiths were dismissed, and though they were relieved, they were not happy. Mr. Griffith wrote,

> "We would like to have had the lawsuit proceed past the point where our daughter would have had to provide her therapy records. We would like to have known who it was that convinced our daughter that we had sexually abused her as a child, tortured her, taken part in satanic rituals and murdered babies.
>
> "We would like to have had our daughter evaluated by the psychiatrist that our attorney had selected. We had hoped the psychiatrist could have made a proper diagnosis and could have advised a proper course of treatment."[2]

Bob is a former hospital administrator who spent some twenty years with the medical community, looking at issues of malpractice and how to ensure that patients are getting proper care. He told me,

"We've studied this very carefully. She was thirty-three when she had her baby. She was in labor for fifty-six hours, and immediately after that she started showing some paranoid behavior. Within a few months we noticed some delusions. In addition to the complicated delivery, the baby got pneumonia and had to be hospitalized for an additional ten days or so. Christy was stressed out from the delivery and with the baby being in the hospital. While the baby was still in the hospital she was accusing the nurses of drugging the baby. To me it seems obvious she had some kind of serious postpartum depression that should have been taken care of with medication. Had she gotten into the hands of proper medical care, she could have been treated.

"When she visited us some six months later, she got me aside to question whether I had gotten our maid pregnant when we were in the Philippines. Christy would have been what, four or five years old then? And she had a very clear memory of our maid being pregnant, having the baby, and all this sort of thing. In fact, the maid was never pregnant. That was for certain a delusion, and none of this, we never saw any of this prior to her delivery. So I would say that was the beginning."

ANSWER FOURTEEN

Why would anyone believe anything so painful as being sexually abused by a parent if it weren't true?

ANSWER NUMBER FOURTEEN: Because she has an undiagnosed mental condition, such as postpartum depression, that has impaired the "adult child's" judgment and made it difficult for her to accept appropriate help.

LACK OF REGULATIONS FOR THERAPISTS

Though most therapists are well qualified in their chosen specialties, there are incompetent therapists working in many areas. This is true of any profession, even skilled laborers.

It is likely that sexual abuse treatment has attracted more than its fair share of incompetent therapists. This has happened for a number of reasons that interrelate. First, the need for sexual abuse therapists has been hyped up due to mass hysteria. Counseling services are being flooded with requests, both privately and through social services. In order to provide enough therapists, services have had to lower their standards. I constantly hear reports of (and from) counselors-in-training who are not getting adequate supervision.

Second, there is a lot of funding for sexual abuse victims, so that's where the jobs are. People who might have enough skill and training to handle career counseling or other transitional problems (not covered by insurance) have taken jobs where the money is and may be in over their heads. For-profit hospitals have realized the money to be made in programs for "recovering" sexual abuse victims. Those working for the hospitals are pressured to keep the beds filled. Marketing people go out and sell the hospital, and, consciously or unconsciously, the staff therapists who do intake interviews know that they are expected to find enough evidence of severe emotional distress to grant the patient entry into the program. The myths that have grown up about sexual abuse in terms of severe and long-lasting damage have made it a diagnosis that usually serves to justify insured hospital stays for Post-traumatic Stress Disorder (PTSD), Multiple Personality Disorder (MPD), or other disorders that are said to need long-term intensive in-patient treatment. In addition, clients are commonly told that recovery from sexual abuse takes five years or more of outpatient treatment. This guarantees steady income for a therapist for quite a while.

Third, books like *The Courage to Heal* that present an oversimplified understanding of the problems of sexual abuse make it look easy to do sexual abuse therapy. New therapists in the area may fail to look at the big picture because they are so preoccupied with learning the fascinating techniques for recovering memories, bringing out "alters," or cracking the codes of satanic cults. Also, it is very common for victims of sexual abuse to become counselors in sexual abuse programs. A poll taken at the Eastern Regional Conference on Abuse and Multiple Personality found that well over half of the therapists working with "survivors" consider themselves to be survivors of sexual abuse. Many also considered themselves to be survivors of satanic ritual abuse.

Some psychology professionals argue that therapists should not try to work with clients who have been diagnosed with the same disorder that the therapist has had because the therapist will have greater difficulty being objective. Others believe that the only therapist who can truly help the sexually abused is a therapist who has been sexually abused herself. There is some merit in both sides of this argument, but I think the best choice might be a therapist who has not been abused but has worked with many clients who have been. He or she would have the best grasp on the problem while being able to keep some professional objectivity.

Because there are now too many therapists who have slipped into practice without adequate supervision or licensure controls, I believe the rate of error has skyrocketed. Add to this a sense of crusade on the part of many of these therapists, and we have a terrible mess.

PRESERVING YOUR SANITY

Though I will present detailed advice on how to select a good therapist in a later chapter, I would like to suggest a few cautions here and briefly explore what can be lost when therapy goes wrong. As we saw earlier with Aileen, who was encouraged to call her therapist every night, her personal losses were great during her misguided therapy. She lost six years of her life—years that she could have spent building her career (she'd been accepted into a prestigious program and had to drop out); years that she could have spent guiding, nurturing, and enjoying her children; her last few years with her mother; time that she should have spent trying to save her marriage—and a great deal of money that her whole family needed.

I understand the retractors' sense of loss. I too lost years of productivity because my therapists assumed they knew more than they did. When I married in 1975, my therapist had told my husband I would always have terrible mood swings and nothing could be done about it. In fact, something could be done about it, but the therapist was not up on the latest research. Anti-depressant medication was available then, but it would be another ten years before anyone would prescribe it for me.

When therapists fail to widen their vision and expertise through continuing-education courses in new areas of research, they may go on using the least effective methods available and may fail to diagnose properly. If a therapist has only enough time to keep up in his or her specialty, then he or she should make it a point to work in a group practice that includes therapists in other specialties.

What are some basic principles you should keep in mind when selecting a therapist?

CAUTIONS!

1. Ask the therapist to explain his or her credentials. Is she a counselor, psychotherapist, social worker, psychologist, or psychiatrist?

2. Go to a group that has a variety of specialists and uses a psychiatrist as a consultant when making a diagnosis.

3. Avoid any therapist who advertises as a specialist in sexual abuse unless you have always remembered being sexually abused.

4. Be wary of joining any kind of "survivor" group, especially a self-help group that is not run or advised by a licensed therapist.

5. Don't agree to hospitalization unless you can establish that you are free to check out at any time if you don't feel the program is benefiting you.

Some of the reasoning behind these cautions needs little explanation, but I'll elaborate on each of them briefly. It is not commonly known that licensing rules for therapists vary greatly from state to state. A *credential* for training, such as hypnotic techniques, is not a license, and can often mean very little in terms of expertise. Credentials are commonly handed out at seminars where "experts" address an audience of hundreds. The experts may have no direct contact with the student, but the student takes home a certificate and receives continuing-education credit for nothing more than attendance.

In order to obtain a *license* the therapist has to take certain courses, pass a test, and be closely supervised for the first year or so. However, the license can represent many, widely varying levels of competence. School counselors, social workers, para-professionals, nurses, and psychologists all can obtain licenses from their respective professions. Ask your therapist what he or she was required to do for the license.

Be aware that *psychotherapists* may have no training whatsoever. The term psychotherapist does not indicate the depth or breadth of education. It is just a euphemism, a professional-sounding word that was made up to make therapists, counselors, and advisers of any kind sound more knowledgeable. There is no governing body of psychotherapists regulating who may use that title. It is only *psychologists* who have a doctorate in psychology, and *psychiatrists* who are medical doctors and also have the equivalent of a doctorate in psychology.

Do not go to a therapist who specializes in a certain disorder unless you have been previously diagnosed by a psychiatrist or psychologist who has a more general practice. We all tend to see what we are looking for. If you really want an objective opinion on what is wrong with you, don't seek out a narrowly trained person, whether his training is in alcoholism, codependency, eating disorders, sexual abuse, or anything else.

Be cautious about joining any kind of survivor group. As we heard from Melody, who started her own group for survivors of sexual abuse, all you need to do is hang up a sign. There is no guarantee that anyone in such a group is any healthier than you are, and if the group does not have good leadership, it can be very damaging.

Finally, don't agree to go into a hospital program until you understand what the rules are about leaving. As mentioned earlier, many retractors were convinced that they could not leave undesirable hospital programs without becoming responsible for thousands of dollars in hospital debts. This is generally not true. One may leave "against medical advice" and the insurance will most often pay up to the day when you leave. Individual policies may differ, so you should become familiar with what yours provides for. You have a right to know, before you go in, just what pressures you will be facing.

THE GRIFFITH HOME

The Griffith kids described a warm, secure childhood, filled with wholesome activities. The family went camping, rock hunting, bowling, and on Scout outings and sat around a dinner table every night talking over their day. They were a military family: the up side was that they had a secure family income that put all the kids through college, but the down side was continuously having to uproot themselves and make all new friends. The Griffiths had lived in twelve different places in twenty-three years while the kids were growing up.

THE GRIFFITH FAMILY

Mother: Lorna, Age 64   Father: Bob, Age 63

Marty	Tracey	Christy*	Chuck
Age 44	Age 41	Age 39	Age 36

*The accusing daughter.

I was able to interview Christy, the accusing daughter, but she requested that I not use her interview. I will just mention that when I had asked Christy how she perceived her family before she had "recovered memories," her description was very similar to her siblings'. Christy, too, painted a picture of parents involved with their children in wholesome activities. Christy even admitted to having adored her dad.

Chuck, the youngest brother, told me, "In comparison with other families, I thought we really had our stuff together. Dad is a professional person; we had money for anything we wanted, and compared to my peers, my parents did a better job of providing for us. There was no alcohol or any problems like that. My dad managed to support three of us in college at the same time. I felt really fortunate."

Tracy, Christy's older sister, confirmed that the only excess in terms of discipline was when her mom went a little overboard with the technique she says she learned from the Catholic Church: shaming. "It got to be for me and my brothers that we could shame ourselves. I didn't want to feel that awful feeling, so I walked a narrow, straight, rigid line and never veered off this path of righteousness. But my sister, Christy, was never affected by shaming."

Tracy remembers using a similar method on her father with great success: "While I was in high school my father had a really crazy boss. He'd come home stressed out, and he'd want a drink. Little Suzy Homemaker that I was, I'd make him a drink. I thought it was really cool for a few days. Then it seemed to me that he wanted a drink every day. I got upset and told him I didn't think it was good for him, and he quit. He honored my request. I think they tried real hard to be good parents."

Tracy and Christy were close friends as well as sisters throughout their early childhood, but Christy became such a rebel in high school that Tracy no longer had anything in common with her. "I don't think my parents knew how to deal with her," Tracy commented. "They probably should have come down real hard on her. When she got caught smoking pot in her bedroom, they were as confused as the rest of us."

The Griffiths confirmed that Christy was more difficult than the other children, but they never thought of her as being deviant. "My mother often said that Christy was different," Bob, the father, recalls. But he and his wife, Lorna, didn't make much of it. Lorna told me, "She didn't really do anything that bad, and we just thought, well, you know, she's different, didn't want to conform, didn't want to listen to us, but she didn't do any of the bad things. And the others were such model children, we didn't think it was fair to compare her with them."

"Christy was more outspoken," Bob added. "If someone would make a suggestion, she'd be the one that said there's another way to do it. But she got real good grades like the rest of them, so we just let her little rebellions go by."

Both Chuck and Tracy remember that when the family moved from Arizona to West Virginia, Christy seemed hit the hardest by the move. "She had established some real bonded friendships in Arizona," Tracy recalls. "Then West Virginia was a real culture shock. We'd come from Tucson, a fair-sized city with a very liberal population, and there we were in the hills, in a real rural community where people are not very sophisticated."

The college the girls attended in West Virginia was disappointing, too. Both girls felt a campus in Arizona would have been much more exciting. Christy seemed to go about creating her own excitement. "In high school she had been Miss Popular," Tracy told me, "but by the time she got to college she was kind of a hippy. She was doing drugs. One time I asked her how many men there had been, and she told me it was around ninety. She said she fell in love with every single one of them. She thought every one of them would be, I don't know, maybe Prince Charming. And every single one of them broke her heart."

Everyone in the family also agreed that though Christy was a rebel in the context of the family, she was a follower among her friends. She didn't seem to be able to think for herself or risk ever disagreeing with her crowd.

EXPANDING ACCUSATIONS

In November 1989, one year after the birth of her baby, Christy had her first "memories" of being sexually abused by her father.

At that point Bob was the only one who had been accused, and his other children were searching their hearts and their memories trying to determine if their father could have possibly abused their sister. But when the siblings did not rally unconditionally to Christy's side, she began to strike out at the larger circle. Chuck told me,

"I was almost starting to believe her. She was talking about repressed memories. She thought maybe she was abused, and every time we talked she was more positive. It was beginning to seem possible, up until the point where she accused me. If she hadn't accused me, there would always have been some doubt in my mind.

[Chuck was living in California with his wife and children at this time. He recalled: "In early 1990 she called and said she might have been abused. Then she was sure she was abused. We spoke on the phone a number of times, and it seemed we were getting closer. She asked if she could put me in her will as a guardian for her daughter.

"She was trying to elicit my support, or at least confirm that I had been abused. I couldn't confirm that for her. Then she called Child Protective Services (CPS) in San Joaquin County, California, and also the local police, accusing me of having abused my own children. That was the end of that. I haven't talked to her since. I felt betrayed, and I don't think I'll ever forgive her for that."

Fortunately, Child Protective Services (CPS) was circumspect. CPS representatives talked to the children at their school first and then made a home visit. The CPS people were quickly satisfied that there was no evidence of abuse. However, Christy had not only called CPS about her brothers, Marty and Chuck, and her sister, Tracy, to report them for child abuse, she also called the police in each town to inform them that her siblings and parents were all members of a satanic cult and had murdered people. "She called and had us investigated by the West Virginia State Police Criminal Investigation Division," her father told me. "She'd even called the FBI to report her memories of me murdering and burying people here on the farm. As a matter of fact she even told them exactly where the bodies were buried. A friend of ours on the police force told us that the FBI did actually come and look for the bodies."

INTERGENERATIONAL ABUSE

The notion of intergenerational abuse has been behind many painful accusations among family members. Unfortunately, those who rant about the intergenerational nature of abuse don't seem to have looked at the studies. Though it is true that many, if not most, parents who abuse their children were also abused as children, it is not true that most parents who were abused as children will abuse their own. In fact, the majority do not.

However, the belief that abuse runs in families, more often than not, has set sibling against sibling.

DILEMMAS FACING SIBLINGS

1. GUILT AND CONFUSION OVER WHO TO BELIEVE

a. The sibling is their peer. The kids traditionally stick together in a family. Their first impulse is to believe the sib, not the parent.

b. They are exposed to the same media hype about sexual abuse and have become preconditioned to accept any accusation of sexual abuse no matter how improbable.

c. If other troubles have existed in the family, such as alcoholism or violence, the siblings are even more prone to believe an accusation.

d. They can feel "crazy" no matter what. If the abuse is true, how could they have missed it? If the abuse is not true, how could they have allowed themselves to be swayed to believe it?

e. Whatever position they take, they will be betraying someone they love.

2. ANXIETY ABOUT HOW TO ACT

a. If they do not believe the sibling and they say so, the sibling may cut off all contact with the family.

b. If they do not challenge the sibling's accusation, they collude in supporting the sibling's distorted reality, perhaps prolonging their illness.

c. If they do not challenge the sibling's accusation, the parents may feel the remaining sibs are failing to be supportive of them at a crucial time.

d. If they do challenge the sibling's accusation, that sibling may accuse them of abuse, or report them to child protective services for the inevitable "intergenerational abuse."

e. If they do not give "testimony" to their belief in the parents' innocence, extended family may take the accusing sibling's story as truth.

f. If the sibling is suicidal, there is the fear that any challenge will push them over the edge. If the parent has failing health at the same time, it is a treacherous no-win situation.

g. If they tell others outside the family about the situation, they help spread the rumors. If they don't tell, they look as though they are hiding a family secret.

In the case of the Griffiths, social workers and police were mobilized in three states to respond to groundless accusations of sexual abuse. This is not an uncommon story among families. No wonder social workers do not have time to get to all the children who are really being abused! In one family the children were actually taken away, abruptly pulled out of the home without warning. It was a warm, caring home, and the children, both under ten, were terrified by the procedure. It took three months for the wheels of child-protective services to turn and slowly complete the investigation that allowed the parents to have the children back. The daughter, four years old, was traumatized by this. Once outgoing, she came home withdrawn and always on edge. How did this tragedy get set in motion? A sister who had recovered "repressed memories" had reported them, though she had not seen the children in years.

There is great potential for children to be traumatized by some of these "good" intentions. At the very least, sex must be a hideous monster to them. On the news, they hear about people dying from sexual contact (for example, from AIDS), and worried parents read them books about being molested. In accused families children invariably witness tense arguments about alleged sexual contact. To the child's eyes sex becomes dangerous, frightening, and painful. At the same time, the child has lost all perspective about what is normal sexual behavior.

Lucille, the sibling of another retractor, explained a conflict she had had with an accusing sib over their children:

"I have a ten-year-old boy, and she has a seven-year-old boy. She thinks that my son sexually abused her son, so she doesn't allow her kids around my kids anymore. Her little boy is really hyper.

"This happened about two years ago. She asked her little boy, 'Bobby, did anybody ever touch your private parts?' And she said that he said, 'Kevin does: he rubs me up and down.' Now I don't know what my son did, if anything, but kids touch each other sometimes. My husband and I were so worried about this, we had a meeting with our pediatrician about it.

"The pediatrician said it was totally normal; you wouldn't believe the things that kids do. Jessica thinks that my father abused Kevin when he was an infant, abused her kids when they were infants, and that they're all running around abusing one another now. She thinks my son has major problems.

"Kevin says Bobby's lying. He did admit to taking the little girl next door into the toy room and making her lift up her dress because they were playing doctor. He told me a few things like that, but he never touched Bobby. Jessica says he's a masterful liar.

"Then, I caught my little girl playing doctor with another little girl. My little girl was telling this other little girl to put this doll inside her vagina. I got all upset, thinking, 'What if Jessica's right?' So we made an appointment with a child psychologist who's an expert on child sexual abuse. He said the same thing as my pediatrician: 'You wouldn't believe the things we have to pull out of little girls.' They put things here and there; it doesn't mean they were sexually abused. My husband said, 'You won't be satisfied until you prove your kids have been sexually abused.' I was getting nuts about it. It's real easy to fall into.

"I got this little coloring book about bad touching, and I went over it with Kevin. I said, 'Kevin, has anybody ever touched you? If anybody does, tell Mommy.' He had nightmares for two nights after that. There was stuff in there about not talking to strangers. I just decided to leave him alone."

THE CHILD SEXUAL BEHAVIOR INVENTORY

What sexual behaviors are common and normal in children? The increase in interest in childhood sexual abuse has spurred some new research into children's sexuality. Dr. William H. Friedrich and Dr. Patricia Grambsch, both from the Mayo Clinic, headed up a study of 880 children, ages two to twelve, who had never been sexually abused to see what sexual behaviors normally occur in children. A checklist called the Child Sexual Behavior Inventory (CSBI) was used to determine at what age children exhibit certain sexual behaviors, and how common each behavior is in children who haven't been sexually abused. Later, this sample of unmolested children was compared with a study of 276 known sexually abused children by using the CSBI again.[3]

I have constructed the following chart using their research, which shows how behaviors range from most common to least common. Behaviors are listed in descending order of frequency and are broken into smaller categories by the percentage of children (boys and girls combined) who engage in the activities:

CHILD SEXUAL BEHAVIOR[4]

Column I   *Column II*

MOST COMMON

About 50 to 65 percent of all children
- Are shy with strange men.
- Walk around in underwear.
- Walk around nude.
- Play with opposite-sex toys.
- Scratch their crotches.
- Touch genitalia at home.
- Undress in front of others.

[Percentage among sexually abused children who exhibit these behaviors: about 40 to 50 percent]

About 20 to 40 percent
- Are shy about undressing.
- Sit with crotch exposed.
- Kiss nonfamily adults.
- Kiss nonfamily children.
- Touch breasts.
- Try to look at people undressing.
- Are interested in the opposite sex.

[Percentage among sexually abused children: about 30 to 50 percent]

About 10 to 20 percent
- Touch genitalia in public.
- Show genitalia to adults.
- Look at nude pictures.
- Masturbate with hand.
- Pretend to be opposite sex.
- Stand too close.
- Talk flirtatiously.
- Are overly aggressive, or overly passive.

[Percentage among sexually abused children: about 15 to 40 percent]

About 5 to 10 percent
- Use sexual words.
- Show genitalia to children.
- Hug strange adults.
- Are overly friendly with strange men.
- Rub body against people.
- Touch others' genitalia.
- Dress like the opposite sex.
- Talk about sexual acts.
- Want to be the opposite sex.
- Imitate sexual behavior with dolls (girls).
- Ask to watch sexually explicit television (boys).

[Percentage among sexually abused children: about 10 to 40 percent]

Fewer than 3 percent
- Undress other people.
- French-kiss.
- Make sexual sounds.
- Imitate intercourse.
- Insert objects in vagina/anus.
- Masturbate with object.
- Ask to engage in sex acts.
- Put mouth on genitalia.

[Percentage among sexually abused children: about 10 to 25 percent]

LEAST COMMON

The most important thing to remember about this chart is that all of these behaviors are displayed by some children who have never been sexually abused, so that none of these behaviors are certain indicators of sexual abuse. Only in the last two categories (Column II) is there any significant difference between the number of children who have not been sexually abused and those who have been. We can see that the behaviors in the last two groups are displayed much more often by children who have been sexually abused, so they might serve as warning signs.

CHILDREN'S SEXUALITY

According to Jeffrey Victor, sociologist and author of *Human Sexuality: A Social Psychological Approach*, the United States is one of the most sexually restrictive societies in the world. Our customs are still influenced by Victorian beliefs that children should be protected from knowledge about sex. Victor's book was written in 1980, when practices such as masturbation were just beginning to be accepted in children after a century of severe restriction. Child-rearing books of the 1800s warned that masturbation would result in insanity and advised parents to tie the child's legs to opposite sides of the crib so that he couldn't rub his thighs together and possibly stimulate himself!

Meanwhile, out in the East Arctic, Inuit (Eskimo) children are encouraged to experiment with sexual intercourse when they are five years old. Researchers who have studied more sexually open societies have found that during childhood sexual activities often follow a sequential pattern that leads to intercourse. Sexual play among children begins with self-stimulation and moves on to mutual masturbation with a partner, and then on to attempts at heterosexual intercourse. In some societies, parents even tutor children in how to achieve sexual pleasure. The parents believe that children must practice sex so that they will have a satisfying adult sex life.[5] We in America believe in practicing many other activities that our children engage in—from washing the dishes to playing an instrument—so why do we find sexual practice so shocking in our children?

Dr. Harold Lief, Emeritus Professor of Psychiatry at the University of Pennsylvania, has expertise in human sexuality and its effect on mental health. During a telephone interview he spoke of a very interesting set of cross-cultural studies that had been done by James Prescott of the University of Buffalo. Prescott discovered that in societies where there is an absence of sexual rehearsal in childhood, where there are the most repressive sexual customs for children, there is also the most violence. Sexually permissive societies have the least violence.[6]

Victor defines common sexual behavior for children at various ages and stages. Infant boys commonly have erections, and infant girls experience vaginal lubrication. According to Kinsey, children are capable of achieving orgasm at age five, though boys do not ejaculate. It is not surprising to learn that masturbation is much more common in boys, age four to fourteen, than in girls. One study of children, age three to six, found that only 14 percent of the girls knew a word for the female genitals, but many of them knew a boy had a *penis* . One interesting research project compared the sex knowledge of American seven-year-olds with that of Swedish seven-year-olds. None of the American children knew about sexual intercourse, but all of the Swedish children did. While the Swedish children's illustrations of where babies come from showed pictures of parents cuddling in bed, the American children showed frightening scenes of doctors brandishing long knives, at the ready to cut the baby out of mommy's tummy.[7]

Even in the best of times American parents have been anxious about their children's sexuality and reluctant to discuss sex with their children. Children sense this anxiety and often feel shamed if they are caught masturbating. There really is no acceptable form of sexual expression for children in our society. It isn't any wonder that parents interpret normal sexual behavior in children to be signs of sexual abuse.

Our panicked, anxious, fearful responses to our children's sexual play, which has been heightened by the sexual abuse scare, are certain to have a very negative effect on the sexuality of the next generation. It's certainly having an immediate effect on the role models—school professionals— whom our children observe in the place where kids spend so many of their waking hours.

Beth Hansen, the sibling of an accusing daughter, is also a school counselor, and she has seen the effect of the Sexual Abuse Recovery Movement in the schools: "I work in an elementary school, and I've been advised not even to hold a kid's hand walking down a hall. I told my professor, 'Look, I work with kindergartners, first and second graders. They want to hold your hand. What if they take my hand?' And my professor said, 'Don't take it. Drop their hand.'

"I can't hug them or touch them. Finally, this year I decided that I refuse to sit in a room with a child who's crying and not give him a hug or comfort him in some way. I have a million dollars' liability insurance. If I get called on the carpet for giving the kid a hug, I'm just going to do that."

What a sterile world, where simple displays of affection are suspect.

PARENTING TIPS

Dr. Lief offered some perspectives and advice to parents who are trying to negotiate the muddy waters of physical care of their children and "bad touching." To begin with, Lief explained, there are two factors that come into play when one is trying to determine what action by a parent might be sexually abusive: (1) violation of the child's boundaries and (2) sexual arousal in the parent. Some people would interpret hugging, kissing, touching, and caressing as an invasion of the child's boundary, while others would see this as simple affection or attachment. If one of the child's orifices is penetrated, you've got an obvious case of sexual abuse, but when it comes to caressing it's a much grayer area.

Whether it is a violation depends on the intent of the parent and the perception of the child, but even if we could know what is inside each of their heads, we would still not have a clear-cut case. An adult may have sexual intent that a child doesn't recognize; like a tree falling in an empty forest, is it sexual abuse if the abused doesn't think so? On the other hand, an adult may intend no sexual abuse, but the child might perceive the behavior as a violation.

Such ambiguous situations lend themselves to the greatest risk of misinterpretation in therapy twenty years later. If a child never interpreted sleeping with her father after her parents divorced (simply lying there cuddling with no sexual contact whatsoever) as sexual abuse, but a therapist tells her it is incest, the whole impact of the experience can be changed by this relabeling.

"There are so many instances that can be open to different interpretations," Dr. Lief told me. "The parents walk around nude, or the parent and child may take a bath together, and it may be perfectly innocent, but a therapist with a certain mind-set might reinterpret it as abuse. The therapist needs to try to understand the basic relationship between the parent and the child. Is it a loving one? You really have to do a motivational analysis of the experience."

Lief also gave an example of "emotional" or "covert" incest: "I remember treating a family where the father was very intrusive in asking his thirteen-year-old daughter about her sexual feelings—what she felt like when she was with boys, whether or not she masturbated. Even though he never touched her or fondled her, these probing questions were very intrusive. His whole attitude was such that he evoked feelings of sexual arousal and extreme discomfort in the child."

I asked Dr. Lief how he thought the sexual abuse focus currently in the media would affect the way parents today treat their children. "This whole thing through the eighties has made a lot of parents ultra-careful and inhibited about what might be natural behavior. Kissing, touching, cuddling are natural and vital to the child. A lot of families—I have no idea how many—restrain their spontaneous desires for physical affection."

Lief offers this advice: "If the child is clothed and you're just holding him, or hugging him, or holding him up in the air and swinging him around, it's natural and wholesome. A parent doesn't need to worry about changing an infant's diapers and cleaning the child's genitalia. However, if the parent finds himself or herself getting sexually aroused, that's a warning sign."

The parent should be guided by his or her own sexual reactions and also by the reactions of the child. If a preschool child looks over-stimulated, perhaps by the sight of a naked parent, then it's time to cover up. On the other hand, some reactions should not create alarm. It is perfectly natural for a baby or toddler-age boy to have erections while being bathed. The mother should just ignore this unless the child asks about it. What kind of response should the parent give?

"First of all, there should be naming of the organ. It should be called the penis, not the peewee, or whatever. Then the main thing is to say to the child that it's perfectly natural and normal, and every little boy has this experience, and let it go at that." If the parent does not feel aroused, there is no need to stop bathing the child.

Dr. Lief warns against overreacting to a child's sexual behaviors. A child should not be scolded or punished for masturbating. "You know they used to make kids wear mittens, tie their hands down when going to bed, that sort of thing. Kids play with themselves from birth on. During infancy I wouldn't take any notice of it at all. If the child is over two and it gets to be a nuisance, I would tell the child to do it in his bedroom so he doesn't embarrass others."

When judging displays of sexuality or deciding on rules about nudity, parents need to keep in mind the context and the individual child's personality. Dr. Lief recalled going to a nudist camp as a child and his shock at all the nudity around him since he was not used to it. "Most of the kids seemed to think nothing of it. And the chances are that they grew up feeling pretty good about their bodies. But I'm sure that some of the children were over-stimulated by that. It depends on the child's reaction. The point is that the mother or father and the child have to be comfortable with the situation. If you see signs of anxiety, then back off."

DOCUMENTED DELUSIONS

I was able to look at the third edition of Christy Griffith's history of abuse which she mailed out to all the relatives, neighbors, and friends to sound the alarm about her parents. She felt that all the people Bob and Lorna came in contact with should be warned about their "satanic cult activities" so that their children could be spared. Hence, she mailed out copies of a 59-page document chronicling all her alledged abuse in great detail. She began with a letter to the recipient explaining that the account she was sending proves that both her brother, Chuck, and her father are dangerous child molesters. (For the record, Chuck was eleven and Christy, fourteen, the first time he allegedly raped her.)

The book is divided into sections that cover each location where they lived. Though the location changes, not much else does. There are repetitive stories of her father taking her into a closet to rape her. The closet is usually located in the family room where everyone else is eating popcorn and watching television. They never notice the father and Christy slinking off to the closet. Neither does she comment on why she kept going to the closet without a fight or whimper. I think she must have come up with the bizarre scenario because her siblings had protested that they were always together, so when could it have happened? – The answer: It happened while we were all together, but you either didn't notice or chose not to intercede.

The table of contents of Christy's accusations has over one hundred entries, presented in chronological order from age three to about age thirty. Her first memory is a puzzling account of mom bringing Christy's baby brother, Chuck, home from the hospital. According to Christy, her sister, Tracy, informs her that the baby is Tracy's and Daddy's. Christy seems to think that is some sort of confession of the secret of her brother's birth, but Tracy would have only been five years old at the time.

The document rambles on and ends with present proofs of the abuse Christy and her siblings must have suffered as children. She enumerates all the symptoms of abuse she sees in herself and her grown siblings. I reprint below an excerpt from the proofs of Christy's earlier abuse:

"When alone, I feel paranoid, especially if I hear a sound like someone might be around that I can't see. I am always suspicious if I don't know what my husband is doing. I am always wondering if he is doing something sexual or having an affair.

"I have some phobias that are associated with the abuse. Being uncovered or partly uncovered at night makes me afraid that someone will grab that part of my body. Snakes, I have a phobia at times when I sit down on the toilet, that a snake or rat will come up and enter my body. Heights, I'm afraid that I will throw myself off. Sharp objects, I'm afraid that I will stab or cut someone else or myself.

"If something happens around the house that I can't explain, I misplace something or overlook something, I think my husband is deliberately trying to trick me, upset me or make me think I'm crazy.

"I have stomachaches and gas. I have headaches and sinus congestion. I get dizzy and have had blackouts. I have had severe menstrual cramps. My shoulders are permanently tense. All these stress-related disorders could be directly linked to the stress of child abuse."

We can see that Christy's "memories" do indeed show that she is fearful and suspicious, but there is nothing about her description that points to sexual abuse *per se*. These are common stress reactions coupled with an uncommon degree of paranoia. The final paragraph, which lists very mundane physical ailments, is offered as possible proof of her childhood sexual abuse. It sounds as if she has been doing reading on "body memories," a theory that links all physical twitches or discomforts to hidden memories of sexual abuse. In a study done by Susan E. Smith, author of *Survivor Psychology*, therapists linked the site of pain to an imagined, past, physical contact.[8] For example, menstrual cramps may be caused by the body's memory of candles being rammed up the vaginal opening in a satanic ritual.

THE SISTER'S STORY

Ironically, Christy's sister, Tracy, was the first in the family to go into therapy. Tracy's therapist also raised the issue of childhood sexual abuse, but she was not as pushy about it as Christy's therapist may have been. (Or perhaps, as Tracy speculates, Christy kept switching therapists—six in three years—because she couldn't find one who would unconditionally support her accusations.)

Tracy explained,

"I used to go to ACOA. I was never an 'adult child' of alcoholics; my parents weren't alcoholics, but I knew I was an 'adult child' of something. So I went. Incest is pretty big in that community. It's big with some therapists. I don't think people are running around incest-scared, like a witch hunt, but it is an issue that's discussed, because it is real; it has happened to a lot of women. I know nine women who really were incested.

"I had three years of therapy myself, following a divorce, and part of that process was trying to understand what was wrong with me. One of the questions I was asked, which is kind of typical with all women in therapy, was whether or not I was a victim of incest. I explored that issue with my sister. What do you remember? What happened? Could this have happened without our remembering?—things like that. She says that because of the conversations that we had, a seed was planted in her mind that triggered her memories.

"My therapist said things like, 'Other women whom I have known with your symptoms have been incest survivors. I wonder if you are.' Since she was someone that I had absolute trust in, I considered her questions very seriously. It became a question that I felt I had to have an answer to. I knew something was terribly wrong with me, but I didn't know what. Incest was the explanation that was offered to me. I had all the symptoms. It would explain why my life was so miserable, except that I had no memories of it at all.

"I knew that 'memories' aren't always reliable indicators of the truth; things do happen to people that they don't remember. So, if something is terribly wrong and you don't know why, you wonder if something horrible did happen that you don't remember.

"While in therapy, I did an enormous amount of very hard work, and now I'm a fairly healthy person. I explored every feeling, every memory, every detail of my past and present life, and, at the end of three years, I was done. If incest had been a reality, I would have known. I would have remembered.

"I have since found out what is wrong with me. I have a brain-chemistry imbalance that has been treated successfully with anti-depressants for three years now. I found the answer to the question, 'What is wrong with me?' For a long time, when life was so unbearable for me, I looked endlessly for the answer to that question.

"I think my sister is also looking for the answer to that question. When you are so desperate for relief from the pain, you look everywhere. It's an all-consuming thing. Every breathing moment you hunt for reasons why things are the way they are. The list in my head of what could have possibly gone wrong included all the people that I have ever known, all the traumas that ever happened. Of course that list included my father and my mother, as well as my husband, my kids, and everything and everybody else."

SURVIVOR PSYCHOLOGY

Susan E. Smith explores the way the recovery culture has contributed to the forming of a "survivor psychology" that is dangerously coercive in its methods. Formerly a personal-defense instructor who taught skills to many rape victims, Smith has long questioned the abuse of power. She considers the current methods being used by therapists to be a rape of the mind. As Smith sees it, "The seeds of victimization are sown in the destruction of emotional and intellectual boundaries. The first line of defense is knowing your own mind and retaining the ability to think critically. The slogan of the recovery movement is, 'Think with your heart, not with your head.' "[9]

The erosion of critical thinking in psychotherapy circles began with some of the absurd notions of recovery gurus like John Bradshaw, who cited bogus statistics off the top of his head. An entertaining orator who attracted thousands to recovery conferences all over the United States, Bradshaw didn't seem to feel any moral responsibility to differentiate fact from opinion for his listeners. He stated with authority that 95 percent of American families are dysfunctional and have the "soul murder" of their children as their main goal.

I remember watching this movement develop. It began with meetings for Adult Children of Alcoholics (ACOAs), but many other baby-boomers found that the "symptoms" of ACOAs also fit them. These meetings were the first to allow, and even encourage, nonprofessionals to attend what were billed as training seminars for therapists working with ACOAs. At an

ACOA conference I attended in San Francisco in 1990, at least a third of the audience were "adult children" who had come for personal-growth reasons. This inclusiveness, though seemingly very democratic, is a boundary violation that has served to inhibit the professional development of the therapists attending. As Sherrill Mulhern pointed out in her analysis of the social dynamics at satanic abuse training sessions, a therapist does not feel free to challenge the speaker's assumptions about satanic abuse if she knows that one-third of the people in the room are making the same assumptions.

The original, genuine ACOAs were the lucky ones. They earned the right to everyone's admiration for surviving years in an alcoholic home where they were physically neglected, emotionally abandoned, and beaten. They had real battle scars to which they could point.

Because alcohol consumption was a very popular pastime with parents in the '50s and '60s, those "adult children" who had had parents who drank moderately began to slip into the cozy definition of ACOAs when they became frustrated with life's disappointments. Baby-boomer "adult children" of nondrinking parents who never used corporal punishment began to feel very left out. They needed a link, a disease, a justification that would not only help them feel included with the ACOAs, but also explain their angst in this time of sociological and economic turmoil. Initially, it had been enough to claim you had grown up in a dysfunctional home, but when others told stories of their physical abuse and all you could report were disappointments such as never getting the roller skates you wanted when you were nine, some stronger excuse was needed.

Though the professed inclusiveness of the movement meant you would be welcome at the meetings, and it was standard rhetoric to recognize everyone's suffering, regardless of what they might have actually suffered, we all know a rubber snake when we see one. When the longing to be accepted met up with the lack of genuine hardship, hardships needed to be created. Sexual abuse was the "perfect crime." The purported amnesic nature of the trauma allowed for contradictions between one's former stories of growing up in middle-class privilege and the new stories of rediscovered, horrendous abuse that qualified one for top pity positions in the hierarchy of the wounded "adult children."

It was a new kind of midlife crisis. Baby boomers were coming up against the realization that their lives were half over, and they hadn't become great filmmakers, Nobel Prize winners, concert pianists, or astronauts and probably never would. Where former midlife sufferers had to come to terms with the fact that they weren't as bright or unique as they had once thought they were, baby-boomers dodged that psychological crisis by telling themselves that they would have become President of the United States if only their potential hadn't been pulverized by the trauma of childhood sexual abuse.

TRACY'S CONCLUSIONS

When Tracy Griffith asked herself, "What is wrong in my life?" and faced up to the reality of her human limitations, as millions before her have had to do, she gave up the easy out of being able to say it was all her parents' fault. She told me,

"I am able to make a definitive statement to myself about the truth: Incest didn't happen. Even though we don't remember everything that has happened in our past, we can make decisions about it using the best information we have. I spent a month at my parent's house this summer, and then my parents came to see me. I spent a lot of time with my dad. It just becomes more and more cemented in my mind that it could not possibly have happened. He really is a gentle, loving man."

Tracy has since tried to have a rational, step-by-step discussion with her sister about the improbability of their father's having committed incest with her, but Tracy finds that Christy just can't respond to reason:

"She just couldn't or wouldn't, I don't know which. She decides what is true and twists reality to fit it. Her truths change too, not based on new information but on some need for a different truth. The decisions she makes are unshakable, but the information she uses is illogical.

"For example, she is certain that her husband is having an affair with a sixty-five-year-old co-worker. I know Stephen. He is a very truthful man. I asked him straight out if he was having an affair, and he said no. I believe him. Christy also believes she had a baby when she was eleven, and I know that isn't true, because I was there. [In our interview, Christy told me that she is retrieving repressed memories of her husband's infidelity in the *present*! She believes she represses moments in her current life as they occur.]

"When I visited her this summer, she told me that she has multiple personality. She believes this because one time she was on her couch and she just knew she was a man, right then and there. Her friends were there and asked her to describe her experience. She couldn't describe anything that seemed to point to a multiple personality. But somehow she has been able to make the jump from, 'I feel like a man lying on the couch' to 'I am a man, and I have a multiple personality.'

"When she talked about it, it was as if she found it all very interesting and unique, not painful. The people I know who were incested don't think it's at all fun. They dread their memories because they are so painful.

"My opinion, and I bet I'm right, is that when she grew up into an adult, life was not what she expected. We were taught that there was one right man—a Prince Charming—waiting out there for us. I know she is not satisfied in her marriage. Her husband is not Prince Charming, not Jesus Christ, not her savior; he is just a man. She had given up everything she had—career, friends—to move to TM [Transcendental Meditation], headquarters. The TM people were going to save the world, but the world didn't get saved.

"When she was a teenager I remember her talking about how special her first baby was going to be. She had seen him in a dream, and his name was going to be Benjamin. But she aborted her first baby because she didn't know the father well. Then, when she had her baby, not her first baby and not a boy, delivery was a nightmare. She refused pain medication for the first fifty-some hours. So I think she ended up at middle age, and her life was not what she thought it was going to be.

"I went through the same thing. We had very unrealistic expectations about what adulthood was supposed to be. So, in trying to understand what went wrong, the assumption is: 'It must be someone else's fault, because I've done everything I can possibly do to make my life work and it isn't.' I think she is fighting taking responsibility for her life. She doesn't want to have to fix her marriage or manage her disease.

"When we were little, our dad was our hero. You always knew he would rescue you if you were in big trouble. He was the cornerstone of the family that we could all fall back on, that kept us going, that made us a family. I wonder if Christy is somehow trying to engage him in a rescue attempt, trying to get her childhood daddy back. Also, if he is her designated savior and she feels that he has failed, her anger would be directed at him.

"But she is the only one who can make a life for herself; she has to save herself. As long as you're a victim you don't have to take responsibility. If you are an incest survivor and have multiple personality, then nothing is your fault; you have an excuse for not being OK. I doubt that all this is a conscious process; it's probably a very subconscious attempt at survival. But still, we have to become aware of why we do what we do and take responsibility for it."

FORGIVENESS OR TRUST?

I asked Tracy what she thought would happen if Christy gave up her "memories" and came back to the family. Would they forgive her?

"In a heartbeat," she answered immediately and then gave the idea serious thought: "My older brother Marty would probably have a hard time, and I think Chuck was really, really wounded. I think it would be real hard for him to come around."

Tracy is right about her brothers. Marty told me he hasn't spoken to Christy since she reported him to child-protective services, and he has made sure that she does not have his new address or phone number. He can easily live without her. Chuck's sentiments are similar, but he gets to the real crux of the matter: trust. Chuck explained,

"My older brother has taken the attitude that we've wasted a lot of time and effort and he's not going to let this person dictate what he does and take up more of his time. Marty feels she's not to be trusted; she's not somebody that he's going to have any contact with in the future. He wants to just forget her and move on with his life.

"From my point of view, she's caused a lot of pain and done a lot of damage and many, many years will have to pass with her behaving normally before we can have any kind of relationship.

"She caused me some inconvenience and embarrassment; I could forget about that. My concern is, if she has any contact with me or my family, then she can go to the police again and say, 'I saw those children yesterday; this is what they told me.' My goal is that she doesn't have any contact with my children, until they're eighteen years old."

But what about the parents? Can they forgive and forget?

"My mother is standing there with open arms, waiting for the moment to happen," Tracy told me. "I think my dad might take a little longer. It's hard to say how long, but it would eventually happen."

In the course of our conversation Tracy told me a little bit about her parents' background. They both grew up poor and in harsh environments. They have really made something of themselves: "My father grew up in this little community where life was very hard. For him to go into the military and become a person who's made it, I think is very remarkable."

You have to admire that. Her father became a professional. Her mother got to be an officer's wife, which was probably beyond her childhood expectations. But more important, they made time to play with their children, and they managed to put them all through college. In the course of their lives the Griffith parents have taken giant steps of which they should be able to feel proud.

Tracy and I agreed that this is what is most tragic—for her parents to have put that much effort into being better parents, only to be accused of something so heinous in their "golden years." It's just so unfair.

SUMMARY POINTS

1. The growing hysteria over sexual abuse has created a skyrocketing demand for sexual abuse therapists. Counseling services struggling to meet this demand have had to lower their standards. There are no certification requirements for treating sexual abuse, so counselors with backgrounds in unrelated fields are moving into these jobs and are often in over their heads.

2. Swelling demand for Sexual Abuse Recovery Therapy, underwritten by insurance coverage, has created a growth opportunity. For-profit hospitals and private practitioners are going after this potential market by advertising Sexual Abuse Recovery treatment and, in so doing, creating a temptation, conscious or unconscious, to find enough evidence of sexual abuse to warrant long-term treatment.

3. Books like *The Courage to Heal* present an oversimplified understanding of the problems of sexual abuse and make it seem easy to do sexual abuse therapy. Therapists who depend on such

literature are misled by its uncomplicated, formulaic methods of diagnosis and treatment.

4. It is very common for victims of sexual abuse, real or imagined, to become counselors in sexual abuse programs. Their desire to help others like themselves, however commendable, makes objectivity difficult in diagnosing and treating suspected cases of sexual abuse.

5. When choosing a therapist ask very careful and specific questions about her qualifications. A *credential* is not a license and can often mean very little in terms of expertise. Even a *license* is no guarantee a therapist is competent in every area, and in some states therapists may operate without any license.

6. The title *psychotherapist* has no legal meaning; it is a professional sounding word that was made up to make therapists, counselors, and advisers of any kind sound more knowledgeable.

7. Don't agree to go into a hospital program until you understand what the rules are about leaving. Remember, you may leave "against medical advice," and your insurance company must pay up to the day when you leave.

8. Although many parents who abuse their children were also abused as children, it does not follow that everyone who was abused will in turn abuse their own children. Most do learn from their parents' mistakes.

9. Sexual abuse of children is real, horrible, and finally being acknowledged. Unfortunately, the "discovery" of this dark side of humanity has led to an almost paranoiac reaction to any sign of sexual behavior in children. In the United States, the sexual abuse scare has caused parents to regard perfectly normal sexual "play" as somehow pathological.

10. Hysteria over sexual abuse and unclear definitions of "covert" incest have led frightened parents to curtail and question their own expressions of affection.

11. The slogan of the Recovery Movement ("Think with your heart, not with your head") has led to an erosion of critical thinking in psychotherapy circles; also, the inclusion of non-professional,

"recovering" adults at professional conferences inhibits mental health practitioners from challenging the ideas of the speakers.

12. Why would anyone believe anything so painful as being sexually abused by a parent if it weren't true?
   • Because she has a mental disturbance that prevents her from seeking out or heeding the advice of competent mental health professionals.

THIRTEEN

Perspective
and Proportion

*"We've all made parenting mistakes. But the issue we
are fighting isn't whether or not there is family dysfunction. We are objecting to accusations of the most
heinous crimes one person can commit against
another."*[1]

— Pamela Freyd, Director, FMSF

An interest in the issue of sexual abuse accusations and society's
response to them had begun teasing at the back of my mind in the late '80s. I
was in therapy during the height of the ACOA (Adult Children of Alcoholics) movement, and completed therapy about the time that delayed
trauma from childhood sexual abuse began to replace trauma from alcoholism as the most frequent self-diagnosis. I saw two friends who had made
accusations of long-forgotten sexual abuse get swept along in the tide of the
Sexual Abuse Recovery Movement. For one, the machinery she had set in
motion leaped out of her grasp. Some lives were ruined before she realized
her mistake, and there was nothing she could do to set it right. The other
started out with emotional turmoil clearly connected to current life events
and gradually became convinced that she had been a victim of sexual
abuse. I saw her mental health deteriorate rapidly, and I was disturbed
by this.

I wondered not only about the advisability of digging for memories of
sexual abuse, but also at the extreme reactions people were reporting. I'd
had a number of "inappropriate" sexual encounters with adult males during
late childhood and adolescence. To name a few: At age eleven, a teacher

ran his hand up my leg to my bottom as I stood at his desk (he was fired); at age twelve, I received daily obscene phone calls from a pervert in the area (he was arrested); at thirteen, I accepted a ride with a stranger and found myself on a deserted dirt road fighting off his sexual advances; at fourteen, the father of a family I babysat for propositioned me while driving me home; and at sixteen, a high school teacher cornered me in an empty corridor and suggested that we meet. I was like a magnet for this type of attention because my father was extremely distant and I longed for male attention. These incidents were all little blips of disturbance in my life. They did communicate the idea of women as sexual objects, but the traumatic impact was about a one on a scale of ten, whereas one beating by my father would easily register a five.

I wondered how much consensus there is about what constitutes traumatic sexual abuse. What does the average parent of this generation think is sexually inappropriate? What were the standards of the baby boomers' parents? When it comes to gray areas like emotional or covert incest, can we expect our parents to have known what behaviors would now be considered deviant?

I decided to devise an opinion poll and try it out on parents of varying ages to see what they would regard as sexually inappropriate between parent and child. I gave this test to 42 adults, in three church congregations, two in the mid-Ohio valley and the other in upstate New York. The respondents were asked to rate ten family scenarios that were related to sexuality. The incidents on the test were all based on true stories, altered only by the limitations of normal memory deterioration. (I will not be including them here and have destroyed the survey because some of the subjects of the stories felt they might be recognized.) Subjects were asked to rate the incidents by selecting one of the following terms: Very healthy, Somewhat healthy, Neutral or Irrelevant, Somewhat dysfunctional, Very dysfunctional.

My poll was simply an *opinion* poll. There were no right answers that I had in mind. I was trying to determine if there is any consensus of opinion that we can assume would be the result of the respondent's personal judgment. The results showed that there was no uniform agreement on the deviancy or health of the parents' behaviors in any of the scenarios. Numerical results are given in an endnote.[2]

My survey wasn't scientific; nor did it represent a psychological evaluation of what is healthy or dysfunctional in families addressing topics related to sexuality. It simply shows us whether or not we can easily reach

consensus on what is sexually appropriate and what is sexually dysfunctional. It appears that there is no consensus. The respondents' opinions
covered the whole range of choices and rarely showed any clear agreement. Apparently what seems obviously sexually deviant to some is
regarded as healthy by others.

I MEET THE FMSF

I'd been marveling at the growing sexual hysteria for a couple of years
(in fact I was writing a novel on the subject) when I came across an ad for
the False Memory Syndrome Foundation (FMSF) in the October 1992
issue of my church magazine. I don't remember exactly what the ad said,
but they seemed to be raising some of the same questions that had started
echoing in my mind. There was an 800 number and I called. It took quite a
while to make contact because at that time the FMSF was a small office,
something like a closet with an answering machine, and was staffed
entirely by volunteers. I left messages on their machine, they left messages
on mine, and after about two weeks we finally connected. I thought they
were rational and well informed. They were indeed interested in my
questions. I needed information for my novel, but I also saw the possibilities for a nonfiction book. Of course, I wondered if they might be a
group of well-organized perpetrators. I felt that I could get a better sense of
who they were and what they stood for by meeting the volunteers in
person.

I went to Philadelphia in March of 1993. By this time the FMSF had
about 2,000 members and had just opened a real office. Parents had come
forward to staff the office on a more steady basis, and they were trying
frantically to deal with the perpetual onslaught of phone calls. I planned to
spend a few days there just nosing around. The director, Pamela Freyd,
took time to answer my questions and I was invited to explore the files, the
mail, all but the confidential parent forms.

The staff responded warmly to questions and debate. It was an atmosphere that welcomed inquiry, and everything about the place said, "Explore. We have nothing to hide. We will help you in any way we can."

My memory of this openness of the FMSF has influenced me more and
more as I have continued my investigations for this book. I have had several
so-called "scholars" – authors and professors of respected institutions who
are invested in repressed memory theory – refuse me permission to quote

them. In so doing, they have blocked the opportunity for free debate about and discussion of their ideas. There have even been efforts to prevent me from attending certain professional conference sessions and warnings that I had better not quote any of the proceedings. I cannot help but wonder what the recovered memory therapists and proponents are hiding—why they feel that their "proofs" and theories can stand no scrutiny.

THE SHOULDS

In her classic book *Passages*, Gail Sheehy posits that our twenties are characterized by doing what we *should*.[3] We are still governed by parental messages, both internal and external. Even if we don't get along with our parents and deliberately try to defy what they think we should do, we are bound up in doing the polar opposite, in a reactionary way, instead of understanding what we each want because of our own desires. It isn't until our thirties that we begin to look at what we really want and follow our own star. For many, this is an extremely difficult passage, because it means that we must break away from our parents if we have failed to do so before then. It's a common phenomenon that when we are trying to break a compelling dependency, we tend to vilify the person we are dependent upon. Lovers do this at the end of affairs. Most children do this in junior high, finding fault with everything their parents do, wear, or say.

The longer the dependency has been established, the greater the force needed to break it.

ANSWER NUMBER FIFTEEN:

Why would anyone believe anything so painful as being sexually abused by a parent, if it were not true?

ANSWER NUMBER FIFTEEN: Because his or her unresolved and unconfronted conflicts with significant others have built up to a crisis level, and the adult child has an unconscious need to create distance until he or she can learn better conflict-resolution skills.

The deepest conflictual passage we each have to face is the separation from our parents. Until we have negotiated our new status as adults, we are still vulnerable to feeling as if we must obey our parents' every request. If we defiantly refuse, we may expend as much emotional energy in our refusal as we would physical energy in fulfilling their requests. Throughout many generations and across many cultures, obligations to parents have been one of life's burdens. It is a rare family that manages to work together, incorporate new spouses, and agree harmoniously about how the grandchildren should be raised. The extended family has long been a key source of conflict in family life, but now the pressures have multiplied.

Our life spans have increased so much that many couples find themselves paying their children's college tuitions while paying their parents' rest home expenses. Added to this tremendous financial pressure is the pressure of our shrinking incomes which causes most couples to each hold full-time jobs, and single mothers to cave in to poverty.

The system is imploding.

In the affluent '50s and '60s, middle-class families may have been able to provide for three generations, but that is no longer possible. Those who are approaching middle age in this country must unburden themselves of responsibility for their parents as well as responsibility for their children when they reach adulthood. In many ways, we live in an "every man for himself" economy.

However, we are not just talking about money. We cannot "afford" the emotional cost of being responsible for three generations either. When adults find it impossible to break overly dependent ties with their parents, chances are that they will have difficulty breaking these ties with their children, too. Letting go without lashing out is a difficult skill. When baby-boomers cannot accomplish mature independence from their parents, they sometimes resort to more brutal rejection.

A recovered memory of sexual abuse fits the bill perfectly. Not only does it provide a socially sanctioned reason to abandon our obligations to aging parents, it gives us an excuse to be "inadequate." Most therapists generally advise their clients to try to lower their stress while undergoing therapy. Clients need some unstructured time for contemplation and the self-discoveries of therapy can be very tiring.

Cause and effect can become confused. The therapist tells his client to slow down her life (and recovering memories of repressed sexual abuse is reputed to be very stressful so the warnings are given great emphasis in recovered memory therapy). The client may give up volunteer positions, ask for fewer hours at work, hire household help, tell the kids they'll have to help out more, and let the extended family know that they are "not well" and no one should expect them to host the family holiday dinner this year. As the client adjusts her responsibilities downward, the therapist is simultaneously digging for repressed memories.

The client feels relief and believes the relief comes from uncovering repressed memories. However, it is just as likely that the relief has come from suddenly having more free time and less stress in her life.

Recovered Memory Therapy has not been the cure, stress reduction has been the cure.

A SEXUALIZED RELATIONSHIP

The second coming of Woodstock serves as a reminder of how much the sexual atmosphere and mores have changed since the '60s. We have come full circle from repressed sexuality that was a holdover from the Victorian age (and sexually transmitted diseases such as syphilis that once had no cure); to free love, streaking, and cohabitation; back to a "highly controlled" sexuality backed by liberals and conservatives alike as we struggle with the threat of AIDS.

Though we all pledged that we (unlike the generation before us) weren't going to treat sex as if it were secret or dirty, the reality of AIDS has returned sex to the "dark side." Coupled with the fear of sexual abuse, these dark images of sex have become all-pervasive. As a result, the rules on what is sexually inappropriate have changed radically in the past twenty years. So-called "sexualized incidents" between parent and child are based on very stringent, almost hypervigilant judgments about family habits and behaviors. Stories by survivors who have not yet recovered memories of actual sexual abuse make much of comments, looks, common medical procedures such as enemas or anal thermometers, and any number of family customs surrounding nudity. Yet, how could we expect our parents to have foreseen what they should or shouldn't have said, as determined by future mores?

It is like a sport where the rules have been changed halfway through the game. One team (the adult children) has access to the rules; they know where they are written and have been informed of and reminded about the changes several times, by word-of-mouth. The other team (the parents) have not even been told that the rules have changed.

The only way the parents' team can discover a rule change is to violate that rule. When they violate the unknown rule and are penalized, they might suspect there are other rules they don't know about, but they cannot avoid future penalties for the other unstated rules. They must either risk breaking more rules and being penalized, or stop playing the game. However, the penalty for forfeit is ten years' expulsion from the sport.

ALCOHOLISM

Pernicious hindsight, such as the belief that parents should have known what we would find sexually inappropriate today, began with the Adult Children of Alcoholics Movement. It is one thing to realize what our parents' drinking and their violent or neglectful behaviors during our childhoods have done to us in the long run. It took most ACOAs years of therapy to make this connection. But once we have the insight, we seem to expect that our parents were born knowing that parental alcoholism damages children and that they deliberately ruined our childhoods anyway. We fail to take into account the culture in which our parents lived. People didn't go jogging after work in the 1950s; they had a few drinks.

As one parent told me:

> "The culture has changed so much since I was growing up. Drinking was sophisticated. If you look at old movies, they are all standing around with drinks in their hands. When we were in our forties, I realized that we were drinking too much. We discussed it, and Jeffrey cut back on his drinking a lot. Then he gradually began to drink more and more again, until I felt like I'd lost my best friend."

The typical alcoholic family situation is part and parcel of the times during which this generation's parents reached adulthood. Parents who are now in their fifties and sixties find themselves in a double bind. The social rules regarding drinking, smoking, and sex have changed drastically in the past twenty years. Perhaps half of the accused families had within them a parent who was a recovered alcoholic. For their generation, quitting drinking is a very laudable action. Not only must they overcome physical addiction, but also, because drinking was part of their culture growing up and throughout adulthood, it is uncommon for their peers to stop drinking. This makes their struggle much more lonely. They are under more pressure to drink at parties with their peers than a thirty-year-old would be among his or her friends.

Excessive alcohol consumption is a social problem that is finally turning around. It has been culture-bound, yet in each family that had a problem drinker, the complaining children have perceived this as a fairly special personal problem that they endured in their childhood home. The individual parents are being held accountable for going along with traditions of the day that they did not recognize were destructive. Remember Ruth Ann O'Neill's description of "cocktail hour"?

This generation of parents has experienced two blows. First, they stumbled into the freedom to drink and smoke and by so doing provided the statistics that show how seriously these habits damage one's health. They suffer from cancer and alcoholism in huge numbers. Society had not protected them, and they were chosen to be the first generation to suffer the physical and mental health repercussions of alcohol consumption.

Many overcame the drinking and some the smoking, but as they restored their health and sanity, they began to be barraged with criticism. Now that they had changed their destructive behavior, they were repeatedly asked to defend their past mistakes. This is their reward.

Similarly, they have been caught in a sexual mores trap. They were all to be virgins when they married (the women anyway). Sex between consenting males and females was a shameful secret unless they were married. They grew up in an era of extreme sexual repression, and many vowed not to raise their children that way. Up until ten years ago, the trend was toward sexual liberation. All this changed suddenly as the specter of AIDS outgrew ever-increasing boundaries. Now it is common knowledge that even responsible heterosexuals can get AIDS. As FMSF Director Pamela Freyd wisely observed,

> "The sexual mores have changed with the threat of AIDS. This generation is the first to grow up believing that they could have sexual freedom, only to find out that sex has then become associated with death.
>
> "The sexual hysteria, the extreme obsession with sexual abuse, has grown in tandem with the spreading of AIDS.
>
> "At the same time, chlamydia has become almost epidemic among people who were very sexually active in this generation. It's a very uncomfortable thing. Most people wouldn't tell their therapist that their venereal disease is acting up again."

Dr. Pamela Freyd makes a valid point. It might very well be that the discomforts of chlamydia are often a source of the vaginal sensations Sexual Abuse Recovery therapists are attributing to body memories.

The energy behind the discoveries of ever more sexual abuse is tinged with raw fear. Is it really death we fear, not sex? AIDS has changed everything. We are heading back toward a puritanical attitude. Twenty years ago I thought I would raise my children to be uninhibited and unafraid of sex. When my son was small I was focused on helping him glory in his own body and enjoy his nakedness. My worries were about sexual repression. Now my worries are about AIDS.

SEX EDUCATION

Unfortunately, there has not been as much emphasis on sex education as there has been on sex abuse education, or sex abuse therapy. In many cases, those with sexual problems simply need good information on sexual functioning. The panic over sex abuse has created such a demand for therapy that therapists have not had time to get fully educated. Any therapist treating clients for suspected or even confirmed sexual abuse should have a firm knowledge of what is normal in terms of sexual development. Instead, they rush to take courses in hypnosis (that don't include theory and cautions explaining the limitations of hypnosis), and read popular books on sexual abuse that espouse theories, that have never been scientifically tested, as if they were already proven truths. Then therapists with spotty educations become part of the problem.

The therapists who diagnose sexual abuse often state that they find it in 75 to 80% of their patients. Some argue that their caseloads break down this way because that is how common sexual abuse is. Others point out that when a therapist gets a reputation for dealing with a certain problem, she naturally attracts a high percentage of patients with that particular problem because she comes to be seen as an expert, and clients often come by word-of-mouth recommendations from other clients. The latter is a sensible explanation, but we can't ignore the possibility of therapists looking for what they expect to find and losing objectivity in doing so. Exaggerated and distorted statistics (see Chapter One) have made incestuous abuse seem far more common than it is. Like John Bradshaw's estimates of the number of dysfunctional families, the figures get inflated with every retelling. As Pamela Freyd has stated:

"You can look at any of the FMS families for family dysfunction and you are probably going to find family dysfunction. We've all made parenting mistakes. But the issue we are fighting isn't whether or not there is family dysfunction. We are objecting to accusations of the most heinous crimes one person can commit against another. Parents are being accused of criminal acts, based on so-called repressed memories, and this theory has never been scientifically proved."

Once accused, every reaction of the parents is read as a guilty response. There is nothing they can do to shake the certainty of the diagnosing therapist. Some therapists argue that they must support their patients' reality, as though reality is subjective.

Many aspects of each of our lives can be unique to us because of our personal interpretation or perceptions of events. This has to do with our internal reality. Yes, I might believe someone meant to purposely harm me when they never even thought of doing so, and this belief will color my relationship with the accused person ever after that. I may even provoke them to begin to plot against me.

However, most of what happens can be verified and defined in objective terms. Though *my truth* can exist as a perception or opinion, there is still an objective truth that is based on facts.

Either a given father has molested his daughter or he has not. If he did, he should go to jail; if he did not, his daughter cannot be cured of something that did not happen. She needs to be cured of her delusions, instead. The objective reality is not irrelevant.

A THEORY OF RELATIVITY

Laundry lists in books like *Courage to Heal* and *Secret Survivors* give the impression that any type of sexual abuse is likely to be devastating and need years of therapy to heal. I asked Dr. Lief, the psychiatrist who specializes in sexuality we met in Chapter Twelve, to elaborate on the relative harm of various types of sexual abuse.

"All the literature on sexual abuse was reviewed in the 1991 annual issue of the American Psychiatric Association, and in one article the conclusion is that about twenty-eight percent of children who have been sexually abused, not just they're imagining it, it's been corroborated as abuse, twenty-eight percent suffer no ill consequences. That's very hard for the sex abuse industry to accept, because they assume that any child who's been abused is inevitably damaged. That's not true. We don't know why some children go through such an experience without any apparent damage and others are severely damaged, psychologically and emotionally, by these experiences. That in itself is research that needs to be done."[4]

Lief believes that a person who is basically stable, has good coping skills and ego strength, can form a good love relationship, and can work well with others will be more able to put memories of sexual abuse in their proper place if the therapist doesn't make too much of it. On the other hand, someone with a genetic psychological disorder, or someone who comes from an extremely disturbed family, who may have been sexually abused and has borderline personality disorder, may have years and years of treatment ahead of him. However, Lief pointed out that anyone with borderline personality disorder would probably need years of treatment even if he or she hasn't been sexually abused.

"If there's sex abuse, there's probably been some shame and humiliation, perhaps even physical and emotional abuse. If there's just sexual abuse without physical abuse, there is a better chance of recovering. If you have sexual abuse and physical/emotional abuse, then obviously the child is going to have a more difficult time dealing with it."

Lief talked about one of his unusual cases—an example that breaks all the rules.

"I had in analysis a young woman who was in her late twenties, and she had been sleeping with her father since the age of fifteen—for twelve years—following her mother's death. The father and daughter had a loving relationship. She was in analysis with me and did very well and has been a very productive person subsequently. She's married and has children. She wasn't disturbed except for being overly dependent on the father—but he was dependent on her too. Through analysis she was able to stop acting out her feelings toward her father.

"Whenever I mention this case in a lecture I am faced with a lot of resentment from therapists who are involved in sex abuse cases themselves, because that goes counter to their feelings or belief systems that every case inevitably traumatizes a life. I've treated lots of cases of women who were sexually abused. I don't look for a connection between adult psychopathology and child sexual abuse. Sexual abuse is just one factor affecting a patient. To me there are no telltale signs of previous sexual abuse. The notion that someone has all the classic signs of sexual abuse is preposterous."

VICTIMS ALL!

Why has my generation (the baby boomers) chosen to use sexual abuse as the metaphor that justifies our breaking away from our parents? Dr. Lief believes there are three primary social forces that are contributing to this phenomenon. "One is the whole growth of victimology—the need to see oneself as a victim," Lief told me. "There's even a professional journal of victimology." Lief's second social force is the women's movement. Though the women's movement has made significant progress in showing the world that women are as capable as men, there is a segment that continues to see women first and foremost as victims.

"This whole business of sex abuse is certainly gender-oriented and -related," Lief pointed out. "Several years ago I went to a professional meeting at the APA on sex abuse, and it was jammed. There must have been a thousand people in the audience, and I looked around to see that I was one of eight, ten, twelve men out of a thousand. The rest were women.

"The third major social force that plays into this sexual abuse phenomenon is the Recovery Movement, the twelve-step Movement, self-help groups growing up like wild mushrooms, for everything under the sun. The conjunction of those three social forces— victimology, feminism, and recovery—have laid the groundwork for all these theories of sexual abuse to really take hold."

I wondered aloud to Dr. Lief if another social force is a reactionary effort to reverse the sexual liberation movement. During the 1969 Woodstock music festival, adults and children walked about naked and everyone thought it was beautiful—the mark of a new, more advanced society. Now those parents would be locked up for sexual abuse. Dr. Lief recalled a conversation he had with a colleague back in 1970.

"Clark Vincent, Chairman of the Department of Behavioral Sciences at Bowmen-Gray Medical School in Winston-Salem, said that in thirty years the children of these boomers who were 'acting out' at Woodstock and in Berkeley would be the most repressed and repressive generation we have seen in this century. In other words, he was certain that the pendulum would swing in the other direction, and it's happened."

Dr. Lief has been speaking out on this issue for a couple of years now. Recently, he was booed off the stage at McGill University in Montreal. The dissenters (most of whom were accusing adults) were outsiders, not students. According to a Montreal medical journal article, about thirty off-campus adult demonstrators screamed abuse and rattled noisemakers so that the students and other attendees could not hear Dr. Lief speak. Indeed, they continued to make so much noise each time he attempted to speak that he could not be heard and the talk was canceled.

"I've now given the talk four times, in three of the hospitals in this area at professional meetings, and the first time, I got the most resistance because it was primarily a group of women counselors who were engaged in sex abuse therapy. So they were the most hostile.

"The second time I gave it was in a large hospital with a dissociative disorders unit, and so I got some hostility. Some of the residents were enraged at what I said. When you attack satanic sex abuse you, directly or indirectly, attack the whole concept of multiple personality disorder, because about twenty-five percent of MPD cases are alleged to have satanic sex abuse. I got a lot of resentment.

"I get polarized points of view. People say, 'I think everybody should have heard this. I'm so glad that you said these things. Somebody needs to say it.' Then I also get, 'How can you say these things? MPD really exists, satanic sex abuse really exists.' You're either with them or against them—this sort of a semi-paranoid reaction."

RIGIDITY AND POLARIZATION

When we say that no one ever lies about being sexually abused, we are ascribing to an extreme. "Never" and "always" are extremes that are rarely true. People lie about everything under the sun—why wouldn't some people lie, misremember, or have delusions about sexual abuse? There are documented cases of people being mistaken about sexual abuse, even realizing that what they once wholeheartedly believed about being sexually abused was a totally false memory. Why do some therapists continue to insist that all reports of sexual abuse are factual?

It's my guess that they fear that straying from an absolutist position could be dangerous to victims of real sexual abuse. They believe the end (strong unquestioned legislation against sexual abuse) justifies the means (shouting down any challenges that some reported sexual abuse may be false). Better to believe a few who might not have been sexually abused, they reason, than to disbelieve anyone who has actually been sexually abused.

Therapists and social workers have fought for years to get society to believe that children are sexually abused. They don't want to lose any of that ground. They fear the admission that even one accusation of sexual abuse could be false will put the first crack in the glass, and years of progress will be shattered. It is understandable that they would rigidly adhere to extreme positions in order to protect their clients.

But the dogma has been spread too far and wide. Research shows that it is not true that all people with eating disorders were once sexually abused, but some therapists are preaching this. Some go so far as to believe that all mental illnesses or depression are caused by sexual abuse. If you need therapy, you must have been sexually abused, is their reasoning.

If a reformed alcoholic who could have handled moderate drinking is convinced to never drink again—he hasn't missed much. Alcohol is bad for anyone's body. He'll be better off without it. If overzealous pacifists convince a formerly abusive parent, and even some parents who would have never been abusive, never to spank their children, nothing is lost. There are many better ways to discipline. But if a client becomes convinced she was sexually abused when she was not, great harm can be done not only to the client, but also to the falsely accused parents or siblings. Indeed, in some cases of false accusations, harm is done to many innocent bystanders, and the relationship between the client and his or her family can be irreparably damaged. As we saw earlier, Aileen's mother died believing she was still accused of sexual abuse by her beloved daughter. Aileen regrets this and is justifiably angry at all she and her children have lost.

This is why we need to push ourselves to think more discriminately about sexual abuse. It is fine for a therapist to decide that he or she will not express any doubt when a client reveals a story of sexual abuse—particularly, if it is the therapist's general style to be more supportive than challenging. But it is not necessary to publicly maintain the stance that no one ever lies about sexual abuse. This encourages and maintains dangerous absolutist thinking. It is a position that is not open to new information.

Here is Dr. Lief's prediction:

> "The whole situation will change when these events take place: when the insurance companies turn back claims and refuse to pay for therapy, especially for multiple personality disorder based on satanic sex abuse, and when parents or recanters sue their therapists."

In modern America, money is what ultimately causes change in our culture.

NEW TRAUMA THEORIES

Therapists and organizations who vociferously ascribe to the notion of repressed memories of sexual abuse are constantly asked the question: "But how could someone forget being sexually abused?" There are scores of women who have been sexually abused and have never forgotten. They are similarly baffled. Many report their frustration over all the group therapy time devoted to helping other clients recover memories of sexual abuse when those who have never forgotten just want to focus on getting on with their lives.

A common explanation that has been offered is that the trauma of being sexually abused by a trusted parent is much deeper because the relationship is closer and the child is dependent on the parent for bread and bed. Another explanation which is repeatedly posited is that only the very worst experiences are forgotten. This implies that those who have not forgotten their abuse have not really suffered very much, or that they have suffered much more than they remember (but they forgot the worst parts.) However, these theories are based on conjecture, not research or careful investigation.

In addition, I find the theories oversimplified. The forgetting of sexual abuse is reputed to be a very sophisticated defense mechanism, but if we give this serious thought, we will realize that forgetting traumatic experiences is not an effective way to avoid future exploitation or harm. As a major defense, forgetting instead of heightening one's awareness in moments of danger would leave one more vulnerable. Any species that defended itself this way would become extinct!

I find myself bristling at these theories because they do not jibe with my personal experience with trauma. My father had a mood disorder and would frequently go into an uncontrollable rage, smashing toys and beating anyone within reach. I don't remember specific beatings before my adolescence, but I do remember being perpetually aware of the potential for violence.

One of the known survival mechanisms triggered with repeated trauma is a heightened awareness of warning signs. We might not remember the specifics of the abuse, but we sure want to remember anything that might help us avoid the abuse next time. By the time I was five I had learned to read the signs of an impending beating well enough to hide in the closet before I could be grabbed and beaten. My memories then are mostly of being in a closet, long clothes hanging in front me, hiding me. But as I call up that image, which has never been forgotten, I know I am standing in the closet because my father is raging outside.

Our defense mechanisms, or our survival instincts, would be very poor indeed if they erased all memory of a traumatic event simply because we were dependent on the perpetrator. This is what we are asked to believe about reports of sexual abuse that allegedly took place repeatedly across a span of ten years and were totally repressed at the time they each occurred. Event occurs: total erasure. Event occurs again: total erasure.

We start each day with no knowledge of the perils of the day before. We are not capable of learning from our experiences. We are helpless to do anything to circumvent further damage because the earlier experience has been totally forgotten.

In reality, there are a million ways for a sentient being to deal with a dangerous situation once warned. The greater our level of awareness, the greater our protection. It is not logical from a survival point of view that memory would be totally blocked.

I know my father's ragings and beatings took place throughout my childhood years, but I have only a few clear images, like snapshots kept as reminders. My father punches my brother's bad leg so that he will fall down immediately and be unable to get away from my father's blows. I keep this snapshot to help me remember how important it is to get out of sight immediately. I don't remember every blow inflicted on me. In fact, I can only think of a few blows I remember. That was not the important part. Getting away was what was important.

I do remember that when I was hit, I never felt any pain. All my consciousness was directed at finding an escape route, or the pain had been obliterated by my own rage. The lack of pain enabled me to get out of the situation as quickly as possible. That is what a survival defense does. Children have enough cunning to know how to manipulate adults to get them to keep on giving food and shelter. Serial amnesias of serial abuses don't contribute to survival in any way that I can see.

Right now there are many political activists working to help change laws so that adult children can sue their parents and send them to jail without the burden of having to prove that the abuse actually took place. They would do better to focus on the legislature that protects those who are children right now. Though it is true that we need strong public examples (such as Father Porter) that show that sexual abusers cannot get away with abusing children, resources once available for children are now being drained off to treat and defend adults. Will we wait until today's children are tomorrow's adults before we address their sexual abuse?

Yes, I remember that I had no rights as a child. I was born in 1947, and as I grew up my father had the right to discipline me any way he chose until I was eighteen years old—legally an adult who could then press charges of assault and battery against him. The situation for children is better now, but it has not been changed by women exploring their pain with their therapists. It has been changed by social action outside a therapist's office. If we want to save the children, we must stop acting like children and start using our power as adults.

SUMMARY POINTS

1. When a client begins therapy with a Sexual Abuse Recovery therapist the diagnosis of sexual abuse has already been made; the search for evidence then begins. Therapist and client scrutinize the parents' behavior for evidence of "covert incest" or a "sexualized relationship." Past actions are examined under a distorted lens— and biased therapists generally find what they are looking for.

2. When the rules on what is sexually inappropriate between parent and child become as stringent as they are now, can we really expect our parents to have known what they should or shouldn't have said?

3. Sexual abuse recovery books give the impression that any type of sexual abuse is likely to be devastating and need years of therapy to heal. This is a broad and false overgeneralization. Many factors enter into how badly early sexual abuse will affect a person later in life.

4. The conjunction of three social forces—the victimology movement (the need to see oneself as a victim), the feminist movement, and the recovery movement—have combined to create the sexual abuse recovery phenomenon.

5. Therapists and social workers have fought for years to get society to believe that children are sexually abused. They fear admitting that even one accusation of sexual abuse could be false will destroy years of progress. They fail to see that the persecution of innocent people will do much to damage the credibility of true victims of sexual abuse.

FOURTEEN

Turning   Points

*Before you do anything, you must first decide what is
more important to you: to be* right, *or to have a* relationship *with the accusing child.*

ELIZABETH CARLSON, a retractor

WHO WE ARE IS shaped by the stories we tell about ourselves.

Psychologists have long been familiar with the concept of self-fulfilling
prophecies, and literature has used that concept as a theme for millennia.
Most Eastern religions recommend chanting phrases and suggest that focusing our energy in this way will create desired changes in our lives. Pop
psychology has borrowed this chanting idea and urges everyone to start the
day with "affirmations," generally positive phrases about ourselves or
wishes for what we hope will happen. As the theory goes, chanting affirmations creates spiritual energy that will make our dreams come true.

Repeatedly focusing on any outcome really will increase its chances of
happening. We all respond to sincere praise, and sincerely praising our
strengths each morning will boost our self-esteem. But what if our self-
messages are negative? What if our "affirmations" are really curses?

Renée Frederickson, in her book *Repressed Memories: A Journey
to Recovery from Sexual Abuse*, recommends that readers who have
no memories of being abused, but have personal problems such as "failed
relationships, depression, anxiety, addictions, career struggles, and eating
disorders," try to get "memories" of sexual abuse by chanting an "affirmation." Frederickson states, "Try saying to yourself three or four times a
day for one week, 'I believe this problem is about my repressed memories
of abuse.' "[1]

But this is just the beginning of Frederickson's plan. In addition to chanting this "affirmation" four times a day, she recommends total submersion in the sexual abuse subculture and enough activities to keep the client busy all day. She recommends that the reader volunteer to be a listener for other clients trying to get "memories" of sexual abuse. The clients guide each other as they each try to make memories of abuse surface. They each look for signs of sexual abuse in their dreams, write about sexual abuse in their journals "as if" they have been abused, and attend to "bothersome" (Frederickson's term) bodily sensations that may be "body memories" of abuse.

Frederickson's vision is pervasively negative. Each chapter ends with a section entitled "Empowering Yourself," where she describes activities for the reader in search of his or her forgotten abusive past. At the end of Chapter Four she describes a process for constructing a family genogram. The reader is to construct a family tree that goes back several generations and is to note any dysfunctional behaviors. Frederickson tells the reader, "Err on the side of overstating problems, rather than on the side of denial." For your nuclear family you are to label each family member either "O" for offender, "D" for denier, or "V" for victim. There are no other choices. *All family members must be seen as playing one of these roles, including the reader who is doing the labeling!* If you aren't an offender, then you must be a denier or a victim. Since Frederickson's advice is to all readers, we must assume that she sees every family as a collection of offenders, deniers, and victims. There are no optimists, philanthropists, nurturers, or even supportive people in Frederickson's reality.

Who could help but become depressed and obsessed if surrounded with people who ascribe to this philosophy of life?

Frederickson's book is just a distillation of the many other sources on the market that instruct how to get memories of sexual abuse. *The Courage to Heal* is similar in approach, as it assures readers that, even if they never get memories of sexual abuse, they can still count themselves among the sexually abused. There are absolutely no elimination criteria. As I have noted earlier, these survivor manuals list symptoms so broad and vague that no one can claim not to have them, and yet there is no list of properties that indicates that a problem's cause is probably something other than sexual abuse. Therefore, everyone who considers this possibility will conclude that he or she must have been sexually abused.

As we have seen through the stories of retractors, being a victim of sexual abuse is an incredibly negative lifestyle. The belief system allows no room for doubts, and the convert is unlikely to come upon contradictory opinions because the treatment keeps him or her in constant contact with like-minded people. There is total submersion in the "victim identity." This is not good therapy or even healthy for those who always remembered being abused or for those who have corroboration.

Self-absorption and relentless dwelling on what has gone wrong in our lives is considered pathological. It is evidence of a distorted kind of thinking that leads to major depression. Frederickson is prescribing that her readers schedule and plan to submerse themselves in pathological thinking and behavior that leads to major depression.

Memory research shows that when we try to remember something from the past, our minds have only stored fragments. To create a memory with detail, our minds search other memories and borrow bits and pieces to "flesh out" the recollection. Then the recollection is stored with these added elements. The mind cannot distinguish between the original details and any that were added later through borrowing or imagination. This means that as believers do these exercises to conjure up memories, they are actually rewriting the histories of their lives.

This is not constructive or healthy for anyone.

THE KANE FAMILY STORY

Though Frank and his daughter, Maura, lived in the same house throughout her accusations, Frank knew nothing about them for a year. The daughter actually came up with her suspicions before seeing a therapist. She had been depressed and started reading self-help books. A recently converted, born-again Christian, the daughter was reading books about sexual abuse that were supported by Scripture.

THE KANE FAMILY

Mother: Bernice, Age 49   Father: Frank, Age 53

Maura	Gary	Greg
Age 27	Age 24	Age 23

"One of the books had a list of 150 symptoms," Frank told me. "The title of the book was *Freeing Your Mind from Memories that Bind* (Here's

Life Publishers, 1988). It had instructions such as 'Think of dark places and dark rooms in your life. Look at old pictures and see when you first started looking sad.' She also had a friend who had had memories."

Maura, now age twenty-seven, told me, "I guess it all started because I was searching to find out why I was the way I was. I had been very unhappy. I didn't really have any close relationships. I didn't know how to make friends. I stutter, and I had a lot of fears. I'd always been a loner, but my depression got really bad after I lost my job."

In early 1991, Maura went to a talk at a women's group meeting:

> "This lady who had been sexually abused, but had never forgotten, said that a lot of us in the audience had been sexually abused, too, but we just didn't remember it. It was like a light went off inside of me.
>
> "My emotions said I was abused. I had my answer, I had something to blame it on now. I felt special, like this set me apart from everyone else. Immediately, I started to get worse. The same day I felt uncontrollable anger and started crying uncontrollably. I felt the violation emotionally, and I felt it physically, like it was happening right then."

ANSWER SIXTEEN

Why would anyone believe anything so painful as being sexually abused by a parent if it weren't true?

ANSWER NUMBER SIXTEEN: Because she has become isolated and depressed due to current life problems, but an honored authority told her repressed memories of incest are the most common cause of deep unhappiness.

Though Maura did not tell her father what was going on, her mother, Bernice, supported her and became increasingly worried about her daughter's mental state. In the fall of 1991, Bernice decided to take Maura to a Christian therapist. Bernice explained:

> "My daughter had these alarming symptoms, and the therapist believed Maura had been sexually abused. I supported Maura because I knew that she needed me to. Maura was really hurting, and she was very unstable.

"When she first told me I felt disbelief, but she was so fragile that I couldn't really question her too much. And I had some doubts about my husband, because Frank had been depressed for most of our married life. I thought maybe it was the result of something like this, while another side of me said he just never could have done something like that. Frank was away at a research program. When he did come home, it was hell for me. I felt so split."

Maura elaborated regarding this time:

"I worked with that therapist for about five weeks. I was a mess, but every time I left her office I felt worse. She didn't help me. After five weeks she told me that I was well enough to confront my father—that she couldn't go any further with me unless I did.

"I wanted to know how to cope, to get through each day, and she told me that this was the next thing to do to get better. So I wrote my father this letter. I didn't feel it was very accusatory—like I've heard others confront their parents. It was a very gentle, forgiving letter. I really thought that he would feel relieved that he wouldn't have to hold this guilt inside him any longer. I thought it would bring our family together. But it didn't."

Maura's mother confirmed,

"We sent the letter with good intentions. I thought Frank would finally be able to talk about it and make amends, so our family could be close again. I guess we were just awfully naive. If I'd realized what would happen to our family as a result, I would not have advised Maura to write the letter. Maura told him that she was ready to forgive him, but that just made him angrier because he had nothing to be forgiven for."

REWRITING THE STORY

What if the speaker who had been sexually abused, but had never forgotten it, had stuck to her own truth—that, based on her personal experience, one doesn't forget sexual abuse?

A twist of a phrase, an assumption based on "rumor," and we have begun to fabricate a whole new "truth." Feeling is fine, but sometimes we need to use our heads.

Cognitive therapy is a therapeutic method that teaches clients new ways of thinking. We can learn to reinterpret things in a less negative way by taking a look from a different angle. We can consider how the incidents might have been neutral or positive.

My family's guiding philosophy was "Get them before they get you." My father, who was born in Poland, grew up in a city slum, very poor, at a time when "Pollacks" were a hated minority. "Get them before they get you" may have been a realistic guideline during his childhood. But as a young adult he married and built a house in a quiet, new, suburban development populated by second-generation Poles, and Italians and an assortment of other ethnic groups who had attained middle-class status. Most of the people in our neighborhood made the transition from victim (of ethnic prejudice) to accepted member of the American melting-pot family quite smoothly, but my father never stopped seeing himself as a victim. He continued to believe that everyone was out to get him, regardless of proof to the contrary.

He worked hard to obtain the money to move to the suburbs, but he didn't benefit from the move because his mind, his perceptions, had not moved.

When we wrap ourselves up in a negative reality, we are prevented from seeing the positive influences around us. It's true that sexual abuse is rampant and incest is much more common than we ever imagined. But that is not the end of the story. Only one-third of children who were abused grow up to be abusive parents. That means that two-thirds don't![2] I think that is a proof positive of the ability of people not only to grow toward health with each generation, but also to triumph over the effects of abuse.

There is great power in calling up the positive. If you want to win a race you shouldn't chant "I always lose; I always lose; I always lose" while waiting for the gun to go off.

In even the most depraved lives there are positive moments or influences. Grieving the negative is necessary, but honoring the gifts of life is even more important. This is where time in therapy needs to be spent.

If your therapist has spent more time and energy focusing on the negative possibilities than he or she has on your current life problems and possible solutions, you need to stop and think about whether this has helped you or harmed you. It may be time to reevaluate the therapeutic approach and consider changing therapists.

Many retractors admitted having doubts about their accusations of sexual abuse many times before they decided to quit their destructive therapy. Why hadn't they left sooner? As we have seen, most had developed an extreme dependency on the therapist as well as on women in their support groups. They knew by then that if they expressed doubt about the accusations, they would be shunned by the group and possibly abandoned by the therapist. They would be going it alone when they felt intensely vulnerable. Some saved up their strength as they developed more certainty about their doubts; others were forced out on their own resources when their insurance coverage ended. In all cases, the transition was difficult.

YVETTE—LEAVING THE GROUP

Yvette, whom we met in Chapters Three and Six, was feeling vague doubts. She seemed to be "stuck" in therapy. At the same time, her insurance had run out, and although her therapist, Dr. Galinski, had offered her a reduced fee, the weekly payments were double what her copayment had been with insurance. She'd been checking into starting back to school and learned that she qualified for state-funded therapy sessions with a participating therapist. She'd visited the participating therapist closest to her home to see if she felt she could work with him and found Dr. Fields to be a refreshing change. When Yvette told Dr. Galinski that she was thinking of transferring, the therapist seemed angry and reminded Yvette that she could not continue in group (which Yvette could afford) if she was not in individual therapy with Dr. Galinski. Yvette was not happy with this, but she understood her therapist's reasons, and they agreed that the next group session would be Yvette's last. Yvette told me,

"I was about fifteen minutes late. When I got there the other women were acting cold. I started trying to get caught up with them. I found out that Laura's mother had died, and the next day her brother committed suicide. So I thought, 'No wonder everyone's acting so strange.' Then my therapist said, 'I think it's time you told the other women your decision.' So I told them that I was going to change to a therapist nearer to me, and it meant I couldn't come to group anymore.

"Laura and Nancy started saying, 'What are you running away from?' So I explained about the insurance and the drive and all that, but they kept it up. They were really angry with me. They were grilling me for the whole hour and a half.

"When the session was over, we usually hug each other before we leave, so I reached over to hug Laura, and she drew back and said, 'I don't want to hurt your back.' Then I turned toward Janice, and she turned her back on me and went over to Dr. Galinski, then out the door. When I went into the women's room, Janice was in there, and she said to me, 'I want you to keep thinking about this.'

"Usually we laugh and chitchat after group, but there was all this tension. We started out to the parking lot, and Laura came by and made some sarcastic remark. I was in shock. These were people who had said they really cared about me. And there they all were, attacking me. I thought, 'Did I just imagine that they were my friends before?' I couldn't understand why they were so angry with me. They acted like I was leaving the group just to hurt them.

"I didn't want to leave the group, but at the same time there's a part of me that feels like it's time to move on. I have to think about what's best for me right now. Whether I'm wrong or right, I have to try this change and learn from my own mistakes. At first I felt so guilty, but by the time I got home I was angry."

Yvette has experienced a typical reaction, not just in incest survivors' groups but in any group that comes together for a shared purpose. When someone leaves, the other members are liable to perceive it as a rejection of not only them, but also the group's values and purpose. Even if someone is moving to a new town, or has some other reason that is clearly not a judgment of the group, people tend to feel abandoned. Yvette's guilt may also have clouded her perceptions somewhat. It is very unprofessional for a therapist to take a client's departure personally. He should be able to let clients go with his blessing, but therapists are human, too. Dr. Galinski may have felt rejected and failed to hide it.

The departure was not easy for Yvette, but a few months later, she had no regrets. The program funding her current therapy limits her visits to twenty a year. Her new therapist, Dr. Fields, is letting her schedule her visits on an "as needed" basis, generally every other week, so that Yvette will not use up her appointments and find she has none left if a crisis strikes. She feels proud that Dr. Fields trusts her judgment about when she needs therapy.

At the same time, Yvette has started attending junior college. She doesn't have a particular direction yet, but in the first semester she was able to learn about a number of programs that sound exciting to her. It's been twenty years since Yvette's brother molested her. As she sees it, it's time to get on with her life.

EVALUATING YOUR THERAPY

Deciding if you need to end therapy or change therapists can be extremely difficult. For many of the retractors this was their first experience in therapy, so they did not have any previous experience against which to measure their current therapy. How can you tell when therapy is going well or when it is of little benefit? Painful feelings or regression do not always mean therapy is going badly. Therapy, by its very nature, is likely to be quite painful at times, and it is common to regress for a spell while struggling with old hurts.

Although you may still have moments of pure misery, you should be able to look back after six months and see that, overall, you are stronger, are clearer about your problems, and have some sense of forward progress. An excellent resource for not only evaluating your current therapy, but also for selecting a new therapist, is *The Consumer's Guide to Psychotherapy*, by Jack Engler and Daniel Goleman (Simon & Schuster, 1992).[3]

If you are considering changing therapists, or if you are a family member who would like to seek therapy or find a therapist you can consult about a false accusation, here are some things to consider. Engler and Goleman recommend that before you choose a therapist, you should interview several. Customs vary, but many therapists will offer to see you for a "get acquainted" appointment without charge. Good therapists should be asking themselves, "Do I have the expertise needed to help this person?"

You should be trying to determine how comfortable you feel with the therapist. Does he or she make it easy for you to talk about yourself? Does the therapist welcome questions? Did he or she use a lot of confusing terms or jargon that left you not knowing what was said? Be cautious if the therapist seems disrespectful, cold, excessively sympathetic or solicitous, or condescending. Similarly, a good therapist will not come on so strong that you are overwhelmed, offer clever or quick interpretations of your problem, talk more than you do, or seem overly eager to please. Be especially suspicious if the therapist immediately thinks you fit the profile for his or her "specialty." The therapist should be trying to get a feel for you as an individual, not trying to pigeonhole you right away.

Consider your specific needs in terms of your personality. Do you feel you would do better with someone who quietly waits for you to speak or with someone who actively draws you out? Do you prefer a therapist to behave more like a parent or more like a peer? Would you do better with a therapist who is very affirming or one who is very challenging? Does it matter to you if the therapist is a man or a woman? Young or old? You want the best match you can find—someone it will be easy for you to trust.

If you decide to see one of the therapists on a regular basis, you should both know from the start what your goals are, how long the therapist thinks it will take to achieve those goals, what methods the therapist uses, and which methods he or she thinks will work best with you. This should be a *dialogue* with the therapist considering your thoughts and feelings, as opposed to the therapist's dictating what will be best for you because he or she is the expert. You also need to know how much the sessions will cost, and what will happen if your insurance runs out.

It is wise for you to see a medical doctor for a physical examination to rule out conditions that mimic mental illness, such as diabetes, or an inherited psychological problem, such as a mood disorder, which would require medication along with the therapy. Your therapist should show awareness about these problems.

The most important piece of advice that Engler and Goleman offer is that you should establish, from the start, a time for periodic evaluations of your progress in therapy. Even the best therapist can be the wrong therapist for some clients. Any good therapist will not mind setting a time with you for evaluations of the therapy. For example, you can propose that after eight sessions you schedule a session evaluating your therapy to see if you might need a change in approach, or even a change in therapist. When these evaluations have been agreed upon beforehand, the therapist is less likely to feel defensive when you suggest having an evaluation session, and you don't have to struggle to introduce a topic that you think will be offensive.

For some of you, these recommendations will be hindsight at this point. You may be in therapy already and wishing that you could stop and evaluate where it is going. Don't feel guilty. This is a reasonable desire. You may even want to consult another therapist to get a second opinion. Engler and Goleman suggest that your therapist will feel more comfortable if you tell him or her before you consult another therapist. If you think you like the basic method and philosophy but aren't sure if you and your therapist are a good "fit," consult someone who is familiar with your therapist's approach. For example, if your current therapist believes in family systems therapy, consult with a family systems therapist in another group.

However, if you have been working with someone who specializes in sexual abuse, but you did not have "memories" of sexual abuse when you entered therapy, you need to get a neutral opinion from someone who does not specialize in sexual abuse. A very experienced, licensed psychologist or psychiatrist with a general practice would be your best bet. If you feel as if you need a totally new approach, try someone who is very "eclectic" or borrows from many therapy disciplines. A few quick questions in a pre-appointment phone call could help you narrow choices down.

If your current therapist seems angry, hurt, or defensive at the suggestion that you want to speak to someone else, beware. Your therapist should not be that emotionally vested in you. Also, if your therapist makes dire predictions about what will happen to you or tells you that you are just resisting therapy or are "in denial," be aware that this is very unprofessional. Do not let yourself be discouraged from seeking a second opinion about how your therapy is going. If the therapeutic relationship is healthy, your consultation will probably affirm that.

RECOVERING FROM RECOVERY

Frank's daughter Maura can now look back on her experience with some objectivity. Maura explained,

"I continued with that first therapist for about a month after I'd sent the letter. She tried to take me back—to do memory regression with me—starting from the womb. I couldn't get memories. She told me to do automatic writing, and it was scary what I started writing. I would write all this angry stuff, and my writing got younger and younger. When I was really angry I would just scribble. I began to feel like a bad spirit had taken me over—that it wasn't really me.

"Finally, in October of '92 I started with a new therapist. I still believed that my father had sexually abused me, although I didn't have any memories. This therapist said, 'Let's not look into your past right now. Let's just help you to cope day to day.' It was like an answer to prayer.

"She was a Christian counselor, and she would pray with me. All my feelings, my depression—we prayed about them, and I started to feel better. She gave me practical guidance. She told my mother to get me up in the morning and fix me breakfast. I needed that. I needed to get out of bed and feel cared for. My mother would encourage me to talk, and I began to pull out of it.

"First, my pride broke. I thought, 'Even if he did abuse me, it's not worth destroying my family.' But I hated admitting that I might be wrong. As soon as I gave up my pride, I knew that it had never happened. I've stuttered all my life. My mother has been seriously ill most of my life. She had a serious kind of arthritis, and then she had an ulcer from the medication that she had to take. My father has suffered from chronic depression. They each had withdrawn from me in some way, and I realized that that was what had caused my feelings of loneliness and uncertainty. I had wanted my father's affirmations, and I hadn't gotten that.

"I feel that I'm done with therapy now. My church has been incredibly supportive; my new boss is really good to me, and my family is behind me. I'm not as shy as I used to be. I feel like God loves me and has led me out of this deception."

CUTTING OFF CONTACT

It is common knowledge in conflict-resolution training techniques that when feelings of conflict are very intense, the best solution might be for the two parties to take a break from each other until each person feels more calm and ready to talk. "Adult children" who request "emotional space" from parents in the form of having no contact for a while may be making a constructive, healthy request. Still, cutting off contact with one's parents is not easy. Parents generally put up a lot of resistance, and the adult child is riddled with guilt. Though I don't recommend the approach, many adult children have found it less difficult to break the tie if they have an unquestionably legitimate reason (such as incest) to cut off, or if they can goad their parents into angrily cutting off contact themselves. In the late sixties and early seventies the preferred method was to become a "hippie" and join a cult that espoused values that were very different from the traditional values of the parents. Many parents stepped right into the trap, telling their children they must either quit the ashram or quit the family.

The parents whose children chose to abandon the family's values felt like failed parents. However, contrary to what they might have thought at the time, they had not failed to make their children feel loved, they had failed to teach their children to question overly simple solutions to complex problems. The "all emotional problems are caused by childhood sexual abuse" doctrine is another one of those simple answers to complex questions.

Parents concerned about reestablishing contact with their estranged adult children can learn a lot from those who have studied the mass exit from the family that took place in the '70s. Exit counselors, the professionals who counseled these young adults when they began to doubt their new systems of belief, can show us what helps adult children return to the family and what pushes them further away. As I mentioned earlier, *Radical Departures: Desperate Detours to Growing Up*, by Dr. Saul Levine, as well as *Combatting Cult Mind Control*, by Steven Hassan, and *The Wrong Way Home*, by Dr. Arthur J. Deikman, offers answers to the questions: Why would anyone give up everything for an unfounded belief? Is there a certain personality that is prone to joining groups with rigid belief systems? How do I break the hold these people have over my child?

In Chapter One we began to understand the mystery of why many of the accusing daughters had been exceptionally close to the parents, perhaps even the "favorite." The daughters had often felt suffocated by closeness and needed a "radical departure" to break away. The adult children had typically felt overprotected or that their parents had been too involved in their lives and had failed to open the way for the children to discover things on their own. Accusations of sexual abuse had become their radical departure.

I have distilled the advice of the exit counselors and the retractors into the following one-page chart to serve as a simple reference for the family that is waiting and hoping for the return of a sibling or adult child.

CHANGES

So what made people like retractor Melody Gavigan recognize that they had not really been abused? The retractors' answers vary, but the stories of their turning points do echo the advice given by exit counselors. Melody could see that she was getting worse, not better. She knew that all the psychotropic medications she was taking were making it difficult for

DOS AND DON'TS FOR FAMILIES OF ACCUSING CHILDREN

DO DO THIS

Keep in touch in small, non-threatening ways.

Be sympathetic to your child's pain and supportive of her in other aspects of her life.

Remind your child of good times in the past in a conversational (not preachy) way.

Encourage your child's dreams and plans for the future.

Let it be known that you would like a family session with a neutral therapist.

Keep your child informed of major family events such as a marriage or the death of a grandparent.

Respect your child's need for space to think things through.

Be very gentle with your child when she is having doubts about the accusation.

Try to have one family member stay in "nonjudgmental" contact.

Seek therapy for support and an inside view.

Learn all you can about the movement and the therapist. Act curious but concerned.

Admit to and express a willingness to discuss every accusation that is at all true.

Stay active in a support group of people who understand the problem.

Keep a file of all correspondence with your accusing child.

Think through what you will do when your child calls to ask for forgiveness. Humility helps.

When your child "returns" be sensitive to how vulnerable he or she is during the transition.

DON'T DO THIS

Don't exhibit anger with your accusing child. Her mind is not her own.

Don't send literature you think your child might find "interesting." That triggers resistance.

Don't sue or threaten the therapist unless you have given up all hope of reconciliation.

Don't criticize your child's therapy or therapist.

Don't force other family members to take sides.

Don't hide the accusation. Take the shame out of the accusation by being the first to tell your relatives and friends.

Don't pay the accusing therapist's bills. Many accusing children give up the "memories" when the money runs out and they leave that therapist.

Don't call or send a barrage of mail if your child has asked for minimum contact.

Don't neglect your own needs or the needs of other family members.

on't be confrontational or condescending.

Don't "jump the gun" when your child shows signs that he or she is doubting the memories. Deep change takes time.

Don't insist on an apology as a condition for reconciliation. It will come in time.

Don't turn on your spouse or other family members when the stress is great.

Don't insist the accusing child tell you all the grimy details. That story has been reinforced too much already.

Don't let pride get in the way of your reestablishing a relationship with your child.

her to think. One medication had even caused her to have terrifying hallucinations. She decided to rid her system of medication, and as soon as her mind began to clear, she signed up for a psychology class at a nearby college. When she learned in class that memory is a chemical process and most of our memories are lost forever and can't be retrieved, she began to have doubts about her "recovered memories." Then, while "computer-talking" over the Prodigy network, Melody came upon the story of retractor Lynn Gondolf. As soon as Melody read what had happened to Lynn, Melody felt certain that her "memories" were false, too.

Indeed, many of the retractors began to doubt their memories when they came across information about False Memory Syndrome or destructive cults. These were usually random occurrences: A retractor would come upon a television program or newspaper article that described False Memory Syndrome or discussed the controversy over repressed memory. Suddenly she had the opinion of an expert to stack up against the word of the therapist who had convinced her that she had been abused. Exposure to contradictory information was a key turning point for every retractor, but they all admitted that *if their parents had been the ones to give them that information, they would not have read it*. They would have trashed it immediately, because they had been warned by their therapists that parents will try to convince you of their innocence. Some even believed that their parents were satanists out to destroy them. The accusing child had to be strong in his or her resistance to avoid being destroyed by the parents.

A second major factor that influenced retractors to give up their "memories" was having a close relationship with at least one family member or feeling certain that he or she would be forgiven for the accusation. Their wise parents had not given up or given in to their own rage at being falsely accused. During any contact they could have with their child, they expressed their support or concern. This did not mean that they had to pretend to believe an accusation of sexual abuse. None of the parents of retractors I spoke to had accepted the "memories" as reality.

Instead, the parents generally believed that the accusing child was a victim of misleading therapy, and the parents' anger was directed toward the therapist, not the adult child. As a result, they could genuinely sympathize with their children's obvious pain, regardless of whether the memories were real. The parents continued to offer unconditional love.

In many cases, both parents had been accused, or at least the retractor was angry at both because one was the "perpetrator" and the other was guilty of "allowing" it to happen. If the child had no contact with the parents, there was often a sibling who had managed to be nonjudgmental and keep in touch by not directly challenging the belief. The lesson here is Don't get angry at your accusing child or encourage her brothers and sisters to defend your honor; don't insist that the accusing child take back her accusation as a condition for a relationship with you, and don't get in a hammerlock by trying to straighten out the problem when the accusing child is obviously resistant.

Steven Hassan recommends that, instead, you remind that child of his or her best self. Sidestep the issue by talking about fond old times, or about present career and family happenings, or plans for the future—focusing on the better future ahead—when he or she is done with therapy. As they used to say in the sixties, "Make love, not war." By helping your child or sibling remember better family times, or focus on some of his or her current concerns outside of the sexual abuse issue, you are creating some neutral ground, a safety zone in your relationship.

Basic steps to resolving any conflict are looking for common ground, abandoning the arrogance of always being right, and being the first to offer a concession to the opponent's viewpoint. One retractor said to me, "If only my mother could have admitted what she *did* do wrong. I know now that she didn't sexually abuse me, but we still don't have a close relationship because I can't talk to her about the ways she did hurt me." Steven Hassan points out the importance of understanding your "lost" child's perspective and the influences on him or her. Try making a first move toward reconciliation by admitting some of the mistakes you made as a parent. In so doing, you show your openness to constructive criticism and your remorse for your failings.

I have met about forty or fifty of the families in the FMSF. Many are actually model, healthy families, and knowing that we all make mistakes, they have no trouble admitting that there are a few things they wish they had done differently with their children; others are normal families who may have disciplined a little too harshly or failed to be supportive enough to give their children the high self-esteem they would need to stand up to the pressures of today's world; some are truly troubled families, perhaps with an alcoholic parent who created pain and havoc in the family. All the honest families know that even though they did not sexually abuse their children, there are some complaints about the families that are valid.

The last generation, by this I mean the parents being accused now, was taught never to criticize or contradict their parents. By watching their parents, they often picked up the message that parents should never admit to mistakes because admission weakens their authority. Those are out-moded beliefs.

If you are the parent of an accusing child, show a willingness to understand your adult child's perspective. Read some of the literature your adult children are reading on families. My book *How to Avoid Your Parents' Mistakes when You Raise Your Children* could be classified under recovery literature but takes a much more rational and neutral approach than that classification suggests. For example, I don't promote the idea, by dividing the world into the black-and-white categories of healthy or dysfunctional, that most families are hopelessly messed up. I talk about the vast middle group—the average families who have done their share of wrong things but also have done enough right things to balance it out.

Take a step toward your child or sibling by showing your desire to understand her world and strive to be a quiet, supportive, steady presence waiting in the wings. The retractors told me that they noticed these little efforts of their parents even in the midst of their own greatest anger. One retractor, who had told her mother that she didn't want her to come over or call, was secretly pleased when her mother would send her cards with very short notes that shared a tidbit about another family member or simply said, "I'm thinking of you and wishing you well."

BREATHING ROOM

If you are a parent who suspects you may have overparented your child so that the child felt he or she had to resort to a "radical departure," then your most important task right now is to support your adult child's right to make his or her own decisions. Show your willingness to back off and give him or her space to sort things out. Sometimes "nothing" is the hardest thing to do, but there are times when "nothing" is exactly what we must do. Otherwise you run the risk of pushing the accusing child really to dig in her heels and fight to uphold the veracity of her "repressed memories."

Steve Hassan, exit counselor, ex-Moonie, and author of *Combatting Cult Mind Control*, wisely points out that all you really have control over is your own actions, your own responses.[4] He cautions parents to take care of themselves during this stressful time. All the experts and retractors agreed that it is wise for the rest of the family to get counseling.

"What?" you might be saying right now—"go to one of those maniac therapists? You've got to be kidding!" Most therapists are not maniacs, and what goes on in good therapy is something you need to be informed about anyway. What better way is there to learn about what good therapy is supposed to be like? By seeking support and guidance from a therapist you can get a feel for what your accusing child may have been seeking.

But more important, there is generally so much family stress created by the accusation that many families cannot be support enough for one another. A counselor offers some sympathetic understanding and can be a critical resource for understanding what is happening with your son or daughter in various stages of therapy. Some retractors have held on to their mistaken beliefs for as long as ten years!

If all your energy is focused on changing your adult child's mind, you are likely to neglect yourself, your spouse, and your other children. Ten years is a long time to put everyone and everything else on a back burner. For the health of yourself and everyone else in your family, you need to take this all as calmly as possible. It is better to get in touch with the fact that this is not really your *personal* problem, the result of your *personal* failing, which you must *personally* solve.

Many factors have contributed to your adult child's taking up the belief that he or she is a victim of incest. We have touched on many of these. The world is an increasingly complex place. The media—television, magazines, and movies—model impossible levels of competency. Networks of family or friends are often unavailable when the stress becomes too much for today's adults—simply because most careers demand frequent geographic relocations. Family is often far away, and there is no time to make friends. Melody Gavigan started a group for incest survivors so that she could make new friends in her new town. Self-help support groups have become the social milieu that has replaced meeting other adults through church or neighborhood block parties. At the same time, the uncovering of astonishing numbers of verifiable accounts of sexual abuse has created a hysteria that has spurred a destructive overzealousness. So *you* didn't personally create this problem. Many good parents have been falsely accused of sexual abuse.

HEALING BEGINS

Frank Kane was out of town participating in a health program when he received the letter of accusation from his daughter, Maura. This was in September of 1991, before the FMSF existed. He felt terribly alone.

Fortunately for Frank, he had the support of his two sons, Gary and Greg, both in their early twenties. By a happy coincidence, Gary had mailed his father a beautiful letter thanking him for being such a wonderful father, coach, and friend to Gary as he was growing up. The letter had arrived a few days before Maura's letter of accusation.

Gary had just gone away to his first year at chiropractic college. He was shocked when he heard his father's news:

"I found a message on my answering machine from my father. He sounded upset, but merely said, 'I got your letter, and I'm looking forward to seeing you this weekend.' It seemed very odd, but I assumed my father was still emotional about my heading off to school.

"When I visited my father at the facility where he was involved in a health study, much of what we talked about consisted of awkward small talk. I could tell that something was bothering him. As I prepared to leave, he told me he needed to tell me something. He began to cry.

"He then proceeded to tell me that my sister, Maura, had accused him of sexual abuse. He handed me a letter that I read in disbelief. The writing was Maura's, but the words were so foreign as to what I believed she would ever say. The letter cut me so deep that anger gripped me. It seemed so heartless and uncaring, and I wept with my father.

"For weeks afterward my studying was hindered; each time I picked up a textbook or searched my notes, I would think, 'How can they believe this?' "

Bernice explained,

"When Frank first called home after he got the letter, it was just wrenching. It's impossible to describe how painful this was for all of us. I love my husband, but I've had to love Maura also. He would get angry, and rightfully so—he was innocent.

"There was a part of me that knew all along that Frank hadn't done anything. Maura really hadn't had any 'memories.' She just had feelings and these things they call 'body memories.' She was confused, and I was confused. Maura has since told me that if I hadn't supported her, she doesn't think she would have made it through. I knew all along that Frank was stronger than Maura, and she needed me to support her. But I could see he was in such pain—Oh, God, it was awful."

As soon as Frank got back in town, he went to see the therapist. Frank told me about this visit:

"I confronted the therapist and learned that she didn't even know about the traumatic events that had recently occurred in my daughter's life. Maura had expected to marry this boy, and he had sent her a birthday card with the announcement that he had decided to marry someone else. The therapist didn't even know about this."

Neither did the therapist realize that Maura had lost her last job and had not been able to find another one. A third problem that deeply affected Maura had gone unaddressed: Maura had had a problem with stammering ever since she was a toddler, and she was feeling very down about being twenty-five, unmarried, unemployed, and socially handicapped.

Frank also took along a list of questions to ask the therapist and found that her background in psychotherapy was very limited. He came home and told his daughter this. Unbeknownst to Frank, when the daughter next went to the therapist, the therapist told Maura that she wasn't sure that the father had molested her.

Maura was totally confused at this point, upset that the therapist had insisted that she write the letter to her father and was now changing her mind. Maura didn't want to tell her father about the therapist's doubts, but she stopped seeing this therapist immediately.

Greg still lived at home, so when Frank returned from his health program, he was not totally alone with his wife and accusing daughter. The accusation hung over the house for a year while Frank tried to treat his daughter as if nothing had happened because he believed that she was having serious mental problems, and he didn't want to make them worse. "I never felt like this was really Maura. This was something that had taken her over," Frank told me. Maura spent most of her time shut up in her room.

Frank became increasingly worried about his daughter and decided to consult a psychiatrist at Beth Israel Hospital. The psychiatrist saw each parent and then the daughter, in turn, and at the end he announced that he did not believe any sexual abuse had taken place.

What were the accusations? Maura had never really gotten any "memories." Although her letter to her father said that he had committed incest and rape, she told him that she was sure there had been no penetration. The only memory she had been able to dredge up in a year's time was a memory of herself as an infant, lying in her crib. Her father had come in and wiggled her toes and recited, "This little piggy went to market." Then he had run his finger up her leg.

After the family visit to the psychiatrist, Maura decided to go back into therapy with a new therapist. This therapist focused on Maura's problems in the here and now. This was November of 1992, and about the same time Frank saw a program on the first few falsely accused parents who had gone public. He immediately contacted the FMSF 800 number and started receiving literature. His wife refused to read it, so Frank sat and read it to her. Although Frank found the literature very comforting and affirming, it didn't seem to turn his wife's head. Frank told me,

"What finally broke the spell was a service at my wife's church. The pastor and his wife each spoke about false memory syndrome. They had three people in their church who they believed were having 'false memories,' including my daughter. The pastor and his wife got up in the pulpit and said that this was an evil sent to break up families.

"It hit my wife and daughter right between the eyes. [Greg later told him that Maura had hurriedly left the church right after the service.] First, they thought that I had gotten to the pastor and his wife, but I hadn't."

As a matter of fact, Frank's wife's fundamentalist church had been a bone of contention between them for more than a year. Frank had believed that church friends might have planted the ideas of sexual abuse in his daughter. The last person he would have gone to talk to was his wife's minister.

"The pastor and his wife had seen a program on television and immediately made the connection with what was happening with Maura," Frank elaborated. "They were aware that Maura had been having problems for a long time and that she wasn't getting any better."

The pastor's wife came up to Frank's wife after the meeting and told her that she wanted to see both the mother and Maura the next day. They had a two-hour session, during which Maura became extremely upset. Suddenly Maura's mind cleared. Three days later, as Easter approached, Maura gave her father a beautiful card—butterflies in flight on the cover and the words, "God is a changer. . . ."

Frank and Maura gave me permission to print her letter:

Dear Daddy,

I love you very much. I am writing to say that I am sorry for what I've done to you and our family. I have made a grave mistake. I finally realize how deceiving our minds can be. My life back then was in turmoil and I was very confused.

I will not pass the blame to any other. I take full responsibility because God has given each of us a will and choices to make. I made a bad choice.

It has so saddened me to see you crushed by my actions.

And I'm sorry that all this time has gone by to get me to this place of humility and honesty.

God vindicates the innocent. He sees your innocence and I finally see it too.

I love you very much,

Maura

"After I got that card it was as if the weight of the world came off my shoulders," Frank told me. "For the next several days I was totally wiped out, like I'd been run over by a steam roller. I hadn't realized how much tension and pressure had built up."

One Sunday in December of 1993, Frank, Maura, and Bernice all went to New York where they were interviewed by Channel Nine. "Then Maura spoke to an open meeting," Frank reported. "She told the crowd, 'I could never have come out of this without the support of my family.' She pointed toward us sitting in the audience, and everyone in the hall—over a hundred and fifty people—cheered and applauded for us."

FORGIVENESS IS A TWO-WAY STREET

I interviewed Elizabeth Carlson, a retractor, who has spoken to hundreds of accused parents about how families can turn this situation around and heal. Elizabeth told me:

"There are pretty much three trains of thought that I've come across with parents. Some of them say they want absolutely nothing to do with the child again because the child has absolutely destroyed their lives. Some say they are willing to have the child back in their lives, but the child has to come back with a fully certified, bona fide apology. The third is, 'We'd do anything to have our child back in our life.' I think parents have to make their own personal decision about that and maybe get some therapy to help them make that decision.

[Elizabeth tried to describe the accusing child's frame of mind:] "They're stuck, so stuck and brainwashed and cut off from family and this and that, they're looking for answers of any kind to help them with their problems, their depression, their low self-esteem, their eating disorder, whatever brought them into therapy to begin with—especially if they're on psychotropic drugs.

"They're constantly told that dredging up 'memories' and cutting off contact is the only way they'll ever get better. You believe that you're on the brink of insanity and that if you believe all this garbage and do what you're supposed to do, only then can you get better. For a while you go through a period of a temporary high. It's like, 'This is the answer!'

"My therapist threatened that she would abandon me if I didn't do the 'work,' that I would continue to get sick, that I would end up in endless mental illness, chronic incarceration in a state mental institution, lose my children—the dire predictions were endless. If parents can really take this into their hearts and really understand that their child is under all this pressure and fear and negative influence, maybe they can find it easier to forgive."

Another retractor, whom we'll call Dee, talked about how her parents responded to her first cautious attempts to resume contact while she was still confused about her "memories":

"My mom and dad had both ended up in counseling because of the accusation, and my mom really grew. She came to me with a long list of things she wanted me to forgive her for. That was so renewing for me. Mom's just one of those people who wanted a happy family. She grew up in a painful family; she was physically abused and her dad was real, real stern, and she always wanted his love.

"Because she so wanted a happy family she became really manipulative in trying to make that happen. A lot of my feelings and pain got ignored or swept under the carpet, because that was too painful for her to look at. When we talked about this it was so easy to forgive her. It's what I wanted to do anyway. It's hard to forgive people who don't come in and ask for it. I needed that.

[Dee's father had never been told exactly what her accusations were; he just knew that his daughter had cut off contact.] "When I was still in the middle of it, he would get drunk and call me and say, 'Now, what was it I was supposed to have done to you?' Thinking back on that, it breaks my heart. I've gone to him many times since and asked him to forgive me. He just says, 'I've already forgiven you. I know your mind wasn't yours and the therapist was controlling you.' "

If you are beginning to doubt that your parent sexually abused you, but you still feel a great deal of anger, you probably need to sort out what things your parents did do that made you so angry. Whether or not you ultimately decide you were sexually abused, in the end you will have to forgive your parents for whatever they did in order to move forward with your own life. This isn't a social rule, it's a spiritual rule. Forgiving your parents—seeing them as mortals who made mistakes rather than as powerful people who intentionally harmed their children—is a developmental milestone.

For me, what made it possible to forgive my parents was learning about their childhoods, and thinking about their character strengths and weaknesses. I developed compassion for my father, whose own parents had both died by the time he was five years old. I suspect that his stepfather beat him brutally. I remembered that my mother's mother, who lived with us for a number of years, was negative, critical, and nervous. She hadn't wanted any children but had had one for her husband's sake. I can imagine how my mother felt, never being able to draw a positive comment from her mother.

I know my father was bright but had learning disabilities, so that he did very poorly in school and dropped out in the ninth grade. I know that my mother never had any ambition beyond getting married and so was totally incapable of understanding or supporting my academic driveness.

I could also find reasons why I should not let them off the hook. After all, I made it my business to become a better parent—why couldn't they? I'll take no excuses!

That's where perspective comes in. I believe that my mother and father were better parents than their parents had been. They just didn't seem to be good enough to give me what I felt and still feel that I need.

There are a number of ways I could interpret the story of my childhood. I could look at what I didn't get, my hardships, and dwell on that, bitter to the end of my days; or I could look at what I made of it, could indeed make a point of making something positive of it. Some might call it "denial." Some might call it identifying with the perpetrator. I prefer to think of it as the series of challenges that has made me who I am today: the "something better" my parents made out of their own childhood pain.

I actually believe that I developed great strength of character from coping with and eventually standing up to my father. My terror at his ragings had made me a consciously peaceful person dedicated to conflict resolution. Conflicts will always be there. Everyone must face difficulties. This is a great learning that many of the retractors have shared with me. They got well when they realized that everyone has problems and challenges. Their sickness grew out of an expectation that life's troubles would not have visited them if they had not been deprived in some way.

RESOURCES FOR QUESTIONERS

Below is a list of organizations that can respond to "survivors" who are beginning to doubt their "memories":

THE SOUNDING BOARD
PO BOX 4668
PARKERSBURG, WV 26101

A newsletter for retractors or those who doubt their "memories." It contains personal stories and articles with information about good-therapy vs. poor-therapy practices. Write for details about a subscription.

STOP ABC
PO BOX 68292
SEATTLE, WA 98168
(206) 243-2723

"Stop Abuse by Counselors" was formed to collect information about unethical practices by counselors and to direct callers toward the resources they need to rectify therapist-induced damage. Director: Shirley Siegel.

FMSF
3401 MARKET STREET, SUITE 130
PHILADELPHIA, PA 19104-3315
(215) 387-1865

The False Memory Syndrome Foundation has sympathetic listeners who are willing to hear your doubts about your abuse and provide you with information that can help you decide whether you are experiencing "false memories." If you get a recording, state that you are a questioner or retractor (whichever is appropriate), and ask to be called by Janet.

FEELING SPECIAL

Dr. Ganaway and I discussed the sense of *entitlement* that is characteristic of many of his patients who came to believe they had been sexually or satanically abused. Some of the retractors told me that for as long as they can remember, they have had an incredible need for attention. Some even recognized that they had been the child in the family who had gotten the most attention, but nothing was ever enough. This need was so great that even the most attentive parent could not have satisfied it.

"When someone has an insatiable need like that," Ganaway explained, "one always feels disappointed. The only way he or she knows for achieving a sense of self-worth is to have it validated continuously by others, to constantly look to others to tell one that he or she is a valued person, even a very special person." Ganaway has found that this character type is often diagnosed as MPD and worries that the "glamour" attached to this diagnosis may either cause the person to imitate it or make the person feel an even stronger sense of entitlement. Seeing oneself as someone who was tortured by a satanic cult and survived may also be a way of reassuring oneself that one is special, practically indestructible.

"People who have come through our program have dealt with death over and over again, hundreds of times," Ganaway told me. "They will put themselves close to it and then pull themselves back from it. Some might say these people have a death wish, but to me it has more a flavor of counterphobia. If you're afraid of snakes you become a snake handler; if they're afraid of death, the more times they can bring themselves right to the brink of it, the more they convince themselves they are an exception to the rule."

This made me think about people who come out of an accident in which they came close to death. Often they have a feeling of being blessed. It may change their whole lives. They may set out to understand what special mission God has for them on earth that caused them to be spared. Others may simply say, "Whew! That was a close one!" We are talking about reframing our life stories in a new, more positive way. Is it possible that Ganaway's patients could begin to see their illness and continued survival as a blessing in disguise?

Ganaway thinks that this feeling of being entitled does contain the shadow of being a "chosen" one:

"Those who feel that a narrowly escaped disaster is a sign that they have a special mission in life may have been folks who were struggling for a sense of purpose. They may have questioned their self-worth, and all of a sudden they feel they have been chosen by God. Almost all the folks that I have worked with, whether or not they have come to the conclusion that they had these 'memories,' are definitely struggling with issues of identity."

Elizabeth Carlson remembered how her search for identity and self-worth played itself out in her struggle:

"We pull things from the outside, and say to ourselves, 'I cooked a good meal; that makes me a good wife. I sewed the kids some clothes and played with them; that makes me a good mother. I'm involved in the community; that makes me a good person'—not from the inside. If I'm not doing things, I don't feel good about myself. Anybody who has any kind of an identity crisis is going to fall between the cracks. So many of us do. How many of us get parented to know who we really are and what we want from life? It's something we have to sort out for ourselves later."

Many retractors admitted to having identity problems or the sense of entitlement. They told me that they hadn't taken their problems in stride, realizing that everyone must deal with problems. Since they did not see the connection between their behavior and their problems, they became preoccupied with finding a reason in their past for *why* they had troubles, as if finding out why would make the troubles go away.

Now they talk about living their lives, dealing with what comes their way—mere mortals, just like everybody else. They no longer expect that they will be excused from life's homework. As one retractor told me, "I had to grow up."

THE BROTHERS' STORY

Greg, Maura's younger brother, was twenty years old and living at home when the crisis with his older sister began. Greg told me,

"It was real hard for me. Maura was having dreams in the middle of the night and screaming. My mother would get up and run into her room. I knew something was wrong, but I had no idea what it was. My sister started dropping hints, but I didn't pick up on them. She'd say things like, 'Maybe I was sexually abused.' She didn't have any idea what might have happened or who could have done it. I'd just sit there with my mouth hanging open. I didn't know what to make of it.

"That first weekend after I found out that Maura had accused my dad, I went on a church retreat. The only way I could fall asleep was to buzz scriptures around in my head to get my mind off of it. I was just an absolute mess.

"Maura would make comments about how sad her childhood had been, and Gary and I were like, 'What are you talking about?' My father was a great, great father. He would go out of his way to do everything for us. This was really hard on my brother because he was six hours away, and there was nothing he could do."

[Gary, the middle child and older son, was particularly saddened by the family troubles on his wedding day. He told me:] "If I thought Christmas and Thanksgiving had been awkward, I hadn't seen anything yet. Everyone acted as if nothing was happening. No one knew of the accusations except for our family, and all the guests thought that it was a storybook day.

"It was a great, exciting day, but it would have been so much fuller and more joyous if we didn't have this hanging over our heads."

[Greg, Maura's younger brother, had sorely missed having his brother at home.] "I was in shock [he told me, as he described the dreamlike quality of living with the accusation]. I felt totally alone. I felt like everything had just crumbled. I didn't think my father had done it, but I had seen warning signs that something was seriously wrong with Maura, and now I was really afraid for her and our family.

"Toward the end I would just be around the house, and all of a sudden I would hear screaming. It was real scary. One time, I had just gone to visit my grandfather who was in the hospital. He was losing his mind, and he started yelling at me. I was really upset by this, and when I left there I had to pick up Maura.

"I was late, and she was very agitated. I said, 'I had a hard time with Grandpa.' As we were going down the street she started banging on the dashboard and screaming at the top of her lungs. I had to pull over, and then she said, 'I guess I haven't been able to handle this anger yet.'

"There were times when I would just break down and cry. Right before I finally left the house in February (two months before my sister snapped out of it), things had been building up and building up. Maura had gotten off the phone with somebody, and she slammed the phone down and ran into her room and started screaming at the top of her lungs.

"I was in my room and I just blew up. I started slamming my door, like I was trying to show her how upsetting it was when someone loses control like that. I started screaming at her, 'Don't you realize you're destroying me? You're tearing this family apart!'

"And Maura yells back at me, 'I'm not angry at you.'

"I felt like she was telling me I had no right to object because she wasn't angry at *me*. I just tore off my glasses and threw them across the room. I bashed my radio and threw it across the room. I yanked my bed out—I just lost it.

"My father came upstairs, and he started hugging me and trying to calm me down. I remember my mother saying, 'We need to get help for this family.' But I knew the help she was talking about was going to a therapist and talking about how my father had sexually abused my sister. I thought, 'Give me a break! You need to get *your* head straightened.'

"A few days later I moved in with friends. I think that might have woken my mother up a little. The family really was being destroyed. I'd left the house.

"Meanwhile my father remained at home. What had really amazed me throughout this whole thing was that my father tried so hard to treat my sister normally. When she came downstairs he would say, 'Maura, would you like some tea?' It was just so sad.

"A couple of months later, in April, I was attending Bible school, and the pastor's wife said something about a show she had seen on false accusations of sexual abuse. My sister wasn't there, so I wrote the pastor's wife a note asking her to please bring this up before the congregation at a service.

"Just a few days later, both the pastor and his wife spoke out about it from the pulpit. I looked over at my mother and sister, and I could see it hit them like a ton of bricks. The next day they had a counseling session, and Maura started crying and was getting ready to leave. My mother told her to sit down and hear the pastor's wife out.

"My mother described it as, all of sudden they just knew that they were wrong."

THE QUESTION OF TRUST

If you return to your family of origin, you need to keep in mind that it may take your siblings and parents quite a while to forgive you. Even then, they may have reservations about you for a long time. You may have to spend as many years proving yourself trustworthy as you spent making accusations. Many siblings have told me that they worry they may never be able to trust the accusing sibling again. As the siblings see it, the stories of incest and satanic rituals came out of nowhere. When we can find no sensible explanation for something, when it seems to have just happened randomly, when we cannot establish cause and effect, we feel helpless and frightened. If we cannot understand how something happened, we cannot imagine how we will prevent it from happening in the future.

We can understand why a brother whose sister reported him for sexually abusing his children when there was no truth to the accusation told us that he will never let his sister be with his children again.

On a deeper level, some siblings felt they would never want to confide in that sibling again—that there will always be a barrier. They had this uneasy feeling that anything they said could somehow be used against them later. It is the unpredictability, the unfoundedness of the accusation, that has destroyed their belief in their own ability to judge when the accusing sibling can be trusted. Their senses apparently deceived them in the past. How can they ever again be certain they know that person?

There is a difference between forgiveness and trust, and forgiveness may be the best some families can achieve in the aftermath of a false accusation.

ALL'S WELL THAT ENDS WELL

Greg Kane told me,

"Things are 99 percent back to where they were, but there's still this reserve. Because my mother and sister swallowed this thing so quickly and so fully, I don't feel like I can really trust them yet. I trust Maura in the sense that I feel like I can get close to her. She's done a complete turn-around, and she sounds so clear when she talks about it. It's not like I'm afraid she's going to change her mind about the abuse again. There's just that 1 percent of reservation that some other idea could take them over.

"If you'd asked me if I thought I could ever trust my mother and sister again while all this was going on, I would have said, 'no way.' But in a strange way it seems like the family is a lot closer now than we have been in two or three years. When we get together, there's this feeling of, 'We survived that one, so we can survive anything as a family.'

"This Christmas we won't have to fake it, like last year. We all tried to act normal, but in the middle of opening a present I'd think, 'Oh, my God. I can't believe what she thinks about my father!' "

[Gary Kane described his relief once his sister had retracted her accusation. He told me: "There was joy again in my home, and I was so proud of my sister, mother, and father. They have come together in forgiveness and are now using the experience we endured to help set others free from the grip of False Memory Syndrome."

Maura's mother, Bernice, also feels the tremendous sense of relief and joy:

"I've met some other FMS parents now, and some of them have been estranged from their children for ten years or more. I feel grateful and blessed that this only went on for a year and a half with us. I really feel like God was watching over us.

"I get a knot in my stomach every time I talk about it, but I know that we must tell our story. It's such an awful deception. It has to be brought into the light.

"I can really see the rainbow at the end there, and it's so good!"

SUMMARY POINTS

1. Self-absorption and relentless dwelling on what has gone wrong in our lives is considered pathological. It is evidence of a dis-

distorted kind of thinking that creates or perpetuates major depression. Yet sexual abuse recovery self-help books recommend total immersion in a victim identity.

2. The checklists of "symptoms" found in sexual abuse recovery books are so broad and vague that no one can claim not to have many of them.

3. Cognitive therapy is a therapeutic method that teaches clients new ways of thinking. We can learn to reinterpret things in a less negative way by taking a look from a different angle. Sexual Abuse Recovery Therapy is cognitive therapy turned on its head—the client is encouraged to reinterpret things in a negative way in order to support the assumption of sexual abuse.

4. If your therapist has spent more time and energy focusing on the negative possibilities than he or she has on your current life problems and possible solutions, you need to stop and think about whether this has helped you or harmed you.

5. You, as a mental health consumer, have the right and responsibility to evaluate your therapy periodically. You should be able to look back after six months and see that, overall, you are stronger, are clearer about your problems, and have some sense of forward progress. Such evaluation sessions should be built into the therapy schedule.

6. Not all therapists and clients are good fits. Not all therapy styles suit everyone. It is OK to say, "I don't feel this is working for me." A therapist who feels threatened by questions is not a good therapist. It is up to you to decide what is good for you. It is your power and your right.

7. While exposure to contradictory information is a key turning point for retractors, any information that comes from the parent will be rejected out of hand. If you are an accused parent, don't try to "educate" the accusing child. It's hard to do nothing, but sometimes that's exactly what we have to do.

8. Don't get angry at the accusing child or encourage her brothers and sisters to defend your honor. Having contact with at least one family member who takes a neutral position can offer the accuser a way back into the family.

9. Try in any way, no matter how small, to express your love and your sympathy for the accuser's pain. Take a step toward your child or sibling by showing your desire to understand his or her world and strive to be a quiet, supportive, steady presence waiting in the wings.

10. Consider counseling for yourself during this painful period. A good therapist will feel supportive, give you insight into what went wrong between you and your child, and help you understand better how to reach your accusing son or daughter.

11. If you are having doubts about your "memories" but you still feel a great deal of anger, you probably need to sort out what other things your parents did that made you so angry. Whether or not you ultimately decide you were sexually abused, you need to forgive your parents before you can grow emotionally. Letting go of "the right to retaliate" is healthier than nursing grievances.

12. Why would anyone believe anything so painful as being sexually abused by a parent if it weren't true?
  - Because he has become isolated and depressed due to current life problems, and an honored "authority" told him repressed memories of incest were the most common cause of deep unhappiness.

First, Do No Harm

IN THE COURSE OF this book I have presented many reasons why someone might "recover" repressed memories of sexual abuse that are not true. I have gathered them together in the chart below so that the reader can review these ideas quickly. However, these answers are still not the whole story. They are just some of the contributing factors to False Memory Syndrome, and all of these reasons exist in a social context that supports them. I elaborate on some additional factors below.

SIXTEEN REASONS WHY

***Why would anyone believe anything so painful
as being sexually abused by a parent
if it weren't true?***

ANSWER NUMBER ONE: Because it explains why he or she cannot meet the modern social demand to manage careers, marriages, and children without the support of appropriate social programs. (Chapter One)

ANSWER NUMBER TWO: Because it is a simple, neat explanation for a lifetime of inner turmoil and disappointment that has not been caused by any known or acknowledged trauma. (Chapter One)

ANSWER NUMBER THREE: Because it provides a compelling and guilt-free reason for separating from his or her family and ends those uncomfortable feelings of ambivalence. (Chapter One)

ANSWER NUMBER FOUR: Because it provides a sense of belonging and acceptance that he has been searching for all of his life. (Chapter Two)

ANSWER NUMBER FIVE: Because someone in authority has said that belief is the only road to mental health. (Chapter Four)

ANSWER NUMBER SIX: Because no questioning of the treatment is allowed. The clients are judged not competent to decide whether their "memories" are true. Doubting is regarded as proof of their "denial" and resistance to getting well. (Chapter Four)

ANSWER NUMBER SEVEN: Because it is a socially sanctioned excuse for escaping responsibility for one's own mistakes or failing to grow up emotionally. (Chapter Five)

ANSWER NUMBER EIGHT: Because he feels trapped, punished, and isolated in an inpatient program and believes he must play the "repressed memory game" in order to gain his freedom. (Chapter Five)

ANSWER NUMBER NINE: Because the therapist has used coercion and his or her aura of expertise to override the client's perceptions and convince the client that her memory cannot be trusted. (Chapter Five)

ANSWER NUMBER TEN: Because many therapists have failed to study the history of psychiatric practices, theory, and past grave errors; these therapists do not realize that they can be mistaken. (Chapter Eight)

ANSWER NUMBER ELEVEN: Because he or she finds focusing on a fantasy of satanic abuse to be less painful than the mundane reality of parental neglect and emotional abandonment. (Chapter Nine)

ANSWER NUMBER TWELVE: Because it provides one simple, graspable reason for being unhappy when he or she "has it all." (Chapter Ten)

ANSWER NUMBER THIRTEEN: Because it's less painful to blame someone else than to examine one's own personal failings and do all the arduous work of changing from within. (Chapter Eleven)

ANSWER NUMBER FOURTEEN: Because she has an undiagnosed mental condition, such as postpartum depression, that has impaired the adult child's judgment and made it difficult for her to accept appropriate help. (Chapter Twelve)

ANSWER NUMBER FIFTEEN: Because his or her unresolved and unconfronted conflicts with significant others have built up to a crisis level, and the adult child has an unconscious need to create distance until he or she can learn better conflict-resolution skills. (Chapter Thirteen)

ANSWER NUMBER SIXTEEN: Because she has become isolated and depressed due to current life problems, and an honored authority told her repressed memories of incest are a common cause of deep unhappiness. (Chapter Fourteen)

As we have seen from the personal stories presented here, clients come to their "memories" through many means. The idea that the source of one's problems is repressed memories of sexual abuse, correct or not, has become accepted. As Tracy, a practicing therapist and a very sensible person, told her story (Chapter Twelve), she mentioned in passing that she went into therapy, and being a troubled female, she just naturally thought she should clear up the possibility of repressed memories of incest. She implied that this is a common component in many women's psychological difficulties.

Similarly, Paula (Chapter Three), who is trying very hard to keep a level head and practice good therapy, did not feel it was suggestive for her therapist to tell her that many other women with her symptoms have learned that they had repressed memories of sexual abuse. The therapist stated that she saw several red flags of possible abuse.

I see a red flag, too. If, during the second session, this therapist is mentioning to clients that they should consider repressed memories of sexual abuse as a possible cause of their depression, it is no wonder that she has many clients with the same symptoms from sexual abuse. With this approach we cannot know how many of her clients really have false memories of sexual abuse that they have dutifully recovered.

One of the "logical" reasons that convinced Paula she should consider this line of thought was that she had had weight problems and never felt truly feminine. Not only have studies shown that there is no correlation between eating disorders and past sexual abuse, most women in this country feel overweight and have trouble controlling their appetites so that they can keep their weight within the acceptable poundage range of the American female. For twenty years feminist literature has been complaining about the impossible standards for women's weight in the USA. Remember Twiggy? Are we now to believe that, it isn't the weight standards at all, it is repressed memories of sexual abuse causing so many women to be overweight?

But therapists are not the only disseminators of this myth. Articles in popular magazines and television talk shows have "educated" the public about this theory while failing to make clear the hypothetical nature of the assumption. This subject gives these shows terrific ratings because it capitalizes on the watcher's morbid curiosity not only about sex, but also about the misfortunes of others.

Of course, most people who are troubled or interested in psychological problems read self-help books, and most of the retractors have read dozens of them. Indeed, Maura Kane's florid "symptoms" were mostly attributable to descriptions she had read in recovery books. Recovery books are dangerous because they generally are not well researched, nor do they make distinctions between fact and opinion in the assumptions they discuss. Therapists may not be able to stop their clients from reading these books and contaminating their thinking, but therapists can teach critical-thinking skills so that their clients are not so susceptible.

Clients need to be taught how to determine the difference between fact and opinion, cause and effect, and healthy skepticism versus naive credulity. Therapists should have their clients bring in the books they are reading and show the therapists the passages that influenced the clients' opinions. The therapists should talk to the client about why the information is or is not reliable.

However, one of the most effective methods of spreading misinformation about repressed memories has been word of mouth. Past generations talked about the weather, but the most popular topic now is mental health. It is no longer shameful to be in therapy. In fact, it is socially stigmatizing never to have had therapy. It implies that the person thinks he or she is perfect. Anyone who has contact with the Recovery Movement also knows that it is considered arrogant to say you are healed. We are all supposed to be in perpetual "recovery."

A number of the more traditional therapists with whom I have spoken point toward the Recovery Movement as a major contributor to the false memory problem. Many of the concepts originally conceived and introduced by Alcoholics Anonymous (AA) were very applicable to other addictions, but, when every undisciplined, ill-considered, or irritating human habit began to be labeled an addiction, we entered shaky ground.

The founders of AA designed a program for quitting booze and staying off it. They never meant their program to do anything else. Their procedures and steps created a formula that helped many recover from alcoholism, but all psychological problems cannot be solved by this formula. For example, denial is a very common denominator in addiction, and one should be on the alert for it when dealing with an alcohol or drug abuser. But when the problem is relationship difficulties, depression, or panic attacks and there is no substance abuse involved, the concept of denial does not necessarily apply. In alcohol abuse treatment, often, if you can get a person to stop drinking, the rest of the problems take care of themselves. Even when women have been sexually abused, reliving the trauma in the therapist's office is not likely to solve the whole problem.

Another contributing factor to poor-therapy practice is that some therapists are working outside the field for which they were trained. While a few years back alcohol recovery programs were the big money-makers in for-profit hospitals, the most lucrative counseling jobs are now in sexual abuse "recovery." Indeed, a job as a sexual abuse counselor may be the only opening a displaced alcohol abuse therapist can find. The demand for sex abuse counselors is so great now that even therapists who wouldn't have dreamed of practicing in a field for which they had not been trained are scrambling to meet this demand.

Unfortunately, many sexual abuse recovery therapists hold the view that all the client's problems can be traced to dysfunctional family behaviors. If the client can't remember anything bad enough to account for her symptoms, then the cause must have been something so traumatic that the client repressed it. Since, in their view, the only thing traumatic enough to warrant repression is childhood sexual abuse, the client's lack of "memories" is regarded as proof of the "memories" existence. Add to this the recent popularity of Multiple Personality Disorder (MPD) as a diagnosis. Add to this the conviction that childhood sexual abuse is the primary cause of MPD, and you can understand the frequent diagnosis of "MPD due to decades-delayed memories of childhood sexual abuse."

Recovery gurus seem to promise that if we go to the right meetings and say the right words, we will get fixed. M. Scott Peck, the author of the best-selling book *The Road Less Traveled*, devoted his whole book to helping the reader reconcile himself or herself to the fact that suffering is part of life. Nonetheless, it is an optimistic book about facing our problems and moving on.

But the prevailing American attitude is that rather than worrying about the rise of crime and what we can do to alleviate social problems, we should all take a break from social responsibility while we heal our inner child.

THERAPIST AS VICTIM

The most popular and common psychological problem during the 1970s was low self-esteem. In the 1980s it was dysfunctionality within families of origin. Now the fad is repressed memories of sexual abuse. As long as the therapeutic community stretches definitions to be more inclusive, more and more people can qualify as victims. For example, now anyone can be an MPD victim, since the criteria spelled out in the DSM-III-R have been rejected by experts like Braun for being too restrictive.

On the other hand, I want to make it clear that my book is not about vilifying therapists or therapy. I have had to write about some very serious malpractice on the part of some therapists because these things happened. Further, I have needed to point out what some therapists do to contribute to the problem of "false memories." Though probably not serious enough to be considered malpractice, some techniques are being misused by ill-informed therapists. These therapists need to take a long, hard look at what they are doing and at the assumptions on which their approaches are based.

The FMSF has been targeting therapists as the perpetrators of false memory syndrome, but this is a misguided and oversimplified explanation for the phenomenon. Therapists are an obvious target, because whether the accusing child has come to the therapy with memories or suspicions or has recovered memories in therapy, most clients have entered therapy before they make any accusations.

I had also assumed the therapists were to blame until, early on in my research, a therapist from Florida (a hotbed of sexual abuse therapy programs) told me that 80 percent of her clients now *arrive* with the concern that they might have repressed memories of sexual abuse. B. L. Dumar, a Florida therapist and alcohol abuse counselor, who, up until about five years ago, found that clients' suspicions of repressed memories of sexual abuse were rare, though she did have some clients who had previously remembered abuse they needed to explore.

Because clients are often referred to Dumar because they have drinking problems, she always insists that they concentrate on getting sober first. She has found that, during therapy with those who have never forgotten sexual abuse, the abuse memories eventually come up again and can be discussed more fruitfully once the client has quit drinking and become relatively stable. This is the only approach Dumar takes, since bringing up traumatic material when the client has not yet gotten a good grip on sobriety would lower the client's emotional stamina.

Serendipitously, Dumar also discovered that the majority of those who have vague suspicions of sexual abuse, generally stimulated by popular psychology books they have read or by talk shows they have seen, gradually come to believe that they are merely that: vague suspicions. As the clients work through their current real-life problems, and the pressures in their lives are relieved, they no longer have to search for some reason to explain why their lives have been in such a mess.

By being better informed and circumspect in their approach, therapists can stop being the fall guys and become part of the solution.

A MORAL IMPERATIVE

Therapists are between a rock and a hard place on this issue. As they have rightfully complained, suspicion expressed by the therapist about the client's "story" can hinder the forming of a therapeutic alliance. In addition, therapists need to be nonjudgmental in order to get people to open up.

It is easy to see the difficulty for therapists, but being nonjudgmental has now become politically correct. The popular culture has absorbed the therapist's anathema to making judgments regarding other people's beliefs, opinions, or behavior. However, we cannot each have our own "reality." Some things are wrong, and some things are right. For example, it is wrong to kill someone because you don't like the color of his or her skin.

A failure to make judgments is amoral. A failure to express judgments is irresponsible. Silence gives consent.

Judith Herman doesn't talk about having to retrieve repressed memories of sexual abuse in her books or her lectures. Yet, she was a speaker at the 1993 Eastern Regional Conference (ERC) on Abuse and Multiple Personality, where about a third of the attendees and speakers were talking about retrieval methods to get at not only "repressed memories" of sexual abuse but also "repressed memories" of satanic abuse. Herman never publicly expressed any doubts about these methods or ideas. By her silence, Herman lost an important opportunity to lead.

Indeed, the whole association has shirked its moral responsibility to make and express any judgment about how therapy is being carried out by some colleagues. At the 1992 ERC there was a "town meeting" or open forum to discuss the veracity of satanic abuse and satanic abuse therapy. Though many therapists in the crowd were concerned that pursuing and publicly backing the notion of satanic abuse could reflect badly on the profession, in the end the group decided to agree to disagree. The ERC now seems to have a policy of not criticizing colleagues, regardless of the unsoundness of their beliefs or practices.

Herman speaks out as a feminist on the issue of sexual abuse. Why is she not also speaking out against therapists' abuse of women? "Recovered memory" therapy is crippling for many. It causes them to become less functional, less capable of living in the real world and competing for jobs. This is a feminist issue.

We need to begin to make judgments again. It is our moral imperative. I believe that many of the "repressed memory" therapists and their techniques are *wrong*. They irresponsibly damage clients and their families.

Further, I do not believe that there is a satanic conspiracy. I believe that both the clients and the therapists who believe this are wrong. They are not only incorrect, it is bad therapy to promote a paranoid belief. These therapists are harming patients. This is morally wrong.

Therapists who do good therapy need to take a stand. It is wrong for them to "live and let live," standing idly by while others do harm in the name of therapy.

It is the therapists' moral responsibility to push for legislation and regulation that require adequate training and licensing procedures for anyone who plans to do therapy. If therapists do not want to be lumped in with incompetent counselors and blamed for problems, they must take a stand and take action now!

Notes

NOTES TO INTRODUCTION

1. Elizabeth Godley, "Memories of Abuse: A Recanter's Tale," *San Francisco Examiner*, April 6, 1993, section A, p. 6. Reprinted with permission of the author.

2. Ellen Bass and Laura Davis, *The Courage to Heal: A Guide for Women Survivors of Child Sexual Abuse*, second revised edition (New York: HarperPerennial, 1992), p. 82.

3. "They Told Me I Was Raped by Satan," television program: *The Jane Whitney Show*, broadcast November 11, 1992, River Tower Productions, Inc. Transcript from Burelle's Information Services, P.O. Box 7, Livingston, NJ 07039, p. 6.

4. Terence W. Campbell, Ph.D., Clinical and Forensic Psychologist, Sterling Heights, MI.

Rosalind Cartwright, Ph.D., Director of Sleep Disorder Clinic, Rush Presbyterian St. Luke's Medical Center, Chicago, IL.

Jean Chapman, Ph.D., Professor of Psychology, University of Wisconsin.

Loren Chapman, Ph.D., Professor Emeritus of Psychology, University of Wisconsin.

Robyn M. Dawes, Ph.D., Professor of Social Sciences, Carnegie Mellon University.

David F. Dinges, Ph.D., Associate Professor of Psychology, University of Pennsylvania

Fred Frankel, M.B.Ch.B.,D.P.M., Professor of Psychiatry, Harvard Medical School, Cambridge, MA

George K. Ganaway, M.D., Clinical Assistant Professor of Psychiatry, Emory University, Atlanta, GA

Martin Gardner, Author, Hendersonville, NC

Rochel Gelman, Ph.D., Professor of Psychology, University of California, Los Angeles

Henry Gleitman, Ph.D., Professor of Psychology, University of Pennsylvania

Lila Gleitman, Ph.D., Professor of Psychology, University of Pennsylvania

Richard Green, M.D., J.D., Professor of Psychiatry and Biobehavioral Sciences, University of California, Los Angeles

David A. Halperin, M.D., Associate Clinical Professor of Psychiatry, Mt. Sinai School of Medicine, NY

Ernest Hilgard, Ph.D., Emeritus Professor of Psychology, Stanford

John Hockman, M.D., Assistant Clinical Professor of Psychiatry, University of California, Los Angeles Medical School

David S. Holmes, Ph.D., Professor of Psychiatry, University of Kansas

Philip S. Holzman, Ph.D., Professor of Psychiatry, Harvard University, Cambridge, MA

John Kihlstrom, Ph.D., Professor of Psychology, University of Arizona

Harold Lief, M.D., Emeritus Professor of Psychiatry, University of Pennsylvania

Elizabeth Loftus, Ph.D., Professor of Psychology, University of Washington

Paul McHugh, M.D., Phipps Professor of Psychiatry, Johns Hopkins University, Baltimore, MD

Harold Merskey, D.M., Professor of Psychiatry, University of Western Ontario, Canada

Ulric Neisser, Ph.D., Woodruff Professor of Psychology, Emory University, Atlanta, GA

Richard Ofshe, Ph.D., Professor of Sociology, University of California at Berkeley

Martin Orne, M.D., Ph.D., Professor of Psychiatry, University of Pennsylvania

Loren Pankratz, Ph.D., Professor of Psychiatry, Oregon Health Sciences University, Portland, OR

Campbell Perry, Ph.D., Professor of Psychology, Concordia University, Montreal, Canada

Michael A. Persinger, Ph.D., Professor of Psychology, Laurentian University, Sudbury, Ontario, Canada

August Piper, Psychiatrist, Seattle, WA

Harrison Pope, Jr., M.D., Associate Professor of Psychiatry, Harvard Medical School, Cambridge, MA

James Randi, Author and Magician, Plantation, FL

Carolyn Saari, Ph.D., Professor of Social Work, Loyola University, Chicago, IL

Theodore Sarbin, Ph.D., Professor Emeritus of Psychology and Criminology, University of California, Santa Cruz

Thomas A. Sebeok, Ph.D., Professor Emeritus of Linguistics and Semiotics, Indiana University

Louise Shoemaker, Ph.D., Professor of Social Work, University of Pennsylvania

Margaret Singer, Ph.D., Emeritus Professor of Psychology, University of California at Berkeley

Ralph Slovenko, J.D., Ph.D., Professor of Law and Psychiatry, Wayne State University Law School, Detroit, MI

Donald Spence, Ph.D., Professor of Psychiatry, Robert Wood Johnson Medical Center, Princeton, NJ

Jeffrey Victor, Ph.D., Professor of Sociology, Jamestown Community College, Jamestown, NY

Hollida Wakefield, M.A., Psychologist, Institute of Psychological Therapies,

Louis Jolyon West, M.D., Professor of Psychiatry, University of California, Los Angeles.

Richard Ofshe and Ethan Watters, "Making Monsters—Psychotherapy's New Error: Repressed Memory, Multiple Personality and Satanic Abuse," *Society*, Mar./Apr. 1993, p. 16.

6. Susan Asher, a Provo therapist, as quoted in *The Utah Daily Herald*, September 5, 1992.

7. "They Told Me . . . ," p. 5.

NOTES TO CHAPTER ONE

1. "Roseanne and Tom Arnold," television program, "The Oprah Winfrey Show," broadcast November 8, 1991, Harpo Productions, Inc.

2. "Too Scared to Remember," television program, "The Oprah Winfrey Show," broadcast January 17, 1991, Harpo Productions, Inc. Transcript #1134 from Journal Graphics, 1535 Grant Street, Denver, CO 80203, p. 3.

3. Linda Meyer Williams and David Finkelhor, *The Characteristics of Incestuous Fathers*, Family Research Laboratory, University of New Hampshire, Durham, NH, July 31, 1992, p. 4. This report can be obtained by calling (603) 862-1888.

4. Diana E. H. Russell, *The Secret Trauma: Incest in the Lives of Girls and Women* (New York: Basic Books, 1986), p. 72.

5. Judith Lewis Herman, *Father-Daughter Incest* (Cambridge, MA: Harvard University Press, 1981), p. 13.

6. *The Secret Trauma*, p. 60.

7. *The Characteristics of Incestuous Fathers*, p. 4.

8. E. Sue Blume, *Secret Survivors: Uncovering Incest and Its Aftereffects in Women* (New York: Ballantine Books, 1991), p. xxii.

9. John F. Kihlstrom, "The Recovery of Memory in the Laboratory and Clinic," paper presented at the 1993 joint convention of the Rocky Mountain Psychological Association and the Western Psychological Association, Phoenix, April 1993. Correspondence concerning this paper should be addressed to John F. Kihlstrom, Amnesia & Cognition Unit, Department of Psychology, University of Arizona, Tucson, AZ 85721.

10. Saul V. Levine, *Radical Departures: Desperate Detours to Growing Up* (New York: Harcourt Brace Jovanovich, Inc., 1984), p. xx.

NOTES TO CHAPTER TWO

1. *Funk & Wagnalls Standard Dictionary,* Second Edition (New York: Harper Paperbacks, 1993).

2. Susan E. Smith, " 'Body Memories' and Other Pseudo-Scientific Notions of Survivor Psychology,' " paper presented at the False Memory Syndrome Foundation Conference ("Memory and Reality: An Emerging Crisis"), Valley Forge, PA, April 1993.

3. Judith Lewis Herman, *Father-Daughter Incest* (Cambridge, MA: Harvard University Press, 1981), p. 119.

4. All quotes in this section are from the *D Magazine* article "Abuse of Trust" by Glenna Whitley, January 1992, pp. 36–39.

5. End quotes from Glenna Whitley's "Abuse of Trust."

NOTES TO CHAPTER THREE

1. Melody Gavigan, "My Recovery from 'Recovery,' " in *True Stories of False Memories*, edited by Eleanor Goldstein and Kevin Farmer (Boca Raton, FL: SirS Books, 1993), pp. 266–270.

2. Martha L. Rogers, Ph.D., "The Recovered Memory Controversy: Scientific Foundations: Part 1," *The Orange County Psychologist*, January 1994.

3. Judith Lewis Herman, *Father-Daughter Incest* (Cambridge, MA: Harvard University Press, 1981), pp. 28–29.

4. David Finkelhor, "Long Term Effects of Childhood Victimization in a Nonclinical Sample," unpublished manuscript, University of New Hampshire, 1980.)

5. Linda Meyer Williams and David Finkelhor, "The Characteristics of Incestuous Fathers," *Family Research Laboratory*, University of New Hampshire, July 31, 1992, p. 2.

6. *Father-Daughter Incest*, p. 179.

7. Judith Lewis Herman, *Trauma and Recovery* (New York: Basic Books, 1992), p. 180.

NOTES TO CHAPTER FOUR

1. Michael Yapko, "The Seductions of Memory," *Family Therapy Networker*, Sept./Oct. 1993, p. 33.

2. Paul Simpson, telephone interview with author, May 26, 1993.

3. John Kihlstrom, "False Memory Syndrome," pamphlet from the FMS Foundation, Philadelphia, Pennsylvania, 1993.

4. George Ganaway, "Town Meeting: Delayed Memory Controversy in Adult Survivors," audiotape of talk given at the Fifth Annual Eastern Regional Conference on Abuse and Multiple Personality, Washington, D.C., June 3–8, 1993,

Audio Transcripts, Ltd. (703) 549-7334, catalogue #834-93-40. All quotes in this section are from this tape.

5. Michael Yapko, "Repression and Reality: How Accurate Are Memories of Childhood Trauma?," audiotape of talk given at the Sixteenth Annual Family Therapy Network Symposium, Washington, D.C., March 1993, The Resource Link (800)241-7785, catalogue #713-218-A&B.

6. "Repression and Reality."

7. "The Seductions of Memory," p. 35.

8. Roberta Strauss Feuerlicht, *Joe McCarthy and McCarthyism: The Hate that Haunts America* (New York: McGraw-Hill, 1972), p. 49.

9. *Joe McCarthy*, p. 54.

10. *Joe McCarthy*, pp. 68–72.

11. "The Seductions of Memory," p. 32.

12. All quotes in this section are from "Repression and Reality."

13. Martha Rogers, from a panel discussion, "Legal Issues: What Do Lawyers Need? What Do Scientists Have?," audiotape of a panel discussion given at the False Memory Syndrome Foundation Conference ("Memory and Reality: Emerging Crisis"), Valley Forge, Pennsylvania, April 1993, Aaron Video (216) 243-2221.

14. Simpson, telephone interview.

15. Paul Simpson can be reached at Today's Family Life Counseling and Educational Center, 7355 North Oracle Blvd., Suite #201, Tucson, Arizona 85704, (602) 297-2273.

NOTES TO CHAPTER FIVE

1. Andrew Meacham, "Call Me Mom," *Changes Magazine*, August 1992, p. 62.

2. Judith Herman, *Trauma and Recovery* (New York: Basic Books, 1992), p. 83.

3. *Trauma and Recovery*, p. 116.

4. "Call Me Mom," p. 56–63.

5. Renee Frederickson, *Repressed Memories: A Journey to Recovery from Sexual Abuse* (New York: Simon & Schuster, 1992), p. 52.

6. *Repressed Memories*, p. 84.

7. *Repressed Memories*, p. 86.

8. *Repressed Memories*, pp. 97 & 106.

9. *Repressed Memories*, pp. 125–27.

10. *Repressed Memories*, p. 141.

11. *Repressed Memories*, pp. 144–46.

12. *Repressed Memories*, pp. 150–151.

13. *Repressed Memories*, pp. 154–156.

14. *Repressed Memories*, pp. 152–153.

15. Susan E. Smith, "Body Memories and Other Pseudo-Scientific Notions of 'Survivor Psychology,' " paper presented to FMSF Conference ("Memory and Reality: Emerging Crisis"), Valley Forge, Pennsylvania, April 1993, p. 12.

16. "Body Memories," pp. 15–17.

17. "Body Memories," p. 19.

NOTES TO CHAPTER SIX

1. Henry Gleitman, "Reflections on Memory," audiotape of talk given at the False Memory Syndrome Foundation Conference ("Memory and Reality: An Emerging Crisis"), Valley Forge, Pennsylvania, April 18, 1993, Aaron Video (216) 243-2221.

2. All of the studies mentioned in this section come from *Human Memory: Theory and Practice*, by Alan Baddeley (Boston: Allyn and Bacon, 1990), pp. 390–395.

3. Ulric Neisser, "Memory with a Grain of Salt," audiotape of talk given at the False Memory Syndrome Foundation Conference ("Memory and Reality: An Emerging Crisis"), Valley Forge, Pennsylvania, April 16, 1993, Aaron Video (216) 243-2221.

4. Elizabeth Loftus, "Memory Distortions," paper presented at FMSF Conference ("Memory and Reality: An Emerging Crisis"), Valley Forge, Pennsylvania, April 1993.

5. Anonymous, "Surviving 'Therapy,' " *True Stories of False Memories*, edited by Eleanor Goldstein and Kevin Farmer (Boca Raton, Fl: SirS Books), 1993, pp. 285–332. This very detailed account should be read by anyone who seeks to know how anyone who was not sexually abused could come to believe that he or she was sexually abused.

6. "Surviving 'Therapy,' " p. 306.

7. "Surviving 'Therapy,' " p. 329.

8. David Spiegel, "Dissociation and Trauma," in *Dissociative Disorders: A Clinical Review*, ed. David Spiegel (Lutherville, MD: Sidran Press, 1993).

9. Edward J. Frischholz, "The Relationship Among Dissociation, Hypnosis, and Child Abuse in the Development of Multiple Personality Disorder," *Childhood Antecedents of Multiple Personality*, ed. Richard P. Kluft (Washington, DC: American Psychiatric Press, 1985).

10. George Ganaway, telephone interview with author, June 12, 1993.

11. Council on Scientific Affairs, "Scientific Status of Refreshing Recollection by the Use of Hypnosis," *Journal of the American Medical Association* (*JAMA*) 253, no. 13, April 5, 1985, p. 1918.

12. Sigmund Freud, *A Case of Hysteria, Three Essays on Sexuality, and Other Works* (London: Hogarth Press, 1953), p. 274.

13. "Scientific Status of Refreshing Recollection," p. 1921.

14. The full decision tree is in Martha L. Rogers, "Evaluating Adult Litigants Who Allege Injuries from Child Sexual Abuse: Clinical Assessment Methods for Traumatic Memories," a talk presented to the Fourth Annual Meeting of the American Psychological Society, San Diego, California, June 20, 1992. The text was also published in *Issues in Child Abuse Accusation* 4, no. 4, Fall 1992, pp. 221–238.

15. Paul McHugh, "Perspectives on Recovered Memories: Trauma, Conflict, and Deficit or Detachment vs. Attachment," audiotape of talk given at the False Memory Syndrome Foundation Conference ("Memory and Reality: An Emerging Crisis"), Valley Forge, Pennsylvania, April 1993, Aaron Video (216)243–2221.

NOTES TO CHAPTER SEVEN

1. Richard Ofshe and Ethan Watters, "Making Monsters," *Society* 30 (April 1993): 4–16.

2. Alan Baddeley, *Human Memory: Theory and Practice* (Boston: Allyn and Bacon, 1990), pp. 386–388.

3. Linda Meyer Williams, "Recall of Childhood Trauma: A Prospective Study of Women's Memories of Child Sexual Abuse," paper presented at the Annual Meeting of the American Society of Criminology, Phoenix, Arizona, October 27, 1993.

4. Linda Meyer Williams, "Adult Memories of Childhood Abuse: Preliminary Findings from a Longitudinal Study," *The Advisor*, Summer 1992, no. 5, pp. 19–20.

5. Chuck Haga and Paul McEnroe, "Sins of the Father," *The Minneapolis Star Tribune*, July 19, 1992, Sec. A, p. 14.

6. "Sins of the Father," pp. 1, 14, 15.

7. Martha Sawyer Allen, "Ex-priest Admits Abusing Children," *The Minneapolis Star Tribune*, July 15, 1992, Sec. A: pp. 1, 6.

8. Staff, "Porter Gets 18–20 Years for Molesting Children," *The Minneapolis Star Tribune*, December 7, 1993, Sec. A: pp. 1, 13.

9. Kenneth Woodward, Carolyn Friday, and Karen Springen, "The Sins of the Father," *Newsweek*, June 1, 1992, pp. 60–61.

10. David Spiegel, "Dissociation and Trauma," *Dissociative Disorders: A Clinical Review*, ed. David Spiegel (Lutherville, MD: Sidran Press, 1993).

11. Derived from T. H. Holmes and R. H. Rahe, "The Social Readjustment Rating Scale," *Journal of Psychosomatic Research* 11 (Pergamon Press, Ltd. 1967), pp. 213–218.

12. Study by L. Nadel and S. Zola-Martin, "Infantile Amnesia: A Neurobiological Perspective," *Infant Memory (Advances in the Study of Communication and Affect, Volume 9)*, ed. M. Moscovitch (New York: Plenum, 1984).

13. "Making Monsters," p. 3.

14. Frank W. Putnam, "Dissociative Phenomena," *Dissociative Disorders: A Clinical Review*, ed. David Spiegel (Lutherville, MD: Sidran Press, 1993), p. 3.

15. "Dissociative Phenomena," p. 4.

16. Thomas A. Harris, *I'm OK—You're OK* (New York: Avon Books, 1967), p. 38.

NOTES TO CHAPTER EIGHT

1. As quoted in Chris Costner Sizemore, *A Mind of My Own* (New York: William Morrow, 1989), p. 117.

2. Bennett G. Braun and Roberta G. Sachs, "The Development of Multiple Personality Disorder: Predisposing, Precipitating, and Perpetuating Factors," *Childhood Antecedents of Multiple Personality*, ed. Richard P. Kluft (Washington, D.C.: American Psychiatric Press, 1985).

3. "Development of Multiple Personality Disorder," p. 40.

4. "Development of Multiple Personality Disorder," p. 42.

5. "Development of Multiple Personality Disorder," pp. 41–42.

6. Richard P. Kluft, "Childhood Multiple Personality Disorder: Predictors, Clinical Findings, and Treatment Results," *Childhood Antecedents of Multiple Personality*, ed. Richard P. Kluft, (Washington, D.C.: American Psychiatric Press, 1985), p. 168.

7. Eve was a pseudonym for Chris Sizemore, author of two books about her life: Chris Costner Sizemore and Elen Sain Pittillo, *I'm Eve* (Garden City, NY: Doubleday & Company, 1977); and Chris Costner Sizemore, *A Mind of My Own* (New York: William Morrow, 1989).

8. Corbett H. Thigpen and Hervey M. Cleckley, *The Three Faces of Eve*, rev. ed. (Augusta, GA: published by the authors, 1992).

9. John Taylor, "The Lost Daughter," *Esquire*, March 1994, p. 84. All material about Sybil's relationship with Dr. Spiegel presented here is from Taylor's article.

10. "The Lost Daughter," p. 84.

11. Carol S. North, Jo-Ellyn M. Ryall, Daniel A. Ricci, and Richard D. Wetzel, *Multiple Personalities, Multiple Disorders: Psychiatric Classification and Media Influence* (New York: Oxford University Press, 1993).

12. Paul R. McHugh, "Multiple Personality Disorder," *The Harvard Mental Health Letter* 10, no. 3 (September 1993), pp. 4–6.

13. Elizabeth Carlson, "Through the Wringer: Panel of People Who Rejected False Memories," audiotape from the False Memory Syndrome Foundation Conference ("Memory and Reality: Emerging Crisis"), Valley Forge, Pennsylvania, April 1993, Aaron Video, (216) 243-2221.

14. George K. Ganaway, "Dissociative Disorders and Psychodynamic Theory: Trauma Versus Conflict and Deficit," paper presented at the False Memory Syndrome Foundation Conference ("Memory and Reality: An Emerging Crisis"), Valley Forge, Pennsylvania, April 1993, p. xx.

NOTES TO CHAPTER NINE

1. Lawrence W. Klein, "Controversies Around Recovered Memories of Incest and Ritualistic Abuse," audiotape of talk given to Conference at the Center for Mental Health at Foote Hospital, 205 North East Avenue, Jackson, Michigan 49201, (517) 788-4858, on August 7, 1993.

2. Frank W. Putnam, "Satanic Ritual Abuse: Critical Issues and Alternative Hypotheses," audiotape of panel discussion at the Seventh International Conference on Multiple Personality and Dissociative States, Chicago, Illinois, 1989, audio transcripts, (703) 549-334, catalogue #595-90-11a.

3. George K. Ganaway, "Satanic Ritual Abuse."

4. George K. Ganaway, telephone interview, June 12, 1993. All quotes in this section are from this interview.

5. Sherrill Mulhern, "Satanic Ritual Abuse."

6. Kenneth V. Lanning, *Investigator's Guide to Allegations of "Ritual" Child Abuse* (Quantico, VA: Behavioral Science Unit, National Center for the Analysis of Violent Crime, Federal Bureau of Investigation, FBI Academy, January, 1992), p. 1.

7. Mulhern, "Satanic Ritual Abuse."

8. Ganaway, telephone interview. All quotes in this section are from this interview.

9. Jeffrey S. Victor, *Satanic Panic* (Chicago, IL: Open Court, 1993).

10. Information about Lynn Gondolf's experience comes from a number of sources: Glenna Whitley, "Abuse of Trust," *D Magazine*, January 1992, pp. 36–39; "They Told Me I Was Raped by Satan," television program, *The Jane Whitney Show,* River Tower Productions, Inc., November 11, 1992, transcript, Burelle's Information Services, P.O. Box 7, Livingston, New Jersey 07039; and "Through the Wringer: A Panel of People Who Rejected False Memories," False Memory Syndrome Conference ("Memory and Reality: An Emerging Crisis"), Valley Forge, Pennsylvania, April 1993, Aaron Video, (216) 243-2221.

11. "They Told Me I Was Raped by Satan," p. 6.

12. Lynn Gondolf, "Through the Wringer."

13. Eileen Goldman, telephone interview with author, 1993.

14. "Controversies Around Recovered Memories."

15. Correspondence with Klein March 30, 1994.

16. "Controversies Around Recovered Memories."

NOTES TO CHAPTER TEN

1. Stephen Landman, audiotape of talk given at a conference, "Controversies Around Recovered Memories of Incest and Ritualistic Abuse," Ann Arbor,

Michigan, August 7, 1993. Tape available from the Center for Mental Health at Foote Hospital, 205 North East Ave., Jackson, Michigan 49201, (517) 788-4858.

2. "It Can Happen to Anyone," *The False Memory Syndrome Phenomenon*, collection of articles compiled by the FMS Foundation, 3508 Market St., Suite 128, Philadelphia, Pennsylvania 19104, 1993, p. 41.

3. Endnote information on this article is being withheld to protect Doreen's privacy.

NOTES TO CHAPTER ELEVEN

1. This chart, based on Stanley Turecki's temperamental variables as explained in his book, *The Difficult Child* (Bantam Books, 1985), was first published in *How to Avoid Your Parents' Mistakes When You Raise Your Children*, Claudette Wassil-Grimm (Simon & Schuster, 1990), p. 294.

NOTES TO CHAPTER TWELVE

1. FMS Foundation Newsletter, Jan. 8, 1993; Vol. 2, no. 1: pp. 3–6.

2. FMS Foundation Newsletter, Jan. 8, 1993; Vol. 2, no. 1: pp. 3–6.

3. William N. Friedrich and Patricia Grambsch, "Child Sexual Behavior Inventory: Normative and Clinical Comparisons," *Psychological Assessment*, 1992; Vol. 4, no. 3: pp. 303–11. Information for this section also came from the following sources: William N. Friedrich, "Sexual Behavior in Sexually Abused Children," *Violence Update*, January 1993; vol. 3, no. 5: pp. 1, 7–11; and William N. Friedrich, Patricia Grambsch, Daniel Broughton, James Kuiper, and Robert L. Beilke, "Normative Sexual Behavior in children," *Pediatrics*, vol. 88, no. 3: September 1991; p. 460.

4. Information derived from William Friedrich, "Sexual Behavior in Sexually Abused Children," pp. 1, 7–11.

5. Jeffrey Victor, *Human Sexuality: A Social Psychological Approach* (Englewood Cliffs, NJ: Prentice Hall, Inc., 1980), pp. 178–192.

6. This and all other information from Dr. Lief comes from a telephone interview with the author on March 24, 1993.

7. Human Sexuality, p. 179 +.

8. Susan E. Smith, *Survivor Psychology—How the Mental Health Missionaries of a Pseudo-Science Cult are Raping Minds and Ruining Families* (Boca Raton, FL: SirS-Books, in press).

9. Susan E. Smith, "Body Memories and Other Pseudoscientific Notions of Survivor Psychology," revised version of paper presented at the False Memory Syndrome Foundation Conference ("Memory and Reality: An Emerging Crisis," Valley Forge, PA, April 16–18, 1993.

NOTES TO CHAPTER THIRTEEN

1. This and other comments by Dr. Pamela Freyd in this chapter from my telephone interview with her on September 12, 1993.

2. Survey results out of 42 returns A = Very Healthy, B = Somewhat Healthy, C = Neutral or Irrelevant, D = Somewhat Dysfunctional, E = Very dysfunctional:

Scenario One: A-13, B-6, C-12, D-9, E-2

Scenario Two: A-4, B-9, C-18, D-9, E-2

Scenario Three: A-1, B-5, C-9, D-23, E-4

Scenario Four: A-4, B-16, C-6, D-10, E-6

Scenario Five: A-11, B-12, C-9, D-7, E-3

Scenario Six: A-16, B-14, C-7, D-5, E-0

Scenario Seven: A-22, B-8, C-4, D-3, E-5

Scenario Eight: A-4, B-5, C-15, D-15, E-3

Scenario Nine: A-18, B-8, C-7, D-7, E-2

Scenario Ten: A-27, B-8, C-2, D-2, E-3

The 42 respondents were self-selected from three different church groups all located in somewhat rural areas. Of these, 18 defined themselves as "liberal," 17 as "moderate," 1 "conservative," and 7 "other." Twenty were males, 22 females. There were 5 respondents between the ages of 20 and 27; 3 between the ages of 28 and 35; 8 between age 36 and 43; 10 between age 44 and 51; and 16 were over 51 years of age (the age of most accused parents). All but three were parents.

3. Gail Sheehy, *"Passages: Predictable Crises of Adult Life* (New York: Bantam Books, 1976), p. 120.

4. This and other comments by Dr. Lief in this chapter are from my telephone interview with him on March 24, 1993.

NOTES TO CHAPTER FOURTEEN

1. Renee Frederickson, *Repressed Memories: A Journey to Recovery from Sexual Abuse* (New York: Simon & Schuster, 1992), pp. 30–32.

2. Jack Engler and Daniel Goleman, *The Consumer's Guide to Psychotherapy* (New York: Simon & Schuster, Fireside, 1992), p. 409.

3. Advice in this section is based on selected recommendations given in *The Consumer's Guide to Psychotherapy*, Part One.

4. Steven Hassan, *Combatting Cult Mind Control* (Rochester, VT: Park Street Press), 1990.

Bibliography

BOOKS

AMBERT, ANNE-MARIE. (1992) *The Effect of Children on Parents*. New York: Haworth Press.

BADDELEY, ALAN. (1990) *Human Memory: Theory and Practice*. Needham Heights, MA: Allyn and Bacon.

BAKER, ROBERT A. (1992) *Hidden Memories: Voices and Visions from Within*. Buffalo, NY: Prometheus Books.

BASS, ELLEN AND DAVIS, LAURA. (1992) *The Courage to Heal: A Guide for Women Survivors of Child Sexual Abuse*, second revised edition. New York: HarperCollins.

BLUME, E. SUE. (1991) *Secret Survivors: Uncovering Incest and Its Aftereffects in Women*. New York: Ballantine Books.

BRAUN, BENNETT G. AND SACHS, ROBERTA G. (1985) "The Development of Multiple Personality Disorder: Predisposing, Precipitating, and Perpetuating Factors" in *Childhood Antecedents of Multiple Personality Disorder*, edited by Richard P. Kluft. Washington, DC: American Psychiatric Press.

CALOF, DAVID L. WITH LELOO, MARY. (1993) *Multiple Personality and Dissociation*. Park Ridge, IL: Parkside Publishing.

CHASE, TRUDDI. (1987) *When Rabbit Howls*. New York: Dutton.

CHESLER, PHYLLIS. (1972) *Women and Madness*. Garden City, NY: Doubleday. Reprint with new introduction. New York: Harcourt Brace Jovanovitch.

CONWAY, FLO AND SIEGELMAN, JIM. (1979) *Snapping: America's Epidemic of Sudden Personality Change*. New York: Dell.

COURTOIS, CHRISTINE. (1988) *Healing the Incest Wound: Adult Survivors in Therapy*. New York: W.W. Norton.

DEIKMAN, ARTHUR J. (1990) *The Wrong Way Home: Uncovering the Patterns of Cult Behavior in American Society*. Boston: Beacon Press.

ENGLER, JACK AND GOLEMAN, JACK. (1992) *The Consumer's Guide to Psychotherapy*. New York: Simon & Schuster, Fireside.

FEURERLICHT, ROBERTA STRAUSS. (1972) *Joe McCarthy and McCarthyism: The Hate That Haunts America*. New York: McGraw-Hill.

FREDRICKSON, RENÉE. (1992) *Repressed Memories: A Journey to Recovery from Sexual Abuse*. New York: Simon & Schuster.

FREUD, SIGMUND. (1953) *A Case of Hysteria, Three Essays on Sexuality, and Other Works*. London: Hogarth Press.

FRISCHHOLZ, EDWARD J. (1985) "The Relationship Among Dissociation, Hypnosis, and Child Abuse in the Development of Multiple Personality Disorder" in *Childhood Antecedents of Multiple Personality Disorder*, edited by Richard P. Kluft. Washington, DC: American Psychiatric Press.

FUNK & WAGNALLS–STANDARD DICTIONARY, SECOND EDITION. New York: Harper Paperbacks.

GARDNER, RICHARD A. (1991) *Sex Abuse Hysteria: Salem Witch Trials Revisited*. Cresskill, NJ: Creative Therapeutics.

——. (1992) *True and False Accusations of Child Sex Abuse*. Cresskill, NJ: Creative Therapeutics.

GOLDSTEIN, ELEANOR WITH FARMER, KEVIN. (1992) *Confabulations: False Memories–Destroying Families*. Boca Raton, FL: SirS Books.

GOLDSTEIN, ELEANOR WITH FARMER, KEVIN. (1993) *True Stories of False Memories*. Boca Raton, FL: SirS Books.

HARRIS, THOMAS A. (1967) *I'm OK–You're OK*. New York, NY: Avon Books.

HASSAN, STEVEN. (1990) *Combatting Cult Mind Control*. Rochester, VT: Park Street Press.

HECHLER, DAVID. (1988) *The Battle and the Backlash: The Child Sexual Abuse War*. Lexington, MA: Lexington Books.

HERMAN, JUDITH LEWIS. (1981) *Father-Daughter Incest*. Cambridge, MA: Harvard University Press.

—— (1992) *Trauma and Recovery: The Aftermath of Violence–from Domestic Abuse to Political Terror*. New York: HarperCollins.

HILLMAN, JAMES AND VENTURA, MICHAEL. (1992) *We've Had a Hundred Years of Psychotherapy and the World's Getting Worse*. New York: HarperCollins.

JENKINS, PHILIP AND MAIER, DANIEL. (1991) "Occult Survivors: The Making of a Myth" in *The Satanism Scare*, edited by James T. Richardson *et al.* New York: Aldine de Gruyter.

KATZ, DONALD. (1992) *Home Fires: An Intimate Portrait of One Middle Class Family in Postwar America*. New York: HarperCollins.

KATZ, STAN J. AND LIU, AIMEE E. (1991) *The Codependency Conspiracy: How to Break the Recovery Habit and Take Charge of Your Life*. New York: Warner Books.

KLUFT, RICHARD P., editor. (1985) *Childhood Antecedents of Multiple Personality Disorder*. Washington, DC: American Psychiatric Press.

KRAMER, PETER D. (1993) *Listening to Prozac*. New York,: Viking.

LEVINE, SAUL V. (1984) *Radical Departures: Desperate Detours to Growing Up*. New York: Harcourt Brace Jovanovich, Inc.

LIVELY, EDWIN AND VIRGINIA. (1991) *Sexual Development of Young Children*. Albany, NY: Delmar.

LOFTUS, ELIZABETH. (1979) *Eyewitness Testimony*. Cambridge, MA: Harvard University Press.

———. (1991) *Witness for the Defense: The Accused, the Eyewitness, and the Expert Who Puts Memory on Trial*. New York: St. Martin's Press.

MULHERN, SHERRILL. (1991) "Satanism and Psychotherapy: A Rumor in Search of an Inquisition" in *The Satanism Scare*, edited by James T. Richardson, *et al*. New York: Aldine de Gruyter.

NADEL, L. AND ZOLA-MARTIN, S. (1984) "Infantile Amnesia: A Neurobiological Perspective" in *Infant Memory (Advances in the Study of Communication and Affect)*, Volume 9, edited by M. Moscovitch. New York: Plenum.

NORTH, CAROL S.; RICCI, DANIEL A., RYALL, JO-ELLYN M.; AND WETZEL, RICHARD D., editors. (1993) *Multiple Personalities, Multiple Disorders*. New York: Oxford University Press.

PUTNAM, FRANK W. (1993) "Dissociative Phenomena" in *Dissociative Disorders, a Clinial Review*, edited by David Spiegel. Lutherville, MD: Sidran Press.

REED, GRAHAM. (1972) *The Psychology of Anomalous Experience: A Cognitive Approach*. London: Hutchinson & Co.

RICHARDSON, JAMES T.; BEST, JOEL, and BROMLEY, DAVID G., editors. (1991) *The Satanism Scare*. New York: Aldine de Gruyter.

RUSSELL, DIANA E. H. (1986) *The Secret Trauma: Incest in the Lives of Girls and Women*. New York: Basic Books.

SCHANK, ROGER C. (1990) *Tell Me a Story: A New Look at Real and Artificial Memory*. New York: Macmillan.

SCHREIBER, FLORA RHETA. (1974) *Sybil*. New York, NY: Warner Books.

SINGER, JEROME L. AND SWITZER, ELLEN. (1980) *Mind-Play: The Creative Uses of Fantasy*. Englewood Cliffs, NJ: Prentice-Hall.

SINGER, JEROME, L., editor (1990) *Repression and Dissociation: Implications for Personality Theory, Psychopathology and Health*. Chicago, IL: University of Chicago Press.

SIZEMORE, CHRIS COSTNER. (1989) *A Mind of My Own*. New York: William Morrow.

SIZEMORE, CHRIS COSTNER AND PITTILLO, ELEN SAIN. (1977) *I'm Eve*. Garden City, NY: Doubleday & Company.

SMITH, MICHELLE AND PAZDER, LAWRENCE. (1981) *Michelle Remembers*. New York: Simon & Schuster.

SMITH, SUSAN. (in press) *Survivor Psychology—How the Mental Health Missionaries of a Psuedo-Science Cult Are Raping Minds and Ruining Families*. Boca Raton, FL: SirS Books.

SPIEGEL, DAVID. (1993) "Dissociation and Trauma" in *Dissociative Disorders, a Clinical Review*, edited by David Spiegel. Lutherville, MD: Sidran Press.

TAVRIS, CAROL. (1992) *The Mismeasure of Woman*. New York: Simon & Schuster.

TERR, LENORE. (1990) *Too Scared to Cry: How Trauma Affects Children . . . and Ultimately Us All*. New York: Basic Books.

THIGPEN, CORBETT H. AND CLECKLEY, HARVEY M. (1992) *The Three Faces of Eve*. Published by the authors. For copies write to The Three Faces of Eve, PO Box 2619, Augusta, Georgia 30904-2619.

VICTOR, JEFFREY S. (1993) *Satanic Panic: The Creation of a Contemporary Legend*. Chicago, IL: Open Court.

WAKEFIELD, HOLLIDA; UNDERWAGER, RALPH; LEGRAND, ROSS; ERICKSON, JOSEPH, AND SAMPLES, CHRISTINE. (1988) *Accusations of Child Sexual Abuse*. Springfield, IL: Charles C. Thomas.

WASSIL-GRIMM, CLAUDETTE. (1990) *How to Avoid Your Parent's Mistakes When You Raise Your Children*. New York: Simon & Schuster.

——. (1994) *Where's Daddy?* New York: Overlook Press.

GOVERNMENT PUBLICATIONS

LANNING, KENNETH V. (1992) *Investigator's Guide to Allegations of "Ritual" Child Abuse*. Quantico, VA: Federal Bureau of Investigation.

SAN DIEGO COUNTY GRAND JURY. (1992) *Child Sexual Abuse, Assault, and Molest Issues, Report No. 8*. San Diego, CA:

WASHINGTON STATE INSTITUTE FOR PUBLIC POLICY, COMMUNITY PROTECTION RESEARCH PROJECT. (1992) *Findings from the Community Protection Project: A Chartbook*. Olympia, WA:

TV, VIDEO, AND AUDIO

BARRETT, MARY JO. "The Systemic Treatment of Child Abuse," Part 1. Audiotape of talk given at the sixteenth Annual Family Therapy Network Symposium, March 1993. Catalogue #713-118-A & B from The Resource Link, (800) 241-7785.

"Bearing Witness to Memories of a Murder." Television program, "Larry King Live," broadcast October 29, 1991. Cable News Network, Inc. Guest, Eileen Franklin, author of *Sins of the Father*. Transcript #418 from Journal Graphics, 1535 Grant Street, Denver, CO 80203.

BECK, PHYLLIS W.; SLOVENKO, RALPH; EMON, RANDONY; GARVER, STEVEN, AND MACLEAN, HARRY N. "Legal Issues: Did the Crime Occur?" Audiotape of panel discussion at the False Memory Syndrome Foundation Conference ("Memory and Reality: An Emerging Crisis"), Valley Forge, PA, April 1993. Tape available from Aaron Video, (216) 243-2221.

BERLINER, LUCY. *See* deRivera, Joseph.

BRODIE, LAURA. *See* Richette, Lisa.

BREWSTER, ANDRE. *See* Richette Lisa.

BURGESS, ANNE W.; Ganaway, George K.; Kluft, Richard P.; Lowenstein, Richard J.; and Courtois, Christine A. "Town Meeting: Delayed Memory Controversy in Adult Survivors." Audiotape of panel discussion at the Fifth Annual Eastern Regional Conference on Abuse and Multiple Personality, Alexandria, VA, June 1993. Catalogue #40-834-93 from Audio Transcripts, Ltd., (703)549-7334.

CALOF, DAVID and Yapko, Michael. "Repression and Reality: How Accurate Are Memories of Childhood Trauma?" Audiotape of debate at the sixteenth Annual Family Therapy Network Symposium, March 1993. Catalogue #12843-93 from The Resource Link, (800)241-7785.

"A Child Cries 'Wolf.' " Television program, "The Maury Povich Show," broadcast November 14, 1991. Maury Povich Productions. Transcript #47 from Journal Graphics, 1535 Grant Street, Denver, CO 80203.

"The Coming of Age – Brain Storms." Television program, "CNN Specials," broadcast May 21, 1993. Cable News Network, Inc. Transcript #182 from Journal Graphics, 1535 Grant Street, Denver, CO 80203.

COURTOIS, CHRISTINE A. *See* Burgess, Anne W.

COURTOIS, CHRISTINE A. *See* Turkus, Joan A.

CRABTREE, ADAM G. "Treatment of Multiple Personality Before 'Eve.' " Audiotape of talk given at the Fifth Annual Eastern Regional Conference on Abuse and Multiple Personality, Alexandria, VA, June 1993. Catalogue #12-834-93 from Audio Transcripts, Ltd., (703) 549-7334.

"Dark Memories." Television program, "ABC News Prime Time Live," broadcast September 17, 1992. American Broadcast Company, Inc. Transcript #263 from Journal Graphics, 1535 Grant Street, Denver, CO 80203.

DERIVERA, JOSEPH; Berliner, Lucy; Victor, Jeffrey; Smith, Susan; and Leggett, Jack. "Epidemiography of FMS." Audiotape of talks given at the False Memory Syndrome Foundation Conference ("Memory and Reality: An Emerging Crisis"), Valley Forge, PA, April 1993. Tape available from Aaron Video, (216) 243-2221.

"Devilish Deeds." Television program, "ABC News Prime Time Live," broadcast January 7, 1993. American Broadcast Company, Inc. Transcript #279 from Journal Graphics, 1535 Grant Street, Denver, CO 80203.

DINGES, DALE P. *See* Seligman, Martin.

FRANKEL, FRED H. *See* Lief, Harold I.

FREYD, JENNIFER J. "Controversies Around Recovered Memories of Incest and Ritualistic Abuse." Audiotape of talk given at a Conference, Ann Arbor, MI, August 1993. Tape available from the Center for Mental Health, Foote Hospital, 205 North East Avenue, Jackson, MI 49201, (517) 788-4858.

FREYD, PETER and GLEITMAN, HENRY. "Some Reflections on Memory." Audiotape of talks given at the False Memory Syndrome Foundation Conference ("Memory and Reality: An Emerging Crisis"), Valley Forge, PA, April 1993. Tape available Aaron Video, (216) 243-2221.

GANAWAY, GEORGE K. "Controversies Around Recovered Memories of Incest and Ritualistic Abuse." Audiotape of talk given at a Conference, Ann Arbor, MI, August 1993. Tape available from the Center for Mental Health, Foote Hospital, 205 North East Avenue, Jackson, MI 49201, (517) 788-4858.

GANAWAY, GEORGE K.; MULHERN, SHERRIL, AND PUTNAM, GEORGE. "Satanic Ritual Abuse: Critical Issues and Alternative Hypotheses." Audiotape of panel discussion at the Seventh International Conference on Multiple Personality and Dissociative States, Chicago, IL, 1989. Catalogue #595-90-11a from Audio Transcripts, Ltd., (703) 549-7334.

GANAWAY, GEORGE K. See Burgess, Anne W.

GANAWAY, GEORGE K. See Lief, Harold I.

GLEITMAN, HENRY. See Freyd, Peter.

GOLDSTEIN, ELEANOR and SINGER, MARGARET. "Through the Wringer: Panel of People Who Rejected False Memories." Audiotape of talks given at the False Memory Syndrome Foundation Conference ("Memory and Reality: An Emerging Crisis"), Valley Forge, PA, April 1993. Tape available from Aaron Video, (216) 243-2221.

GONDOLF, LYNN. See Goldstein, Eleanor.

GREEN, RICHARD. See Richette, Lisa.

HARGRAVE, TERRY. "Forgiveness: Healing Intergenerational Wounds." Audiotape of talk given at the Sixteenth Annual Family Therapy Network Symposium, March 1993. Catalogue #713-218-A & B from The Resource Link, (800) 241-7785.

HUBBLE, MARK AND DUNCAN, BARRY. "Reality Versus the Therapy Industry." Audiotape of talk given at the Sixteenth Annual Family Therapy Network Symposium, March 1993. Catalogue #713-407-A & B from The Resource Link, (800) 241-7785.

KIRSCHNER, ADILE AND SAM, AND RAPAPORT, RICHARD L. "Disclosure and Confrontation." Audiotape of talk given at the Fifth Annual Eastern Regional Conference on Abuse and Multiple Personality, Alexandria, VA, June 1993. Catalogue #06-834-93 from Audio Transcripts Ltd., (703) 549-7334.

KISCIELNY, ROBERT. SEE RICHETTE, LISA.

KLEIN, LAWRENCE R. "Controversies Around Recovered Memories of Incest and Ritualistic Abuse." Audiotape of talk given at conference, Ann Arbor, MI, August 1993. Tape available from the Center for Mental Health, Foote Hospital, 205 North East Avenue, Jackson, MI 49201, (517) 788-4858.

KLUFT, RICHARD P. *See* Burgess, Anne W.

KLUFT, RICHARD P.; ROSS, COLIN A., AND TURKUS, JOAN A. "Town Meeting: the Ritual Abuse Controversy." Audiotape of panel discussion at the Fourth Annual Eastern Regional Conference on Abuse and Multiple Personality, June 1992. Catalogue #22-742-92 from Audio Transcripts, Ltd., (703) 549-7334.

LEGGETT, JACK. *See* deRivera, Joseph.

LIEF, HAROLD I.; MCHUGH, PAUL; GANAWAY, GEORGE K., AND FRANKEL, FRED H. "Perspectives on Recovered Memories: Trauma, Conflict, and Deficit or Detachment vs. Attachment." Audiotape of talks given at the False Memory Syndrome Foundation Conference ("Memory and Reality: An Emerging Crisis"), Valley Forge, PA, April 1993. Catalogue tape available from Aaron Video, (216) 243-2221.

LIPTON, ANITA. *See* Richette, Lisa.

LOWENSTEIN, RICHARD J. *See* Burgess, Anne W.

MCHUGH, PAUL. *See* Lief, Harold I.

MELTZER, RUTH. *See* Whybrow, Peter.

"Memories of Abuse." Television program, "Sonya Live," broadcast May 3, 1993. Cable News Network, Inc. Transcript #288 from Journal Graphics, 1535 Grant Street, Denver, CO 80203.

MULHERN, SHERRIL. *See* Ganaway, George K., "Satanic Ritual Abuse."

NEISSER, ULRIC. "Memory with a Grain of Salt." Audiotape of talk given at the False Memory Syndrome Foundation Conference ("Memory and Reality: An Emerging Crisis"), Valley Forge, PA, April 1993. Catalogue tape available from Aaron Video, (216) 243-2221.

O'HANION, WILLIAM HUDSON. "Frozen in Time: A Solution-Focused Approach to Sexual Abuse." Audiotape of talk given at the Sixteenth Annual Family Therapy Network Symposium, March 1993. Catalogue #713-321-A & B from The Resource Link, (800) 241-7785.

ORE, MARTIN. *See* Seligman, Martin.

PERRY, CAMPBELL. *See* Loftus, Elizabeth.

PUTNAM, FRANK W. *See* Ganaway, George K., "Satanic Ritual Abuse."

"Repressed Memory." Television program, *Good Morning America,* show #1621 broadcast August 31, 1992. American Broadcast Company, Inc. Transcript #1621 from Journal Graphics, 1535 Grant Street, Denver, CO 80203.

"Repressed Memories Stir Difficult Controversy." Television program, "CNN Morning News," broadcast May 3, 1993. Cable News Network, Inc. Transcript #302, segment 1, from Journal Graphics, 1535 Grant Street, Denver, CO 80203.

RICHETTE, LISA; LIPTON, ANITA; KISCIELNY, ROBERT; BREWSTER, ANDRE; ROGERS, MARTHA; BRODIE, LAURA; CRAING, WILLIAM B., AND GREEN, RICHARD. "Legal Issues: What Do Lawyers Need? What Do Scientists Have?" Audiotape of talks given at the False Memory Syndrome Foundation Conference ("Memory and Reality: An Emerging Crisis"), Valley Forge, PA, April 1993. Catalogue tape available from Aaron Video, (216) 243-2221.

ROGERS, MARTHA. *See* Richette, Lisa.

"Roseanne and Tom Arnold." Television program, *The Oprah Winfrey Show*, broadcast November 8, 1991. Harpo Productions, Inc. Transcript tape available from Journal Graphics, 1535 Grant Street, Denver, CO 80203.

ROSS, COLIN A. *See* Kluft, Richard P.

SELIGMAN, MARTIN; DINGES, DALE F.; ORE, MARTIN; PERRY, CAMPBELL, AND LOFTUS, ELIZABETH. "Memory: The Research to Date." Audiotape of talks given at the False Memory Syndrome Foundation Conference ("Memory and Reality: An Emerging Crisis"), Valley Forge, PA, April 1993. Catalogue tape available from Aaron Video, (216) 243-2221.

SINGER, MARGARET. *See* Goldstein, Eleanor.

SMITH, SUSAN. *See* deRivera, Joseph.

TAMARKIN, CIVIA. "Professional's Forum: Investigative Issues in Ritual Abuse Cases." Audiotape of talk given at the Fifth Annual Eastern Regional Conference on Abuse and Multiple Personality, Alexandria, VA, June 1993. Catalogue #50-834-93-A & B from Audio Transcripts, Ltd., (703) 549-7334.

"They Told Me I Was Raped by Satan." Television program, *The Jane Whitney Show*, broadcast November 11, 1992. River Tower Productions, Inc. Transcript, from Burelle's Information Services, P.O. Box 7, Livingston, NJ 07030.

"Too Scared to Remember." Television program, *The Oprah Winfrey Show*, broadcast January 17, 1991. Harpo Productions. Transcript #1134, p. 3., from Journal Graphics, 1535 Grant Street, Denver, CO 80203.

TURKUS, JOAN A., AND COURTOIS, CHRISTINE A. "The Dissociative Mental Health Professional as Client and Therapist." Audiotape of talks given at the Fifth Annual Eastern Regional Conference on Abuse and Multiple Personality, Alexandria, VA, June 1993. Catalogue #27-834-93 from Audio Transcripts, Ltd., (703) 549-7334.

TURKUS, JOAN A. *See* Kluft, Richard P.

VICTOR, JEFFREY. *See* deRivera, Joseph.

WHYBROW, PETER AND MELTZER, RUTH. "A Mental Health Crisis." Audiotape of talks given at the False Memory Syndrome Foundation Conference ("Memory and Reality: An Emerging Crisis"), Valley Forge, PA, April 1993. Catalogue tape available from Aaron Video, (216) 243-2221.

YAPKO, MICHAEL. *See* Calof, David.

ARTICLES AND PAPERS

ALLEN, MARTHA SAWYER. (1993)"Ex-priest Admits Abusing Children." *Minneapolis Star Tribune*, July 15, section A: 1, 6.

ALLISON, MARIA RUTH. (1992) "When You Suspect Child Abuse." *Networker*, May/June: 54–57.

ANDREAS, STEVE. (1992) "Embedding the Message." *Networker*, May/June: 59–62.

BALDWIN, LEIGH. (1993) "Delayed Memories: A Survivor's Search for the Truth." *Moving Forward*, Volume 2, Number 4: 4–5.

BARRETT, MARY JO AND TREPPER TERRY. (1992) "Unmasking the Incestous Family." *Networker*, May/June: 39–46.

BLYSKAL, JEFF. (1993) "Head Hunt: How to Find the Right Psychotherapist—for the Right Price." *New York* January 11: 28–38.

BRYAN, BARBARA. (1993) "History, Hysteria, and Tapeworms." Paper presented at Charlottesville, VA: National Child Abuse Defense and Resource Center. August 21.

BRZUSTOWICZ, RICHARD, AND CSICSERY, GEORGE PAUL. (1993) "The Remembrance of Crimes Past." *Heterodoxy* January: 7.

CALLAHAN, JEAN. (1992) "Leaving The Ashram." *Common Boundary* July/August: 32–38.

CAMPBELL, TERRENCE W. (1992) "Diagnosing Incest: The Problem of False Positives and Their Consequences." *Issues in Child Abuse Accusations* Volume 4, Number 4: 161–168.

COLEMAN, LEE. (1992) "Creating 'Memories' of Sexual Abuse." *Issues in Child Abuse Accusations* Volume 4, Number 4: 169–76.

CONAWAY, JANELLE. (1993) "Journey to the Dark Side." *Albuquerque Journal*. July 18, section C: 1.

Council on Scientific Affairs. (1985) "Council Report: Scientific Status of Refreshing Recollection by the Use of Hypnosis." *Journal of the American Medical Association* Volume 253, Number 13, April 5: 1918–23.

COURTOIS, CHRISTINE A. (1992) "The Memory Retrieval Process in Incest Survivor Therapy." *Journal of Child Sexual Abuse* Volume 1, Number 1: 15–29.

DALY, LAWRENCE W. AND PACIFICO, J. FRANK. (1991) "Opening the Doors to the Past: Decade-Delayed Disclosures of Memories of Years Gone By." *Champion Magazine* December: 43–47.

DAWES, ROBYN M. (1991) "Biases of Retrospection." *Issues In Child Abuse Accusations* Volume 1, Number 3: 25–28.

——. (1992) "Why Believe That for Which There Is No Good Evidence?" *Issues In Child Abuse Accusations* Volume 4, Number 4: 214–18.

DEMAUSE, LLOYD, editor. (1991) *The Journal of Psychohistory* Volume 19, Number 2: Fall. New York: Association for Psychohistory, Inc.

——. (1992) *The Journal of Psychohistory* Volume 19, Number 3: Winter. New York: Association for Psychohistory, Inc.

DERIVERA, JOSEPH. (1993) " 'Trauma Hunt' Perils Therapy." *The Cleveland Plain Dealer* May 19: Forum/Essay & Comment Section.

DOE, REBECCA. (1992) "The Nightmare That May Never End." *Issues in Child Abuse Accusations* Volume 4, Number 4: 248–50.

EMON, RANDY. (1993) "Occult Cop." Text of talk given at the False Memory Syndrome Foundation Conference ("Memory and Reality: An Emerging Crisis"), Valley Forge, PA, April.

EVERY, MARY. (1992) "Memories, True or False?" *Santa Barbara News Press* October 18.

False Memory Syndrome Foundation. (1993) "Family Survey Results." False Memory Syndrome Foundation, Philadelphia, PA, Summer.

——. (1993) "Summary of Legal Survey Data." Presented at False Memory Syndrome Foundation Conference, (Memory and Reality: Emerging Crisis.), Valley Forge, PA, April 17.

False Memory Syndrome Foundation Newsletter. (1993) Volume 2, Number 8, January 8: 3–6.

FINKELHOR, DAVID. (1980) "Long Term Effects of Childhood Victimization in a Non-clinical Sample." Unpublished manuscript.

FORREST, MARGOT SILK. (1992) *The Healing Woman* Volume 1, Number 8.

FREEMAN, KERIAN. (1992) "The Hurt with No Name." *Networker* May/June: 27–31.

FRIEDRICH, WILLIAM N. (1993) *Violence Update* Volume 3, Number 5, January: 1, 7–11.

—— and Grambsch, Patricia. (1992) "Child Sexual Behavior Inventory: Normative and Clinical Comparisons." *Psychological Assessment* Volume 4, Number 3: 303–11.

GANAWAY, GEORGE K. (1993) "Dissociative Disorders and Psychodynamic Theory: Trauma Versus Conflict and Deficit." Paper presented at the False Memory Syndrome Foundation Conference ("Memory and Reality: An Emerging Crisis"), Valley Forge, PA, April 17.

GARDNER, RICHARD A. (1992) "Belated Realization of Child Sexual Abuse by an Adult." *Issues in Child Abuse Accusations* Volume 4, Number 4: 177–95.

——. (1993) "Modern Witch Hunt–Child Abuse Charges." *Wall Street Journal* February 22: Leisure & Arts Section.

GARRY, MARYANNE AND LOFTUS ELIZABETH F. (1993) "Women Who Remember Too Much." Paper presented at the False Memory Syndrome Foundation Conference ("Memory and Reality: An Emerging Crisis"), Valley Forge, PA, April 17.

GODLEY, ELIZABETH. (1993) "Memories of Abuse: A Recanter's Tale." *San Francisco Examiner* April 6.

GOLEMAN, DANIEL. (1992) "Childhood Trauma: Memory or Invention." *New York Times* July 21, Section B: 5.

GONDOLF, LYNNE PRICE. (1992) "Traumatic Therapy." *Issues in Child Abuse Accusations* Volume 4, Number 4: 239–245.

GOOD, ERICA E. WITH WAGNER, BETSY. (1993) "Does Psychotherapy Work?" *U.S. News & World Report* May 24: 57–59, 61, 63–65.

GRIGG, WILLIAM NORMAN. (1992) "The Politics of Child Abuse." *The New American* September 7.

GRINSPOON, LESTER. (1993) "Child Abuse—Parts 1 & 3." *The Harvard Mental Health Letter* Volume 9, Number 1: 1–5; Number 11: 1–3 & 10.

HAGA, CHUCK, and McEnroe, Paul. (1992) "Sins of the Father." *Minneapolis Star Tribune* July 19, section A: 1, 14–15.

HARRINGTON, MAUREEN. (1993) "Did Fantasy or Fact Put Dad in Jail." *The Denver Post* July 6, section F: 1.

HERMAN, JUDITH LEWIS, AND HARVEY, MARY R. "The False Memory Debate: Social Science or Social Backlash." *The Harvard Mental Health Letter* Volume 9, Number 10: 4–6.

—— and Schatzow, Emily. (1987) "Recovery and Verification of Memories of Childhood Sexual Trauma." *Psychoanalytic Psychology* Volume 4, Number 1: 1–14.

HOCHMAN, JOHN. (1984) "Iatrogenic Symptoms Associated with a Therapy Cult: Examination of an Extinct 'New Psychotherapy' with Respect to Psychiatric Deterioration and Brainwashing." *Psychiatry* Volume 47, Number 4: 366–77.

KIHLSTROM, JOHN F. "The Recovery of Memory in the Laboratory and Clinic," paper presented at the 1993 joint convention of the Rocky Mountain Psychological Association and the Western Psychological Association, Phoenix, April 1993. Correspondence concerning this paper should be addressed to John F. Kihlstrom, Amnesia & Cognition Unit, Department of Psychology, University of Arizona, Tucson, AZ 85721.

LARIMER, TIM. (1992) "Blaming Mom: Why It's Gone Too Far." *The Washington Times; USA Weekend* May 8–10.

LAWRENCE, LANA R. (1993) "Backlash: A Look at the Abuse-Related Amnesia and Delayed Memory Controversy." *Moving Forward* Volume 2, Number 4: 1,10–11,14.

——. (1993) "FMS Foundation Asks Underwager and Wakefield to Resign from Advisory Board, Then Changes Position." *Moving Forward* 2, no. 4: 12–13.

——. (1993) *Moving Forward* 2, no. 2.

——. (1993) "What They Said: 'Interview: Hollida Wakefield and Ralph Underwager,' " *Paidika*, Winter, *Moving Forward* Volume 2, Number 4: 13.

—— AND REILLY, MARY ANNE. (1993) "Corroboration and Evaluation of Delayed Memories of Abuse." *Moving Forward* Volume 2, Number 4: 15–16.

LETICH, LARRY. (1992) "Profiles of the Perpetrators." *Networker* May/June: 47.

LOFTUS, ELIZABETH F. (1992) "The Reality of Repressed Memories." Expanded version of talk given to the American Psychological Association, Washington, DC, August. Please address all correspondence to Elizabeth Loftus, Department of Psychology, University of Washington, Seattle, WA 98195.

———. (1993) "Repressed Memories of Childhood Trauma: Are They Genuine?" *The Harvard Mental Health Newsletter* Volume 9, Number 9: 4–5.

———. (1993) "A Trip Down Memory Lame." *The Washington Post National Weekly Edition.* July 5–11: 25.

MAKIN, KIRK. (1993) "Memories of Abuse: Real or Imagined?" *The Globe and Mail* July 3, section A: 1.

MARKOWITZ, LAURA M. (1992) "Reclaiming The Light." *Networker* May/June: 17–24.

McHUGH, PAUL R. (1993) "History and the Pitfalls of Practice" Talk given at the False Memory Syndrome Foundation Conference ("Memory and Reality: An Emerging Crisis") Valley Forge, PA, April 1993.

———. (1993) "Multiple Personality Disorder." *The Harvard Mental Health Letter* Volume 10, Number 3, September: 4–6.

MEACHAM, ANDREW. (1992) "Call Me Mom." *Changes* August: 56–63.

——— (1993) "Study Disputes Link between Eating Disorders, Sexual Abuse" *Changes* April: 22.

MESIC, PENELOPE. (1992) "Presence of Minds." *Chicago* September: 101–103, 122, 126–130.

MEYER, EUGENE L. (1993) "Father Accused of Sex Abuse Goes on Trial." *Washington Post* August 20: section C: 1.

NATHAN, DEBBIE. (1992) "Cry Incest." *Playboy* October: 84, 86, 88, 162, 164.

OFSHE, RICHARD J. (1992) "Inadvertent Hypnosis During Interrogation: False Confession Due to Dissociative State: Misidentified Multiple Personality and the Satanic Cult Hypothesis." *The International Journal of Clinical and Experimental Hypnosis* Volume 40, Number 3: 125–155.

——— and Watters Ethan. (1993) "Making Monsters—Psychotherapy's New Error: Repressed Memory, Multiple Personality and Satanic Abuse." *Society* Volume 30, Number 3, March/April: 4–16.

OKERBLOM, JIM. (1992) "Satanism: Truth vs. Myth/Video Alleges That Children Take Part in Bizarre Rituals." *San Diego Union* Jan. 18.

OLIO, KAREN A. (1993) "Comparing Apples and Oranges: Comments on Susan Ouellette's 'Memory and Perception.' " Karen A. Olio, 2 Lowndes Avenue, Norwalk, CT 06854.

———. (1993)"The Truth Behind the False Memory Syndrome." Karen A. Olio, 2 Lowndes Avenue, Norwalk, CT 06854.

—— (1993) "Truth in Memory: Comments on Elizabeth Loftus's 'Reality of Repressed Memory.' " Karen A. Olio, 2 Lowndes Avenue, Norwalk, CT 06854.

—— AND CORNELL, WILLIAM F. (1993) "Making Meaning Not Monsters: Reflections on the Delayed Memory Controversy." Olio & Cornell, 2 Lowndes Avenue, Norwalk, CT 06854.

ORNE, MARTIN. (1983) "Hypnosis 'Useful in Medicine, Dangerous in Court.' " Interview in *U.S. News & World Report* December 12.

PERRY, CAMPBELL. (1993) "The Problem of Hypnosis as a Time Machine." Paper presented at the False Memory Syndrome Foundation Conference ("Memory and Reality: An Emerging Crisis"), Valley Forge, PA, April.

POPE, HARRISON G. AND HUDSON, JAMIES I. (1992) "Is Childhood Abuse a Risk Factor for Bulimia Nervosa?" *American Journal of Psychiatry* Volume 149, Number 4, April: 455–463.

ROBERTS, SUSAN C. (1992) "Multiple Realities." *Common Boundary* May/June: 24–31.

ROGERS, MARTHA L. (1992) "Evaluating Adult Litigants Who Allege Injuries from Child Sexual Abuse: Clinical Assessment Methods for Traumatic Memories." Paper presented at the Fourth Annual Meeting of the American Psychological Society, San Diego, CA, June 20.

—— . (1994) "The Recovered Memory Controversy: Scientific Foundations: Part 1." *The Orange County Psychologist* January.

SAFRAN, CLAIRE. (1993) "Dangerous Obsession." *McCall's* June: 98, 102, 105–106, 109, 155.

SALTER, ANNA C. (1992) *Accuracy of Expert Testimony in Child Sexual Abuse Cases: A Case Study of Ralph Underwager and Holida Wakefield.* Anna C. Salter, 1 Court Street, Lebanon, NH 03766.

SCHWARTZ, RICHARD. (1992) "Rescuing the Exiles." *Networker* May/June: 33–37, 75.

SHAPIRO, LAURA, WITH ROSENBERG, DEBRA, LAUREMAN, JOHN F., AND SPARKMAN, ROBIN. (1993) "Rush to Judgement." *Newsweek* April 19: 54–60.

SIFFORD, DARREL. (1991) "Accusations of Sex Abuse, Years Later." *Philadelphia Inquirer* November 24.

—— . (1992) "Perilous Journey: The Labyrinth of Past Sexual Abuse." *Philadelphia Inquirer* February 13.

—— . (1992) "When Tales of Sex Abuse Aren't True." *Philadelphia Inquirer* January 5.

SLOVENKO, RALPH. (1993) "The Effect of Return of Memory in Sexual Abuse Cases on Statute of Limitations and the Justification for a Counter Attack." Talk given at the False Memory Syndrome Foundation Conference ("Memory and Reality: An Emerging Crisis"), Valley Forge, PA, April 16.

SMITH, SUSAN E. (1993) " 'Body Memories' and Other Pseudo-Scientific Notions of 'Survivor Psychology.' " Revised version of paper presented at the False Memory Foundation Conference ("Memory and Reality: An Emerging Crisis"), Valley Forge, PA, April 16–18, revised May 5.

SPRINGS, FERN E. and Friedich, William N. "Health Consequences of Sexual Abuse." *The Harvard Mental Health Newsletter* Volume 9, Number 7: 7. (Reprinted from *Mayo Clinic Proceedings*, Volume 67: 527–532.)

STAFF. (1993) "Porter Gets 18–20 Years for Molesting Children." *Minneapolis Star Tribune* December 7, section A: 1, 13.

TARVIS, CAROL. (1993) "Beware the Incest-Survivor Machine." *The New York Times* January 3, Book Review Section: 1, 16–17.

TAYLOR, BILL. (1992) "Therapist Turned Patient's World Upside Down." *Toronto Star* May 19: section C: 1.

*TOLAND, KELLY; HOFFMAN, HUNTER, AND LOFTUS, ELIZABETH (19:) "How Suggestion Plays Tricks With Memory." *Human Suggestibility: Advances in Theory, Research, and Application*, edited by Jon F. Schumaker (New York: Routledge). 1991.

Utah Daily Herald (1992) September 5, 1992.

VAN DERBUR (ATLER), MARILYN. (1991) "The Darkest Secret." *People* Volume 6, October: 88–94.

——. (1991) "Say Incest Out Loud." *McCall's* September: 78, 80, 82–83, 148–149, 151.

WAKEFIELD, HOLLIDA, AND UNDERWAGER RALPH. (1992) "Magic, Mischief, and Memories: Remembering Repressed Abuse." Wakefield and Underwager, Institute for Psychological Therapies, Northfield, MN.

——. "Recovered Memories of Alleged Sexual Abuse: Lawsuits Against Parents." *Behavioral Sciences and the Law* in press.

——. (1992) "Response to Salter." Wakefield and Underwager, Institute for Psychological Therapies, Northfield, MN.

——. (1992) "Uncovering Memories of Alleged Sexual Abuse: The Therapists Who Do It." *Issues in Child Abuse Accusations* Volume 4, Number 4: 197–213.

WAKEFIELD, JOSEPH. (1992) "Recovered Memories of Alleged Sexual Abuse: Memory as Production and Reproduction." *Issues in Child Abuse Accusations* Volume 4, Number 4: 219–220.

WARTIK, NANCY. (1993) "A Question of Abuse." *American Health* May: 62–67.

WATERS, ETHAN. (1993) "Doors of Memories." *Mother Jones* January/February: 24–29, 76–77.

WHITLEY, GLENNA. (1992) "Abuse of Trust." *D Magazine* January: 36–39.

WILLIAMS, LINDA MEYER. (1992) "Adult Memories of Childhood Abuse: Preliminary Findings from a Longitudinal Study." *The Advisor* Summer, Number 5: 19–20.

—— and Finkelhor, David. (1992) "The Characteristics of Incestuous Fathers." Report done for the National Center on Child Abuse and Neglect. July 31, Family Research Laboratory, University of New Hampshire, Durham, NC (603) 862-1888.

WRIGHT, LAWRENCE. (1993) "Remembering Satan—Parts 1 & 2." *The New Yorker* May 17: 60–81; May 24: 54–55, 58–66, 68–76.

YATES, ALAYNE. (1989) "Current Perspectives on the Eating Disorders: 1. History, Psychological and Biological Aspects." *Journal of the American Academy of Childhood and Adolescent Psychiatry*, Volume 28, Number 6: 813–828.

PHONE INTERVIEWS:

GANAWAY, GEORGE. Telephone interview with author, June 12, 1993.

GOLDMAN, LINDA. Telephone interview with author, 1993.

LIEF, HAROLD. Telephone interview with author, March 28, 1993.

SIMPSON, PAUL. Telephone interview with author, May 26, 1993.

FREYD, PAMELA. Telephone interview with author September 11, 1993.